WHEN ONE DOOR CLOSES

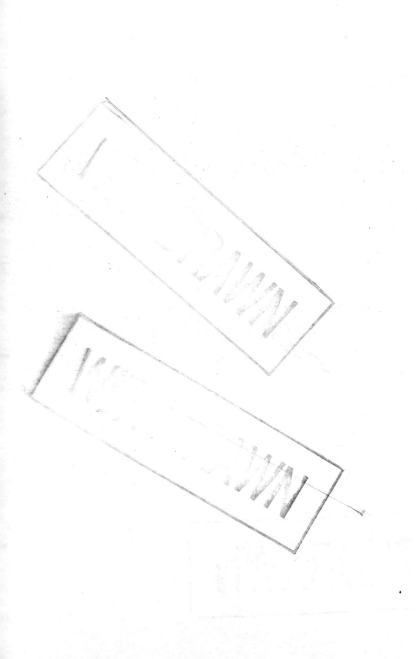

WHEN ONE DOOR CLOSES

Peter Sissons

biteback ᵛᵛᵛ

First published in Great Britain in 2010 by
Biteback Publishing Ltd
Westminster Tower
3 Albert Embankment
London
SE1 7SP

ISBN 978-1-84954-075-9

10 9 8 7 6 5 4 3 2 1

A CIP catalogue record for this book is available from the British Library.

Set in Adobe Garamond Pro
Jacket design: Soapbox
Plate section design: Antonello Sticca
Printed and bound in Great Britain by TJ International, Padstow, Cornwall

For Sylvia

Contents

List of Illustrations

Preface

When I finally packed it in as a news broadcaster, the question I was asked most often was 'When are you going to write it all down?'

There were two problems. For someone whose stock-in-trade was writing a 200-word news story for a national bulletin, it was a daunting task. How on earth was I going to break the habit of a lifetime and write tens of thousands of words? And secondly, there could be no prospect of writing it *all* down. Life's too short. I decided to write down what I most wanted to write about.

The big problem was getting started. Two things happened that meant I couldn't put it off any longer: my wife Sylvia went through the mass of material I had hoarded during my career – cuttings, letters, jottings, articles and photographs – put them into different boxes in some kind of order, and stacked them around my desk at home. I marvelled at how little I had thrown away, yet day after day those boxes sat there reproachfully.

Then out of the blue came the letter that kick-started everything. It was from the distinguished literary agent Michael Sissons, and said simply 'I hear that you are writing your memoirs. Can we keep it in the family?' Well, even though we are not related, Michael gave me what I needed – encouragement, wise suggestions... and a deadline. Fiona Petheram, his cheerful and perceptive assistant, also made me feel that this was something they believed in. Both seemed a lot happier when I actually produced some text. Here's the result.

I did not keep a comprehensive diary, but among all the stuff that I didn't throw away were my pocket diaries with my assignments, lunches and appointments in them. They were very useful in establishing chronology. But the major source for this book is memory; and not just my own, which is vivid enough on most of the events described. No, the secret weapon is my wife's memory. Sylvia has prodigious powers of recall, and was an observer, confidante and adviser throughout my working life. In my last few years at the BBC I also took to writing myself the occasional aide-memoire after an event or experience that I felt particularly strongly about. But if any of these sources are in error, then the responsibility must remain mine and mine alone.

One decision that I had to take was how much of the book I should submit to the scrutiny of old friends, colleagues and mentors. I decided that I wouldn't, not because I don't have the utmost respect for their views, but because I wanted this book to be mine and mine alone. There is one exception to this: the lengthy chapter on my experience as chairman of *Question Time*. To be absolutely certain that my memory and observations had been as fair, accurate and impartial as possible, and not coloured by some of the scars I picked up, I asked Audrey Bradley to look it over. Audrey, who worked on *Question Time* for fifteen years, made some suggestions which I incorporated, and gave me the assurance of her approval. I am as grateful to her today as I was for her support and advice when we worked together. My gratitude also goes to my old friend Reg Turnill, whose insights and good humour helped me refine the conclusions to this book.

These acknowledgements would not be complete without registering my sincere thanks and appreciation to Iain Dale and Biteback Publishing. Iain, besides being a great encouragement, made sure I had an excellent editor, Sam Carter – an alumnus incidentally of my old Oxford college. Sam made few suggestions that I didn't act upon, and that weren't an improvement on my initial effort. My thanks to him also.

Finally, when you set out to write something like this, it reminds you of the many people you've relied on, and who invested a little bit of themselves in you: ITN's great editors, Geoffrey Cox, Nigel Ryan, David Nicholas, Stewart Purvis and Richard Tait and many other unsung heroes like Frank Miles, Derek Dowsett and Chris Barlow. At the BBC, Ron Neil and Tony Hall and exceptional programme editors like Eileen Fitt, Jonathan Baker and Kevin Bakhurst . Then there's Sue Knight and

Sue Ayton, whose agency loyally represents so many news presenters, but whose very first customer from among them was me.

I have mentioned Sylvia, to whom I owe so much. But we are both fortunate in our three children, Michael, Jonathan and Kate, who could always be relied upon to put my ups and downs into perspective with humour and loving support. And last but not least, you will get to know a little in this book of my three brothers, Clifford, John and David. For me, our closeness has always been another great strength and comfort.

January 2011

Introduction

I never saw the soldier who shot me, even though he was no more than ten yards away. In the baking afternoon heat of the Nigerian bush, the only warning I got was a rustle of twigs and grass, and the clatter-click of a fresh magazine being banged into an automatic rifle. Instinctively, I dived head first into the cover of a shell-hole.

But I was a second too late. With both legs angled in the air, one round, just one round, of a long, deafening burst of machine gun fire, tore through both my thighs.

No pain, just a sickening, tearing jab.

My first thought was that I might just be OK.

That didn't last long.

Clatter-click again. Another magazine loaded.

I pressed myself into the burnt and putrid earth of the shallow depression, the panic welling up inside me. A pause. Then, as I winced and twitched in fear, the bullets again exploded in my direction, sprayed wider, some kicking up the rim of soil inches from my face.

Silence again. Movement in the bush, but now going away from me. I had just had his parting shots.

Relief swept over me. I waited a couple of minutes, then slowly and silently rolled over onto my back. What I saw turned relief into angry resignation. From my waist to my knees, my beige slacks were soaked in blood. I had never seen so much blood. The inside of my right leg was a gaping exit wound, torn fabric laced into torn flesh. Soil from the crater rim was trickling into it, as more blood oozed out, making a sort of red mud. I felt faint, and accepted that I was likely to die.

Unknown to me, one of my companions in the small group of reporters I had set off with that morning was already dead – shot in the back as he stood up to take a picture. As night fell, half conscious, weakened by loss of blood and in increasing pain, I was lying next to his corpse. We bounced along together on the floor of a truck which was slowly negotiating potholes on a tortuous sixty-mile drive to safety and the beginnings of medical help.

The traumatic events of the ambush on that October day, more than forty years ago, are still vivid in my memory. I was a 26-year-old TV reporter with Britain's newest and most exciting TV news programme – ITN's *News at Ten*. I had been reporting less than two years, after a thirty-month apprenticeship as a graduate trainee, writing scripts, doing voiceovers and news casting the late-night headlines. I suppose that today it would be called a meteoric rise and it was judged by my superiors that I had a promising career ahead as one of ITN's small, prestigious and glamorous group of top international correspondents. The assignment in Biafra was not my first taste of war – I had acquitted myself well in the aftermath of the Six-Day War in the Middle East the year before. As an up-and-coming reporter, the world was at my feet. Then, one high velocity 7.62mm round changed everything.

I remember that day for more mundane reasons. Every day since my close encounter with the grim reaper, the pain of my wounds has remained with me. For the first few years it was severe, requiring powerful painkillers to enable me to go on working. Gradually the pain eased. But to this day it is always there in the background, and any long period on my feet makes it much worse. The pills are always in my briefcase. Despite numerous skin grafts, there's also the disfigurement of scarring, and highly visible wasting of my left leg because of nerve damage.

My injuries sustained in that ambush in the Biafran war could have ended my career there and then. Foreign correspondents covering the world's trouble spots have to be fit, they have to be able to run, they have to be reasonably nimble – anything less could put them and, more importantly, the camera crew accompanying them at risk. However good my surgeons – and they were very good – I would never again be in that league physically.

And yet, it was not the end of my career – quite the opposite. Never has there been a truer saying than as one door closes, another opens. The new door was opened for me by the big guns of Britain's trade union movement, their battles throughout the 1970s with the governments of Heath, Wilson and Callaghan, and the consequent massive economic damage that was inflicted on the nation.

After more than a year of operations and grafts and a pioneering tendon transplant, I held out hopes of going out again on the big foreign assignments. But wiser heads than mine saw the opening for me before I did. As industrial hostilities opened, I was sent to a different front line, but this one was in my own country. In my new role as ITN's Industrial Editor, I spent the best part of the 1970s reporting the decade's biggest domestic story – the trench warfare between government and unions, and the nation's fight for economic survival. It kept me on television night after night. I grew up as a reporter, presenter and – more and more – as a newscaster. My reporting, I believe, also generally earned the respect of all sides during this deeply divisive period. I learned the meaning and the importance of journalistic balance.

So it was that after the cordite, blood and muck of that Nigerian ambush, my career path took off in a way undreamt of at the time. I spent another twenty years at ITN, years that were to end in the most remarkable acrimony when the BBC poached me in 1989. At the time I was on the crest of a wave, presenting ITN's acclaimed *Channel Four News*, and part of ITN's response was to sue me in person for damaging the programme by leaving. Writs flew, and as the date for a full court hearing approached, the BBC settled by paying ITN a transfer fee – something unknown in news broadcasting. For the next twenty years I settled down to a new working life and journalistic culture at the BBC's imposing but soulless Television Centre. But how lucky can you get? With both employers – inside and outside the commercial sector – I did the sort of work that the hundreds of thousands of young people trying to get into television journalism would have killed for. I got to present practically every terrestrial network news bulletin on all channels. At ITN I reported for, co-anchored or anchored many special programmes – on elections, Budgets and America's space programme. I was chosen to be the launch presenter for the ground-breaking *Channel Four News* and helped it win three BAFTA awards with some landmark television journalism. I chaired the only face-to-face debate during the year-long miners' strike between the miners' leader and the Coal Board chief. And I was the first reporter let into the nuclear facility at Sellafield, being given unconditional and unrestricted access to this most secretive place. Once *Channel Four News* had recovered from its disastrous and depressing launch, I found that I had become a hot property, and the BBC came sniffing around more than once. The first move they made, under conditions of great secrecy, was when John Birt, then the BBC's Deputy Director General, offered me the job of BBC Political Editor. I turned it down, a year or two later choosing another BBC offer that I *couldn't* refuse – to succeed Sir Robin Day as chairman of the BBC's flagship discussion programme *Question Time*, one of the toughest challenges in the business.

On *Question Time*, despite many unsettling changes in the production team, I helped to keep the programme as popular as ever, and its panels as compelling. I persuaded the Lord Chief Justice of England to appear – the first and only time the holder of that office has appeared on such a programme. We began to take the programme around the country regularly, addressing the great regional concerns as well as national issues. Also at the BBC, besides the privilege of sitting in Sir Robin's chair, at various times I presented all the main national news bulletins – the *Six*, the *Nine*, and the *Ten*, and deputised for Sir David Frost on countless occasions on *Breakfast with Frost*. I was on duty the day that Diana, Princess of Wales was killed, and when the Queen Mother died. On the latter occasion, carrying out the BBC's orders not to wear a black tie, I was shocked to become, in certain quarters, an overnight hate figure. I have been Newscaster of the Year, been voted best front of camera performer by the Guild of Broadcast Journalists and won the top award of the Royal Television Society, the Judges' Award.

News was my life; it defined me as a person. But I knew the day would come when I would want to bring down the curtain.

About a year before I actually left the BBC at the end of June 2009, I told the head of the newsroom at the BBC that I was seeing out what would probably be my last contract. By then I had wound down considerably, confined to shifts on the BBC News Channel, formerly BBC News 24.

I decided on a low-key exit, and kept my plans secret from all but one or two senior colleagues. I had been to many leaving parties at the BBC, and decided I didn't want one; some can be rather forced affairs. On one such occasion, as the drink flowed, a management figure who a few minutes previously had made a speech lamenting the departure of the retiring colleague was telling anyone who would listen what a shit he was. Better not to have a leaving do, particularly as I was not sure how I would have been affected if it were for me.

As the day of my last appearance drew nearer, I wondered how to sign off. Should I steal a few final seconds to make a little speech to the viewers, looking them in the eye and saying a tearful goodbye, Hollywood style? I toyed with the idea, and decided that would just be self indulgent. So I just did what I always do, signing off as normal. It was only as I unclipped the microphone and took out my earpiece that the significance of the moment hit me. After forty-five years it was all over. I walked the few yards from the studio to the make-up room. While I cleaned off the powder and foundation, I told the make-up artist on duty that it was the last time I would have to do it. She started to cry. It crossed my mind that I should go into the newsroom, fling a pile of papers in the air and yell 'I'm off!'

A few more paces, and I was in that vast newsroom. A final glance around. Everyone preoccupied at terminals and keyboards. I could have stripped naked and no one would have looked up. My usual desk was already occupied – 'hot desking', as they call it, means no one gets permanent ownership of a work station. I pushed my few bits and pieces into my briefcase, walked to the car park, swung the Volvo out into Wood Lane for the last time, and headed for home. Behind me, inside Television Centre, the mighty BBC multimedia news factory ground on into the night.

After spending so many weeks wondering how I would react, I felt no sadness. I had clearly made the right decision to go. But as I negotiated the traffic round Shepherd's Bush Green, the thoughts came crowding in.

Would I miss the scores of excellent colleagues with whom I had worked at the BBC? The reality was that all but one or two of my generation had already retired. I had worked more recently with several good young producers, but I had older suits than some of them. What they had in common was that they were all looking for leadership, and all they got was management. Come to think of it, although, as a senior presenter, I once had easy access to the BBC's bosses, I didn't now know more than one or two of the people who were in charge of the BBC's journalism. I'd certainly never held a conversation with the Director of News in the five years she'd been in post, and she was rarely seen in the newsroom. If I'd had that leaving party and she'd turned up to make the valedictory speech, I think someone would have had to introduce us. It would have been embarrassing. It was, indeed, time to go.

But if I felt little emotion about leaving the place, I didn't feel empty. My working life had been far too eventful for that. I just had no particular feelings about leaving the BBC.

Forty-four years and ten months previously I had walked into another newsroom, in another journalistic world. At the age of twenty-two, fresh from Oxford, I had been taken on as a graduate trainee at the fledgling Independent Television News. Being one of only two ITN trainees recruited that year was the first and the greatest thing ever to happen to me in my professional life.

The contrast with the BBC I was now leaving could not be greater. Excitement was in the air. ITN was expanding – indeed for the twenty-five years I was at ITN the company grew, year by year. Jobs were secure. There was an esprit de corps, which exists to this day among the ITN pensioners and veterans of that era. We were frontiersmen and women, making the running, and writing the handbook about how TV news should be presented and how we should report on the world. Broadcast political reporting was practically re-invented, with Robin Day pioneering the art of the modern interview. ITN's mission was to drag broadcast news into a new era, and all my formative years in TV journalism were spent helping to make those changes happen. The shared purpose was never inscribed anywhere but in the psyche of the people who worked at ITN, and it ran deep among them. It was the sort of spirit that I imagine you'd find in a crack regiment. It's only a small thing, but after I left ITN, in 1989, I was invariably sent two pocket diaries at the end of each year for my use in the next, an ITN one, and a BBC one. In twenty years at the BBC, I always had an ITN diary in my pocket.

And never far from my mind were the parting words from my Editor at ITN – that I should remember that the BBC wasn't poaching me because of what I could offer them, but for the damage it could cause the successful programme I was leaving. The BBC has enormous strengths and great power. But for me it never found the secret of generating the loyalty that the ITN I knew was capable of inspiring. I know for certain it wasn't always like that at the BBC. Generations of men and women dedicated their working lives to the Corporation. I know many of them personally. Some were almost married to the place. For them, the BBC *was* their life, and their loyalty was legendary.

So why do I want to write about it all? I have read memoirs by some in TV news, which, once I have put their books down, I have found them very difficult to pick up again. Each book of this type could easily have been re-titled *All the wonderful things I've done in Television*. What I *wanted* to know is not so much what they've done, but what they have learned about their industry, how they broke into it, how they survived in it, and what advice would they give to the tens of thousands of youngsters who aspire to join it. Who were their role models? What are their regrets? How would they judge their own strengths and weaknesses? Where is broadcast news going? Is it any longer, with its format of short segments crammed into twenty or twenty-five minutes, up to the task of reporting the complexity of the modern world in a balanced way?

I hope I can also bring the perspective of someone who had two professional lifetimes – one in independent, commercial television; the other in the world's greatest public service broadcaster. Throughout that time, of course, my personal views were largely – and rightly – suppressed, constrained by strict guidelines requiring balance and impartiality. Indeed, in my case, all that became a lifetime's habit, as well as a professional requirement. That can now be cast off, but I hope with not too much reckless abandon. Oh, I don't know...

My story, like many of my generation and background, is of someone who made his own luck, without the cocoon of family money and contacts, social elevation or of an expensive private education. Many of us were born during the war, and knew the hardship of the post-war years. We can be emotional people, which, however hard we strive to be detached, can colour our reporting. But it also puts us close to the pulse of the mass of the people we are supposed to serve. And most of us can't believe the good fortune that has allowed us to spend our working lives doing something undreamt of by our forebears, and which has actually been enjoyable.

Chapter 1

My Liverpool Home

I had the best possible start in life. No posh house, no silver spoon, no money, my home city in ruins; but my generation were not ground down by it. We were the Beatles generation. I was born in Liverpool in 1942, six months after the final raids by the Luftwaffe which had turned large tracts of the city into a wasteland. Enemy bombers were under instructions to destroy Liverpool, not least because it was the headquarters of the war being waged against their U-boats in the Atlantic. All my earliest memories were of endless bomb sites, ruined churches, queues for everything, the grimness of a city that had suffered more extensive damage from German bombs than anywhere apart from London.

I am the third of four boys – two born before the war, one during, and one after. Our mother, Elsie, was the granddaughter of James McWilliam, the pier master at Princes Dock, the first dock next to the Pier Head on the right, as you face the Mersey. (Not many people know it was named, not after royalty, but after Princes Foods, whose gateway it was to the UK.) Elsie was brought up by her grandparents, and spent her early childhood in the imposing Georgian house that used to stand next to the Pier Head, but which was destroyed in the blitz. Its twin, the pier master's house on the Albert Dock, can be seen to this day. She had a gentle, compassionate nature, which never deserted her. I remember her telling me how she and her friends used to play in the local cemetery, and after a big funeral would go around the poorer graves giving each a little bunch of flowers from the generous pile of floral tributes left behind by the departing cortège.

My father, George Robert Percival Sissons, I know little about. I was never close to him. I do know he was born in Rotherham, but I know next to nothing about the family he came from. (Indeed, for years I believed that the family name Sissons wasn't a Yorkshire name at all but a French import. I now know it is an ancient Anglo-Saxon surname, first recorded in the seventh century.)

George left school when he was thirteen and went to sea with the Larrinaga Steamship company of Liverpool. It was a famous old shipping line, with ships registered in sail and steam for more than 200 years. Neither of my parents had anything that could be called secondary education. Both attended the same inner city primary school, Granby Street, in the heart of Toxteth, but ten years apart. Granby Street School, in one of Liverpool's poorest areas, gave them both copper-plate handwriting, meticulous grammar and spelling, and a lifetime ability with numbers. My mother, who left school when she was fourteen, always vowed that her children would have a proper education, and later made great sacrifices to make sure we all went to university. My father believed children should leave school as soon as possible, as he had done, and start working for a living. He had no interest that I could discern in any reading or learning beyond the basics. Music and art were strangers to him. The only books he ever opened were navy or navigational manuals. He laughed a lot at comedians on the radio, like Tommy Handley and Al Read.

My parents met when my mother was working in the beauty department at Lewis's, the City's biggest store, and my father walked through in his merchant navy uniform. She was a striking natural red-head, and for many years her photo adorned the window of a leading Liverpool photographer, Fred Ash of Bold Street. Elsie lied about her age for most of her life. She didn't want anyone to know she married at seventeen, and always said she was older than she was. I only found out her true age from the plate on her coffin.

Before I, her third child, came along, life was already hard for her, as it was for many women during wartime. A husband at sea for months and then years on end, barely enough money for essentials, no welfare state, and two little boys, Clifford and John, to bring up. A day or two after the declaration of war on 3 September 1939, her eldest boy Clifford, not yet six years of age, didn't come home from school. Without warning, he had been labelled, issued with a gas mask, taken to the local station, and with the rest of the school placed on a train to north Wales, out of range of possible German bombing raids. There, in a bare village hall, total strangers picked out the children they wished to billet, starting with the most attractive. Cliff, peering in bewilderment through his wire spectacles, was one of the last chosen.

A few weeks later, Elsie was evacuated also, with two-year-old John – but to a farm ten miles from where Cliff had been placed. The family was reunited for two days at Christmas, when they were allowed back home because father had a couple of days' leave. Then, for the whole of a bitter winter, it was back to separation in Wales. There were no air raids on Liverpool during that time, but it was April before their pointless evacuation ended. The German bombers did come, but four months after they'd returned home, and by then the only refuge on offer was an air-raid shelter.

For someone whose husband's absences at sea effectively made her a single mother, with no structure of social services to lean on, it was, for Elsie Sissons, a time of many tears and much sacrifice. And it got worse. Unknown to Elsie, the evacuation of her and her son John to that Welsh farm nearly cost John his life – the nice farm milk he'd been drinking straight from the cow had gave him tuberculosis of the lymph glands in his neck. A few months after returning from Wales, with John now three, his mother noticed the lump. The tragedy was that the tuberculosis was misdiagnosed as Hodgkin's Disease, a form of cancer far less survivable than it is today, so all through the Liverpool blitz of 1940 and 1941 my mother had to take her little son John in and out of hospital for aggressive radiotherapy which he didn't need. That unnecessary treatment started a ticking time bomb. Twelve years later it triggered cancer of the thyroid, and my mother and father were told that John, by now fifteen, had only six months to live – news they kept from him. Against the odds, he has survived and thrived, not least due to a cheerful determination to live life to the full – but that prognosis in his teens put paid to his ambition to be a doctor. No one thought he would last the course.

I was born on 17 July 1942, in Smithdown Road Hospital, formerly a workhouse, and now replaced by an Asda supermarket. A few days before I was due, my mother was desperate because she had no one to look after Cliff and John while she went into hospital – my father had sailed back to the war from a still-smouldering Liverpool waterfront some weeks earlier. In one of the local shops it all became too much for her and she burst into tears. A kind lady – a total stranger – asked her what the problem was. On being told, there and then she took in Cliff and John and looked after them until mother came out of hospital with me, her new baby.

By the time I was born, John was on the mend, but then there was another hammer blow. Having found a lump in John's neck two years before, my mother found me very listless in my pram, with a lump in my groin. I was only three months old. It was diagnosed as an abscess, and operated on as an emergency in Alder Hey hospital. In hospital I developed paratyphoid and mum was told that I was not expected to live. She told me many years later that I was so emaciated that when she folded back the hospital blanket covering me she folded my little body back with it. I still have the scars on my arms and legs where intravenous drips kept me alive. My eldest brother, Cliff, lost count of the times when, first with John and then with me, my mother would return from visiting us in hospital sobbing her heart out. To add to her agony, some time before I was born she miscarried a baby girl. She wanted a girl so much. But her grief was kept largely to herself.

As we grew up, the constant additional worry, of course, was money. After paying the rent there was often nothing left, and she concealed from us her visits to the pawn shop, where she occasionally parted with the only thing of value she owned, her engagement ring. New clothes or new shoes were a rarity – mother was an expert at making do and mending, as clothes were passed down from child to child and between families. Food was simple – cheap cuts like scrag end of lamb, stewed with vegetables – but always tasty, and our diets were supplemented with free orange juice and cod liver oil from the government. We weren't always in the best of health. Childhood diseases like measles were common, and we were almost encouraged to catch them to get it over with when other children in the street were infected.

In early years my life – and that of other kids – was blighted by the recurrence of two complaints in particular, then euphemistically called 'heat spots' and 'bilious attacks'. It was only many years later that I found out that the former were actually flea bites, and the latter was common food poisoning, caused by the lack of any facility to store fresh food.

By now my mother and we three boys were living in a tiny three-bedroomed terraced house, Number 4, Ingleton Road, a few yards from Penny Lane Hill, at the point where the main railway line passes under the road. Ingleton Road is about 100 yards long, with a red-brick terrace on either side, and behind each terrace is a 'back entry', a narrow cobbled lane. The hallmark of a well-kept house in Ingleton Road, as it was throughout most northern towns, was a spotless front doorstep. At least once a week, in a ritual performed on hands and knees, the step had to be 'stoned' – abraded by the housewife with a flat stone until it looked like new. Anything less signalled a lack of pride in hearth and home.

Our local shops were in Penny Lane. The house originally had no bathroom, but my parents had a bath put into the smallest bedroom, and we three boys all shared the second bedroom. The lavatory was at the end of the small backyard. Under the beds, we had some copious chamber-pots. The only source of heating and hot water was a black cast-iron range in the kitchen. Upstairs, the house was cold. In the winter of 1947, when the snow lay three feet deep outside, it was like an icebox.

My earliest memories are of the VE day party in the street, when I was just under three years of age. A Union Jack paper hat, rows of trestle tables, jam sandwiches, jelly and evaporated milk.

I also remember my brothers taking me in my pushchair to a huge open space in Liverpool, known as The Mystery, where German and Italian prisoners-of-war were encamped. My brothers swapped Woodbines and chocolate for their badges and medals. In the house there was a boxful of wartime relics – mostly tail fins from incendiary bombs which had been picked out of the street after air raids. In The Mystery, there were also a number of barrage balloons, tied to their trailers. I burst into tears when John threatened to stick a pin in one of them.

I remember well the day the father I had never seen came back from the war. We knew he was coming. I had talked about it with other children in the street. One or two told me, matter of fact, that their fathers would not be coming home. They had gone to heaven instead. It was a sunny summer day, and we were all playing outside, when down the short street he came – in his lieutenant's uniform, and carrying his kitbag and an enormous net full of coconuts, things none of us had ever seen before. I knew he was my father, because someone said so. But, in reality, he was a stranger.

And then it became a day I'd rather forget, and which coloured my relationship with him for the rest of his life.

That evening, relaxing with his young family for the first time in more than three years, my father lost his temper with me, the three-year-old son he'd just met. I said something cheeky when he suggested it was my bedtime – I think the words I used to him were 'Who do you think you are?' His response was violent and, for me, painful. I got what he called 'a good thrashing'. It was to remain my father's stock response to a cheeky or insubordinate child for many years, and it killed our relationship before it had a chance to begin. Some have suggested that my memory of that day – the memory of a small child – was not my own, but must have been recounted to me subsequently, colouring my judgement. But the event was so vivid, and so instantly traumatic, that I simply don't believe that can be the case. I could never have written about it while my mother was alive, but despite her attempts in later life to mitigate the damage, I felt not a shred of affection for my father after that incident on the day I first met him. I believe that the attitude of my brothers mellowed with time, but mine didn't.

My relationship with my mother was a total contrast. She was a saint. She brought us up simply and well, making great personal sacrifices. Crucially, for all of us, she believed that the best thing that could happen for her boys was a good education. As soon as I could read, I read constantly. I always had three or four books on the go from the public library, and spent many hours browsing its shelves. All four of us – my younger brother David was born when I was seven – went to university, and two became doctors. Cliff blazed the trail, qualifying in Medicine at Liverpool University. John wanted to do the same, but was discouraged because of his dire cancer prognosis, although he was kept in the dark about it. He read Classics at London University. I went to Oxford, and David also qualified in Medicine at Liverpool. I and my brothers owe our mother everything. I miss her every day.

Despite the shadow cast by my relationship with my father, I had, for the most part, a happy, carefree childhood.

At the age of five I went to the primary school both my elder brothers had attended, Dovedale Road School, just off Penny Lane, and a few hundred yards from our house. There was quite a build-up to the big day, with my mother announcing finally that today was the day Peter Goes to School. All went well, we played with a sand table for most of the time, and I loved the nice motherly teacher, Miss Thomas.

The next day was more of a shock to my young system – I hadn't realised you had to go to school *every* day.

Dovedale Road was a traditional combined primary and junior school, built in 1908, which gave practically all its intake a good grounding in the basics. A mixture of red brick, institutional tiling and corrugated iron, inside its iron-railinged playgrounds stood the brick and concrete air raid shelters erected in 1940. They were there until recently.

When I joined the school, a boy named John Lennon was in the year ahead of me. After I'd been there a year, the new intake included one George Harrison. Besides having half the Beatles, also at Dovedale Road at that time was a boy called Jimmy Tarbuck, who, less than fifteen years later, was to burst onto the national scene, via the stage of the London Palladium, and become a comic legend. In later life, none of us remembered knowing any one of the others at Dovedale, but years later a photograph came to light of a group of youngsters on the beach at the school's annual camp on the Isle of Man. The *Daily Mail*, which published it, had identified George, John and Jimmy, and asked its readers if they knew any of the others. As soon as my wife and I saw it, we knew one of the others was me.

Dovedale Road, with a catchment area that included some of the poorest parts of Liverpool, as well as middle-class Mossley Hill, was bursting at the seams after the war, as the products of the baby boom flooded in. There were fifty children in my class – and that was not uncommon. Looking after dozens of lively kids, and others clearly traumatised by bereavement or other wartime experiences, was tough work for the teaching staff – some teachers had so little energy left towards the end of the day that they instructed their classes to rest their heads on the desk for ten minutes until the bell went. And when the children did, you could hear a pin drop. Despite the class sizes, most teachers appeared to have little problem with discipline. If things got rowdy, we were all commanded to put our hands on our heads. It usually restored order, or at least gave the teacher a breathing space. In our class we had one child, Stanley Williams, who helped to give the teacher a break with his gripping stories. Stanley was a gifted story teller. He came to the front of the class, usually egged on by the rest of us, and, completely off the cuff, told fantastic tales of the adventures of Tom Thumb. Stanley deputised for our grateful and exhausted class teacher on many occasions, and held us spellbound. Fifty years later he wrote to me, with some moving memories of that time. He had become a schoolmaster in Scotland. What lucky kids he taught!

When, at Dovedale Road, we moved from the Infants to the Juniors, discipline became more of a problem, with one or two teachers relying on fear to keep order. The choice of weapon of one teacher in particular was a short frayed cane, used on your hands or the back of your legs, and used often. Someone remarked to me in later life that if that teacher had done that today, he'd probably have gone to jail. He certainly would have lost his job. Many years later, when I had become well known, I was invited to send my good wishes to the said teacher as he reached some milestone of old age. I'm afraid I made an excuse not to. Those recollections of reddened hands and raw legs marred how I recalled my days at Dovedale Road. And not just mine – many years later, in July 2000, my wife and I were paying our annual visit to the Hampton Court Flower Show.

It was the press day, and wasn't very crowded, and suddenly I bumped into a vaguely familiar figure, grey and pale, wearing gardening clothes and a pork-pie hat. But he recognised me first. It was George Harrison, with his wife Olivia, looking for plants for their garden.

Seven months earlier, a crazed attacker, Michael Abram, had broken into their Oxfordshire home, and tried to kill them both. George had been repeatedly stabbed and badly wounded, Olivia less so, and their assailant was then awaiting trial. Sylvia and I, and George and Olivia, sat down in the shade of a large tree, I got us some tea, and we chatted for well over an hour. We talked about our memories of primary school and I mentioned the teacher with the addiction to corporal punishment. George knew instantly who I was talking about, and mentioned his experience with another at Dovedale who was also fond of using a stick. He said he'd gone home after school one day with weals on his wrists after being hit for some minor offence. Seeing the damage, his dad went straight round to the school, confronted the teacher, and threatened to knock his block off. It was the last time George was punished in that way.

However, what really shocked me that day, sitting in the afternoon sunshine at Hampton Court, was learning from George Harrison in graphic detail how close he had come to death on that December night when Abram broke into his house intent on murdering him. I had, as a news presenter, reported the attack and the trial. But that was different from hearing at first hand, and in horrific detail, how he and Olivia literally fought a bloody battle for their lives; how it was more than twenty minutes before the police arrived; how George believed he was going to die, as he was repeatedly stabbed, with Olivia raining blows on the attacker with anything that came to hand, to try to beat him off. If Olivia hadn't been there, George would have been dead.

And burglary wasn't the motive either. The police told George that after they'd overpowered Abram and were driving him away, he kept asking the officers one question: 'I did kill him, didn't I?'

Although our lives had developed in totally different ways, it was remarkable how easily George Harrison and I picked up on the events of our formative years. It was obvious to me that for those of us who belonged to that group of children, in that part of Liverpool, at that time, there remained so much that we would have in common for the rest of our lives. I count myself fortunate to have been one of them. Our values, our experiences, our innocence, the hardships our parents endured, and the sacrifices they made for us, tied us together. We were allowed to grow up, to have a childhood, without being bombarded by the cult of shallow celebrity. In his letter to me, all those years later, Stanley Williams – the Tom Thumb story teller – wrote movingly of those days. 'Together,' he wrote, 'we enjoyed the unsurpassed sponsorship of a victorious post-war society which valued education only a little less than it did its children, who were seen as the inheritors of a new age of prosperity and peace.'

Stanley's theory was that there was a 'gene pool' of exceptionally gifted pupils who attended Dovedale Road in the late 1940s and early 1950s – many of whom grew up to make significant, some immense, contributions to our culture.

In our street, as in many others, from morning 'til night, on days when there was no school, we 'played out' until, as the shadows lengthened, and the street lights came on, our mothers called us in. Even after school, it was a quickly gulped-down tea, then out of the door to play. And there was no suggestion that that wasn't safe – that just wasn't an issue.

All could play in the street because cars were rarely seen. Any oddball, suspicious strangers who hung around were usually seen off with ridicule or a well-aimed football. We had the self-confidence of street survivors with a sense of humour, constantly reinventing our own pastimes. We fished with bent pins and garden canes in the park lake, and were sometimes chased home by the park keeper.

During the long days of the school holidays, we became even more ingenious. We organised our own funfair, with used bus tickets as currency, devising a ghost train with an old pushchair through the air-raid shelters that stood in line at the back of our houses. Going on a proper family holiday somewhere was practically unknown, although Dovedale Road School for many years arranged that week-long Isle of Man camp, from which no pupil was excluded, even if they couldn't afford the modest amount it cost. Family outings usually involved a day out to New Brighton, on what passed for a beach, reached by ferry across the Mersey. Hobbies had to be cheap – stamp collecting or noting down the numbers of the many locomotives, some very famous, that thundered along the line at the end of the road. My eldest brother tried keeping mice; you only needed a couple, and within weeks you had hundreds. Unfortunately, he came home from school one day to find that they had all escaped. Within days, the talk of the street was the mysterious rodent infestation and the Penny Lane chandlers had sold out of mousetraps. He never did own up.

No one had a telephone. But kids in adjacent houses tried to improvise even that ... with two cocoa tins and a piece of string. Most houses had a radio of varying reliability and reception, but the word television meant nothing to us. On Saturday mornings the kids in the street were gathered together by a couple of the older girls, and off we went to the Grand cinema, Saturday Morning Club, in Smithdown Road, admission 3d. Our heroes were Flash Gordon and Roy Rogers.

One shadow over the Sissons childhood was our father's allotment. After years at sea, he became obsessed with land-locked pursuits, especially those that might also save money. So in our tiny backyard he kept battery hens, and a mile away he rented an allotment. The hens were fed mounds of smelly mash to stimulate egg production, which also stimulated large mounds of steaming droppings. For some reason he chose Sunday mornings to muck out the hens, and then one of us kids had to put the stuff in a wheelbarrow and push it to the allotment.

We hated doing it. Pushing a barrow-load of stinking manure through the streets of genteel Mossley Hill, often passing our sniggering friends dressed in their Sunday best, who were off to chapel or church. It took many years before I put the shame of it all behind me, and could learn to see the point of gardening. Even today, although I love my garden, it would take more than the point of a gun to make me have an allotment. Or hens.

But perhaps the most significant thing about those early years was that I can't remember ever being bored. And I was not alone in that. No child I knew, in the Liverpool of the late 1940s and 1950s, sat around waiting to be entertained. We made our own entertainment, and revelled in it. And the entertainment we made wasn't second-best to 'proper' entertainment – but as good as, if not better than. What kept us occupied and amused took many forms. One development actually changed the face of entertainment across the world, as hundreds of Liverpool kids, inspired by the new sound of rock 'n' roll then sweeping in from America, started making their own music – connecting the new idiom to the sentiments drawn from their own roots, their own experiences, even perhaps from their own gene pool. And, as we know, although some became better at it than others, it redefined the culture of a city and a generation. A look at the front page of the *Liverpool Echo* of the late 1950s, which carried hundreds of small-ads for different bands and groups, gives a vivid snapshot of what was going on.

The big milestone for all of us in the state education system was the eleven-plus, the exam that decided whether a child would go to one of Liverpool's many excellent and long-established grammar schools, or be assigned to the secondary modern or technical system. The theory was that a decision could be made at that age, on the results of one exam, whether a child had academic qualities (with the prospect of going on to higher education) or should go down the path to a shorter and more general, practical education. The designers of the 1944 Education Act may not have meant the second option to be perceived as second best, but the staff of Dovedale Road left no one in any doubt what their view was. On the day of the eleven-plus results, the whole school was assembled, and the head teacher read out, one by one, the names of those who had passed. As the names were read out, the lucky ones went up to the platform, to the applause of staff and pupils. They were allowed the rest of the day off, to go home and tell their mothers.

Those whose names were not read out knew only too well that they were failures.

The reward for many kids who passed the exam was a new bike – if your parents could afford it. Mine couldn't. Instead, they bought me a second-hand one, a shiny Raleigh with a red frame, and I was thrilled. A few weeks later, one Saturday morning, I went to the shops for my mother and left the bike outside the butcher's. When I came out, a man was looking closely at it. It had been stolen from him some months before. The police were briefly involved, and the bike was given back. My parents never got their £10 back, and I never got another bike of my own.

I had sat the eleven-plus early in 1953 at the grammar school that I aspired to attend – the Liverpool Institute High School for Boys. It was an easy choice for my parents to make, as both my older brothers had gone there, and my elder brother John was still in the sixth form when I arrived.

The Institute was a school with a great tradition. The building, with its frontage of classical columns in a street of tall and elegant Georgian houses, was completed in 1837, and though it had seen better days, and was increasingly overcrowded, boasted many striking features, including a horseshoe-shaped hall with a gallery. It had been, it is said, one of Charles Dickens's favourite lecture venues. The whole place was daunting for a new boy. The staff wore their academic gowns, and the prefects wore the short, commoners' gowns as worn at Oxford. The head boy got to wear a scholar's gown, adorned down the front with a double stripe of green ribbon. The laboratories, lecture rooms and most of the classrooms and desks were straight out of the nineteenth century.

The headmaster, the last of the great Institute Heads, was J. R. Edwards MA – dapper, ramrod straight, immaculately groomed, feared but respected – even his footfall on a corridor enough to silence the most rowdy class. He was an Oxford classicist who himself taught the classical sixth. Both my brothers before me had read Latin, Greek and Ancient History, so I had no say in the matter – it was the Classics for me, for the next eight years. The Institute had standards. To get your name on the Honours Board, just inside the magnificent iron gates of the entrance hall, it was not enough to have got a place at a university. You had to get an Open Award at Oxford or Cambridge – a scholarship or an exhibition.

In its heyday the Institute got plenty of those. In 1961, the year I left the school, it won eleven Open Awards to Oxford or Cambridge, nine of them in Mathematics – something no other school in the country could boast.

This great school served well most of the boys who attended it, although right from entry at eleven the boys were streamed by ability, and the less fortunate – even though they'd just passed the eleven-plus – found themselves on a slower track from which it was hard to escape.

But the school's reputation for top-end results kept the intake growing. It was built to accommodate 600 pupils. By 1960 it had about a thousand. But the left-wing educational ideologues were circling, and by 1980 the Institute was literally falling apart, systematically and deliberately starved of resources for political reasons. When a council effectively controlled by the Militant Tendency took power in Liverpool in 1983 the school was killed off, and closed in 1985. Ironically, it was Sir Keith Joseph, Margaret Thatcher's Education Secretary, who had to sign the death warrant. I was there on the July night that we performed the last rites. The highlight was an appearance by the legendary J. R. Edwards himself, who spoke with dignity, but with barely disguised bitterness and sorrow, at the great school's demise.

I spoke too, as did other old boys Bill Kenwright and Steve Norris. There was no sign of another famous alumnus, Derek Hatton, darling of the Militants, who had helped to put the knife in. He wasn't the darling of anybody in the great decaying hall of his old school that night.

By great good fortune, however, the long-term survival of the Liverpool Institute, and its eventual restoration, refurbishment and rejuvenation, had been assured thirty-two years earlier, on the day I joined the school in September 1953.

Because, on the same day, there was another boy among the new intake – James Paul McCartney. A month before I entered the world in Smithdown Road hospital, he had been born a few miles away in Walton hospital, where his mother was a nurse.

To my knowledge, Paul never forgot the debt he owed to his old school, and the start in life it gave him. Whenever we discuss those days now, he speaks of the place with affection. Part of that was the fine old building itself, a place of uniqueness and style, and Paul was deeply affected when in later years he saw how derelict it had become, and vowed to rescue it. More than that, Paul McCartney was deeply influenced by what went on inside it, and not much more than ten years after it closed he ensured that it opened again as the Liverpool Institute of the Performing Arts.

Paul himself has paid generous tribute to how his development was influenced by some quite special teachers. Foremost among them was Alan Durband, a young teacher of English, who brought to his classes not just a love of texts, but of ideas. Alan, by whom it was also my good fortune to be taught, discussed anything and everything with his pupils. He was an idealist who never pushed his ideas on his pupils. The first time I became aware of the depth of his personal idealism was one winter's night, when my girlfriend Sylvia and I walked up the hill from my home to the small Woolton Cinema. The film was the classic anti-war movie *On the Beach*, based on the Nevil Shute novel, telling the powerful story of a submarine crew who find themselves among the few survivors of a nuclear war. Alan Durband was standing outside the cinema, in the bitter cold, handing out CND leaflets.

But Alan never took his political beliefs into the classroom. He himself had been a pupil at the Liverpool Institute – he'd been Vice Head Boy – and when he left the school after the war he had to choose between National Service in the armed forces or working down the pits in the coal industry. He chose the latter – others were simply conscripted into the pits – and became one of Britain's 48,000 Bevin Boys. But Alan paid a price, with permanent damage to his lungs and heart, which was eventually to shorten his life. He saw the duty of the teacher as not to proselytise, rather to teach his pupils to ask questions, and never to be afraid to ask the obvious or query conventional wisdom.

He never differentiated between highbrow and lowbrow – *all* knowledge was of value. It made all the boys who came under his influence more acute observers of the world around them. There was no question he himself dodged. I remember the news leaking out to his class that Alan had got married the weekend before, and we started to pull his leg about it. Then someone asked him 'Sir, *why* did you get married?' and he thought for a moment and said, 'It was the nesting instinct.' I've never before or since heard a better reason for getting married, or a more expressive defence of the institution. The way he engaged with us was the mark of a great teacher.

Alan's heart finally gave out in 1993 at the early age of sixty-six, but the Sissons family played a small part in him reaching even that age. Five years earlier, his wife Audrey had telephoned to tell me he was desperately ill. I took my eldest brother Cliff, by then an eminent consultant cardiologist, to see him at his cottage near Oswestry. Cliff examined him, arranged for some further tests, and totally changed his medication and care regime. That day, and many subsequent visits to Cliff's out-patient clinics, transformed and extended Alan's life, giving the educational and artistic scene which he graced a few more years of this remarkable man.

His legacy is hundreds of fortunate pupils who will never forget him, and the many artistic causes that he fought for – including the founding of Liverpool's Everyman Theatre, which nurtured such talents as Bill Nighy, Pete Postlethwaite, Jonathan Pryce and Julie Walters. He also leaves a collection of translations of Shakespeare's plays into modern English – *Shakespeare Made Easy* – which were born out of his efforts to engage student teachers who themselves couldn't make head or tail of the Bard's works, let alone teach a class about them. Four years before Alan died, he was tickled to get a call, out of the blue, from Dustin Hoffman, who was doing his first Shakespeare as Shylock in the West End. The great American actor, with the help of Alan's *Merchant of Venice* paperback – original text on one page, plain English translation facing it – made a stunning success of his debut.

But Alan's place in folklore is assured by his influence on one boy – James Paul McCartney. At the outset he wasn't to know that in McCartney lay the genius to become a giant of popular culture; he treated all boys the same if they were interested in learning. But he lived long enough to have the satisfaction of knowing that he surely had a hand in Paul McCartney developing to his fullest potential.

With hindsight, I can see clearly now where the roots of my interest in journalism came from. It just became second nature to value good writing, and appreciate the power of words. It wasn't always the case. For a year or two in my teens, after someone gave me a second-hand chemistry set, I dreamed of being a scientist. I set up an elaborate experiment in the kitchen, heating various noxious things in my mother's pan in an attempt to make soap, or hair cream, or some combination of the two. As it heated up, with little help from the gas ring, the mixture dissolved the aluminium pan and its fumes stripped the paint off the ceiling. My mother's support for my education ever taking a scientific route evaporated totally as she contemplated the still fizzing remains of what had been her best pan.

Luckily, the lure of test tubes and retorts was short-lived. And it was finally extinguished in a science lesson at school when a flask in which the teacher was trying to make chlorine exploded. He'd added sulphuric acid to potassium permanganate instead of hydrochloric acid. I still have the bloodstained exercise book I was using at the time and any doubts I had about studying the Classics disappeared in that big bang moment. After all, whoever heard of a Classics master making a life-threatening mistake?

Apart from the debt owed to the great Alan Durband, my own development at the Institute was also deeply influenced by my Classics teachers. Donald 'Fanny' Bentliff was a dedicated and learned man, who looked not unlike 'Chalky' in the famous Giles cartoons, and sometimes, to my shame, we mocked him mercilessly behind his back. Always polite and caring, I will never forget his diplomacy when he discovered that my mother couldn't afford for me to go on the trip he was organising to Rome and Florence. He discreetly paid for the trip, and I paid him back with whatever we could afford, whenever we could. I am not sure that it ever covered the full amount, nor did he press for it.

I and countless others received from him and his meticulous attention to the grammar of Latin and Ancient Greek a knowledge of the structures and derivations of language for which I've been grateful at every turn of my journalistic career. I also picked up a piece of advice which has been invaluable professionally. The Headmaster, J. R. Edwards, was a stickler for his pupils deconstructing a piece of complicated Greek syntax to establish its meaning, and not just being tempted to have a guess at what it meant. He used to say, 'Look at it, and never give up what you do know for what you don't know.' I have never forgotten that advice. In a fast-moving news situation, or during a tricky interview, if you have a feeling that the viewer or listener is being asked to believe something that doesn't quite fit with something that you know for certain, then stick to your guns. You do no one any favours, least of all yourself, by abandoning your better judgement under pressure. That said, it can take a lot of courage, especially if you are a younger reporter or presenter, flatly to contradict a major figure in public life who is being economical with the truth, but if you are sure of your ground, you should do it firmly, and with civility.

Paul McCartney and I were on different tracks at the Institute (he was in the modern languages stream) but school life constantly brought us into contact, and he was always the sort of lively and energetic boy who stood out from the crowd. From early on in the school he developed a reputation as something of a cheeky chappie, quick thinking, always cheerful, very bright and not averse to gently sending-up unsuspecting members of staff.

The one word that you never heard used about Paul was 'malicious'. Later in the school his artwork – colourful, original and bold – covered whole walls of the art room, and at that stage I would have put money on him becoming a successful artist rather than a musician and composer. I can claim to have shared a stage with him, and got more prominent billing, when we both appeared in an Alan Durband production of Shaw's *Saint Joan*. Paul was an assessor, I was Warwick. In the trial scene, his back to the audience, and hidden under a voluminous cloak and hood, McCartney risked a surreptitious drag on a Woodbine, betrayed to his fellow actors only by a wisp of smoke and that distinctive seedy aroma.

A year behind us at the Institute came a new group of boys fresh from the eleven-plus, which included George Harrison. By then John Lennon was starting his third year at another leading Liverpool grammar school, Quarry Bank. None of them knew any of the others, but then George and Paul got chatting one day when they caught the same bus home. They weren't the only kids in Liverpool whose imagination was captured by the new sounds of the mid-1950s. On the last day of each term at the Institute boys were allowed to bring a hobby or pastime to school to amuse themselves, while the staff prepared the school reports. I remember well McCartney and Harrison and other boys bringing their guitars in, twanging away, determined to sound like Bert Weedon or Duane Eddy.

Members of staff were not impressed. Fred Bilson, a young Latin master, admonished Paul thus: 'Always remember, McCartney, there's plenty of people in this sixth form with as much talent as you, or possibly more.' Bilson himself, many years later, confessed that it was 'the daftest thing I ever said in my life to anyone, women included'. Les Morgan, a maths teacher of the old school with a disconcerting squint, wrote on Paul's report: 'He will never earn a living playing the guitar.'

Paul and George didn't particularly stand out at that stage. By far the best guitarist, completely self-taught like the rest of them, was Colin Manley, who like me was in the Classical sixth. Some years later Paul told BBC Radio Merseyside that Colin was brilliant: 'The finest guitarist around Liverpool in the early '60s and he could do all that Chet Atkins stuff with two fingers. All the lads tried to play like that, but only Colin could do it really well.' Colin founded a group called the Remo Four with another close friend of mine, Don Andrew, and went on to play with a number of big names before touring the world with The Swinging Blue Jeans. His many friends and admirers were shocked to learn of his death, just short of his fifty-seventh birthday, in 1999, and they packed the Liverpool Philharmonic Hall in tribute to another boy from the Liverpool Institute who had done his bit to change the face of popular music.

But the real stroke of fate, which had ensured that all other gifted and popular musicians from Liverpool would remain forever in the shadow, was that which brought together Paul McCartney and John Lennon.

I am convinced that the Beatles would never have come into being, and that John Lennon in particular would never have achieved his iconic status, had it not been for Ivan Vaughan, who was born on the same day as Paul McCartney, 18 June 1942.

In 1950, with four boys now in the family, my mother and father had moved out of our tiny rented house in Ingleton Road. They'd done a house swap, which was quite common at that time, for a three-bedroomed council house, with front and back garden, in the leafy suburb of Woolton. The couple with whom we swapped did so because the husband wanted to move closer to his work. He made a living cutting men's hair, and he worked in a barber's shop at the top of Penny Lane. That alone would today have made him a celebrity, immortalised in the McCartney song.

The house in Woolton was not much more than a mile from where Ivan lived, and we often caught the same number 5 bus towards the city centre, getting off at Hope Street, and walking the few hundred yards to school. Ivan became one of my two closest friends at the Liverpool Institute. For many years before important exams we revised our classical set books together at each other's homes. We went on bike rides and to the cinema. During school holidays we hung out together. At school we enjoyed each other's company, and led each other into mischief and practical jokes, mainly played on the staff.

Ivan was in the same class as I throughout our time at the Institute. But Ivan had two characteristics that I lacked. He was a better classicist, and he was totally, outrageously uninhibited in his humour and his attitude to life.

Well over six feet tall, slim and gangly, with his black hair swept into an extravagant 'Tony Curtis', Ivan was the original article. He tried to make his school uniform look as much as possible like a Teddy Boy suit – in fact I'm not so sure it wasn't a Teddy Boy suit. The school badge was never sewn onto the breast pocket, but loosely attached to it with a paper clip. Ivan was seemingly uninfluenced by anyone else – his father had been killed in the war – and at home he seemed to be able to come and go as he pleased. He appeared to have a very understanding mother. Ivan saw humour in everything, but without a streak of meanness. He kept us amused by drawing nonsense cartoons, and passing them round the class. He had no role models, although he did routinely try to impersonate Robert Mitchum. Once, drawing himself up to his full height, he towered over one of his teachers, and drawled 'I know you think I'm soft sir, but I'm hard, damned hard.' He got away with it because he was highly intelligent, and his class work was always done conscientiously and to a high standard. But I have never met anyone who was so entertainingly unpredictable in his everyday conduct.

He painted his name in two feet high red letters on the front upstairs bay window of their house, outside his bedroom. He painted his shoes in glossy yellow paint, to the despair of his mother, because he only had one pair. He played mercilessly on the sensitivities of his teachers to the hidden poverty among some children. If you were absent from school for any reason at the Institute, you had to present an Absence Card, filled in with the reason for your absence, and signed by one of your parents. From time to time Ivan would take a day off, but duly presented his Absence Card. On it, under 'reason for absence', he'd have written 'shoes at the menders'. It worked every time – no teacher at the Liverpool Institute dared take issue with that.

The relevance of Ivan Vaughan to the Beatles story, is, of course, that Ivan lived next door to John Lennon. As John Lennon's career progressed, he became a cult figure for millions. His sketches and poems, his laconic humour and his every pronouncement were seized upon as evidence of a unique genius. There is no doubt that in his lyrics and music that description is fitting. But as a personality, and as a thinker, for me and for many of my close friends at the Liverpool Institute, Ivan was the original article. There was little evidence that John Lennon rubbed off on Ivan Vaughan, but plenty that it worked the other way round.

Lennon lived in Menlove Avenue with his mother's sister, Aunt Mimi. Ivan lived in the adjacent Vale Road. Their houses in fact were back to back – separated by their small back gardens. It is well documented how the two of them formed a primitive, skiffle-type group, the Quarrymen. Ivan, although he had no musical ability, played the bass, made of a broom handle, some twine and a tea-chest. The Quarrymen, however, became good enough to take some bookings, one of which was to play at the annual garden fete of St Peter's Church in Woolton, on 6 July 1957. In itself, it was quite a departure for the fête – a ritual, pillars-of-the-community type of event – to book that sort of entertainment. I was there that day, being a member of the St Peter's Youth Club, and in those days a regular church-goer. The Quarrymen attracted a curious crowd, mainly of the younger element. Ivan had told me they were going to be playing, and I felt I'd better have a look, but I, like most people there, left distinctly unimpressed.

I wasn't the only one from our school curious about this new group. McCartney had also turned up. He knew Ivan. Ivan introduced him to John. The band could only be improved, and Paul was a better guitarist than any of them. The rest is history.

Taking the Quarrymen forward meant that there was no place for Ivan. But he continued on the fringes, talking them up, and trying to get people to go to hear them because of his friendship with John. Ivan got very excited when he found out that my eldest brother had saved up and bought a tape-recorder, a rarity in those days.

I got back to our house in Woolton one day to be told by my mother that Ivan and John Lennon had knocked on the front door and asked if they could borrow it. She sent them away with a flea in their ear. My mother liked Ivan very much, but had no time for Lennon.

In those days, around Woolton village, John had acquired something of a reputation as a teenage troublemaker. But I sometimes wish that she *had* lent them the tape recorder, and that they'd brought it back a week later with hours of early Lennon music and songs on the reels of tape. And that one day we could have discovered them...

The future Beatles continued to flit in and out of my life. A year after that historic performance by the Quarrymen behind St Peter's Church, John Lennon's mother Julia was killed by a car in Menlove Avenue as she crossed the road after visiting her sister Mimi. I was a passenger on a number 5 bus which was caught up in the chaos at the scene within minutes of it happening.

Ivan Vaughan and John Lennon, while both were neighbours, got up to all sorts of scrapes. Perhaps the most daring involved their two schools, Quarry Bank and the Liverpool Institute. Ivan confided the planning to me: he was going to go along to Quarry Bank one day, and be introduced by John Lennon as a new boy. Sure enough, come the day, there was no Ivan in our class – he was sitting in Lennon's class, five miles away, having detached his Institute badge. For a whole day Quarry Bank were taken in – his name was put on the register, and he was issued with all the books. By the time the deception was rumbled, Ivan was back at the Institute. An angry Quarry Bank headmaster complained to our own J. R. Edwards. Edwards the disciplinarian sent for Ivan. His punishment was a mild rebuke. In private Edwards, I am told, was not displeased that the Institute had put one over on the old rival, Quarry Bank.

Although Lennon and Vaughan remained friends for many years, Ivan was also to develop a lasting and very close relationship with McCartney, who was not slow to put his hand in his pocket with generous help for his old friend and his close family when they were in need in later life.

Twenty years later, Ivan contracted Parkinson's disease, which gradually destroyed his life. But while he was fighting it, with considerable courage and lack of self-pity, the BBC made a documentary about him, and how the quality of his life was being helped by the drug L-Dopa. Ivan was teaching at Cambridge at the time, and the documentary was presented by Dr Jonathan Miller. When I watched it, unless I blinked and missed it, the great polymath omitted entirely to mention Ivan's unique claim to fame – that he was the man who made one of the world's great introductions. I have no doubt that Ivan would not have volunteered the information. Indeed, there were many stages in his life when Ivan could have made money out of it. He never did. To Ivan it was no big deal. Ivan died in 1993, the same year as Alan Durband.

My years at the Liverpool Institute were happy ones. It was a school that set high academic standards, yet catered for every non-academic interest, with scores of different societies. It was strong at sport, but it was a football school, not a rugby school. To this day I can't tell you the first rule of rugby. One afternoon a week, every class was timetabled to catch the bus down to the school's excellent playing fields at Mersey

Road, not far from the river, in the suburb of Aigburth. In the winter and spring terms everyone was expected to play football. Two captains from the same class picked their sides alternately, from the assembled boys, and the two sides would play each other. When twenty-two boys had been picked, the rest, known as the Left Overs, had a kick around on their own. I was always in the Left Overs. I was not aware of any psychological damage from my permanent inclusion among football's low achievers, nor did it damage my lifelong affection for the sport.

I was better at cricket, a game I really loved and worked at, and eventually I opened the batting for the First XI. Years later, when I became well known, staff at the school insisted I had been captain of cricket at the Liverpool Institute. It wasn't true, but I was slow to deny it.

I was never tempted to join the Combined Cadet Force, although many did. There was some attraction in the uniform, going on manoeuvres, and being permitted to take your gun home, to learn how to strip it down in your own kitchen. It sounds amazing now, but it was quite common to see schoolboys carrying Lee Enfield rifles and Bren Guns on the bus.

The two big events at the Institute, which took place in alternate years, were the Hobby Show and the School Play. The Hobby Show was an open evening at which the ingenuity of hundreds of boys was on display, in exhibitions and demonstrations. There was also a House one act play competition. The School Play was a major dramatic production, usually with Alan Durband in charge. I never missed an opportunity to act, and on one occasion produced and appeared in the winning one-act play.

For a while I was quite stage-struck, and began to fantasise about a career on the stage and my name in lights. I think it was Alan who suggested that I should talk to a professional actor about it all, so I went to see a fine leading player from the Liverpool Playhouse, Trevor Baxter. As he stood before a blazing fire in his large rented apartment, in a faded but genteel Georgian terrace near the school, I was sold – it was just the sort of place I could see myself living in. Then, pouring a second glass of sherry, he told me about how hard it was for most actors to find work, and how little the vast majority earned. I was unsold. In later life I was to meet Trevor Baxter from time to time, usually at a Bill Kenwright first night. I am not sure he fully appreciated his importance in my life, but, for gently steering me away from attempting to earn a living treading the boards, I am eternally grateful.

I wasn't completely put off acting, however, and did as much of it as I could both at school, and later at university. In the career that opened up for me, many of the skills that an actor needs – such as the ability to hold a pause, to see the worth of not filling every space with words, and not to be afraid of a telling silence – have been of great value.

But at the time I hadn't the faintest idea what lay ahead. It was my good luck that eventually so many things fell into place, and that so many good people encouraged me and my contemporaries to fulfil our potential. There was just one snag at the time.

No one went anywhere if they didn't pass EXAMS.

Chapter 2

The Werld of Werk

Exams – they dominated my life. I spent eight years at the Liverpool Institute, four of them in the sixth form. And most of those years were designed to enable boys to pass exams. No one said it, but despite all the other things the school had to offer, the ethos was that if you didn't pass the exams, you didn't have much of a future. The first major hurdle was O levels, taken at the Institute by those judged to be the brighter boys at the end of their fourth year; and by those thought more fitted for the slower track at the end of their fifth. That fifth year was known as the Remove. It was a slow track to O levels, thereafter a fast track out of the school at sixteen – it being practically unknown for anyone in the Remove to make it to the Sixth Form. That was George Harrison's route through the school. Paul McCartney, in the same year as I, did O levels in four years, the gateway to the Sixth Form. At the Institute you had to be good at exams.

And not just any old exams. The school wasn't interested in entering you for ten or twelve O levels, half of which might be in fringe subjects of little lasting value. They wanted good marks in the core subjects – Maths, modern languages, Latin, Geography, English and so on. They weren't going to waste their money entering you for lesser subjects which were little more than trophies, as some schools seem happy to do today. They also expected this core clutch of O levels all to be passed at the same time – otherwise, again, the route to the sixth form would be closed. For boys who made it into the sixth form there were internal tests at the end of every term to keep them on their toes for the A levels they would sit at the end of their second year. Kids today complain of examitis. It's not a new condition.

I got six good O levels, but didn't pass Maths. I hated Maths, I couldn't do it; I could add up and take away and do mental arithmetic quickly. But the algebra, geometry and trigonometry lost me completely. It might as well have been Aztec on the page before me. Teachers tried. I volunteered to stay behind after school to have things explained to me. They painstakingly went through the equations and the diagrams time after time. I nodded bravely – willing them not to think they were failures as teachers, and not to think me too thick. And then I went away and tried to do the stuff myself and my brain slowly switched off and went into standby mode, waiting for the stimulus of something it could actually cope with.

If I'd had to pass O-level Maths, I would still be trying today. But not so fast – the pass mark then was 40 per cent. Even 30 per cent wouldn't be regarded as a 'fail' today. Surely today I could scrape a 'pass' by spelling my name correctly, doing a few sums, and not writing on both sides of the paper at once...?

But that Maths failure was to haunt me – and nearly cost me my place at Oxford.

O levels, for me and my contemporaries, were an important milestone. As we'd gone through the lower school we'd been a pretty lively and often very mischievous class, which could sometimes be quite badly behaved.

We had our hooligan moments and, as a herd, instinctively knew when a teacher was weak. There were always one or two of them, and once we'd sussed out that they didn't know how to impose themselves on a class, they were lost. One science teacher in particular was goaded mercilessly, even cruelly. The last straw was when someone lit a fire in a waste bin at the back of the laboratory, and he totally lost it. Leaping down from the raised platform at the front of the class with a howl of anger, he tripped and thrust an outstretched arm through the glass panel of a balance case. The broken glass lacerated his arm, and there was blood everywhere. None of us in his class showed any remorse or sympathy. It is an episode of which I am not proud. Perhaps there was an element of poetic justice when that other science teacher blew us all up with his chlorine experiment.

Everything changed after O levels. A total change of gear. Boys were expected to decide whether or not they now wanted to take their education more seriously.

Why did I now spend four years – half my entire time in the school – in the sixth form? I think it was because the expectations that others had of me were always higher than those I had of myself. I wasn't an academic high-flyer, but I had teachers who believed I had other things to offer than sheer academic achievement. They believed that I should go to a good university, and if it took me an extra year or two to get the results needed, they encouraged me to do it. And not just a good university. One member of the Institute's teaching staff, in particular, thought I should go to the best university. No prizes for guessing who that was.

Although he didn't teach me in the sixth form of the Liverpool Institute, I got to know Alan Durband quite well in my sixth form years at the end of the 1950s. He and his wife Audrey lived about half a mile from my home in Woolton, and quite often, after school, he would offer me a lift home in his bubble car. He had a BMW Isetta, in which you sat with only a piece of glass in a flimsy door between you and certain death should the lorry in front suddenly brake. (That was at the same time as the noisy two-stroke engine a few inches behind you was crashing into your spine.) It could be a hair-raising ride. Nonetheless it was Alan's pride and joy, and he regularly used to park it next to the Headmaster's shining new black Ford Consul (state of the art 1950s saloon car, 0 to 60mph in thirty seconds). On those journeys home in the Isetta (never mind 60mph, this was 0 to 30mph in thirty-six seconds) we talked about anything and everything – even gardening, a pastime about which I had become quite phobic, maybe even damaged psychologically by those Sunday mornings pushing steaming barrow loads of hen manure through the streets to father's allotment. Alan was looking for a gardener, however, and the offer of a job mowing his grass and hoeing his weeds, at two shillings and sixpence an hour, was one I couldn't refuse. Besides, I needed the money, and my first taste of earning was the ten shillings a week paid to me by the Durbands.

I was actually mowing his lawn one Saturday afternoon, when he came rushing out, flushed, but with a big smile on his face. His first child, Mark, had just been born in the upstairs bedroom. He gave me an extra five shillings.

My mother was very proud that I was the trusted gardener of one of the best-liked teachers at the City's best grammar school. My father grumbled that I was willing to dig someone else's garden, but not to help him on his sodding allotment. By now, more than ten years after the war, my father was still involved with ships, working as a relief officer for the Harrison Line. The work was not well paid, but very responsible, and sometimes involved two or three weeks away from home, looking after cargo vessels while they were in various ports. His absences lifted a cloud from my life, and I suspect that my mother sometimes welcomed them as well.

Because money was always tight at home, the only cash I had for most of my teens was earned by me in my spare time. Between the age of fifteen and when I left University at twenty-two, I had a succession of part-time and vacation jobs of enormous variety. Not only did they keep me solvent, they were in themselves a fund of experience, absolutely invaluable when I eventually entered broadcast journalism. I have never forgotten the people I met and worked alongside. It gave me early and enduring insights into the human condition. Much of the work was hard, repetitive or boring, or all three, but there was an added bonus – it was in Liverpool.

Working alongside fellow Liverpudlians in factories, bakeries, on the docks, on the buses and delivering the Christmas mail, it came home to me what remarkable people they are. Scousers are people whose sense of humour, and unique take on the hand that fate has dealt them, sets them apart. Stubborn, opinionated, capable of what outsiders see as sometimes disproportionate sentimentality, they've even been accused by none other than the Mayor of London, of having a sense of 'shared tribal grievance about the rest of society'. But for me they are the salt of the earth, and those jobs I had drew me closer to my roots. The subsequent direction that my life took showed that you can take the Scouser out of Liverpool, but you can't take Liverpool out of the Scouser.

My eldest brother Cliff, by now a medical student, showed me the way into this world of vacation work and part-time jobs. Sometimes he juggled two or three of them, and if he had to be in two places at once he turned to me for back-up. In one Christmas vacation he was portering for the Belfast boats and simultaneously holding down another job guarding turkeys at a huge farm on the City outskirts. For a number of nights he left me in charge of the turkey patrol, and I sat all alone huddled over a coke stove until, as dawn broke, he reappeared. There was a shotgun, but thankfully no ammunition, and from time to time I conscientiously prowled around the premises – mesmerised by tens of thousands of dead turkeys hanging from hooks, dripping into great vats of warm blood. I hadn't the faintest idea what I would do if turkey rustlers turned up. Actually, they were cleverer than I thought. Five hundred birds went missing one night, and I didn't see a thing. In Liverpool's docks and factories that sort of loss was known as 'natural shrinkage'.

Anyway, thus blooded – almost literally – in the world of part-time work, I got a taste for it.

Many other jobs followed, and never a school holiday or university vacation was spent without earning money. In particular, Liverpool's large bakeries were always short of part-timers, particularly at night. A regular night shift that I worked involved unpacking huge slabs of lard and wheeling them around the various production lines where pies were made. Industrial relations throughout Liverpool at the time were pretty dire, and the big chain bakeries were no exception. In this one it took the form of lots of dumb insolence by the permanent workers against the bakery supervisors. In extreme cases, a reprimand from a supervisor would be followed by the worker on the receiving end blowing the contents of his nose into the pastry the moment the supervisor's back was turned. Great hilarity among all present, except the unsuspecting, inflexible management.

What struck me as very odd, in the world of Liverpool bakeries, was the management's obsession with accounting for every last cake and pie. No 'natural shrinkage' was allowed by them. If twenty pies or cakes went out to a shop, and only eighteen were sold, two had to be returned to the bakery. My mother, who for a time worked in a cake shop, saw long-serving shop assistants sacked for taking a bite out of a stale cake that the rules dictated had to be returned to the factory. They counted them out, and they counted them back. The phrase wasn't invented during the Falklands War.

Counting the pies back was another of my jobs, which broke up the monotony of unwrapping lard. Once it had been ascertained that all unsold pies and cakes had been accounted for, back at the bakery they had to be placed in large galvanised bins for disposal. I quickly learned that there were ingenious ways of breaking up what would otherwise become tedious routine. Our small cake and pie disposal team would compete at bowling, or throwing them into the bins from a distance. The bigger the distance, the more points you scored. And we invented a summer version of the game, too. Inspired by the clouds of wasps hovering over the bins in the warmer weather, we would hurl stale cream cakes through the swarm, and award each other points for the highest number of wasps we could stick to the wall behind the bins. So the time flew by.

As my teens progressed, however, other, more grown-up jobs opened up for me in the World of Work (or Werld of Werk as we Liverpudlians called it).

Each year there was temporary work delivering the Christmas mail. I loved the great seasonal atmosphere at the large Woolton sorting office, and most of the regular postmen welcomed having an extra pair of hands and legs to help them shift the mounds of envelopes and parcels. I walked miles every day, occasionally even being given a small gratuity by grateful householders. At the outset, being conscientious, I asked one veteran postman what I should do if I found myself at the end of my round with a number of letters that I wasn't able to deliver. He stopped pushing letters into pigeon holes, and leaned towards me. 'The procedure I've always adopted' he said, 'is to find a pillar box on the way back to the sorting office, and post them'. I was also unofficially instructed in how to handle that thorny, or perhaps one should say smelly, problem of the delivery of perishables. I put the advice into practice when, day after day, I took a badly wrapped Christmas goose out on my round, and every day the intended recipient failed to answer the knock. After a week, the goose was practically walking along behind me, so at the end of my shift I lobbed it over a hedge and went home.

Two other jobs completed my Liverpool education: security guard and bus conductor.

It was ridiculously easy to get a job as a security guard. I rang up Securicor's local office in Liverpool and made an appointment to see them. A rather disinterested bloke, who knew absolutely nothing about me, made me sign two forms. One was to certify I was now subject to a 'Fidelity Bond' – a form of insurance against me being a thief. And the other was to enable me to draw my uniform from the stores. I do not recall having to show Securicor any form of ID, nor did I receive any proof from them that I was a Securicor employee apart from the uniform.

My first assignment was to guard a building site on the Wirral. I was to prevent thefts from the site while it was unoccupied overnight. When I arrived at the location, I was met by a Securicor dog handler, who put me in charge of quite the nastiest and most vicious dog I have ever encountered. Or rather, he put the dog in charge of me. As soon as the handler left, and I was alone with the dog, it turned on me and chased me into the small security hut. There I was confined, a growling, vicious, hungry dog outside, until the handler arrived to set me free and control the dog twelve hours later.

The next night, I said I would manage without the dog. From that date I became a cat person.

One night a few days later, I did what I was paid to do. From my vantage point in the hut, I saw my building site actually being burgled – two men climbed in, cut open the gate, and proceeded to carry stuff out to a van. I phoned the police, who turned up and nabbed them with impressive speed. A week or so later I received a witness summons to attend the hearing of the case at Birkenhead magistrate's court. I turned up but wasn't needed, as the culprits pleaded guilty. For taking the day off to go to court, on Securicor's behalf, the company stopped me a day's pay. I didn't think to ask the court to reimburse me, because no one told me I could.

Securicor next introduced me to the world of the Liverpool docks.

For most Liverpudlians, at that time, the docks were off-limits. There were miles of docks, but all were surrounded with high walls, and the only routine access through what was meant to be tight security, was for the dockers and others who worked inside. In later years, the glories of some of the finest maritime architecture in the world would be accessible to all, but not then.

Until 1956 it was possible to ride for seven miles from Dingle to Seaforth on the famous Overhead Railway – the 'Dockers' Umbrella' – and look down and marvel at it all. I remember in early 1953 seeing a more apocalyptic scene from the Overhead Railway – the mighty liner *Empress of Canada* on fire and capsizing in Gladstone Dock – but that's another story. That I was able to get inside the Docks when I did, and to see something of the way they worked and were built, was down to Securicor.

My first task on the docks was to be the watchman – a statutory requirement – on a hazardous cargo that was stacked on the quayside at Huskisson Dock. It was a massive pile of metal drums, each bearing skull and crossbones danger signs and the name of some chemical which was unknown to me. For a week I sat there, perched on one of the barrels, during a cold and windy Easter, for twelve hours at a time. Securicor provided no shelter, and I brought my own food and a flask of tea. Some days the cold bit through my warmest clothing and the rain seeped through the topcoat of my uniform. I exchanged the occasional word with dock workers, read a bit and strolled around to keep my circulation moving. Then I caught the bus home. But for me, none of this time was wasted. It was another, different taste of the real world. Some people didn't do jobs as mind-numbing as this for just a week – they did them for most of their lives.

I wasn't yet to know that I was to become a journalist, but my thoughts and observations of the time were squirreled away and have never left me. Wise journalists never let any experience go to waste – especially if they have a weekly column to fill.

I was then assigned to a general cargo vessel, which had brought tinned food and other stuff from Australia. This was before the age of the container, so all the packing boxes were stacked deep inside the three holds. At the bottom of each hold, I was told, under all the other boxed cargo, was a 12,000 gallon cask of Australian white wine, which would eventually be revealed when the general cargo was removed.

I asked the office what my job would be, and was told that I must stop the dockers from stealing any of the cargo. The ship was being unloaded round the clock and I was assigned the night shift. I duly turned up, a callow youth in an ill-fitting security uniform and peaked hat, and climbed into the first hold. The looks I got from the Liverpool dockers, tough, grizzled and cocky, can be imagined. I was regarded as a joke. But the leader of one of the gangs was deadly serious about what would happen to me if I attempted to do my job.

Without barely bothering to encode what he was saying, he pushed his face close to mine. 'Hello there' he said with a smile, and then, with a hint of menace: 'You won't be seeing anything down here.' With that he gestured with his docker's hook to the crane overhead, which was hoisting a couple of tons of cargo from the hold. 'These things can be a bit unreliable,' he said, 'they've been known to drop a load, and crush someone to death.' I told him I got the message.

The image of all Liverpool dockers as loveable scallywags has eluded me ever since, however much it has kept music-hall comedians in work. To be fair, some of the greatest comedians in Liverpool are the dockers, I know that life on the docks, with family men ruthlessly exploited as casual labour during years of great hardship, stripped working men of their dignity, if not their honesty. They wouldn't be human if that kind of history hadn't left a legacy of resentment, and a feeling of entitlement to some perks of the job. But my exposure to the culture in which they worked was not a pleasant one.

Ten years later I would frequently be back on the Liverpool docks as an ITN correspondent, reporting on yet another crippling strike, increasingly connected with the dockers' resistance to the advent of containerisation, a way of handling cargo favoured by shippers because it is totally secure. And if the disputes weren't about containers, they would be about the practice of 'working the welt', which I also saw at close-hand. The way it worked was like this: two gangs of men would be assigned to unload each hold of a ship. When they arrived for work, one gang would find somewhere where they could put their feet up and go to sleep. The other gang would work for an hour and then change places with the first gang, and so on. After eight hours, everyone would go home, no one having worked more than four hours.

Year after year the employers would buy out the practice with increased pay offers, and year after year agreements to end 'working the welt' were cynically disregarded. But because there were too many dockers for the work available, I also understood the insecurities which led to the practice being perpetuated. Whenever I reported on industrial relations in Liverpool, I did so with a bit more knowledge and experience than most other reporters.

So, on my watch, in that ship, the dockers went about their business, in their time-honoured way, and I let them get on with it. But to be fair, the only part of the cargo I know for certain was stolen came to light when the final packing cases were removed from the last hold, and the mighty 12,000 gallon cask of Australian wine was ready to be lifted out. It was empty. Harry Houdini couldn't have arranged a better vanishing act.

By far the most enjoyable period in this great patchwork of part-time and vacation work were three stints I did working as a Liverpool bus conductor – probably about six months in all, spread over three summers. People have often said I have a gift for handling meetings – not only did I go on to chair BBC's *Question Time*, but I have been in demand fairly constantly for private corporate events, when the *Question Time* format can be reproduced, usually with a management panel facing their employees, or a panel of experts answering questions from fellow professionals. Hand on heart, I count myself lucky that, all those years ago, I had the advantage of being able to cope with busloads of Scousers in my home city. If you can handle that, you can handle anything.

There was no interview for the position of bus conductor. I applied to Liverpool Corporation Passenger Transport, filled in a form, and the job was mine – subject to passing the examination for the PSV (Public Service Vehicle) Conductors' badge.

This involved a week-long course of a few hours a day. I reported for the course to the training centre at the Dingle bus garage, in south Liverpool. There, with a dozen or more other wannabe bus conductors, we learned the essentials – ringing the bell (no banging on the ceiling above the driver in lieu of it), changing the displays showing the destination and route number, and filling in the way bill. And we got to play with those lovely old metal machines, which printed the tickets when you dialled the fare and turned the handle. The course was conducted by a large, shambling bus inspector, with showers of dandruff on his shoulders. He seemed be a caring man and, before we left him, he gave us all tips in self-defence. We would, he said, need to know how to defend ourselves should any passenger turn nasty – the most drastic response being to hit the assailant with our ticket machine. Throwing a handful of small change hard into someone's face was also likely to be effective. In my bus conducting career I needed to resort to neither.

One or two people dropped out of the course, clearly defeated by some of its more challenging aspects. There is no shame in that – it's believed that our former Prime Minister John Major, in his late teens, applied to be a bus conductor at the Brixton garage in south London, and missing out on that job didn't seem to do him any harm at all.

However, my training over, and clutching my brand new plastic PSV badge, (which entitled me to free travel) I caught a bus to the Corporation's transport uniform store, at the depot behind the art deco Littlewood's building in Edge Lane. There I was issued with two pairs of trousers, with a neat red stripe down them, and two lightweight summer jackets. I was ready for action, and reported the next day to the bus garage at Speke, a few miles from my home.

My first outing on a bus was a disaster. I found out too late that I suffered dreadfully from travel sickness. With a busload of morning rush-hour passengers watching in amazement, I leapt off the bus soon after taking command, and threw up all over the pavement.

The next few days I dosed up with travel sickness pills, gradually got the hang of things, and even started to enjoy myself. There was a great spirit among the drivers in the garage and, because I was quite nimble up and down the stairs and fast on the bell, I became quite popular with them. They liked conductors who kept the bus moving. What really impressed me was how skilful most of those bus drivers were. At Speke they had some old Daimler buses, which didn't have speed limiters, and the first couple of buses out at 3.30 in the morning could be a white-knuckle ride as they were raced down to the Pier Head.

But the real test of a bus conductor is the passengers. I learnt all the repartee: someone would ask 'Is this bus going to Speke?' and I'd reply 'It'll be a miracle if it does.' To the enquiry 'Do you stop at the Pier Head?' the mandatory reply was 'We'll all get wet if it doesn't'. It never failed to raise a smile. Well, that's my story. But the real comedians on the buses were the passengers. I really did hear two Scousers talking about their wives' mothers – one said 'My mother in law's an angel', to which his friend replied, 'You're lucky. Mine's still alive.' Late one night a very drunk and heavily painted 'lady of the night', of mature years, started pestering my passengers, walking up and down the bus being mildly offensive. We stopped the bus at the Garston garage, and two young policemen got on. She became a bit violent, so they handcuffed her, and as they did so she told them, in a flash of lucidity, 'That'll be an extra ten quid.'

Those months were one of the formative periods of my life. I learned how to handle busloads of drunks on the way home from a night out, during which most of them had spent everything they had on them, including the bus fare home. At the other end of the day, taking the first busload of workers to the Dunlop factory at the crack of dawn, I was struck at how quiet and subdued, almost cowed, some were, and how most of them clearly hated going to work. Those of us who do something we like for a living don't know we're born.

In these ways, earning some money and learning about life, I spent the time between terms at school and university.

But let's just rewind a little to my sixth form education.

At the end of my second year in the Upper Sixth I passed three A levels – with a distinction in Latin, and passes in Greek and Ancient History. The advice from my Classics teachers was to try to improve these results, by re-taking the exams at the end of a third year in the Sixth thus giving myself a better chance of a place at a top university. Accordingly, in that third year, I took all three subjects again and while waiting for the results was offered a place at Bristol University, to study Latin and Drama. Convinced that that was the best I could hope for, I prepared to leave the school. But my mentor Alan Durband had other ideas. Those were the days, remember, when Liverpool's grammar schools each year sent significant numbers of boys and girls to Oxford and Cambridge – a generation later there were years when Liverpool's state schools sent no pupils at all to those universities.

Against this background, Alan was convinced I could get to Oxford. Furthermore, he confided in my elder brother Cliff that if I stayed on for a fourth year in the sixth Form, the view in the staff common room was that I should be made Head Boy – which would be an enormous boost to my chances of achieving an Oxford place. I was sceptical, but Cliff, privy to the intelligence from Alan Durband, egged me on, and Bristol said they'd hold their place open for me. It was a gamble, but on the last day of term, the day which I had planned to be my last in the school, and at the end of the last assembly, the headmaster J. R. Edwards announced that I would be Head Boy for the coming year.

All I had to do now was repay the faith that had been placed in me. The omens were not great – during the vacation, I got my second lot of A-level results, and they weren't as good as the first.

I know the reason. My life had become full of distractions, some quite pleasant, and I had just tired of taking exams. I'd taken my eye off the ball. I was also doing very little school work in the holidays, preoccupied as I was with putting some money in the bank. I also had quite a growing social life.

Most of that revolved around the youth club at St Peter's Church in Woolton, whose annual fête had witnessed that moment of destiny for Lennon and McCartney. There was a youth club dance once a week, and there were GIRLS. There were excursions to places like Blackpool and Morecambe, places I never tired of going to. Returning years later to report the party conferences, I always found time to ride the trams and walk the Pleasure Beach, reliving those innocent days. I produced plays for the youth club, and played for their cricket team, as well as for the school first XI. It being a church youth club, we were all expected to go to church on Sundays, which became another social event in itself – another opportunity for the boys to sit with the girls, and chat them up as we stood around afterwards.

It was at St Peter's that I met and fell in love with my future wife, Sylvia. Very attractive, dark haired and slim, she was at Calder High School for Girls, and was a year younger than me. Initially, she was always with a group of her school friends, one or two of whom I knew better than her. She came to the dances and turned up occasionally to watch me playing cricket. But I knew there was something special going on when I realised that she was the only person in the group I could focus on. There was no flash of light or celestial choir. We just found ourselves together more and more, and felt thoroughly comfortable with each other. My mother liked Sylvia from the moment she met her, and they always remained very close, sharing many of the same values.

Very early in our relationship, Sylvia and I were drawn closer when one day she telephoned in tears to tell me her father – whom I hadn't met – had been killed. He was a site engineer for a big building firm, and had been struck by a bolt that flew off a machine he was examining. We married a year after I left university, had three children of which we are both very proud, and lived happily ever after. That, however, tells only half the story. As my career unfolded, Sylvia always had an uncanny instinct for how the big stories I was involved with should be handled, what the underlying issues were and the key questions that should be asked. Sometimes she saved me from myself, and I was fortunate to have had that sort of intelligence and support to lean on, an empathy that was there from those early beginnings at St Peter's Church.

I wasn't totally immune to the religious aspects of being part of a church social scene. For a while I became quite religious, and decided to get confirmed, rising early thereafter on Sunday mornings to go to communion. I was chosen occasionally to read the lessons in church, and even discussed with the Rector, Morris Pryce-Jones, the possibility of becoming a clergyman. With hindsight, I can't believe I did that. But the flirtation with such thoughts didn't last too long and nor, after two or three years, did my religious belief itself.

So, there I was at the beginning of the school year in September 1960, Head of School, and great things expected of me. I tried hard to put in extra work on my Classics, knowing how much competition there would be when my time came to travel to Oxford and show what I could do. But I found being Head Boy, of a school with nearly a thousand pupils, had its own pressures. The Headmaster had a heart attack and missed most of that last year, which affected school discipline to some extent, and it fell to me to make sure the prefects were well organised to compensate. I also had to take the lead in many school functions, won a Liverpool University prize for 'Excellence in Speaking Latin Aloud', and made the last ever Latin speech, traditionally made by the Institute Head Boy, at the December prize giving.

Shortly after Christmas, in the bitterly cold winter of early 1961, I caught the train to Oxford to sit the Classics exam at St John's College. It was a total culture shock, like being sent to some kind of nineteenth-century punishment cell. The place was freezing. I was shown to a cold room with a one-bar electric fire, and the bathroom – no hot water – was the other side of the quad. In the room there was simply a printed piece of paper telling me what the exams would be, and when and where I would go to write my papers. There were four or five three-hour exams, sat in a cold room in silence, with a couple of dozen other boys. There was no conversation, no social contact of any kind, just a little 'pass the salt' at mealtimes. Then on the last evening I was summoned before a group of bored looking dons who seemed distinctly unimpressed. They were the only people to whom I spoke more than a few words during my short stay. I travelled back to Liverpool thoroughly depressed, to find the rejection letter on the mat the next morning. Neither St John's, nor any of the five or six other colleges in its group of colleges, had anything to offer me. With hindsight I was amazed that my poor frozen brain had worked at all while I was there.

Back at school they tried to cheer me up, and immediately entered me for the entrance exams at Lincoln College a few weeks later. Same routine, but nicer weather, and a more friendly and polite college. Endless writing, a bit of small talk with other candidates, and I picked up not the slightest sign that they were interested in me. I was right.

One last try. J. R. Edwards, who by now had recovered from his heart attack and was back at school, said I should sit the exams at the final group of colleges to hold such exams in the academic year, that to which his alma mater, University College, belonged. Just before Easter I tried again, sitting the papers in the hall of New College, just round the corner from Univ. By now I felt I had a much better idea of what Oxford expected, was well practised, the weather was sunny, and I was a bit more cheerful. I may even have written some good Latin and Greek, although I never held out hope of an Open Award. A Commonership would suit me fine.

I was interviewed by a friendly group of dons at University College the evening before I left, and the impression I got was that they wanted me. Unlike the panels who had interviewed me at the other colleges, they were fully paid-up human beings. We even discussed what I might study at Univ – Philosophy, Politics and Economics. I told them frankly that I didn't want to study Classics – I'd had my fill of writing Greek prose and studying set books. They appeared to sympathise.

When I returned to Liverpool their letter arrived – the offer of a place at University College, Oxford to study PPE. I was walking on air. It was one of the most important days of my life, and I knew it. Looking back, those three or four months in 1961 were my first real taste of pressure, but I never realised it. At the time it was just hard work.

For the whole of the summer term of 1961, which was gloriously sunny, I had nothing to do. I could have left school, and probably would have done if I hadn't been Head Boy. Instead I played a lot of cricket, enjoyed life, and occasionally began to go into pubs – though not near the school.

Actually, my early euphoria was cut short when another letter landed on my mat from University College. Part of the ritual of being admitted to Oxford University was matriculation, the formal process of being placed on the roll of undergraduates. When you matriculated, you dressed up in cap and gown, dark suit and white tie (known as 'subfusc'), and went through an ancient ceremony. But it was more than a ritual – one of the requirements of matriculating, as the letter reminded me, was to have an O level in Mathematics, and where, it asked, was mine? No Maths, no place – however good your Latin and Greek was. I got a very cold sinking feeling. It meant that within a few weeks I would have to sit yet another exam, in a subject I knew in my bones I would not be able to pass, and that my Oxford dream would be snuffed out.

It was then that I had my first encounter with the good fairy who was to come to my aid on numerous occasions over the next forty years. Re-reading the small print of the matriculation requirements, I noticed that 'a science' would be accepted as a substitute for Maths. I had passed General Science at O level, and I wrote asking the college secretary at University College if that would qualify me. To my great joy, she wrote back saying that it would – but added that the University had ruled that 1961 would be the last year that General Science would be an acceptable Maths substitute. They were slamming that particular door, but I had just squeezed past as it shut.

That summer I spent most of my hard-earned savings. Ever since the bike I was given for passing the eleven-plus was unexpectedly repossessed by its legitimate owner, my main form of transport had been the green Raleigh belonging to my brother Cliff, of which he had less and less need. I rode that bike, with drop-handlebars and Sturmey Archer gears, everywhere. I polished it and cherished it. I endlessly repaired punctures in its thinning tyres, often at the side of the road, but it was never quite mine. One day I decided I would pedal no more. I wanted a scooter.

One of the younger school prefects already had one, and I was very jealous. His name was Steve Norris, and thirty years later he was to be transport minister for London and losing candidate for the London Mayoralty. He became famous, too, for aspects of his colourful social life, which also made great demands on his energy and ingenuity. I had got to know Steve well. He was good company and had an engaging Liverpudlian sense of humour. Two years after me, he too became Head Boy of the School. I turned to Steve for advice on scooters.

I had seen some second-hand scooters in a dealer's showroom a few hundred yards from the Institute, and one evening Steve and I went to have a closer look. The one that took my eye was a Puch SR150, a really lovely looking and powerful scooter in cream and red. At £79 it was out of my reach, but my girlfriend Sylvia's mother kindly offered to lend me the extra I needed, and Steve and I returned a few days later to buy it. (Although I parted with it for just £25 some years later, I wish I'd kept it – it's a classic model which now goes at auction for £3,000 or more.)

I handed over the money, and we wheeled it out into the street. I hadn't the faintest idea how to ride it, but I clung on to Steve and he drove us home. There he became my scooter driving instructor and in a couple of hours, new 'L' plates tied in place, cork crash helmet on my head, I entered my motorised age.

A few weeks later my schooldays were over. I didn't know what lay ahead – apart from a final ten weeks 'on the buses'. I shed a tear as I left the Liverpool Institute. It was an extraordinary place: a classic grammar school that provided the city and the country with a steady stream of professional people and public servants for more than a hundred years. Even that half of the school who didn't go on to higher education received one priceless gift – the Liverpool Institute gave them standards and spirit, while nourishing their individuality. For proof of that, look no further than my friends George Harrison and Paul McCartney. They went on to the highest level of popular culture, enriching the lives of hundreds of millions, and they had not a bad word to say about their school. Like the other Institute boys, they also remained classless, it being a place where you were never aware of the social circumstances of other boys. It was just never an issue.

For me, Oxford was now the great unknown. But I never doubted that my Liverpool education had equipped me to take whatever it could throw at me. Most importantly, in view of the career path that I would eventually take, my education hadn't ended at the school gate. Those varied jobs, working alongside real people in the real world, had given me self-confidence and adaptability. I didn't see it like that at the time. I simply looked forward to the unfamiliar challenges ahead.

Chapter 3

From Oxford to ITN

Getting into Oxford University had been far from plain sailing, but I at least thought that travelling there on my pride and joy, the scooter, would be straightforward and fun. That was before Oxford reminded me of the rules – no motorised transport until the second year. And even then you couldn't take it for granted you'd get permission. I had that joy still to come – and what a performance it was. The Regulations demanded that you had to dress up in cap and gown, and go in person to be vetted by the proctors (responsible for university discipline), pay a small fee, and if they liked the look of you receive from them a small green light that had to be mounted on your car or motorbike, the better for them and the police to identify it as belonging to a member of the university. For now, though, the scooter would have to stay in Liverpool.

So it was that, early on a freezing morning in October 1961, instead of zooming down the A41 I found myself waiting, early, at Rock Ferry Station, just outside Birkenhead, for one of the few through trains from Merseyside to Oxford. A week or two beforehand a British Road Services van had collected my luggage from home, diligently packed by my mother into one of my father's old sea trunks – still with his name stencilled on it: Lt. G. R. P. Sissons RNVR. There were a number of familiar faces on that station platform – other boys from the Institute going up for the first time, and some going back into their second or third years. It seemed quite a popular train. The strange thing was, during my three years at Oxford, I saw only one or two of these former schoolmates again. Most of us went our separate ways, with different interests and new sets of friends.

One or two boys, looking rather embarrassed, were being seen off by their parents. Sylvia went absent from school to wave goodbye to me. Already in her last year at Calder High, she had decided to apply for a place at a teacher training college as near to Oxford as possible. We'd seen each other nearly every day during that summer. There were tears as the train pulled out, made worse by its pungent clouds of smoke and steam and the noise drowning out our goodbyes.

A few hours later, University College made me feel at home. It was a welcoming, friendly place, quite unlike my first awful experience when I sat my exams at St John's ten months previously. Although Univ, founded by William of Durham in 1249, has a strong claim to be the oldest college in Oxford, it is far from being the stuffiest. The first members of the college staff that I and all the newcomers got to know were the porters. Univ's porters ruled the Lodge – the vestibule of a college that you step into off the street. They treated you as if you were grown up, until you demonstrated otherwise. They knew everything that was going on and they made things happen. They were also fiercely loyal to the college. They knew the rules about student conduct and made sure you knew them. The dons treated them with respect. Indeed, it was unacceptable conduct in the college for anyone to be offensive to any of the college servants.

Incidentally, among the new University College undergraduates welcomed that day was someone who was to become more famous than any of us, a young gawky mathematician called Stephen Hawking.

The head porter, the first servant of the college – first in every way – that we all met that afternoon, was Douglas Millin. Douglas had been an NCO in the Second World War, and looked like it – ramrod straight and smartly turned out. But it was his vocabulary which came as a shock to me.

Even though I had grown up in Liverpool, I had rarely heard, let alone used, the 'F' word – and I don't think I'd had a particularly sheltered upbringing. (Just remember the national outrage in 1965 when Kenneth Tynan used the word for the first time on television.) Douglas, however, used it with a frequency that forty years later would have put Gordon Ramsey in the shade, and no one batted an eyelid – although he never used it in the presence of women.

Douglas greeted the new intake as they arrived, and thereafter always remembered their names. If you were a Univ man, you were one of the family. Douglas had a second-in-command, Bernard, who liked to offer the new boys a word of advice from his army days – 'Keep your mouth shut, your bowels open, and trust nobody.'

But what set Douglas Millin apart, and gives him a little place in history, was his friendship with the future President of the United States, Bill Clinton. Clinton, with his friend and future Labor Secretary Robert Reich, arrived at Univ on Rhodes scholarships in 1968, four years after I left. Douglas reportedly looked the two Yanks up and down, and remarked of Reich – who was not the tallest of men, and appeared to be even shorter next to Clinton – 'I didn't know it was possible for America to produce someone that f***ing small.' But that seemed to break the ice, and soon Clinton and Millin were close friends, with Clinton, according to one account, often seen in Douglas's inner sanctum with his feet on his desk, answering his phone, helping to sort the mail and gossiping for hours on end.

Although no one doubted that it was a genuine friendship, it had advantages for the future President, with Douglas, it is said, turning a blind eye on those occasions where Clinton's social life collided with college regulations. By the time Clinton won the presidential nomination in November 1992, Douglas had retired and was in poor health. But when the invitations to the Presidential inauguration in January 1993 went out, the only person invited from Oxford – City or University – was Douglas Millin. Douglas declined the invitation, but two years later the two men met again, when Clinton returned to Oxford to receive an honorary degree. Despite all the calls on the President's time, and the people queuing up to see him, the only person to get a one-on-one chat with him was Douglas. With the Secret Service men outside looking anxiously at their watches, Bill Clinton and Douglas Millin sat for more than an hour in Clinton's old college room, talking about old times. Just think of it – an hour of the undivided attention of the President of the United States. Not even Prime Ministers get that.

There is, remarkably, a Sissons connection here. The room in which they sat, the converted alms houses at the back of the college, had been my room in my second year. When Bill Clinton moved into it five years after me, it enabled me to claim that I and Bill Clinton had been in the same bed, albeit not at the same time.

But I digress. My first term at Univ flew by. I couldn't believe that Oxford only had eight-week terms – by the time British Road Services finally delivered my trunk, it was almost time to start packing it again. I made a lot of new friends, and initially most of them, like me, hailed from northern grammar schools – we tended to stick together. The boys from public schools were friendly enough, but the big divide was that they seemed to have more money to spend than we did. For all the time I was at Oxford I was on a full grant – about £350 a year. My tuition fees, accommodation and main meals were paid for by the government, but everything else had to come out of the grant. Books took a large part of it, then laundry and other college sundries, subscriptions to societies, and a hundred and one other things that meant putting your hand in your pocket.

During the winter months – and Oxford can be one of the coldest places in England – there was the extra expense of keeping warm. The college provided the room, but you had to pay to heat it. The only heating was a two-bar electric fire. To switch on two bars was expensive, and you waited anxiously for your meter to be read at the end of term. So the coldest days were spent swathed in sweaters and in winter I usually slept in one as well.

During the three years I was there, I used to draw £2 a week from the Midland Bank at Carfax, the main crossroads in the town. Out of that I'd buy a small tin of coffee, some margarine, jam and crumpets. What was left might buy a round of beer on a Saturday night and a visit to the cinema.

At first, I envied the undergraduates from the public schools. Their social lives were different, their mantelpieces were always full of invitations to parties, and they could afford to eat out occasionally. Some, after the first year, had cars. One or two had been sent to Oxford as part of a career in the army, and were on officers' pay. Attractive Sloane-like girls seemed to be in and out of their rooms. One lovely blonde in particular, tripping round the quad, regularly took the eye. Her name was Joanna Trollope, who married and later divorced her Univ man.

When I went up to Oxford, the rules about visitors of either sex in all the undergraduate colleges were very strict – at Univ visitors were not allowed in your room after 7 p.m., although in my second year that was extended to 10 p.m. Having a member of the opposite sex in your room overnight was a very serious offence and everyone knew there was a risk of being sent down – expelled permanently from the University – if you broke the rule. You have to remember that in those days there were no mixed sex undergraduate colleges. As a result, transgressions of the segregation rules were often lapped up by the tabloid press.

In one notorious case in my first term, a female undergraduate at St Hilda's College, one of their most promising and brilliant scholars, was caught *in flagrante* with a man in her room during the day – bad enough for her, but also at a time when she should have been at a tutorial. Her punishment was merciless. She was sent down – excluded from the University with no appeal, her life in ruins. The man involved was rusticated by his college   sent down temporarily, able to resume his university career within a few weeks. The story was picked up by one or two newspapers, but quickly forgotten. Now it would be a national scandal, questions in Parliament, or even a matter for the European Court of Human Rights. As I recall, at the time there weren't even any demonstrations about the outcome, although students – led by contemporaries like Tariq Ali – habitually demonstrated about practically anything else. The fuss died down, and we all got on with the exciting business of our new student lives.

Whatever background you came from, the great leveller was the social intercourse in the college's own beer cellar, and at dinner in hall in the evenings, where everyone mixed in. And as we all got drawn into college and university life, with its many societies and interests, the earlier barriers didn't seem so important. I found also, as a Liverpudlian, that I was very much in fashion. The Beatles were starting to get very big, and I even got to meet Paul again briefly when they played at the Carfax Assembly rooms – their only Oxford appearance. The reflected glory did me no end of good among my peers, and delayed the disappearance of my Liverpool accent for some time.

But what really determined any success I had at Oxford, once I'd found my feet, was my tutors. The quality of the teaching, the sheer originality of the thinking, the depth of scholarship, the good humour and concern for one's welfare – all these things were very special, although not immediately appreciated in the excitement of actually being there.

However, they all had one thing in common with the best of the teaching at the Liverpool Institute: they taught you to ask questions, and how to measure whether you were getting the right answers. It was, of course, of enormous advantage that the group in which you were taught was never larger than four or five – and often just two. You were given personal attention, and you were regarded as an asset of the college, but an asset that could be improved. I called it teaching, but it was much more than that.

The fact that you were there at all had already demonstrated you had some intelligence, but what these dons wanted to do was to bring you to realise how you could use it. You could be told which books to read, but books were there not to tell you what to think, but rather to give you the background to take a view of your own – to challenge you to make up your own mind. The three dons I saw most of were Maurice Shock (Politics), David Stout (Economics) and Peter Strawson (Philosophy). Shock awakened in me a fascination with politics and political life which has never left me. Stout frightened me to death with his razor-sharp intelligence, and the huge reading lists he expected us to work our way through. I think he knew I'd never make an economist, but years later he was of enormous help to me when I became ITN's Industrial Editor.

Strawson, one of Oxford's greatest philosophers, and a kindly gentle man, destroyed – without setting out to – what little was left of my religious belief by the remorselessness of his reasoning. From time to time, these brilliant and busy men farmed us out to academics in other colleges for a term or two. For economics tutorials outside Univ, I was sent down the road to Nuffield College, to Dr Singh. Thirty years later, Manmohan Singh, as India's Finance Minister, was credited with liberalising the Indian economy, setting it on the path to globalisation, and in 2004 became its fourteenth Prime Minister. He wasn't a particularly inspiring economics tutor, but you can't win them all.

So, over that first year in Oxford I put the Classics, which had so far dominated my education, out of my mind and concentrated on understanding something of the modern world. At the end of my second term I passed my preliminary exams – which was just as well, because if you failed them you were sent down, without a second chance. What that meant was that I would then have no exams until the final exams – or Schools, as they were called – at the end of my third year. More than two years without exams meant there was plenty of time to do other things. I became involved with acting again, and with journalism for the first time.

University College had one of the best college dramatic societies in the university, Univ Players, and I became its treasurer. I acted, produced, directed and organised. I did not get deeply involved with the main university acting scene, OUDS and ETC, although a number of my friends did.

Univ Players had the talent and the resources to put on some ambitious work, and we did major productions of the relatively recently written *Rhinoceros* by Eugene Ionesco and *Sergeant Musgrave's Dance* by John Arden. But by far our biggest success was with Robert Bolt's *A Man for All Seasons*, likewise a fairly new play at the time. Robert Bolt himself came to see our production at the Oxford Playhouse, in which I played William Roper. It was a very talented company, and a number of those student actors went on to a career in theatre or film. One of them was Michael Johnson, who played the King, and later adopted the professional name of Michael York. But the actor that Bolt singled out for special praise was Michael Emrys Jones, later to act professionally as Michael Elwyn, whom I have now known for nearly fifty years. Michael's Cromwell, said the author, was the finest performance he'd seen in the role.

The director, also lauded by Bolt, was Braham Murray, who went on to years of success as artistic director of the Manchester Royal Exchange Theatre Company. The production secretary, incidentally, was Joanna Trollope, the blonde from the quad.

We took our production of *Rhinoceros* to the Student Drama Festival at Aberystwyth, where, to the amazement of everyone who saw it, the eccentric *Sunday Times* critic and festival adjudicator Harold Hobson rubbished it. Instead he gave the prize to a bone-numbingly awful production by Leeds University of Chekhov's *Three Sisters*. We were very aggrieved, and a lot of unkind things were said about Mr Hobson's faculties.

Much more fun was involved in taking our production of *A Man for All Seasons* for a week's run in Dublin at Trinity College, during an Easter vacation. I organised this, doing the ferry bookings from Liverpool to Dublin for the cast, costumes and props.

Unfortunately, transport costs took most of the money that had been budgeted, so the first task when we arrived was to find somewhere cheaper to stay than we had originally planned. A group of us set off, wandering the streets around Trinity College until we found a tall, dilapidated boarding house, hard by some railway arches. A notice, prominently displayed, said 'Vacancies'. We soon found out why, but it was getting late and beggars can't be choosers. The 'lady' told us she had the right number of vacant beds, it was affordable, so we sent a message back to the rest of the cast to move in.

There were no single rooms – most had three or four beds in them. We gave the few women in the company first pick, then the men scrambled for what was left. I was among the last four, who flung open the door of the last room at the top of the house at the back. There was me (William Roper), Michael York (né Johnson, The King), Adrian Brine (The Common Man) and Philip Bushill-Matthews (Richard Rich). We gazed inside. There, by the dingy light of a bare bulb hanging from the ceiling, we could see only three beds – one of them being a rather rickety-looking double. Michael and Adrian hesitated – fatally. For with one bound – or rather two – Philip and I 'bagged' a single bed each, and sat smugly on them. Michael and Adrian gazed, open-mouthed, at the double bed, theirs for the next week, and we all unpacked.

Because it was so grim and dark in the room, I flung open the grubby curtains, to expose the grubby window panes, but it didn't get any brighter. The reason no light was coming in was that, a few inches from the window was a blackened, sooty wall, and on the top of it, a few feet from our faces, ran the main Dublin to Belfast railway line.

It got worse. The bed linen had clearly not been washed since the last occupants of the room, probably people in the business of delivering coal, had moved out. And in one or two of the creases and crevices of the fabric, I thought I detected minute signs of movement. Other members of the company ran up the stairs reporting similar findings, and asked me, the organiser, to organise them some clean sheets. The 'lady' of the house was sympathetic, and said she would see what she could do. When we all returned from the theatre that night, we found that all the sheets had been freshly ironed, although none of them had been washed.

Dog tired, and with no fight left, we were soon asleep. Then, about two in the morning, the earth moved, and moved, and MOVED. A massive freight train was passing the window, practically close enough to touch. And as the noise reached its crescendo, the rickety double bed rattled, heaved and finally collapsed.

Years later Michael York and Adrian Brine collaborated on an acclaimed book entitled *A Shakespearean Actor Prepares*. There was no mention of how actors might prepare for bagging a bed in an Irish doss-house. In the end we all enjoyed the experience, the breakfasts were good, and life thereafter treated all of us well – especially Bushill-Matthews who went on to become, in the fullness of time, the leader of the Conservatives in the European Parliament.

For me, the acting road was fun, but it led nowhere. The journalism with which I became involved, and at which I first tried my hand, was another matter. I wasn't to know it at the time, but it was the beginning of a journey that made me a household name.

The job wasn't at all grand, and I think I got it only because they could find no one else to do it, but I was offered the position of football correspondent on the Oxford University newspaper, *Cherwell*. It was, however, a subject I knew something about, being a lifelong Liverpool supporter, so it wasn't very taxing. I went to no editorial conferences, and I never even got to meet the sports editor Jonathan Martin – until he became Head of Sport at the BBC many years later. I would simply get a note in my college pigeon hole, asking me to go to a match, and post my copy into the box outside the *Cherwell* office by the appointed deadline. I took to it like a duck to water, especially when it involved talking to people.

In my career I have carried out many thousands of interviews, but the very first was carried out on a rainy and deserted Oxford football field. The player I had been asked to interview was the 22-year-old Bob Wilson, who was just starting his long and glorious Arsenal career as an amateur. He was playing for an FA XI against Oxford University at Iffley Road, and was already being tipped for great things. I reported that he was 'the coldest man on the field when the final whistle went on this one-sided game.' The FA won 4–0, and Wilson had only one direct shot to deal with. I grabbed him afterwards, but he was in such a hurry to get into the warmth of the pavilion that he said nothing worth putting in the paper. Not only was it my first interview ever, it may have been his first experience of being interviewed.

The other big story I was fortunate to report was Oxford United's FA Cup run in early 1964. Oxford United were in the Fourth Division of the Football League, and after beating Brentford in a replay, became only the second club from that division ever to reach the FA Cup fifth round. They were drawn against Blackburn Rovers – who were top of the First Division. In modern terms, it was Accrington Stanley versus Manchester United. There was massive national interest, and a huge build-up. Oxford United were captained by Ron Atkinson, at the beginning of his long and colourful career as player, manager and pundit.

On the day, the tiny Manor Ground at Headington was bursting at the seams. I reported that the Blackburn team, packed with internationals like Bryan Douglas and Mike England, 'trotted out, looking confident and relaxed', and that when play started 'Atkinson followed Douglas as if he were hoping for his autograph'. Oxford United won 3–1, and the shocked Blackburn team trooped off looking as if they had been mugged.

Many years later I spoke to Ron Atkinson about that day, and he could remember every moment. He couldn't recall being interviewed by me, but then he was interviewed by everyone that week. I think his distinctive way with words – 'someone in the England team will have to grab the ball by the horns', 'well, either side could win it, or it could be a draw' – came later.

Oxford United's dream ended in the next round, beaten 2–1 at home by Preston North End, after a typically physical display by Preston's intimidating centre forward Alex Dawson. I concluded my report for *Cherwell* by observing that 'Big Alex, snorting like a buffalo which had just eaten the hunter, led the victorious visitors from the battlefield.' It could have been said by Big Ron himself.

So began my journalistic career. A small beginning, but I was hooked. I was beginning to think that this was what I wanted to do. I loved the challenge of not just writing at a desk, but getting out and reporting what I had seen, turning it into words and conveying an accurate impression to the reader. Even when, eventually, I got to work in television, I never lost my conviction that the words were more important than the pictures, and that a picture should always be set in its context.

There was one other feature of my University life that influenced me greatly – the Oxford Union Debating Society. Shortly after I became an undergraduate, I paid my £20 and became a life member of the Union. Thereafter, nearly every Thursday in term-time for three years, I went along to the debates. Although I spoke from the floor only occasionally, I was never a principal speaker – 'on the paper' as the jargon had it – until I was invited back some years later. Nor did I get involved in University or Union politics.

The real joy during my undergraduate years was watching accomplished debaters in action, and none more accomplished than Brian Walden. Brian had been President of the Union four years earlier, and was frequently invited back because he was such a star turn. He entered Parliament in 1964, winning a seat in his native Midlands, but resisted overtures at various times from Harold Wilson to become a minister. Brian enjoyed the independence of the backbenches, knew how little power or influence he would have as a junior minister, and anyway, he enjoyed the freedom to earn big money from outside interests – for many years he earned more money from the National Association of Bookmakers than he did as an MP. He was, quite simply, the finest debater I have seen, before or since. To see him making a case in full flow, taking interruptions from the floor in his stride, and putting them down with good humour as well as relentless logic, was an education in itself.

Eventually, after being re-elected as an MP four times, he changed careers at the age of forty-five, and in 1977 became one of the best political interviewers I have ever seen, mostly with London Weekend Television. Tough, tenacious, but never rude, hectoring or uncivil, every Walden interview was a masterclass. And he had the disconcerting gift – which I have never seen in any other interviewer – of being able to summarise, without fear of contradiction and with total accuracy, everything his interviewee had said in an interview at any point in it.

Although I was to get to know and admire Robin Day, and eventually succeeded him as chairman of *Question Time*, it was that early exposure to the young Walden at the Oxford Union that first awakened in me an awareness of the forensic skill required to challenge a strongly argued position.

I also discovered the dining room in the Oxford Union. Come to think of it, before I went to Oxford I had never in my life eaten in anything resembling a proper restaurant, with tablecloths and proper cutlery. It was a whole new world, three courses for two shillings and sixpence, in pleasant surroundings, served by Mr Duck, the attentive head waiter. For Sylvia and me it was an occasional treat, for which, I found out much later, we had to thank Michael Heseltine who had been Treasurer of the Union in 1954, and had driven through what he called a 'Brighter Union' policy – renovating the restaurant, and opening up the cellars as a nightclub.

Oxford wasn't all acting, listening, writing and tutorials. In my second year I was able to keep my scooter in Oxford, and visit Sylvia, who by now was enrolled at a very strait-laced all-women teacher training college in Gloucester.

Some such ladies colleges took regulations to extremes, especially in matters of personal morality. There were rumours of one which compelled its young women to push their beds out of their rooms if they had male visitors – as if it were not possible to get up to hanky-panky on the floor. At Gloucester they seemed to be obsessed with how the girls dressed – requiring hats to be worn on teaching practice, to general amusement. When I could, mostly at the weekends, I would ride over the Cotswolds to see Sylvia. On one visit we became formally engaged, although I think we had both accepted for some time that we would marry. We chose a ring, and I bought it for seventeen pounds ten shillings from what was then a little jewellers shop, the inspiration for the Tailor's shop in the famous Beatrix Potter story and now the Beatrix Potter museum.

The ride to Gloucester in the summer was glorious, but in the winter the road could be very hazardous. More than once I had to give up because of snowdrifts, or because I had skidded on ice and damaged the scooter. Warming myself by the log fire in a Cotswold pub and being tended to by a fussing landlady, was a wonderful antidote to all the inconvenience.

By good fortune, I was free from another sort of inconvenience in my second year – the requirement to be back in the college before midnight, when they locked the front gate. For that year I was assigned a bedroom and sitting room in a part of the college, at the back, which was being renovated. A good push opened the temporary gate, and I could come and go at all hours as I pleased. Its quiet location in a college backwater suited me fine, and I can see why it appealed subsequently to Mr Clinton.

As my Univ career progressed, especially in that second year when there were no exams, I took to drink. Well, no more than most undergraduates, but a good night out with college friends became a highlight of the week. Or sometimes two highlights of the week. It was much the same group of northern grammar-school boys as in year one, frequenting the rougher pubs on the fringes of the town where the beer tended to be cheaper and more to our tastes. One or two of my friends could drink prodigious amounts, and once or twice I made the mistake of trying to keep up with them.

However, the drinking episode of which I was most ashamed didn't happen in Oxford, but during the vacation in Liverpool. A fellow Liverpudlian from the same college, a Classicist who later became a brilliant Mandarin scholar, introduced me to Yates' Wine Lodge, and the delights – or more correctly, dangers – of Australian wine. It was a terrible mistake – Australian white wine, in those days, was like a very strong sweet sherry, and was sold in very large schooner glasses. It was also very cheap. I was ill in the street outside and ill on the top deck of a bus going home. It was so awful. Would I ever get another job on the buses again? It was not my finest hour, and it was some years before I would be enticed again inside a Yates' Wine Lodge.

For the record, when I was tempted back, it wasn't to the Liverpool one, but to the Yates' at Blackpool. That was a legendary rendezvous, and one of the most important watering-holes for those reporting Labour Party and TUC conferences. Cheap draught champagne (why was it called that, when it was out of a bottle?) was the tipple of the assembled hacks, and was consumed in great quantities with no ill effects, and I wished I'd discovered it sooner.

In my third year at Oxford I didn't have a room in college, and had to move into lodgings. But I was really lucky to be offered a room at a house in north Oxford by a young Univ don who, like me, had been educated at the Liverpool Institute, where he was an exact contemporary of my eldest brother Cliff. His name was Ronald Oxburgh, and he and his wife Ursula looked after me as if I was one of the family.

They also welcomed and fed Sylvia when she visited. Ron was a geologist, and he and Ursula liked lots of fresh air and the simple life. After lecturing at Oxford, he became a Professor at Cambridge, President of Queen's College, Chief Scientific Adviser to the Ministry of Defence, Fellow of the Royal Society, Rector of Imperial College, Chairman of Royal Dutch Shell, Governor of the BBC and Baron Oxburgh of Liverpool. He once gave Sylvia and me dinner at Queen's – in the very room where Richard III had dined. But at Oxford he was 'Ron' and he went everywhere on his bike.

It suddenly dawned on me, and many others in that third year, that we'd better do some work, or we would be lucky to get a degree. In the past, at school, there had always been someone to push and bully you into doing the work. At Univ it was up to you. It was a huge change in my life. The work habit was difficult to sustain in the second year, with no exams to aim at. Now, in my final year, it was entirely a matter for me to motivate myself to make a success of my life. As I got down to some serious work, living in lodgings became an advantage because I wasn't constantly distracted by college life. I would dine in hall in the evenings, then spend some hours in the college library.

The library, however, was next to the beer cellar, so invariably I made time for a pint or two before heading back to Ron and Ursula's up the Banbury Road.

As the time for my finals approached – known at Oxford as Schools, because you sat the papers in the Examination Schools in the High Street – all I could think of was how much I didn't know. There were some days of almost blind panic. How can you read all the books you were supposed to have read in the few remaining weeks? Suddenly there was no point in revising any further.

The day of the first exam dawned. I had slept little and awoke early, then it was time to get dressed up for the occasion – cap and gown, dark suit, white bow tie, the uniform known as subfusc. I scootered into town, parked round the back of my college, then walked through the Lodge and turned right for the short walk to the Examination Schools. Then, inside the massive halls, it suddenly hit me – among so many other people I was now totally on my own. I turned over the paper, and wrote and wrote. Over the next few days there were eight three-hour papers.

Then it was over. I put down my pen for the final time. As I did so, I promised myself that I would never sit another examination in my life, a promise that was kept. I walked out into the High Street, which was bathed in the midday sunshine of a glorious June day. Crowds of other undergraduates were noisily opening bottles of champagne. Cars tooted as they drove past. And what did I do? I got on a bus. It just happened to be passing, and was the bus that would take me down the High Street, left at Carfax, and down the Abingdon Road to Univ's sports ground. Still in my subfusc I walked into the pavilion, up to the bar, and ordered the nicest pint I had ever tasted. A few other close friends drifted in, but not much was said. Then we re-filled our glasses and went outside and stretched out on the grass in the summer warmth.

Gradually we began to talk, about our feelings now that our time at Oxford was nearly over, and what lay in store for each of us. We talked until the shadows lengthened. I remember our groundsman and his wife rustled up some sandwiches for us all. We drank more beer, but slowly, and no one became drunk. We got the bus back to college and had a final beer in the cellar, and suddenly everyone was very tired, though not too emotional.

A few weeks earlier I had found time, amid my revision timetable, to do two things. Struck by the realisation that I would shortly have to earn a living, I went to the University Appointments Board to see what was on offer. The answer was … not much. I had left it a bit late. Most of the big industrial, retail and financial companies had already shortlisted their graduate entrants. In any event, I didn't think that sort of life was for me. Could they offer me anything else?

Well, yes. There was just a chance that ITN, the new kid on the block of TV News, would take another graduate trainee that year. Usually they took only one. I was pencilled in to go to London to see ITN for an interview after my finals.

I was by no means confident that ITN would take me. In the previous Easter vacation, I had approached the *Liverpool Daily Post* and *Echo* to see if they could offer me anything. I was shown into the office of the formidable, humourless, chain-smoking Alick Jeans, Chairman and Managing Director. He treated me as if I was something the cat had brought in.

I had also applied for a traineeship with the Thomson Organisation, owners of a number of local and regional newspapers, as well as *The Times*. They said they would let me know.

The second thing I had done that term was to prepare for the eventuality that I might not be able to get a job in journalism at all. Accordingly, I applied for a lectureship in Politics at a technical college at Bridgewater in Somerset. I went for interview, but despite a glowing reference from my tutor Maurice Shock, they rightly appointed, that very day, someone who actually had some experience of teaching. Had they given me the job, however, I could have been a West Country teacher, leading a life a world away from the path I eventually took.

So, as I sat my finals, the only cards I was left holding, and not too confidently at that, were ITN and Thomson.

A day or two after I had sat that last exam, I heard from Thomson. They offered me a graduate traineeship, starting on the *Stockport County Express*. It is a measure of how pessimistic I was about impressing ITN that I wrote to Thomsons and accepted.

Two days later, I was summoned to see the Editor of ITN, Geoffrey Cox, at ITN's offices in the old Air Ministry building at the junction of Aldwych and Kingsway in London. I hitch-hiked to White City, caught the Underground to Holborn, and walked into what had been renamed

Television House. The Editor's secretary, Helen Gane, met me out of the lift, and after a short wait showed me into Geoffrey's office.

He was an impressive man, short of stature but, as I was quickly to appreciate, a giant in journalism. A New Zealand Rhodes Scholar, before the war he had worked as a foreign correspondent for the *News Chronicle*, then the *Daily Express*. He had covered the Spanish Civil War and the rise of Nazism, staying on the continent until the very last moment while the storm clouds of war were gathering. When he returned to Britain, he could have had any big job in Fleet Street. But Geoffrey had seen enough of Nazism to know that what he wanted to do was fight it. He joined the New Zealand Division, which was entrusted with what was to be the heroic, but unsuccessful defence of Crete, during which he was chief intelligence officer to the GOC, General Freyburg. Twice mentioned in dispatches, he fought also in mainland Greece, Libya and Italy.

Geoffrey put me at my ease, and we talked about anything and everything. He seemed interested that one of my special subjects in my PPE course was the Spanish Civil War, which he had seen at first hand.

The interview over, Helen Gane led me back into her office, where she gave me the first-class return rail fare from Oxford. I hitch-hiked back again, having made a good profit on the day, and had my first taste of the ITN expenses system.

Two days later I received a letter from Geoffrey Cox offering me a job at ITN as a graduate trainee on £700 a year, and could I start on 31 August 1964? I wrote immediately to the Thomson Organisation, saying that I had been offered the job I really wanted, at ITN, and I hoped they would understand why I was changing my mind about joining them.

They were not pleased, telling me by reply that I would get nowhere in life if I went around letting people down. The rebuke hurt, but I could live with it.

At the end of term, I said my farewells at Univ. One of the last people I saw, as I left, was a little old man in a Homburg hat standing in the Lodge, waiting for a taxi. It was Earl Attlee, one of the twentieth century's greatest Prime Ministers, who had been a Univ undergraduate sixty years before and, as I found out, had just lost his wife. He'd been at a dinner at his old college. He was completely alone. My new life stretched before me.

I had already learned my examination results – a second class degree. But a few weeks later, before I started work at ITN, I had a letter from

Maurice Shock telling me my marks. I had done badly in Economics and Philosophy, but he said 'your marks in Politics were outstandingly good, with some alpha in every subject. The number of Univ men who have achieved that in the last decade could be counted on my fingers! I hope that you prosper at ITN.'

Having said goodbye to Oxford, I returned to Liverpool for a few weeks. I needed to slow down, catch up on my sleep and share my news with my family. It also suddenly hit me that I would soon be leaving my Liverpool home permanently.

It was not the happiest of homecomings. My mother and eldest brother Cliff sat me down and told me that my father had been unconscious in hospital for some weeks, having suffered a series of heart attacks and strokes. He was being cared for in Birkenhead General Hospital, where Cliff was senior medical registrar. They had not told me about any of this, so as not to distract me from my final Oxford exams. A few days later my mother came into my room very early in the morning to tell me that my father had died.

The last time I saw him was in the hospital mortuary, where I went with Cliff to complete the identification formalities before he could be cremated. I was saddened at the scene, but until then it hadn't really hit me how little I felt for him. I shed no tears. But there was a lump in my throat a week or two later as I left Liverpool and headed for my new life in the capital.

I was intrigued to know why I got the job at ITN, but only plucked up the courage to ask Sir Geoffrey Cox (as he had become) many years later after he and I had both moved on from ITN. I told him that I thought it might have been because I could demonstrate that I knew a bit about the Spanish Civil War, which he had seen at first-hand. He smiled and put his arm round me. 'No Peter,' he said, 'I hired you because I had too many public schoolboys on the payroll. ITN needed a bit of Liverpool rough!'

Chapter 4

This is the Life

I didn't feel like a bit of Liverpool rough when I walked into the ITN newsroom on the morning of Monday 31 August 1964. I felt like the bee's knees. After a farewell tour bossing a Liverpool bus, I had come up to London a few weeks beforehand to stay with the family of a college friend and find somewhere to live. That had been a depressing experience, each morning grabbing the first edition of the *Evening Standard* and traipsing round some of the most ghastly over-priced bedsits. But I struck lucky, securing my own room in a flat-share with two other young professionals at Swiss Cottage. It was a bit dingy, but it was big, full of character, and mine. It also set me back only £4 a week, out of my £64 a month take-home pay. And because of the odd working hours I was to have at ITN, I hardly ever saw my new flatmates. Perfect.

The other big change in my circumstances concerned my mode of personal transport. During the vacation I had traded in my scooter and taken out a hire purchase agreement on something much more grand. Not having the time or inclination to take a driving test, I found out to my joy that there was a class of car that you could drive on the motorcycle licence I already possessed. So, one sunny morning in Liverpool, the ink barely dry on the hire-purchase documents, I drove away from a showroom at the wheel of a brand-new three wheeler Reliant van. Mine was powder blue, but in every other respect the very model of the vehicle that was to give such sterling service in years to come to Trotters International Traders.

I had never before been in charge of anything with a steering wheel and three pedals, so I taught myself to drive it as I went along. In truth, although I never admitted it at the time, it was an awful vehicle. Unstable, a constant oil leak from the day I bought it, and the simplest task underneath the bonnet requiring fingers that were twelve inches long and double-jointed. But it had a fibre-glass body, and this was to save my life.

One evening, driving in the rain back to London from Gloucester with Sylvia (we'd married after I'd been at ITN a year) I fell asleep at the wheel. On the A40 in High Wycombe, with my eyes closing, the van drifted across the road into the path of an oncoming coach full of late-night revellers returning from some sporting function. Just as I woke up, the coach braked and skidded sideways down the wet road towards me. The van, with me helpless at the wheel, hit the coach, bounced off and ploughed through a wall, coming to rest in the front garden of a house. The coach careered in the opposite direction and demolished another garden wall.

If I'd been driving any other vehicle, the impact could have been fatal. Instead, the fibre-glass body absorbed the shock, and simply flew into pieces. I sat there, in that front garden, with nothing of the van left, but still holding onto the steering wheel. I had a small scratch on my nose; Sylvia was totally unhurt. In the road, forty drunks were emerging from the stricken coach, wondering what had happened. They were soon joined by another large group of people who were barely sober – they'd been having a celebration of some kind in the house, in the front garden of which I was now parked with the remains of my van. This second group, whose evening I had interrupted, was composed entirely of trainee policemen. They took Sylvia and me inside, and were very hospitable – after seeing the state of the coach passengers, they assumed we were the innocent parties.

After all the formalities, a kindly policeman gave Sylvia and me a lift back to London. I never saw the remains of the van again. My insurance paid a massive bill for a van, a coach, two garden walls and a lot of landscaping, and a couple of months later I pleaded guilty by letter at the local magistrates' court to careless driving. In every sense – the fine was £20 – I got off lightly. So don't let anyone ever tell you that Del Boy's van was just a useless heap of junk. Mine became one – but not before it had saved my life.

However, all that was still to come when, on the morning of Monday 31 August 1964, I turned up for my first day of work in my new career. ITN occupied the seventh and eighth floors of Television House, at the junction of Kingsway and Aldwych in central London. Television House, formerly Adastral House, had been the home of the Air Ministry during the war. The only clue from the outside that it housed ITN was a small illuminated circular sign fixed to the seventh-floor balcony. I always thought that the lack of ostentation was just right – ITN choosing to announce itself to the world by the quality and style of its broadcasts, not by flashing signs or swanky offices.

Not that it had much option in the matter. Since its launch nine years previously, the ITV companies had never been enthusiasts for ITN, and generally resented having to put money into a news company they didn't want, rather than stuffing it into the pockets of shareholders who were coming to realise that ITV was a licence to print the stuff. Nonetheless, when I joined it, ITN was not only surviving but managing to grow and to carve out a durable place in the affections of the viewing public. It was even beginning to convert those more enlightened ITV moguls who realised they were going to need ITN as a key component in meeting the legal requirement that ITV produce some public service programming of quality.

So I was in the second wave of ITN pioneers. Much of the heavy lifting had already been done, and the key battles for survival had been won, but not without casualties. The first Editor, Aidan Crawley, walked away from the battlefield, in protest at the scarcely veiled hostility of the ITV companies, and their determination to keep ITN in a very small box. But Geoffrey Cox, his successor, had their measure. He had the political skills and the creative vision to win the fight for a quality news service on ITV with mass appeal, and which, crucially, enjoyed the confidence of the Regulator – the Independent Television Authority.

Cox had hired wisely, using well what money he had and surrounding himself with journalists and technicians of flair and dedication. The programmes that ITN made spoke for themselves – and rewrote the rules of journalistic engagement across public life. By 1964, some of the founding stars of ITN had gone – Robin Day, Christopher Chataway, Ian Trethowan, Ludovic Kennedy and Huw Thomas among them. But the strength of an army lies in the quality of the replacements, when key people are lost. In came Alastair Burnet, Peter Snow, Andrew Gardner, Richard Lindley, Alan Hart, John Edwards, Reginald Bosanquet, Gerald Seymour, Michael Nicholson, Sandy Gall, John Whale, Julian Haviland and many more. And I was lucky to have been chosen to join them.

These were the front men of ITN, but behind the scenes they were backed by a formidable bunch of journalists, technicians and cameramen.

And most had one thing in common: they wanted ITN to succeed, despite the sometimes absurd and punitive restrictive practices insisted on by their various unions – the ACTT, NATKE and ETU. For me, a young trainee coming in, this desire for the organisation to succeed manifested itself in the best possible way: experienced journalists and technicians were always ready to help you to learn.

It wasn't always obvious, because bringing newcomers down to earth was a merciless art form. But a surprising number of my new colleagues made very good role models. You looked up to them because they were good. They could be difficult and stroppy, and there were the usual stand-offs and clashes between strong personalities. ITN's first Editor, Aidan Crawley, recounted an occasion when he escorted the members of the Independent Television Authority out of the seventh floor lift for an important visit, to find two of his senior journalists rolling on the floor having a fist-fight. He coolly guided his guests round them, explaining that they seemed to be rather engaged, and that their departments could be visited later.

So although not all colleagues were easy to work with, allowances were made, and there was no shortage of people for a new entrant to this strange life to respect and to learn from. They brought to ITN hard experience in Fleet Street, in the cinema newsreels, in the film industry and in the armed forces. They had a reservoir of knowledge that was not gleaned from expensive media courses, which had yet to be invented, but by putting in the time on stories big and small. Years later, when I was at the BBC, it struck me how few senior people there were to look up to and to learn from, despite the size of the corporation.

It does happen, of course, in any organisation where there is true leadership. The people I have listed above, all strong characters, could just have easily – put together in the same organisation – been a total disaster. But they were well led and no one was in any doubt about what the orders of the day were. The rules of engagement were not written down anywhere at ITN. I once saw an ITN Style Book, a few terse typewritten pages on how to write clearly and economically. In it there was, as I recall, no reminder that writers and reporters should be accurate and balanced, and at all times act ethically. It was taken as read that no one *needed* reminding – a total contrast to the substantial volume of Editorial Guidelines distributed today to everyone at the BBC.

Everyone knew, quite simply, that it was his or her job to get the story, get it before the BBC got it, and tell it in a way that ordinary folk could understand and trust. And before it went on air, it had to satisfy the most exacting standards of balance, impartiality and accuracy. Such standards, of course, were and are laid down by law, for news both on ITV and the BBC. But at ITN, way back in 1964, it was simply the ITN way. In twenty-five years at ITN, during which I and many others learned our trade, none of us was required to go on a single journalistic course. What was required of us was understood, and it came from the top.

Geoffrey Cox gave the game away in his memoirs, when he described the responsibility he carried during the war as Chief Intelligence Officer with the New Zealanders in Crete, where every morning he had to brief the commanders in the field:

> The keen faces around me, drawn with weariness and strain, were of men who were going to base their actions at least in part on what I told them. The lives of the men they commanded and indeed their own would depend upon the accuracy of the information I imparted.

> It was a chastening discipline but a stimulating one. It developed in me a relish for establishing the truth, which is an end in itself. Television properly used provides an invaluable new means of achieving that end.

Geoffrey Cox lived a full life well into his nineties, and on 3 July 2008 – the forty-first anniversary of the first *News at Ten* – many of us gathered in the 'journalists' church', St Brides, just off Fleet Street, for his memorial service. Cox's successor as ITN Editor, Nigel Ryan, delivered what must be one of the most eloquent, affectionate and fitting tributes ever heard there, recalling the mess that Cox inherited, and the route he took out of it. I make no apology for quoting Nigel Ryan at length.

> His [Cox's] immediate task was to inject the iron of professionalism into a threadbare organisation starved of cash, but with a red-blooded pioneering team. At least life wasn't dull. In his first week ITN was falsely accused of faking news and in Africa a freelance cameraman was eaten by a crocodile. Determined to secure ITN's place in the top league Geoffrey sent Robin Day to interview President Nasser at the height of the Suez crisis. After that ITN never looked back.

> As an Editor he embodied the celebrated C. P. Scott dictum 'Opinions are free. Facts are sacred.' He taught his staff to think of the viewer as voter

and the first function of news to provide true information on which the electorate could make up its own mind. The slogan 'We report, You decide' wasn't written by him. But it might have been.

He applied the rules of accuracy and impartiality strictly (more strictly, I think, than they are applied in the rush of today's increasingly live news environment). He hunted down hidden comment with missionary zeal. Adjectives were suspect. He once fired a reporter for describing as 'obscene' the barbed wire fence around a US nuclear bomber base where CND marchers were demonstrating.

He was a stickler for political balance. There was a story he enjoyed telling against himself. After previewing a film about the Holy Land, he asked: 'Any problems?' 'Yes,' came the exasperated reply. 'We've had a protest from a bloke called Pontius Pilate who said his case had not been fairly put.'

David – now Sir David – Nicholas, then his Deputy Editor, later wrote 'Had we been given the opportunity to cover Paradise Lost, we would have sought an interview with God (preferably exclusive)... but we would have carried a reaction from Lucifer too...'

He defined his position as unaligned radical. He saw television as a force for good, and opposed censorship in all its forms...

Geoffrey Cox did not invent the ethos of public service broadcasting. The BBC did that. But he was foursquare behind it. And at a time when the corporation held back he seized the banner and led the charge.

This was the organisation which I had joined as a graduate trainee, and that was the man leading it. Although I knew little about him, it was not long before I knew of his values, because they pervaded the organisation. I had no lofty ideals, no preconceived ideas, but never doubted that I could contribute as long as I learned quickly. I soon found that there was no training scheme as such. You were given things to do, and you were expected to get on with it. Learning was by watching and then trying to do it yourself. If I had to say what was the prevailing ethos at ITN when I joined, I would say it was enthusiasm for the job in hand. Among ITN's 280 or so employees, few appeared to live in fear of the boss, but all knew that serious lapses of journalistic standards put their jobs at risk, as well as the future of the company. There was no room for people who didn't measure up, and people were occasionally fired for major one-off mistakes or consistent incompetence.

On that first day, I was struck by how friendly most people were. The big stars were Andrew Gardner and Peter Snow, and Andrew showed me round. The newsroom was a shabby and untidy workplace, equipped with desks and chairs that had seen better days, typewriters in various stages of obsolescence, and scores of identical beige telephones – so that when a phone rang you had to lift up three or four before you got the right one. It was obvious that what money ITN had to spend had not been spent on office furniture or other physical comforts.

The prevailing smell of the newsroom was cigarette smoke. Half the people there seemed to be smokers. One of the other newscasters, Anthony Brown (father of the BBC's reporter/presenter Ben Brown) used to smoke right through the rehearsal of his bulletins, and on occasion had a drag during transmission – a wisp of smoke from his ashtray being occasionally just visible to an observant viewer. The ITN pub, the White Horse round the corner, was an integral part of ITN life.

The consumption of alcohol was not frowned on, but everyone knew there were limits, and the line was drawn where it interfered with your work, rather than being a social break from everyday tensions and stresses. Nonetheless I was soon amazed at the prodigious amounts that could be drunk by colleagues who seemed totally unaffected by it. In this regard, ITN was little different from nearby Fleet Street, home in the 1950s and 1960s to some of the greatest post-war newspaper journalists, who seemed inspired rather than handicapped by their daily intake.

Towards the end of my first week, I was sent out of the office with a film crew to see how a story was covered. I was assigned to accompany Julian Haviland, who was then serving his apprenticeship as a general reporter before progressing to become one of ITN's most distinguished political editors. There wasn't really a story as such. We went to Heathrow airport where some Hollywood celebrity was expected to be passing through. In those days it was still something of a novelty to see the likes of Grace Kelly or James Stewart on the news, even though they had little to say. Such coverage was common practice for both ITN and the BBC on slow news days and a cheap way of filling a minute of the bulletin, which at that time on either channel ran for more than twelve or thirteen minutes.

No sooner had we arrived at the airport than Haviland and the three-man crew (cameraman, sound recordist and lighting man) disappeared. I was lost. Then I found a film crew, but it was from the BBC, and I fastened on to them. I have to say that I did so partly because *their* reporter was young, blonde and beautiful. We got chatting about reporting and she gave me my first lesson – how to hold a microphone. Don't wave it back and forth during an interview, but hold it equidistant from you and the person you're interviewing. During the course of the afternoon, we struck up a friendship, which exists to this day. Her name was Judith Chalmers. At the time I thought this, the reporter's life, was just the life for me.

I was soon brought down to earth. That Heathrow experience was to be my last taste of life 'on the road' for more than two years.

I was assigned instead to the writers' desk on the ITN bulletins, which at that time were at ten to six and five to nine. The humblest job an ITN writer could do was to write what were called 'spares'. The chief sub, himself supplied from the wires by the copytaster, gave you a sheaf of agency stories that were not likely to make the bulletin, but needed turning into short pieces that could be used to fill the bulletin if a major film failed, or the bulletin was in danger of under-running. None would take more than fifteen or twenty seconds to read. Established writers used to knock off a pile of spares in no time.

On my first day doing this, I laboured away, the pile of reject balls of paper growing higher in my waste-bin.

But then, the moment of truth. Clasping a couple of freshly re-typed short masterpieces, I put them in front of the chief sub, and stood proudly at his elbow. He picked up the first one and read it. He put it to one side. He read the second one, then placed it on top of the first. Then, taking the two pieces of paper in both hands, he crumpled them into a ball and tossed them into the bin – without a word, and without looking at me. I took that as a sign that I had to do better. It hadn't been like that when I was football correspondent of the Oxford University newspaper.

Within a couple of weeks I was taken off the writers' desk on the bulletins and reassigned once more to a job I was to do for the next twelve months. It was to what one might call the graveyard shift in a department of ITN which some unfairly referred to as The Salt Mines. The name of the small department was ITN Syndication. It had three or four writers and a couple of film editors. Its function was to syndicate picture stories that had appeared on the ITN bulletins that day to a few dozen overseas customers – mostly fairly primitive newsrooms in developing countries, but some bigger established English-speaking customers. Syndication could only begin its work once the regular ITN bulletins had finished with the film – which meant working highly unsocial hours, through the late evening and early morning. So now, as all my new chums were going home, I started work.

The writer's job on Syndication was to package the film story in such a way that the overseas customer could use it 'off the peg' with minimum extra work. The film would be delivered to the customer station with a brief 'dope sheet' (explaining why it was a story they might find worth running); an introduction, for the local presenter to read; and a script to be read by a local reporter or commentary voice. This meant that every word of the script that an ITN Syndication writer sent with the film had not just to explain what was going on, but had to hit the shots in the film precisely. The requirement was that, if an overseas presenter or reporter read our script at a steady three words to the second, it would make perfect sense. Across the television industry it's known as writing to film, but standards now are nowhere near as exacting as those we worked to – with pictures increasingly being used as 'wallpaper' over which general points can be made, rather than each shot being explained to the viewer and put in context to carry the story forward.

Over that twelve months I became very good at writing to pictures, and my writing for television generally improved hugely, standing me in good stead for the many news programmes I went on to present. I firmly believe that the presenters of the top news programmes should be among the best writers on those programmes. If not, they are not the complete article. But the improvement I made on ITN Syndication, hunched over a shot-list and a typewriter in the small hours of the night, was something I did not achieve alone.

There were three writers senior to me, without whose help I would have sunk without trace – Frank Miles, Derek Dowsett and Chris Barlow. I owe them everything. Each wrote beautifully and economically, and each went on to become a key production figure as ITN expanded, and an essential part of the many programmes on which they worked. Frank Miles's attention to detail became legendary. As the chief ITN producer specialising in space, Frank's bedtime reading in July 1969 included the massive inches-thick flight plan for the first moon landing, Apollo 11. In it, Frank spotted some NASA timings for the moon landing which didn't make sense, and a correction was duly made when he contacted Mission Control.

At the end of my year on Syndication, I was restored to the main writers' desk for the ITN bulletins. My writing on Syndication had been noticed by the Editor, Geoffrey Cox (not the man to take his eye off any corner of ITN), and he had sent me a number of personal notes congratulating me on scripts I had written. On the bulletin desk there were no more humiliations from the chief sub. Day after day I found myself getting the lead story to write. The other writer vying with me for the unofficial ranking of 'splash sub' was Michael Nicholson, and there was a lot of friendly rivalry between us. We both knew that the next step up for us could be promotion to reporter, and Michael – one of the fiercest ever competitors in the news business – was not best pleased when I beat him to it, but only by a week or two.

Back on Syndication, however, there was a lot of pain when ITN wrapped up the operation to set up a joint newsfilm agency with United Press – UPITN. The small team of expert writers on Syndication were kept in the dark, practically until they got their redundancy notices. The whole thing was bungled by management, and it took the threat of a strike by the other journalists at ITN to sort it out and save the jobs of three men who went on to give ITN many years of invaluable service.

Restored to the main newsroom, I made two other breakthroughs at ITN. Someone had noticed that I had a good broadcasting voice, and I was given the chance to become one of the select few who read the commentaries over newsfilm in the ITN bulletins.

I came to ITN with the vestiges of a Liverpool accent, but I had heard Geoffrey Cox's views on regional accents: he thought they were OK on local programmes, but at ITN he wanted no one's voice to be a distraction in itself. He didn't want ITN voices to be the studied kind of Queen's English that had so characterised the BBC. He wanted voices that gave little or no clue to the background or origin of his reporters and newscasters. Accordingly I worked on removing what was left of my Liverpool accent. I wasn't the first to go down this route – Sue Lawley's origins in the Black Country and Richard Baker's in North London were once evident in their speech, but such tell-tale signs have long been eradicated. My Liverpool roots have been known to reassert themselves vocally, but only after a pint or five.

The commentary voice at ITN was a relic of the cinema newsreel, on which it was modelled. On air, the newscaster read the introduction to a film and an anonymous but distinctive voice read a script over the pictures, telling the story. The commentary was done live from a small booth just off the news studio. I, or one of the other voices, sat there surrounded by the scriptwriters. A tap on the shoulder was the signal to read the next cue – and sometimes a hand over the mouth was the signal to shut up. It was my first taste of live broadcasting. These days, of course, we have what is called the Reporter Package – the whole report, incorporating interviews and graphics, voiced and signed off by the reporter. That was another development pioneered by ITN, but did not become routine until the launch of *News at Ten*.

Having a distinctive voice and using it regularly OUT of vision, it was only a short time before I got the chance to use it IN vision. There were some fourteen different ITV companies, a regional federation of broadcasters, and they required ITN not just to provide the main news bulletins but to furnish them with a late-night summary of the news headlines. The fourteen companies usually operated, for programming purposes, as two or three regional groupings, which meant ITN had to transmit the news headlines at two or three different times late at night. During 1966 I became a regular ITN late-night newscaster, alongside my other duties as writer and voiceover.

For me, they were happy days. I had become established at ITN inside two years, had learned to write for television and had appeared on screen as a newscaster, which also paid £3 extra for every appearance. In the summer the year before, Sylvia and I had married in Liverpool, and were now living in a one-bedroomed flat in Crouch End in north London. It wasn't the greatest place to live, but I had gone to Islington council's rent officer, as one could in those days, who, despite the landlord's protestations, reduced the £6 a week rent to £4 – the same as I had been paying for a flat share at Swiss Cottage. Every weekday morning I drove Sylvia – I still had that van – across Hampstead Heath to her first teaching job at a primary school in Willesden. So we now had two incomes coming in. I also had my first experience of actually being recognised in the street as a result of my appearances on TV.

Around the same time I got in touch with my old school friend Paul McCartney, and invited him over to dinner with Sylvia. I didn't really think he'd accept but, out of the blue one bitter winter's day, he phoned to say he and his girlfriend Jane Asher could come in a couple of days' time on the Saturday night. As it happened, we had already arranged to have dinner on that night with friends from my Oxford days, Dick and Jane Russell. They had a bigger flat than ours and were thrilled – and not a little sceptical – when I said I would be bringing along Paul McCartney and Jane Asher. Dick and Jane's flat was in West Hampstead, not far from McCartney's luxury London house in St John's Wood. But to make sure that Paul found the West Hampstead address I drove with Sylvia – in my Reliant van – to Paul's house, so he could follow us. I parked in the road at St John's Wood and when I buzzed the intercom, Paul invited us in. While we waited for Jane Asher we gazed around us. Two things stick in my mind – it was the first time I had seen a colour television, even though regular transmissions in colour had not then started. And there was a tasteful line of flying ducks on his living room wall.

Then we all set off for our dinner date. I led the way in the van and our guests tailed us in a brand new Aston Martin DB5, already the most iconic car in the world thanks to James Bond.

Getting to West Hampstead in this unlikely convoy was the easy part. It was a bitterly cold night, and our Oxford friends had prepared a warming winter casserole, lots of beef cooked with vegetables. After the introductions, with Paul his usual relaxed self, he glanced into the small kitchen and let slip that he and Jane Asher were vegetarians. Then, as if one disaster wasn't enough, almost immediately it got worse – the heating in the flat conked out. A frantic search found the only available way of saving the evening. An old electric fan heater was placed underneath the dining table, as close as possible to where the less than well padded Asher was to sit, and a bag of brown rice – the only vegetarian food that could be found – was thrown into a pan.

Paul was terrific. He ate a plate of brown rice as if it was a veggie banquet. Asher was quiet and polite as she toyed with hers. You don't get that slender by eating more than a grain at a time. Paul chatted away about anything and everything, but became most animated when he got onto the topic of people who'd tried to overcharge him. He'd had a big row with a TV engineer who'd sent him a bill for £300 for doing, he said, practically nothing to his new set. And the local vet had tried to rip him off for treating his dog and supplying its vegetarian food. Paul was, and is, careful with money. The evening ended with him signing all our

Beatles LPs – James Paul McCartney. And the pair climbed back into the Aston Martin and were gone.

Years later, trying to make conversation, I happened to raise the memory of that evening when I shared a table with Jane Asher at some celebrity evening. She looked straight through me – Paul was not just history, he was erased from her past.

On another occasion I also started to tell the story to Linda McCartney, whom Sylvia and I had got to know well – and got the same look. You raked up Paul's old girlfriends in front of Linda at your peril.

Early in 1967 there was a lot of excitement at ITN. It appeared that Geoffrey Cox, after nearly two years of painstaking lobbying, had finally won the battle for a half-hour news programme. The shortish evening bulletin at 8.55 was going to be replaced, for a trial period of three months, by the *News at Ten*. It was to be yet another revolution led by ITN in British TV News, and the first *News at Ten* was duly broadcast on 3 July 1967. To meet the new challenge ITN had to expand, and expand quickly. Among other things, it needed new reporters. I got my chance, and was appointed to ITN's reporting team a couple of months before *News at Ten* went to air.

When I was called in to be told the news I was thrilled, but I didn't have the heart to tell Michael Nicholson when I got back to the newsroom. He had to wait another two weeks, during which he found it difficult to give me the time of day. When I returned that evening to Crouch End, we had a celebration with our convivial neighbours upstairs. At the end of the evening I was carried down the stairs back to our flat, and was so hung over the next morning that Sylvia had to call the ITN news desk and tell them that I was unwell. To my shame, I missed my first day as a reporter because I had been paralytically drunk. It was my darkest secret for many years. From then on, although I was ill a number of times in ITN employment, it was always in my own time: I didn't miss any rostered day for my remaining twenty-two years at ITN – except when I was shot.

The first story I was given as an ITN reporter was in early May. A young golfer, Peter Oosterhuis, had been chosen to represent Great Britain in the Walker Cup that month. He was barely out of school, so his selection was causing something of a stir. I met him on a golf course in Dulwich, did a brief interview and filmed him holing some putts. It made a minute and a half on the evening bulletin. I learned one small lesson that day. I'd taken the precaution of asking Oosterhuis how he pronounced his name. He said 'Oaster-house' as in Oast House. For years thereafter I heard leading golf commentators pronounce it Ooo-ster-house. Ever since, if in doubt about how someone pronounces his or her name, I've always asked them in person. You'd be surprised how many colleagues don't bother. There was another lesson I learned: I know nothing about golf and have never had the slightest inclination to play it. Yet from that report you'd think I was an expert. Get well briefed, and the viewer will see a trusted friend. Try to make a virtue of your own ignorance, and you may just come over as a bit of a wally.

Two other assignments taught me some valuable lessons soon after my appointment as an ITN reporter. ITN's Assistant Editor in charge of Input – what the BBC call Intake, or News Gathering – was Don Horobin. Don's nose for a story was legendary, and his conspiratorial manner invested each of his hunches and ideas with the aura of being potentially the greatest story ITN had ever covered. At his best, Don was inspired and he had some notable successes, usually stories pursued against the 'better' judgement of initially sceptical reporters. At his worst, he wasted hours of reporting time, having mad obsessions checked out, including, as we will see, the Loch Ness Monster. But the balance sheet was in his favour. Don Horobin, the letters 'ITN' running through him like a stick of Blackpool rock, was responsible for some of ITN's greatest scoops. But however enthusiastic he was about a story, he never let a story go unchecked.

I always got on well with Don. Like some other colleagues who had learned their journalism in the School of Hard Knocks, he was interested only in how hard you were prepared to work to get the story. He didn't care whether you'd been to Eton or Bash Street School. As with all Don's assignments, the chosen reporter was taken to one side and given the brief, usually out of the corner of Don's mouth.

On the day in question, about ten-thirty in the morning, Don called me into his office, closed the door and said just one word – 'drugs'. Well, he did say a few more, promising me that 'drugs' was going to be one of the big stories for many years to come. This was at a time when 'drugs' most certainly wasn't a big story. I'd gone through university without being aware of 'drugs'. But Don was right, and way ahead of his time on the issue. He felt in his water that the drug menace was simmering beneath the surface of our society, and that we should start waking people up to it. And he wanted the story for that night's *News at Ten*. End of briefing.

I went back to my desk and, while a film crew was being assigned and loading their gear, I wondered where on earth to begin. I decided there could be no short-cuts, that this story would not fall into my lap and that if I wanted to find young people on drugs, I should go to where I could find most youngsters in any one place – at least during the daytime. So I took my crew no further than Trafalgar Square. We stopped and spoke to scores of people, found dozens who were users of hard drugs, and a handful who were prepared to talk frankly about it on camera. Some showed the stuff to me, showed their scars, even offered to sell it to me. It was hard work, but I had my story for *News at Ten*. It was an elementary lesson I've never forgotten – if you want to be a reporter, there's no substitute for wearing out a bit of shoe leather, doing your own research and verifying the facts in person.

If anything, the second of the stories that Don threw at me was even more of a challenge. The Pope had just issued an encyclical repeating his opposition to artificial means of birth control – and this at a time when more and more women were being liberated by the invention of the contraceptive pill. 'Matey', said Don, as he slipped his arm around me, and pushed a dog-eared cutting into my hand, 'get out there and find out what Catholic women think about that'. I had five or six hours at most. I began by walking the streets of an area of London with a large Irish population – Kilburn. I knocked at dozens of doors, asking total strangers – all women – whether they were Catholics, whether they were on the pill, what they thought of the Pope, what their husbands thought about it all – intimate questions even for someone you knew well. And when I found someone who would talk, I had to pop the question – would you mind repeating all that on camera for use on tonight's *News at Ten*? I got lots of refusals, some quite abrupt, and maybe I deserved to have my face slapped. But a surprising number were willing to talk frankly, and on camera, about the predicament of the Catholic female and their determination to act in their own interests, regardless of what the Pope said. It made compelling television – an issue brought to life by individual human stories. It was the ITN way.

I believe it was one of the strengths of ITN that it never employed researchers. Nigel Ryan, ITN's third Editor in Chief, a former Reuters man, insisted that a reporter was his or her own best researcher. A good reporter would only have to check the research – so why not do it yourself? Years later, when I was anchoring *Channel Four News*, I made the mistake of relying on some second-hand research for a major interview with a Cabinet minister. I quoted something at the minister as fact, based on the information I had been given, but not checked. It was wrong, he was right, and I was shot down in flames. That preyed on my mind for weeks. If I was going to make mistakes, at least they were going to be *my* mistakes.

The launch of *News at Ten* came too late for ITN to use the new programme to showcase its coverage of the biggest news story of that summer – the Six-Day War in the Middle East – so its war coverage had to be crammed into the regular bulletins. And as a news organisation it was uncharacteristically slow off the mark, Israel's surprise attacks on Egypt on 5 June coming also as a big surprise to the world's broadcasters.

Initially, ITN also found itself over-reliant on material from the new UPITN agency, and it was a few days before it got its own operation up to speed.

A couple of weeks after the war, with the wreckage of its enemies' armies still smouldering on all fronts, I was sent to Israel with an ITN crew to relieve the reporters and crews who'd had practically no sleep for that time and were being pulled out. For me, it was a surreal experience. Not yet twenty-five years of age, the only other time I had flown was on a £47 package holiday to Yugoslavia. Yet here I was with one of ITN's top film crews, Jon Lane and Hugh Thomson, champagne glasses in hand, winging our way to the world's biggest hotspot, in the comfort of a magnificent BOAC VC10. Before I left London, I had been offered no training or advice whatsoever about what I might expect, and how I might minimise any risk in the war zone for which I was now heading. Nor, as I was to find out eventually, was any of us insured by ITN.

Lane and Thomson, of course, had done it all before, and I was fortunate to be with them. We were booked into one of the best hotels in Tel Aviv, The Dan, where we checked in late in the afternoon. Jon and Hugh chatted up the receptionist and promptly got us upgraded, at no extra cost, to the magnificent penthouse suite. Within half an hour they had also found us a driver with a huge white American car – at 50 dollars a day. We went out and got ourselves accredited at the military press office. Then the hard work started.

Before dawn the next day we left Tel Aviv and headed south for the Suez Canal. It was the obvious thing to do if we wanted unlimited pictures of the aftermath of the conflict. From Tel Aviv to El Kantara on the Suez Canal is about 170 miles, and for a hundred miles before we reached the Canal we drove through the wreckage of the Egyptian army. It had been the biggest armoured battle since El Alamein. You couldn't go a hundred yards without passing the remains of an Egyptian tank. And not just wreckage – many had simply been abandoned, the boots of the crew left nearby in the sand so as not to hamper them as they ran away. I climbed into one or two deserted tanks, which seemed to me to be in almost showroom condition although, with hindsight, the risk was that they may have been booby trapped. In the middle of the desert an Egyptian ammunition train had been destroyed, with unexploded ordnance scattered for half a mile around – another hazard we ignored in the quest to get the dramatic pictures that were there for the taking.

In the heat of that day it was time to take a rest, shelter from the sun and sit down. We saw a white-painted building near the railway – perhaps some kind of railway office. We walked round it, then peered in through an opened window. It was a horrific sight, and the smell was worse. Seventeen or eighteen bloated corpses, plainly Egyptian civilians, men, women and one or two children, lay apparently where they had fallen, or been dumped. There wasn't a lot of blood and no tell-tale bullet holes in the walls. They had not been blown to bits and the building was intact. It didn't look as if they had been machine gunned. They might have been killed by a blast outside, and just thrown in there until burial parties could return. The scene was so horrific that we couldn't possibly have used any pictures we took, and it was impossible to establish what had happened. Lane and Thompson were adamant – we couldn't do anything. To this day I wonder whether we missed some kind of atrocity. I could easily have shipped a story to that effect. But in truth, it would probably have taken a lengthy commission of enquiry to establish what happened. Was that better than the snap judgment of a passing TV crew? In the event, we walked away, but I suddenly felt a lot older.

When we reached the Suez Canal it was getting dark and was eerily quiet, even though the Egyptians were dug in on the other side just a couple of hundred yards away.

I then had my first experience of bivouacking for the night. We slept in the open, smothered in mosquito repellent and ate tinned baked beans. Then there was the matter of going to the toilet, and I found that all the best places, in odd corners where one might quietly do one's business, had been used hundreds of times already by passing soldiers. It was disgusting. Just before dawn we were awakened by an Israeli major, who told us we had to get out – they had intelligence that our positions were going to be strafed by some of the few Egyptian jets that had escaped the Israeli destruction. We spent the next few hours watching the sun rise over the desert, and digging ourselves into slit trenches. No jets came.

In the day and a half since we had left Tel Aviv, we had a number of stories 'in the can', including an interview with the first UN observers to arrive. It was time to send our material to London. There were no satellites of course in those days, so everything had to be physically packaged and sent back to base, where the film would be processed and cut to match the commentaries I sent with it. I recorded these on location, as well as some pieces to camera establishing that we were actually there, and rehearsing the recently introduced sign-off: Peter Sissons, ITN (or *News at Ten*) at the Suez Canal (or wherever we happened to be).

The next part of the operation illustrates exactly how far news gathering has come in the last forty years. We drove with our film, undeveloped and sealed in its cans, back to Tel Aviv. With obstacles, potholes and roadblocks, the drive took at least half a day. At the hotel, no time to shower, just to pack the film into clearly labelled bags, include all the scripts, and drive to the airport. Then we would find the queue of people waiting to check in for the flight to London. Now for the tricky bit: one of us would have to identify a reliable amateur courier. Typically, we would approach someone who was well dressed and looked friendly: 'Hello, we're from ITN. I wonder if you could do us a big favour. We need to get this package to London urgently. Could you take it for us? ... You can? That's great. You'll be met at Heathrow by a man carrying an ITN sign. By the way, under no circumstances try to open the package – there's undeveloped film inside. And don't let on to any of the airline staff that we've given it to you, it'll only complicate things.' Few people refused to act as our unpaid couriers in this way. But that was then.

In London, a despatch rider could get from Heathrow to ITN in under half an hour – I believe the record was just over twenty minutes. Then the film had to be processed and edited, and then wait for the next opportunity to transmit it. If all went like clockwork, it was possible to get a story from, say, the Suez Canal onto an ITN bulletin in a day and a half. These days, of course, it is instantaneous. But so must be the judgements of the reporters on the spot. If, in 1967, I had second thoughts about a story or wanted to revise my script, I could catch my package before it went on air, and phone some revised observations. It is a matter for debate whether instantaneous news has given us better, more reliable and considered news.

That summer I spent a number of weeks in Israel, spread over two trips. By chance, on my birthday in July, Lane, Thompson and I were again camped out just across the Suez Canal from the Egyptians. When we awoke, the crew had a birthday surprise for me – a football. In the dawn light we noisily kicked it up and down the road by the side of the canal, until a lazy burst of machine gun fire told us that someone on the other side wanted to get some sleep.

The next time I was to hear a machine gun, it would be different.

Chapter 5

Beating the Bullet

I returned from the Six-Day War to life as a general reporter, checking in each morning with the news desk, and waiting my turn to be assigned to whatever might be going. The glamour of the foreign correspondent, which I had briefly tasted, soon gave way to everyday home assignments. I didn't resent that; because of the strength of ITN's reporting team I was way down the pecking order when it came to the bigger stories, particularly the foreign ones. From time to time I picked up a big story, but not always under propitious circumstances. One day early in October 1967 I was rostered as the late reporter. On a quiet day this often meant that there was little to do except report in at midday, when all the stories had been assigned, and then go with some under-employed colleagues for a long lunch, usually in Charlotte Street a couple of blocks away.

On the day in question, as that pattern unfolded, much cheap red wine flowed, but our revelries were interrupted by a telephone call: would Peter Sissons please go back to the office urgently, there was a breaking story. Somewhat unsteadily I made my way back to the news desk, where I was instructed to go with a crew to interview Barbara Castle, the Minister of Transport. I was told that the minister had just announced the introduction of a device called the breathalyser. Well, when I sat down in front of Mrs Castle half an hour later, frantically chewing mints and sipping black coffee, she didn't need any new-fangled device to tell what my problem was. I pulled myself together, she seemed rather amused by it all, and the arrival of the breathalyser made the lead on *News at Ten*.

A few days later I was trusted with an outside broadcast, live into *News at Ten*, from a large pub on the Esher bypass. I quizzed drinking drivers about whether they felt safe to drive home, then breathalysed them, invariably having to tell hardened and disbelieving boozers that if they attempted to drive with that amount of alcohol in their bloodstream they'd be breaking the law. There had been a rumour that eating pickled onions could also affect the breathalyzer. At my request a lone drinker ate several jars of pickled onions, on the promise that I would breathalyse him, on air, before the programme ended. Gasping for air through half a gallon of onions and vinegar, he wasn't best pleased when we ran out of time and dropped his contribution. However, recoiling from the fumes of his breath, I didn't catch his precise words.

The next year, 1968, saw my first chance to appear as a newscaster on *News at Ten*. On the night in question Reggie Bosanquet was unwell, and I was temporarily promoted from newscasting the late headlines to co-anchoring the main news with Leonard Parkin. I knew in my bones that this was the opportunity that all understudies prayed for, but far from being keyed up all I could think of was that, at last, I would find out first-hand what the newscasters said to each other at the end of the programme – the subject of a national guessing game. The programme went well, without mishaps, and at the end Leonard bade the viewers goodnight. I waited expectantly, but as the camera pulled back and the music played, Leonard turned to me and moved his lips soundlessly. Pathetically, I did the same. But in a way Leonard was just being professional; with a microphone around, he knew that you should always behave as if it may be live, and not say a word unless you'd be happy for the viewer to hear it. That night was a landmark for me. I knew I could perform on the bigger presenting stage, but the next day it was down to earth and back to the job of general TV reporter.

It's a strange life. You can be doing a soft story one day, and the next day be thrown into a situation where you need to dig deep into what talent you have to rise to a challenge that can make or break your career.

That happened to me in the autumn of 1968, when I was given another chance on the big stage of foreign reporting.

The Nigerian Civil War had been in progress for well over a year, with the federal government attempting to crush the breakaway by Nigeria's south eastern province, which the rebel leaders had called Biafra. It was an ugly little war, characterised by what threatened to turn into a humanitarian disaster, as the federal forces tightened the blockade of the core areas under Biafran control. The Biafrans had stoked international sympathy and indignation by skilfully exploiting the plight of their starving and the suffering of their children. But by September, fourteen months after the commencement of hostilities, there was widespread speculation that the Biafrans were heading for defeat.

Coming in to work at Television House on what I thought would just be another day, I was taken to one side by the Foreign Editor and told that ITN wanted me in Nigeria on the next flight, to cover what could turn out to be the endgame in the increasingly bitter, and bloody, civil war. Theoretically, I could have refused – it being always understood that reporters cannot be compelled to put themselves, potentially, in harm's way. However, what was also unspoken was that careers at ITN were not built by saying no to challenging assignments. Not that refusal entered my head. I knew I had to go, and I wanted to go. I armed myself with a sheaf of cuttings from ITN's news information library, went home, packed a bag, kissed Sylvia goodbye, and flew to Lagos.

As in the Middle East, I was accompanied by one of ITN's most experienced film crews, but this time both veterans of the Second World War. Cyril Page had flown primitive Swordfish biplanes from merchantmen converted to makeshift aircraft carriers, and after the war became the BBC's senior cameraman, spending nine months filming in Korea. Archie Howell was also a navy veteran and now one of ITN's most reliable sound recordists. Cyril had a reputation as a man who could arrange anything, as his legendary expenses often testified. But behind this wheeler-dealer facade was a fine and fearless cameraman. Archie also was a top-rate technician, but in temperament was the complete opposite of Cyril: taciturn and reserved, except when something really annoyed him. We didn't talk much on the flight out. I think it was just sinking in that the brief we had, to get to the seat of the action and chronicle how it all ended, might just be something of a tall order.

Nigeria was a shock, at least for me. We couldn't get our gear out of Lagos airport without paying a string of bribes to shameless uniformed officials. The Federal Palace Hotel, supposed to be four or five star, was dirty, tired, run-down and practically empty. The only other people in residence were a small group of correspondents from UK national newspapers, most of whom stayed put in the hotel, filing from there. Some would, quite unscrupulously, pick the brains of any of their number who did venture out to do some actual reporting, and often file the story before their too-helpful rival.

Surreally, in the evenings, the cabaret artiste was the glamorous Lita Roza. She'd been Britain's top female singer in the 1950s, with a string of hits. Here she was looking dejected and bored and singing to an almost empty dining room in an awful hotel.

She didn't sing her most famous track 'How much is that doggie in the window?' of which she famously said: 'I went into the studio and only sung it once and I've never sung it again. It was rubbish.'

I felt really sorry for her. I soon felt even more sorry for myself, when I got the most dreadful diarrhoea after my first meal. But the worst part of that hotel was the lack of communication with the outside world. To get a telephone call to London meant waiting up to two days. If you weren't in your room when the call finally came through, then you missed it. Any and every complaint was met by something along the lines of 'What do you expect? There's a war on.' There wasn't a friendly face in the place. Local telephone calls asking for help from government officials in arranging access to the front line were a waste of time.

Our breakthrough came when we were invited one evening to meet Nigeria's President, General Yakubu Gowon, known to his friends as Jack. This was arranged by the *Daily Express* correspondent, Walter Partington, who seemed to know him quite well. We spent a bizarre evening with Gowon and his cronies looking at Walter's snapshots, which he had taken on a trip inside Biafra. The Nigerian High Command roared with laughter at many of the photos, particularly those of Biafrans in officers' uniforms. The consensus was that the furthest any of the enemy would have got in the Federal Army was lance corporal. But the evening was useful and Gowon, who I found was intelligent and sympathetic, advised us to get to the airport the next morning, where we could hitch a lift on a military transport to Port Harcourt.

Port Harcourt, an important city strategically and economically, principally because of its oil, was now back in Federal hands after being declared Biafran by the rebels at the start of the war. More than 300 miles from Lagos to the south-east, it was the obvious base from which we could now get closer to the fighting as Federal troops tried to press home their advantage.

The next morning we drove early to Lagos airport, which was a hive of military activity with troops assembled for transit to the eastern front. But despite our presidential backing, no one took any notice of our requests to join a flight. For three days we waited at the airport, each evening returning, dejected, to our hotel. On the fourth morning we gave up on the official route and, with the connivance of a friendly pilot, jumped on board an aircraft as it began its take-off run. The pilots of these planes were all Americans and all slightly mad. They had to be, given the aircraft they were flying – totally clapped out DC4s. For their efforts, I was told they were paid thousands of dollars a day, in cash.

As we trundled down the runway, I was aware there were no seats, let alone seat belts. The interior of the aircraft was packed with coffins, and each of the coffins was packed with mortar bombs. Glancing out of the window as we eventually left the ground, I saw rivers of oil running out of the cowling over one of the four engines. The plane flew low, possibly because it wasn't pressurised – the toilet was a hole in the floor – but more likely because it couldn't get any higher. After an hour or so, on the approach to Port Harcourt and with the ground only a few hundred feet below us, we saw a massive, long, burnt scar in the forest. Scattered along it were the remains of a DC4 that had taken off half an hour before us, with forty Federal commandos on board. We flew directly over the wreck, and hit the runway far too heavily for my liking, as the mortar ammunition bounced in its entirely appropriate packaging. But we were on the ground, the cold sweat of fear mixing already with the hot sweat of a stifling tropical day.

By now it was not much more than ten in the morning. A car took us the short drive to the temporary headquarters of the 3rd Marine Commando and its feared – and almost certainly deranged – commander, Colonel Benjamin Adekunle, the Black Scorpion. We'd been beaten to it, however. Already standing outside, looking smug, was a film crew from CBS News, with its reporter Morley Safer. Morley, a Canadian by birth, was eleven years older than me, and already battle hardened by his assignments in Vietnam, where his reporting had earned acclaim. A stills photographer by the name of Priya Ramrahka made up our party. Priya was a good-looking 33-year-old Kenyan Indian, and was working that day under contract to *Time Life*. That made seven of us. But suddenly there was one more. A familiar figure in a pork-pie hat appeared, smiling. It was Partington of the *Express*, who'd also wangled himself along for the ride.

Adekunle had put an open-topped long-wheelbase Land Rover at our disposal, and another accompanying vehicle carrying nine or ten Federal Commandos. There was some light relief when I asked one of them if he knew what the creature on their regimental badge was (it was a blue octopus on a red background). This six foot six battle hardened Nigerian commando scratched his head and said: 'I think it's a spider.'

As the scorching midday sun climbed almost directly above us, we set out along a road that became increasingly rough and uneven, through the bush to the north of Port Harcourt. The road narrowed, and the potholes became deeper and more frequent. It was the road to Owerri, sixty miles distant. What our escort didn't share with us was the lack of intelligence regarding who now was in control of Owerri. It was a small town of strategic importance to the Biafrans, guarding one of the main approaches to Umuahia, now their seat of government. Owerri changed hands a number of times during the later stages of the conflict, but on the day we passed through all was quiet, with Federal troops in occupation. We kept going, turning right out of the town onto the Umuahia road. So far, so good, but not a frame of film in the can.

A few miles outside Owerri, the road widened and the bush either side became less dense – taller trees with high grasses and saplings between. The possibility that it mightn't give much cover didn't cross our minds.

Nor did the possibility of danger when we were brought to a halt by a huge, deep trench dug across the road. We got out of the vehicles and continued on foot. As it happens, we had to leave our big camera, the kind that recorded the sound as well as the picture, in the Land Rover because the camera had developed a fault. It meant that Cyril and Archie were not joined by the sound cable, instead Cyril carried a smaller lightweight Arriflex camera and Archie carried a small reel-to-reel tape recorder. The flexibility that gave them may have saved their lives.

I walked along next to Archie, recording a rather breathless description of our surroundings and how close we believed we were to the Biafran front line. We kept up quite a pace, because time was getting on, and I made a mental note of some pictures I wanted Cyril to shoot on the way back. One of the extraordinary scenes we hurried past in the bush was a clearing, where soldiers had obviously been until recently. There were the remains of a meal, and the ashes of a fire. And two other bizarre sights: in the middle of the small clearing was a wind-up gramophone, with a pile of old 78 rpm records. And a few feet from it was the vehicle in which its owners may have been transporting their primitive sound system, a battered but serviceable Silver Cross pram.

On the way back, I promised myself, it would be the perfect place to do the first to-camera piece of my Biafran assignment, maybe even accompanied by some crackly danceband.

We walked briskly up the road, our Nigerian escort strung out in front of us, totally unaware that we had walked through the front line, such as it was, and were moving deeper into territory held by the Biafrans. We were relaxed and chatty. One shot changed all that. It rang out from several hundred yards ahead. The commandos with us seemed unfazed. Gesturing to us to stop and be quiet, they held a quick conversation among themselves, then one of them moved a dozen yards ahead of us all, dropped down on one knee, and blazed away in the general direction of that single incoming shot. They had caught a glimpse of two or three of the enemy, and seemed convinced there were no more than that. They couldn't have been more wrong. We had walked into an ambush. There was a volley of incoming shots. Someone yelled the blindingly obvious 'take cover!', and we scattered to each side of the road.

The nearest place for me to take cover was on the opposite side of the road to most of the others. Across the road, a few yards away, I glimpsed Cyril standing behind a big tree, coolly winding up his camera. The incoming fire became sporadic, each group of shots greeted by our escort with a deafening burst of automatic fire in response. Morley Safer and his CBS crew managed a piece to camera, him crouching in a shallow ditch. Then, suddenly, all hell broke loose, and none of us could do anything but get as close to the ground as possible and hope. The incoming fire became intense, long bursts of heavy machine gun and Bren gun fire. The commandos we were with were firing thousands of rounds back, guns blazing. Bullets ricocheted off the road and pinged off the trees.

As I pressed myself against the earth on my side of the road, my heart pounding, I lost sight of my colleagues, and they lost contact with me. I knew it was a mistake to get separated from my crew, but to attempt to rejoin them would mean breaking into the open. So driven by instincts of self preservation I crawled a few yards further into the bush, and into a shallow hole. I heard someone say 'we're surrounded'. There was a momentary lull. Then some more shots, and I heard Morley yell 'He's been hit'. At that moment, Priya Ramrahka had stood up and been shot in the back, dying almost instantly. Again the firing became intense, but unknown to me, the rest of my party, under covering fire, had begun crawling back down the road, dragging Ramrahka with them, and were soon round a bend and out of immediate danger. The firing stopped about half an hour after it had started, but I was safe.

So I thought.

Cautiously, I stood up, cracking the dry twigs and leaves around me. Then, no more than ten yards from me, I was aware I had company. I held my breath as whoever it was drew nearer, the only noise being the tell-tale rustling as he parted the dense vegetation in front of him. Then the movement stopped. I still couldn't see him. But the next noise, the metallic double click of a firearm being readied for business, went through me like an electric shock. In one desperate movement I flung myself back into my shallow hole. I went in head first, and as I did, my unseen stalker opened fire.

For a second or two my legs were in the air, and before they hit the ground with the rest of my body, I felt the sickening, numbing, tearing kick of a high velocity bullet going through both of them. I lay on my back in the hole, and what instantly flashed through my mind was not fear, but anger – anger that I was in such a mess, in such a god-awful place. Then came the second burst of fire, from a second magazine, which I'd heard my attacker click into place. The earth around my head fizzed and jumped as the bullets hit. And then again it was quiet. I lay for a minute or two, then raised my head to look at my legs. From the waist to my knees my whiteish slacks had turned red, soaked with blood. It crossed my mind that my little foxhole in the Nigerian bush might just have become my grave. I thought I was losing so much blood that I would soon be unconscious, but when after a short time I still appeared to have my wits about me, I called out. I shouted that I was a British journalist, and that I had been hit. I called three or four times and then lost the strength to do it again, but it was enough. Help was coming.

Why had my attacker lost interest and disappeared? Let me for a moment scroll forward.

More than thirty-five years later, I was given the most extraordinary explanation, which I have no reason to disbelieve. At a lunchtime awards ceremony in London, for the Television and Radio Industries Club, I was introduced to the novelist Frederick Forsyth. A journalist before he started penning his gripping novels, Freddie had been a BBC reporter covering the Biafran war, and had become sympathetic to the Biafran cause. At the same time he had become increasingly unhappy at the restrictions the BBC placed on his reporting of the conflict.

So, in 1968 he walked out on the BBC, put on a uniform, and did his best to help the Biafrans, principally by presenting their case to the world's media. Talking to Freddie at that lunch I said that I didn't think we'd met before. To which he replied that we had in fact come very close to meeting, and then gave me the most amazing account of the circumstances.

Frederick Forsyth recalled how he had been there that day on the road to Umuahia, and had intervened to stop the firing when he discovered that an English person was involved.

He was able to recount to me details of the incident which only someone who had been there could have known. He told me how he had been invited to join a group of rebel soldiers who planned to ambush Federal troops by blocking a road near the contested town of Owerri. They'd dug a deep trench across it, and cut down trees to make it impossible to drive off the road and get round the obstruction. When the trap was sprung on the patrol accompanying me and my colleagues, Freddie was clearly close to the action.

I didn't take a note of what Frederick Forsyth said at that lunch, but he described the moments immediately after I had been hit to Nicholas Hellen of the *Sunday Times*:

> I could not see who was who, but I heard an anguished English voice shouting 'My God! My God! I've been hit.' For all I knew, it could have been an oil worker or a missionary, and I couldn't just stand there. The guy next to me sighted up for a second shot. I pushed his rifle away, so he just shot up into the sky. There was a return of fire from the other side, and we crawled away.

His account, kept to himself for all those years, and now told to me in such a matter-of-fact way, left a deep impression. It felt so inadequate, but I could do no more than shake his hand and thank him.

A few weeks later, however, I received a letter from Morley Safer, the CBS correspondent who had been with me on the day of the ambush thirty years previously. Morley, writing from the New York offices of the CBS flagship *Sixty Minutes*, and by now laden with awards for years of outstanding TV journalism, made it clear that Forsyth's claim had made a totally different impression on him. He'd pinned to his letter a photocopy of Nicholas Hellen's story from the *Sunday Times*, and came straight to the point:

Dear Peter,

Why does instinct, memory, and a fairly good bullshit detector tell me that the enclosed may be more a product of imagination than reality? Bwana Forsyth calms the savage horde and the only person to die in the ambush is the ever-faithful Gunga Din Ramrahka.

Apart from anything else, I cannot imagine Field Marshal Forsyth in charge of anything less than a full division at the time, and while we did take a lot of fire that day, as we both know, two guys with automatic weapons can create a lot of fire, especially if you happen to be on the receiving end.

I suspect in another twenty years, he will take credit for not only saving Sissons, but France, Britain and all Western civilisation.

All good wishes, Morley.

I think if Morley had spoken to Forsyth as I did, he would still have had a bit of fun, but he would not have been so harsh. I have no doubt that the knowledge Freddie had about what happened that afternoon could only have been acquired in person; his graphic language, perhaps laced with poetic licence, was no more than you would expect from such a distinguished thriller writer recalling an event many years later.

As Forsyth and his Biafran friends melted away that day, thirty years earlier, I was in a real mess, but at least I was alive – just.

Three or four of Adekunle's commandos, begged by my friends to try to find me, had returned and had heard my shouts. By the time they got to me, I was drifting in and out of consciousness. The next thing I remember was that they had dragged me out onto the road. Then the firing began again – a couple of the Federal troops had gone a bit further down the road to give covering fire, and just hosed the bush around us. I remember finding the noise not just painful, but distressing. The major in charge took off his webbing and tied tourniquets round the top of my legs. Then cutting away the fabric, he pushed field dressings onto my four wounds, or in the case of the first exit wound, on the inside of my right thigh, deep into the huge hole the spinning bullet had made. I passed out. Cyril and Archie met the soldiers, carrying me back down the road and put that old Silver Cross pram we had seen earlier to good use. I was placed in it, my legs hanging over the end, and wheeled back to our vehicles. Cyril said later that I had begun to scream in pain. It was getting dark.

Our entire party was driven a few miles to a wooden shack, which was doing duty as a field hospital. Outside the hut was a stack of coffins, of which the Nigerians seemed to have a good supply. Inside, in the fading light, my only lifeline was some dressings and antiseptic. I came to, finding myself on a table as an orderly wrapped bandages round the top of my legs. I turned my head to find Ramrahka lying next to me, obviously dead.

The next few hours are a blur, but Cyril Page commandeered an ancient military ambulance and we set out to drive through the night back to Port Harcourt, about seventy miles away. I lay on the floor of the truck, next to Ramrahka. He wasn't in a coffin, because he was a tall man, and they didn't have one big enough. Every time the vehicle went over a big pothole, and there were many, I bounced into his body, which by now was quite cold. The ambulance went straight to Port Harcourt's small hospital, the property of the Shell Oil Company, but commandeered by the military. I was put on the floor of a brightly lit room. Some yards away was an operating table, with an operation in progress. I was struck by the most incredible thirst, and begged for some water. An orderly said that if he gave me some, I would vomit it right up again. I said I didn't care. He helped me to drink, and up it duly came. I went out like a light.

I awoke the next morning in a hospital bed. The 'ward' had no roof and no other patients that I could see, and the sun was getting higher in the sky. My wounds had been cleaned up, or so everyone thought, and heavily bandaged.

Cyril and Archie were there, and seemed relieved when I recognised them. Cyril tried to cheer me up. A small Nigerian plumber or fitter, who appeared to be lost, entered the room. He was wearing oily blue overalls, and carrying a huge sack of spanners and tools.

Cyril walked over to him, took him by the shoulder and guided him to my bedside. 'Here you are, Doctor,' said Cyril, 'you can start operating on him now.'

All that day, Cyril and Archie looked after me, part of the time on the baking Port Harcourt tarmac, swatting away the flies from my stretcher as we waited for transport back to Lagos. We went back the same way as we had come out – on an ageing DC4 full of coffins, but this time the coffins had bodies inside them, not bombs. They had found one into which they could fit Ramrahka, by bending his legs.

In Lagos I was transferred to the University Teaching Hospital, which appeared to be full of war casualties. Had I been a Nigerian soldier, I could well have ended up having my legs amputated, but any thought of that was stopped by the appearance of a consultant orthopaedic surgeon from Winchester, Ken Hesketh, who was flown out by ITN. Ken ensured that the wounds were stabilised, but that nothing drastic was done until I could be assessed back in the UK. I spent a week in hospital in Lagos, lying on my back watching huge red and green lizards walk across the ceiling above my head, not knowing whether they were the real thing or whether I was hallucinating. I needed a lot of blood, and staff at the British Embassy held a blood-donor session on my behalf.

Another donor, who came to see me, was the kindly Angus McDermid, the BBC's Africa correspondent, and I was also visited by Sam Hall, the Reuters correspondent, later to become an ITN reporter himself. When Ken judged me fit to travel, I was taken to Lagos airport by ambulance and there, on the tarmac in the sunshine, saw the beautiful sight of a BOAC VC10, always a special aircraft but never more special than it was for me on that day. A fork-lift truck raised my travel-cot to the door, in which stood a vision – a blonde stewardess so perfect in blue and crisp white. And as I was lifted up from the tarmac, I glimpsed her suspenders and lacy stocking tops and suddenly life seemed much better.

And here's another co-incidence: that senior BOAC stewardess, on what was for her just another flight, was the daughter of the surgeon into whose care I was going back in London, Mr David Trevor, of the Royal National Orthopaedic hospital, later to be President of the Royal College of Surgeons.

I don't remember much of the flight back to Heathrow. The airline had removed six seats to accommodate me in my cot, and Ken Hesketh and the cabin crew worked to keep me comfortable. Ken had a bag of drugs and equipment, which included a bed-bottle. After I had made use of that, he found that he couldn't rinse it out – it wouldn't fit under the tap over the tiny wash-basin in the lavatory. The crew came up with the solution: they rinsed it out with champagne, of which they had plenty on board. By then Ken was entitled to several glasses of the stuff himself, but he had to rely on something stronger to keep me free from pain during the flight.

At Heathrow, I was only dimly aware of a small group of senior people from ITN, who were there to meet me. But the real joy and relief was again to hold the hand of my wife, Sylvia. She had had a deeply distressing time, because of the poor communications with Nigeria, and had been distraught when news reached London of the DC4 that had crashed, killing everyone on board on its approach to Port Harcourt. For many hours she had no way of knowing that it wasn't the aircraft on which I was travelling. Sylvia accompanied me in an ambulance to the Orthopaedic Hospital in central London, where, in a room on the fifth floor, I went into a long sleep.

The next day, my surgeon David Trevor operated, cleaning the wounds and with the help of a small metal detector, removing the bullet that did the damage. It was broken into many pieces scattered through both thighs. I have it in a jar at home, although some fragments are still buried deep in my legs. He also removed, thrust deep into the gaping hole in my right leg and compacted into a tight blood-soaked ball, the field dressing pressed in by the Nigerian major. It was identified as a First World War bismuth and paraffin dressing, a clue to the state of Nigerian Army medical supplies in the field. But it had almost certainly saved me from bleeding to death. There was widespread nerve damage – I had lost the sciatic nerve in my left leg – but no damage to bone. The bullet had missed my femoral artery by less than a centimetre.

I spent the next ten weeks in hospital having a series of skin grafts. But the scarring was the least of my problems. What I didn't know was how superficially my wounds had been cleaned up in Nigeria. Dirt from the road and my foxhole had festered into a serious infection, and it wasn't responding to treatment. My brother Cliff, himself a doctor, was telephoned and given a pessimistic prognosis. They told him that they had used a range of antibiotics, but none had worked. The last shot in their locker was a drug called Pyopen. If that didn't stop the infection, I could die. It did.

It was a slow recovery, but made much more bearable by the closeness of my hospital room to ITN's new headquarters in Wells Street, about a quarter of a mile away. Each day a succession of friends would arrive, usually carrying bottles of wine or beer, which they then proceeded to drink, something I was not allowed to do. Towards the end of my stay, two of them – the newscaster Ivor Mills and producer Steve Wright – decided that a trip to the pub nearby would cheer me up. One evening, unknown to the nursing staff they got me out of bed, put an overcoat round me, and carried me upright, without my feet touching the ground, into the lift, down to the ground floor and into the pub, The Green Man, over the road. There I gratefully sipped my first pint for two months, while back at the hospital there was consternation that I had gone missing and my mug of Ovaltine was going cold next to my empty bed.

The beer had its effect. When Mills and Wright brought me back, I wouldn't have been able to use my legs even if they had been in good condition.

Another visitor was ITN's redoubtable crime correspondent, Tom St John Barry, who brought with him the head of Scotland Yard's firearms squad. During the Umuahia ambush, the sound recordist Archie Howell had kept his tape recorder running, until the tape ran out. The frenzy of firing on that tape was of great interest to the Metropolitan Police, who had found it useful in training recruits to recognise the sound of different types of weapons. It seems that every handgun and automatic ever invented was on it – pistols, Bren guns, sten guns, Tommy guns, Lee Enfields as well as the ubiquitous AK47 – they were all there, some of great vintage.

The empty bottles in the wardrobe in my room, and the crate of them under my bed, were generally overlooked by the nursing staff. That was until I had a visit from my fearsome Auntie Kay. Kay Sissons was a retired senior nurse – a Sister Tutor of the Old School, who in her day had terrorised student nurses in Liverpool. Entering my hospital room, before she'd even taken off her coat, she set about re-making my bed, muttering about the incompetence of modern nurses. Then her blood pressure rose as she stubbed her foot on the crate of empties under the bed. Vowing to go and sort things out with my ward sister, she took off her coat, and as she opened the wardrobe door to hang it up, another pile of empties inside fell out. Auntie Kay did not see the funny side.

During those two and a half months in hospital I was also cheered up by the numbers of people, not just friends and colleagues but complete strangers, who wrote to me. Among the letters I treasure to this day was one from Geoffrey Cox, who had hired me four years previously. Geoffrey, always under-rewarded at ITN, had recently moved on from the ITN editorship to the deputy chairmanship of the new ITV franchise, Yorkshire Television – where he freely admitted that at the age of fifty-eight the money was a great attraction. Geoffrey wished me a speedy and complete recovery, adding that 'you have behaved throughout your time with ITN not only with intelligence, but with courage'. He went on to reflect that 'in comparison with these chaotic African Wars the Spanish Civil War and the Russo/Finnish Wars, in which I did my war corresponding, seemed to have been very orthodox affairs with one's dangers reasonably predictable'.

A week or two before Christmas I could finally go home. I had lost three stone in weight, and wore a calliper on my left leg to hold up my drop-foot, a direct consequence of the sciatic nerve being shot away. The biggest hole in my legs – the exit wound on the inside of my right leg – had still not healed, and I was to return to the hospital regularly for a number of weeks to have the dressings changed until it did. I took home with me a pile of very strong painkillers, which I was to need for many years to come.

That Christmas was spent quietly at home, a new place in Kent where we had moved shortly before I went to Nigeria.

ITN took away my car, the second-hand Vauxhall which had replaced my late lamented Reliant van, and procured for me from British Leyland's press fleet an almost new Austin 1300 with automatic transmission – essential now that I had an almost useless left foot.

In the spring of the following year there was an opportunity to ease myself back into some gentle work. It sounds extraordinary now, but ITN decided to spend a week hunting the Loch Ness Monster. Several camera teams and reporters were despatched to a hotel at Drumnadrochit on the shores of the loch, the hunt was heavily promoted on air, and a series of weighty deadpan reports featuring miniature submarines and all sorts of monster lures appeared on *News at Ten*. It didn't do the ratings any harm, and quite senior people at ITN took the whole thing very seriously, frowning upon anyone who took it frivolously. It was however an excuse for a succession of the company's top people to leave the office and spend a few days visiting the scene of the investigation, and I and my wife were invited to join them. It was little more than a free holiday for us, but I made myself useful ferrying people to and from the airport in my new car. The social life for a few weeks was also very restorative.

Back from Loch Ness, I tried to re-start my reporting career. At first I could undertake nothing too strenuous, but the ideal story fell into my lap. John Lennon and Yoko Ono were attracting a lot of publicity with their campaign for world peace, which seemed to involve little more than lying in bed in some of the world's top hotels. At the end of March they were lying in bed for peace at the Amsterdam Hilton. Pictures had appeared in the press, but no one had obtained a bedside interview. I knew John Lennon of old, and travelled to Amsterdam with an ITN crew. Within a few hours I had a world exclusive, talking to them among the posters and pillows, and getting more than two minutes on *News at Ten*. Well, at least I was back in business.

During that summer I was also able to spend some time reporting from Northern Ireland, where the Troubles were gaining momentum and the security situation was deteriorating by the day, often characterised by vicious rioting. My lack of mobility left me vulnerable in such situations, and my task wasn't made any easier by the fact that my BBC opposite number was Martin Bell. Marking Martin, one of the most diligent, intelligent and energetic of reporters, meant the ITN man had to be on top of his game. But my ITN crews and colleagues at Ulster Television gave me a lot of help and protection, and my confidence began to return. I also got to know Martin well, and the two of us together had our backs to the wall in a number of dodgy situations.

Our work was made no easier by Ian Paisley, who appeared to relish blaming ITN and the BBC for, as he saw it, talking down the Protestant people and being soft on the mainly Catholic civil rights movement. If Bell and I were covering a Paisley rally, he invariably pointed us out at the back of the room and ranted that we were as much their enemies as the Republicans. We felt far from safe. The Paisley of those days could be fearsome – but the Paisley I encountered many years later had mellowed greatly. One night I was flying back from an assignment in Washington DC and, unusually, had been upgraded to Business Class. As I settled back into my seat before take-off, a familiar figure lowered himself into the seat next to me. It was Ian Paisley. I found him a most congenial travelling companion – especially when he plied me with champagne. Alcohol, of course, in Paisley's book is 'The Devil's Milk' but every time the stewardess brought us a glass of champagne, Paisley passed his to me.

In between those first reporting assignments after my injury, I gave some serious thought to my predicament. I reckoned that my career prospects had probably been permanently affected by the injuries that I had sustained on ITN's behalf.

ITN, although they had picked up all my hospital bills, and been generous in other ways, had never suggested any kind of compensation or given me any guarantees as to my future employment. And amazingly neither I, nor any of ITN's other reporters sent into hazardous situations, was insured. What was I to do about it? My first thought was to approach my union, the National Union of Journalists, in which I had been active since joining ITN four years previously. I spoke to a senior official at head office, who suggested I speak to the NUJ's lawyers. This I duly did and was told, in no uncertain terms, that they were not prepared to help me. 'Sorry old boy, these things are just an occupational hazard' was the gist of what they said. I put down the phone, cancelled my NUJ subscription and never re-joined.

My next move was to seek independent legal advice, which was quite clear – I had a case against ITN for compensation. Letters were exchanged with ITN's lawyers, and the situation for a time became quite unpleasant – with ITN's General Manager, Bill Hodgson, telling me they would always find some kind of work for me, but that if I pressed my compensation claim, and they paid up, then I would have to leave.

The matter dragged on for nearly three years, before the ITN board approved a £6,000 ex gratia payment with no conditions attached. The payment recognised that the injury might impede my future earning power, and that I would have some substantial ongoing costs – for example, for many years I had to have my shoes made specially, and every time I changed my car there was the extra cost of automatic transmission. Bill Hodgson subsequently told my wife, on a social occasion, that he deeply regretted the unsympathetic way he had handled the matter. As far as I was concerned, there were no hard feelings, just relief when there was a final settlement, and I could get on with my life and my career.

Just under a year after the Biafra shooting, I went back into hospital for surgery to correct my dropped left foot, so that I could discard the calliper I had to wear. David Trevor at The Royal National Orthopaedic Hospital had perfected a relatively new procedure – a tendon transplant – which had originally been devised for polio victims. This entailed getting under the skin, taking the tendon that inverted the foot – a movement that was still functioning – detaching that tendon and relocating it on the top of the foot. I lost the ability to invert my left foot, while re-gaining the more vital function of waggling it up and down and preventing it dropping and dragging. It was a very good trade-off. To secure the newly moved tendon to the top of my foot, he put a suture through the tendon, then right through my foot, and tied it firmly to a pyjama button. Finally, the whole of my left leg from the knee down was encased in plaster, which had to stay on for ten weeks. As the weeks went by it began to smell noticeably. It got so bad that when I went to the cinema, people would move several rows away from me. But when the plaster came off, and that button – by then embedded in the sole of my foot – was cut away, the operation was a complete success. Forty years later I had to have an MRI scan of my ankle, and it showed David Trevor's handiwork still in perfect condition.

So it was that I was able to resume my life at ITN. I still had a limp, chronic pain, and found it difficult to run for more than a few yards. If I were to go on reporting, I had to accept that I now had serious physical limitations. At the time I saw it as a depressing setback. I was soon to find out that it was a golden opportunity.

Chapter 6

What the Barons did for me

I had a lot of luck during my forty-five years in news. Surviving my injury was a good start. I simply counted myself lucky to be alive. But as the 1970s began, I didn't for a moment believe that by the end of the decade my lack of mobility would actually work to my advantage.

ITN's top foreign reporters and correspondents were kept busy during the 1970s, and did much to enhance ITN's growing reputation, in the process winning a string of richly deserved awards. The Dawson's Field hijackings, the terrorism at the Munich Olympics, Nixon in China, war between India and Pakistan, another war in the Middle East, Watergate, America's humiliation in Vietnam, Turkey's invasion of Cyprus, the death of Mao, the rise and fall of Idi Amin, the Camp David Accords, the Iranian revolution, and much more. It was work that only reporters who were physically fit, and who could look after themselves in tight corners, could undertake.

From my new location on the sidelines of all this, I could have been a very rare presence on the nation's television screens. I was proud of most of my colleagues and felt fortunate to be part of an expanding organisation on top of its game, and increasingly often running rings round the BBC. But as the decade unfolded, one massive, continuing domestic story gave me the opportunity to develop a different high profile career at ITN. That story was the dire state of the British economy, plunged into crisis by the oil shock, and made worse by the month by soaring inflation and massive waves of industrial unrest. My Biafran injuries had closed one door, but opened two new ones. The first to open was my appointment as ITN's Industrial Editor, responsible for all its Labour, Industrial, Economic and Aviation coverage. It gave me status both inside and outside ITN. But the second opportunity it gave to me was to develop an on-screen presence and style. Frequent appearances on *News at Ten* as a specialist home-based reporter led to my being asked from time to time to stand-in for the established newscasters. And as my confidence on-screen grew, I started to newscast regularly across all ITN's programmes.

It didn't happen immediately. At the beginning of 1970, the plaster had not long been taken off my tendon transplant, and I was still sore. It was important for a few months that I didn't put too much extra strain on that weak left foot and rip the relocated tendon from its new anchorage. I needed to get back to work, but preferably sitting down for most of the time. So when I was offered the chance of working as Home News Editor, I jumped at it – although perhaps in my condition, jumped was not the right word. I was temporarily appointed to the small team of news editors, taking my place on their rota, arriving early every morning to make the dispositions of reporters and crews, and staying late to assign stuff for the next day or write the handover for the next on shift. It was a busy and responsible job, which also gave me a close-up view of the professional insecurities and ambitions, and personal weaknesses, of many of my colleagues.

Among those colleagues that I got to know particularly was Ivor Mills, one of ITN's most personable bon-viveurs, who in his youth had the looks of a young Cary Grant. Ivor, incidentally, had the distinction of having a dish on the menu at Bertorelli's Restaurant in Charlotte Street named after him – Scampi Mills. It was large succulent scampi coated in batter and lightly deep-fried, served with mayonnaise and, invariably, chips. That, and the large amounts of wine that accompanied any Mills lunch, left its mark on his waistline – and would have done him even more damage had it not been for the concern of the upstairs waitress in Bertorelli's, Anna. Unfairly but widely regarded as the rudest waitress in London, Anna sometimes refused to serve him with Scampi Mills. 'You're not having that,' she would say in her usual tactful way, 'you are getting too fat'.

Early one morning, as I was starting my shift on the news desk, Ivor was the first reporter to arrive for duty. And as he crossed the practically deserted newsroom, I noticed that he was walking in a rather strange way, indeed he looked positively to be in pain, and after bidding him a cheery 'good morning' I asked him if perhaps he'd come off badly the day before in one of his regular tennis matches with Bosanquet. He drew me to one side and confided that it was all because of his trousers. He'd spent the night, he said, at a rather exotic party, and when he came to leave there was only one pair of trousers left, and they were a rather poor fit. I don't know whether he was having me on, but I suspect he wasn't.

I made what I could of the new job. While the foreign desk, which was next to the home desk, was assigning reporters to the world's hotspots, I had to fill the home news diary. And when there was a lot of heavy foreign news, I was often under pressure to lighten the mix. The great tradition of ITN's 'And Finally' slot was safe with me, and it was with great enthusiasm that I despatched the ever-dependable Ivor one morning to do a story about the world's heaviest cat, which had been found to be living in Folkestone. Ivor came back with the story remarking, as he showed me his scratches, 'That cat's a killer.' The thing about Ivor Mills, who worked as a freelance, was that he would deliver the goods for the news desk whatever the story. Ivor was a hired hand and got on with the job. And if he were sent on a duff story, he would invariably see it as an opportunity to take his camera crew for a good lunch somewhere, while they 'checked it out'. But he was far from being a lightweight.

One evening, there was a late development in a big media story – a bitter dispute in Fleet Street – and Ivor was put into the *News at Ten* studio to explain it and to interview, live, Jocelyn Stevens, the managing director of Express Newspapers. In the brief live interview, Ivor gave Mr Stevens such a rough time that it prompted a rare tribute from a distinguished guest who was watching that night in the control gallery, the Commissioner of the Metropolitan Police. Observed the Commissioner: 'We usually caution them before we interview them like that.' And that was long before Jeremy Paxman was invented. I, and all who worked with him, were very fond of Ivor Mills. When he left ITN to become Head of Public Affairs at the Post Office, he reminded his many friends: 'If ever you want to have an affair in public, I'm your man.' His humour concealed a very serious man, an accomplished classical pianist who studied composition at Queen's University Belfast. In his sixties, his health was broken when he was hit by a motorbike while alighting from a taxi on a London street, and he died relatively young in 1996. I count myself lucky to have known such a colleague.

My news desk duties ended suddenly half way through May 1970, when the Prime Minister, Harold Wilson, asked the Queen to dissolve

Parliament, prior to a general election a month later on 18 June. A general election campaign meant putting every available reporter on the road, and I was given the job of shadowing every movement of one of Labour's most colourful and controversial figures, George Brown. Labour were well prepared for this election, and within hours of the dissolution, I had George Brown's itinerary in my hand. For practically every day for three and a half weeks he was scheduled to speak at five or six market square soapbox meetings plus an evening rally – all in marginal Labour seats, up and down the land, and often many miles apart.

George Brown was an intelligent, charismatic and mercurial politician who had resigned as Foreign Secretary two years before, but remained as the party's deputy leader. His principal weakness was alcohol – the words 'tired and emotional' were coined for him – and although never tainted by sexual scandal, he had been known to pinch the occasional female bottom. He was accompanied throughout the campaign by scores of reporters, cameramen and TV crews. Of the reporters, half were from tabloid newspapers with the sole brief of getting picture and story of George drinking, George falling over, George losing his temper or George attempting to kiss any passing lady admirer. I was told that one tabloid alone had twelve reporters and photographers on the case.

For the next three and a half weeks dozens of cars carrying the panting hacks joined in a madcap race between George's speaking engagements. He was driven, often at breakneck and illegal speeds, in a supercharged black limousine. The rest of us raced to keep up with him. If he made an unscheduled stop, we all stopped. If he swung off the road for a cup of tea, we all had a cup of tea. What he never did was to stop his car to relieve himself – that would have been the picture of pictures for half the pursuing pack. Sometimes we drove in his wake so fast that wheels left the ground going over humpback bridges. The ITN crew travelled in their big Ford; I drove myself in my Austin. That arrangement gave us the flexibility for me to keep an eye on George at one location while the crew raced on ahead to set up for the next. His speeches, across East Anglia, the West Midlands, Essex, Wales and the north west were barnstorming affairs. At the end of the day, after yet another packed rally, and with his voice increasingly hoarse, he must have longed for a drink. But George stayed stone cold sober, with only adrenalin coursing through his veins, and the pursuing pack was cheated. Once or twice they thought they had him, and to my knowledge one or two stories were fabricated by hacks pressurised by their London news desks, but George survived.

It was a glorious summer, and Wilson went into the campaign convinced he would win, his judgement backed by the opinion polls. But during the Brown tour, George, in private, began to confide in those close to him that, in his bones, he knew that Labour would lose. He was right. I stood near him at Derby Town Hall just before midnight on polling day, as the Returning Officer announced that Brown, George, had lost his seat, at Belper.

He was crushed, and retired alone, brushing away our microphones, to his suite in the Railway Hotel and closed the door. One of his staff told me that if he gave an interview to anyone the next day, it would be to me, whom he judged to have played straight with him during the campaign, and whom he had got to like. On that half-promise, I phoned ITN, who spent a small fortune putting electronic links into the Railway Hotel. Overnight, the only available mobile tower to carry the transmission dish was driven down from Scotland. Extra engineers and technicians arrived, all on the legendary rates of 'golden overtime' that were the hallmark of their union, the ACCT.

At ten the next morning all was ready for the exclusive George Brown interview. I walked across the lobby of the Railway Hotel, up the broad staircase, and knocked on his door. After a minute or two, he opened it. He was wearing a silk dressing gown, and there were signs that, at last, he had taken a drink. Thick curtains were still keeping out the daylight and, most extraordinarily, there was music in the room. In the half light of a faded suite in a venerable Midlands railway hotel, which had seen better days, there was the sound of a gramophone. It was a record that had come to be special for a politician who had also seen better days – Frank Sinatra singing 'My Way'.

It was no surprise to me when, years later, he selected this as his top record on *Desert Island Discs*. But on that morning after the 1970 election, although I felt for the first time as a reporter that I was intruding on private grief, I pressed ahead with the job I had to do. I made some sympathetic noises, and told George we could do an interview, live into Day Two of the ITV election coverage, as soon as he was ready. But he did it his way, and told me, in the nicest way, to get lost.

～

That 1970 election, which gave Edward Heath a majority of thirty, focused me as never before on politics. Shortly after arriving at ITN I had worked as a runner on the 1964 election results programme, and had also been involved in a small way in the 1966 coverage. Although I had studied politics at university, a large part of it was the theory of government and the constitution, and how it had evolved. What I now found compelling as a reporter was seeing politics in the raw, on the streets, in rowdy meetings; seeing the pressure groups and lobbyists in action, and how party backers – especially the trade unions – operate. Seeing the fear and the elation of party workers on election night, marvelling at how, just occasionally, the people were able to give to – and take away from – their masters, reminding the politicians just who puts them in power. I was hooked.

The direction I took as a reporter – constrained by my Biafran injuries – might easily have been that of the political correspondent, based at Westminster, and part of the parliamentary lobby. That I didn't was essentially because of the new type of government that came in with Edward Heath, and the trajectory it took to its eventual humiliation and defeat. Its three and a half years in power were meat and drink to reporters specialising in trade union, industrial and economic affairs. And I was to feel completely at home among them. It set me up nicely for the five years after that during which things got even worse under a Labour government.

Let's try and sketch in some of the background.

The laissez-faire economic platform which had brought the Heath government to power was derided as 'Selsdon Man' by Harold Wilson, after the Selsdon Park Hotel in Surrey where the Tory high command had thrashed out the policy. Its main features were less state interference in industry, a revival of free enterprise, and a comprehensive Industrial Relations Act to bring the Unions to heel. At the best of times it would have been a tall order. The Conservatives inherited 6 per cent inflation, pay rises running at 12 per cent, and rising unemployment, yet specifically ruled out any government interference on pay. Employers led the way in resisting pay demands, and within a month of Heath taking over there was a national dock strike. Heath declared a state of emergency, which didn't help at all – 1970 became the worst year for stoppages since 1926, the year of the General Strike.

But as unemployment rose (it passed the million mark on 20 January

1972) and the boom engineered by Heath's Chancellor Anthony Barber to try to reduce it succeeded only in stoking inflation, Heath had to perform a humiliating U-turn. The low point came in 1972, with the bankruptcy and nationalisation of Rolls Royce, and the bail-out of Upper Clyde Shipbuilders. Laissez-faire went screaming into reverse, as lame ducks were basted with large amounts of public money. Heath had to eat his words, and now saw pay restraint as the key to holding down prices, blaming the unions rather than the Barber Boom for the growing crisis. Accordingly, 8 per cent was deemed the unofficial ceiling for pay rises, a limit soon brushed aside by the miners with their first national strike since 1926.

It lasted seven weeks, led to yet another state of emergency plus a three-day working week to conserve electricity, and gave the miners at the end of it most of what they wanted, which was a lot.

Heath ploughed on with the search for a workable incomes policy, initially trying to replace his unofficial ceiling on pay with some kind of national voluntary approach agreed with the TUC leadership. This got no further than 'solemn and binding' undertakings, described by Bernard Ingham in his memoirs as 'a sick joke ... one of the great cons of our time'. Indeed, at a joint news conference between the TUC General Secretary Victor Feather and the Chancellor Anthony Barber, at which 'Mr Solomon Binding' (as it became called) was wheeled out yet again, Mr Feather caught my eye. I was sitting in the front row, and as the Chancellor of the Exchequer droned on about the latest TUC undertaking, the faintest of smiles crossed Mr Feather's lips, and he winked at me. It said it all.

Within months, Heath gave up on Solomon Binding and staked all on a full blown statutory prices and incomes policy.

For a while the statutory approach held, but eventually the dam burst under the pressure of a wave of strikes in key areas – notably the mines, electricity generation and supply, and the railways.

Looking back on it now, even writing it down now in headline form, the magnitude of the crisis, and the pace at which events unfolded, is almost unreal. If you wanted to make your name as an industrial correspondent, it was the ideal time.

Oh, and that wasn't all.

In the background was the hated Industrial Relations Act, a running sore ruining any attempt to build a constructive relationship between both sides of industry and the government. Its crowning fiasco was the imprisonment and release of five dockers' shop stewards – The Pentonville Five.

Their imprisonment was the logical outcome of putting the law at the centre of industrial relations – prison being the ultimate sanction for people determined to defy the law. With the Five banged up there were even moves at the TUC to call a general strike, but riding to the government's rescue came an obscure legal official, the Official Solicitor, who used his even more obscure powers to spring the Five from jail. Although the government itself didn't use the Act again, it rejected Union demands for its repeal, and made no attempt to stop other employers from using it.

For month after month, year after year, there was no let-up from this diet of dire economic, industrial and labour news, and quite early on it was decided to expand ITN's capacity for covering it. When it all began, ITN's industrial correspondent was Richard Dixon, a conscientious and respected reporter, with wide contacts, who was soon to depart to be Director of Public Relations at the CBI. After the 1970 election, as I found myself doing more and more industrial and labour reporting, Richard and I became a two-man team and, when Richard left, I was appointed Industrial Editor. Because there'd probably never before been a government in more intense economic trouble, manifested day in day out, in strikes, short-time working and industrial confrontation, than that Heath government, it was soon obvious that ITN needed further specialist reinforcements. On my recommendation, Michael Green and Giles Smith were hired from Fleet Street, each with strong contact books on both sides of industry.

I had got to know both of them well, both had a crash course in adapting to the demands of television, and they were soon kept busy. During this time I had a close-up view of the development of Heath's new Industrial Relations Court, which was charged, under the controversial Industrial Relations Act, with making the unions legally and financially accountable for their actions. The President of the Court was Sir John Donaldson, later to become Lord Donaldson, the Master of the Rolls. The Industrial Relations Act made him, for a time, the most high-profile judge in England. It also made him, by far, the most politically exposed of the judges, responsible as he was for enforcing a piece of legislation around which political views were polarised. Indeed, he had helped the then Solicitor-General, Sir Geoffrey Howe, to draft the Act. Sir John tried hard to make the new court distinctively different from the rest of the legal system.

On a couple of occasions he asked me to go to see him, to discuss the working of the court, and how it could become more media friendly. I made some suggestions, including the idea that we, radio and television, should be permitted to broadcast, in sound only, excerpts from the proceedings of the court. Donaldson had introduced tape recording instead of manual record-taking of proceedings, but balked at its wider use. Where he did co-operate with the media – and I believe I had some part in persuading him – was in issuing reporters with advance copies of his judgments. It meant that when he returned to court to deliver his judgment in a major case, we didn't have to take a note, and consequently he could be quoted more accurately, which he was concerned to achieve. But key parts of any judgment – such as the precise fines imposed – were kept blank for us to fill in as he reached them. It felt, however, really quite strange to be checking against delivery the findings of a High Court Judge, as if it were some run-of-the-mill political speech.

I and my small team worked hard and few ITN bulletins went by without one, sometimes two, and occasionally all three of us, getting a piece on air. Without doubt it was the unions that kept us most occupied, often staking out late-night cliff-hangers at the headquarters of the latest band of brothers and sisters threatening to bring the country to a halt. We spent many nocturnal hours, for example, at the luxurious, Hampstead HQ of the train drivers' union ASLEF, located in the mansion once owned by Sir Adrian Boult. The members of ASLEF's executive would arrive and settle in for the night, and their amiable but cunning general secretary Ray Buckton would tell the reporters assembled in the impressive ballroom that the decision on whether the strike was on or off could take some time. What we didn't know, and I found out from an impeccable source many years later, was that the decision had usually been taken long before the meeting started, and most of the night was spent by the dozen or so members of the Executive passing the time for dramatic effect – their ordeal lightened by the presence of a substantial drinks cupboard.

But it was during those long nights that the assembled correspondents really got to know each other. My BBC opposite number for many years was Ian Ross, a seasoned correspondent who always knew what was going on, and who kept me on my toes. Although we were in competition with each other, our relationship developed from respect into friendship, and when I moved to *Channel Four News* I played some part in persuading him to leave the BBC and spend the final part of his career with ITN.

The other ritual demanded of the industrial and labour correspondents was attendance at the various union national conferences to watch their Byzantine internal politics in action. That in itself could be a real strain on one's constitution. Not for nothing was the annual conference of the National Union of Mineworkers known among the industrial correspondents as The Intergalactic Drinking Festival.

On one legendary occasion the invitation to a National Union of Mineworkers dinner read '6.30 for 9'. Behind the bar there was only beer and whisky, which hardened NUM men used to consume holding a glass of each, and expect reporters talking with them to do the same.

As the senior of the three ITN industrial correspondents, I kept some perks to myself – and by far the best of these was reporting the development of Concorde, which the Heath government had inherited from the previous administration, and the aircraft's champion, Tony Benn. I jealously guarded the title of aviation correspondent, which was in our department's portfolio. As a result, as the decade progressed, I was on board for all Concorde's landmark flights, to Bahrain, Washington DC, and New York. On the first commercial flight, to Bahrain, I made a small piece of history – becoming the first reporter to conduct a face-to-face interview with a pilot flying an aircraft at twice the speed of sound – the velocity at which a bullet leaves the muzzle of a rifle.

Keeping the company of other aviation correspondents from time to time was an education in itself. They ranged from relative newcomers like me, to the former Battle of Britain pilot Teddy Donaldson, from the *Daily Telegraph*. Some were very, very good. But the main preoccupation of others was hanging on to the many jollies and freebies that came their way. This second category were in the habit of getting together and deciding what story they were all going to file on a particular day. It was safety in numbers – if they were all filing the same story, their news desks would find it more difficult to nail them when it turned out to be without foundation. And the story, when they were short of one, that they always seemed to file was 'Concorde cancelled' or 'Concorde to be scrapped next week' or some such. Concorde, of course, never was cancelled, but whenever it appeared in print, I had to spend countless hours checking it out, or pretending to check it out, before my own news desk decided they could rest easy.

It was around this time that I got to know Freddie Laker quite well. Freddie Laker, or Sir Freddie as James Callaghan made him, was the founding father of cheap air travel, which is taken so much for granted today. In 1971 he had the visionary idea of a low-cost, no frills service to the United States. It would be called Skytrain, and it would ensure that air travel would no longer be the prerogative of the rich. But the established carriers, co-ordinated through the cartel of the International Air Transport Association, fought him tooth and nail. One evening, I got a call from his PA, Robin Flood, asking me to go round to his Mayfair offices. I found him very depressed. Over a drink, he explained his Skytrain idea to me and the political brick wall it had hit, because of the lobbying of the IATA airlines in the UK and the United States.

He asked me if I had any ideas for changing Skytrain's prospects. I told him, off the cuff, and over a whisky or two, that he needed to turn the future of Skytrain 'from a matter of public interest to a matter of public concern'. That phrase hit home. Working men and women on low incomes were the people the other airlines forgot, and there and then Freddie Laker vowed to tell the politicians, in what became a favourite phrase of his, 'that I am going to let the travelling public out of jail'. Subsequently, he bombarded individual MPs with information about Skytrain, defying them to deny it to their constituents. He stepped up the lobbying on the other side of the Atlantic too, winning support from President Carter. It took six years, but he didn't give up, and Skytrain's fleet of DC10s flew for the first time in 1977 – £55 one-way from Gatwick to New York. Branson, Ryanair and Easyjet came later, but Laker blazed the trail, before he was forced out of business after five years by rising oil prices and ruthless undercutting on his transatlantic routes.

But no one could take away from him the achievement of bringing low cost air travel to the masses, and in a speech at his sixtieth birthday party, he was generous enough to acknowledge the advice I had given him about the need to pressurise the politicians and to carry public opinion.

Apart from the aviation correspondents, the other group of specialist reporters I mixed with were the motoring correspondents, who also ranged from the knowledgeable and principled to out and out cynical freeloaders, but all were judged by the car makers to have enormous power. The future of British car manufacturing was another of the threads running through my time as Industrial Editor, and I went on a number of the major product launches, as well as covering the interminable negotiations, damaging strikes and political manoeuvring plaguing the industry.

In 1973, the struggling British Leyland launched the Austin Allegro, subsequently voted the worst British car ever made, and called, even by the British Leyland PR staff the 'All Aggro'. Early models came with a square steering wheel, for no apparent reason. It was also prone to rust and its rear window was known to pop out unexpectedly, usually when the car was jacked up in a way that was not recommended. To launch the car, British Leyland spared no expense. You'd think they were launching a small-car version of a Ferrari and Rolls Royce rolled into one.

Early one morning, planeloads of specially chartered aircraft set off from Heathrow Airport, filled with writers and reporters from every media outlet you could name. Naturally, I thought that this was a job that I should spare Michael Green and Giles Smith the stress of doing. Hundreds of hacks were flown to southern Spain in time for a slap-up lunch at a luxurious hotel, gallons of wine and unlimited platefuls of lobster. There were speeches reminding us what a moment this was in motoring history. Then we were ushered outside to where scores of shining, brand new Allegros were standing in the sunshine. We were thrown the keys, some reporters finding it quite a struggle to catch them, given a map of a twenty-mile scenic route, and told to be back in time for tea.

For me, it was one of the most hair-raising experiences ever, as dozens of unhinged motoring writers vied to carve each other up on winding mountain roads. I got back with the car intact, which is more than I can say for my state of mind. Many of the cars were severely damaged or written off. Some of the writers, having written off one Allegro, hitched a lift back to get another one and start again.

But the crowning moment of the day was yet to come. That evening, British Leyland had taken over most of one of Madrid's most famous locations for flamenco dancing. All the correspondents, me among them, were bussed in, and served a delicious dinner in lovely, refined surroundings. Even more wine flowed. Then the lights were dimmed, and onto the stage stepped the guitarist, followed by one of the most statuesque and beautiful dancers you could ever wish to see. This was the Margot Fonteyn of Flamenco. The place fell silent. Dark haired, aquiline nosed, immaculately dressed in traditional costume, she drew herself up to her full height, raising her castanets, wrists inverted, above her head. And just as the guitarist was about to strike his opening, majestic chord, the silence was broken by the motoring correspondent of a well known tabloid newspaper, who stood up and yelled 'Gerremoff.'

Despite my lack of empathy with some of the motoring fraternity, I got on well with the other industrial correspondents. I was soon invited to join the committee of the Labour and Industrial Correspondents Group – the equivalent, in the 1970s and early 1980s, of the Parliamentary Lobby, and for a time more influential.

Most members of the Group had an advantage over their colleagues in the Lobby because they were close to both sides of industry and particularly the Unions, contacts which were essential against the industrial, economic and political background, and the arcane nature of union politics. In the history of the Labour Party, the trade unions have probably never had more power than during those years. And with Labour in government, many ministers didn't contemplate pursuing policies that would alienate the union bosses, the party's paymasters.

If you could read the union mind, you were ahead of the game politically – and most labour and industrial correspondents enjoyed that advantage. The Labour and Industrial Correspondents Group enjoyed a status at that time that was never repeated. But as union power diminished, so did the importance of the Group, and it is now defunct. But labour and industrial correspondents like Trevor Kavanagh, Peter Hitchens and Richard Littlejohn found themselves well equipped by their experiences to move on to political reporting, carrying the insights that labour reporting in those years had given them.

After a spell as Secretary of the Group, in 1976, I was voted in as Chairman. The principal mark I made as Chairman was to change the rules of the Group to permit the membership of women. There was only one female industrial correspondent, from the *Morning Star*, but I thought it unjust that she would be asked to leave whenever colleagues were invited as The Group to confidential briefings with ministers or union and business leaders.

I thought for a time there might be two women members, when Angela Rippon was seconded to industrial reporting for a few months by the BBC. I remember her turning up on a few crisis doorsteps, and spending many pleasant hours in her company as she proved herself to be a disarming competitor. She was also the only industrial correspondent who wore large earrings and a fur coat. Or at least I think she was.

That was all to come, when, at the end of 1973, the crisis facing the Heath government took a turn for the worse, which is saying something. Many thought it couldn't get any worse.

With the second stage of his Prices and Incomes Policy already having provoked numerous strikes at the beginning of the year, Heath decided to press ahead with Stage 3 in the autumn. This limited pay rises to 7 per cent, far less than the ambitions of key groups of workers like the miners and electricity workers. Their hand had been strengthened by another big increase in the world price of oil, after the Yom Kippur war. Despite tailoring the pay policy to provide exceptions for certain groups, like the miners, it was not enough to avert a national overtime ban in the pits. In December the government declared yet another state of emergency, imposed power cuts to conserve coal, rationed petrol, imposed a 50mph limit on the roads, and put industry on a three-day working week. It was a dire winter.

When the Miners upped the ante and called a national strike, Heath called a snap election. On the morning of 7 February, I was at the NUM headquarters in Euston Road in the office of the president, Joe Gormley, shortly after he got a phone call from Downing Street to inform him that Edward Heath had decided to call a general election. I have never seen anyone look so unconcerned. Heath asked the country 'who governs Britain?' Gormley could have told him the answer there and then.

ITN had just three weeks to prepare for the general election on 28 February.

I was given my election assignment that afternoon – I was to follow the campaign of the Opposition leader, Harold Wilson, and on election night itself I was to be the reporter on the outside broadcast unit at Labour's headquarters, Transport House, in the heart of Westminster.

Wilson's campaign would not be like George Brown's. He would address big, set-piece rallies around the country, returning to London each night to be ready for Labour's news conference the next morning.

Sometimes he travelled by car, driven by his loyal driver Bill Housden. I found it remarkable that as Opposition leader he appeared to have so little security, even though he had already served two terms as Prime Minister. I remember driving myself one evening to a Wilson rally in a big provincial town. A couple of miles from the centre I passed his black Rover, parked on its own in a lay-by. There was no police escort, just Bill in the front seat, and Harold in the back with the light on, going through the pages of his speech. And always smoking a cigar. The pipe was just for the cameras.

On other occasions he travelled by rail, and I would be invited to sit opposite him in his compartment. I have never seen a senior politician more relaxed. He wanted to know about my background and, as a Liverpool MP, liked the fact that I was from the city. He'd also been a don at my old college, which gave us more fertile ground for reminiscence. He wanted to know all about my family and filed away the details in his prodigious memory. Whenever we met subsequently, he asked after them by name. It must have been a personal tragedy when he realised a few years later that his memory was decaying, the real reason for his shock resignation.

But during that election campaign in February 1974, he was on top of his game. He had an instinctive understanding of the medium of television, its importance to the politician seeking election, and the needs of the crews behind the television cameras. Every big Wilson speech at his campaign rallies would contain the forty-five or sixty second sound-bite that he judged the most important point he needed to make on that day, and which he knew would get prominence on the TV bulletins. But to make sure we got it, and had time to get it back to the studio for transmission, he placed it right at the front of his speech. Before he'd even said good evening to his bemused audience, wherever it was, he would launch into the clip he'd sculpted especially for the evening bulletins – on healthcare, defence, taxation, or whatever was the burning topic of the day. That done, he would visibly relax, and explain to his puzzled audience why he'd gone off on that particular tangent.

During that first election campaign, however, there was one occasion where the evening location was so remote – somewhere in East Anglia – that there was no way either the BBC or ITN could cover Wilson's evening speech and get it on to their evening bulletins. Remember, this was before satellites. To be sure of getting pictures on air for a national bulletin, dispatch riders had to carry undeveloped film back to the London base. The alternative was to bike the pictures to a regional station where the film could be developed and edited. From there, the pictures could be beamed back to base across miles of countryside, from relay to relay, or transmitted by landline. However, these regional facilities were often not available at weekends, and this was a Saturday.

So, in mid afternoon, I and the BBC reporter, Keith Graves, went up to Wilson's suite at his hotel to tell him that neither of the two national broadcasters could get that night's keynote campaign speech on air. He thought for a few moments, then told us of his cunning plan. We were invited to set up our cameras in his hotel room, while his driver, Bill, went down to the car to bring his lectern.

Wilson always preferred to use his own lectern, rather than rely on the one provided, which might not have been the right size. Then, with our lights on, and cameras running, he pulled out of his pocket the fifty-second portion of that night's speech that had been tailored for TV and delivered it, in close-up, to the few people in the room with him. BBC and ITN dispatch riders were waiting, and Harold Wilson made the evening TV news, 'addressing a rally tonight in East Anglia'. At the time, neither I, nor Keith Graves, had a problem with what we did – we would have done it for any major politician in a similar situation. Occasionally I wonder if we should have collaborated in deceiving the viewer. But that night, I had other things to worry me – like getting back from that remote part of the country. Motorists were being rationed to no more than two gallons of petrol at any one fill-up, and there were few enough garages open anyway. For many hours, in driving rain, I drove through the dark countryside on the smell in my tank, praying I wouldn't run out of petrol. The country was in a mess.

The result of the election was a political mess – a hung Parliament. Heath tried to form a government with the Liberals, but failed. It was said at the time that he found the demands of their leader, Jeremy Thorpe – which included electoral reform – unacceptable. Many years later he told me over lunch at his home in Salisbury that he had dropped the idea of talking to Thorpe on the advice of the security services. The clear inference was that they knew things about the charismatic but flawed Liberal leader that made him unsuitable as a partner in a ruling coalition.

Wilson formed a minority government, and he acted quickly to end the confrontation that was crippling the economy. On the first morning of the new administration, the new Employment Secretary, Michael Foot, summoned the leaders of the still striking National Union of Mineworkers to his office in St. James's Square. He gave them everything they had been demanding from the Heath government, and more besides. It was all done and dusted in a couple of hours, and the union, some of whose leaders couldn't believe their luck, called off the strike practically there and then. As Mr Foot left the building, on his way to lunch, he stopped for a second to say into my ITN microphone 'You see, Labour government works!'

Another election that year was inevitable. In October Labour managed a majority, but only of three. I reprised my role, accompanying Wilson during the campaign, and staking out Transport House on election night.

Between those two elections, ITN made a revolutionary contribution to the public understanding of the mysteries of the election process – it pioneered the use of computer graphics.

A brilliant computer consultant called Paul McKee had been hired by ITN to help guide the organisation into the computer age. Up until now, the most graphic device that existed for explaining how the movement of votes affected the number of seats the parties won, and the ultimate result of the election, was the primitive 'Swingometer' deployed by the BBC's Robert McKenzie. McKee discovered the existence of a simple computer program that was being used to design the complicated patterns on some types of knitwear – such as Fair Isle pullovers. He rewrote the program so that the piles of stitches became piles of votes, and by linking it with a basic calculating function, it could keep a running total of votes cast for each party.

Other more sophisticated calculations were added, such as the swing between the parties nationally, the national share of the vote, and the outcome in individual seats or groups of seats. So it was that election computer graphics were born. Peter Snow operated the machine, named VT30, in the October election results programme, and again in 1979.

In 1980 he was poached by the BBC, initially to present the newly launched *Newsnight*, but, I suspect, because they too had seen the future of election graphics, and it included the flair, technique and infectious enthusiasm of Peter Snow. At ITN, I was given the formidable challenge of filling Peter's shoes, operating the graphics in the Snow role for the elections of 1983 and 1987.

Five or six weeks after that second election of 1974, on 21 November, with Harold Wilson again installed in Downing Street, he gave an evening drinks party there for the senior reporters who had accompanied him on the campaign trail. Most of his closest aides were present, and Wilson was on good form, puffing on his favourite cigar. We were all put at our ease, many in deep armchairs and sofas, and there was no shortage of drink. Suddenly, I noticed the door at the end of the room open, and a grim-faced Home Secretary, Roy Jenkins, entered. He called the Prime Minister over, and the two conversed in whispers. Marcia Williams, Wilson's political secretary, said something like 'I hope he hasn't come to spoil the party'. He had. The party ended almost immediately on the news he had brought – that the IRA had bombed two pubs in the centre of Birmingham with the loss of nineteen lives. Two other victims died later. It remained for many years the worst terrorist attack in UK history.

From 1974 until the election in 1979, the Labour government, at first under Wilson, and then from April 1976 under James Callaghan, was battered by events, at home and abroad. But it was the home front that eventually did for it, an ill wind that benefited few groups more than the labour and industrial correspondents. The nation became a hotbed of industrial unrest, which was the product both of wage demands chasing the tail of runaway inflation, and employers demanding changes in working practices which the unions feared could only result in more jobs being lost. Pay increases nationally were soon running at 30 per cent, and inflation peaked at 26.9 per cent. Yet the more jobs that were lost as a result, the more militant the unions became.

It wasn't Cabinet meetings that became the weekly focus of attention, but meetings of the TUC General Council, the 'union barons'. It was they who were seen as the most powerful men in the country, and they who set the tone. Many of them lived in fear of the far left among their membership, who could attempt to remove them from their comfortable offices, union houses, and perks that often included fraternal visits to iron curtain countries particularly well endowed with holiday resorts. There were exceptions of course, and not just among leaders on the right, like Frank Chapple and Eric Hammond of the electricians' union. Many correspondents had a sneaking admiration for the leader of the mighty Transport and General Workers Union, Jack Jones, who lived an austere, apparently incorruptible life from his south London council flat (a flat which he was later to buy, when Margaret Thatcher gave him the chance).

Incidentally, it would have been a political earthquake had Jack Jones then been accused of being a Soviet agent, as happened after his death, when he was fingered by the highest ranking KGB defector, Oleg Gordievsky. Jones knew of the suggestions before he died in 2009, and angrily denied them as 'a slur and an outrage'.

During this period, industrial and labour correspondents who were doing their job were among the best informed reporters in the country, and we would occasionally find ourselves being asked by senior politicians, government ministers and captains of industry to read the union mind, and tell them what was going on.

On one occasion, just as I was leaving the office one evening, my phone rang and the caller identified himself as Sir Douglas Wass, the legendary Permanent Secretary to the Treasury, and he invited me to lunch at his club. We had an exchange of views over a very good bottle of wine and he was wonderful company. Then he said something that has stuck in my memory every since – we were discussing, quite indiscreetly, the relative merits of ministers we both knew. Sir Douglas leaned across the table to me. 'The thing to remember about most ministers,' he said, 'is that they are our PR men.' It is widely believed that Sir Douglas Wass was the model for Sir Humphrey Appleby, in *Yes, Minister*. If he wasn't, he should have been.

I have never worked harder than I did during those years. But it is not the big disputes that stick in my mind so much as those moments when you know that something has happened that is extraordinary. You may not, as a reporter, be able to do it justice at the time, but you just know in your bones that things are never going to be the same again.

In February 1975, I'd stepped into a lift in the Palace of Westminster. I was alone, but just as the doors were closing, a blonde middle-aged woman squeezed through them. It was Margaret Thatcher, who had just been elected Conservative leader, after a second ballot of Tory MPs, news I had heard only a couple of hours previously. There, alone with me in that lift, stood the most controversial figure in British politics, and you couldn't have wiped the smile off her face. She simply couldn't unsmile. As we travelled up a few floors, to the Press Gallery, she spoke, but not to me. To herself she kept repeating five words – 'one hundred and forty six'. It was the number of votes that had been declared for her, a clear majority over her four male challengers, a number that had just changed the course of our political history. And I am sure she knew it.

That was a private moment, unlike Denis Healey's brief, fighting speech to the 1976 Labour Party Conference in Blackpool. He'd flown to Blackpool, having aborted his plan to attend an international conference of finance ministers, while actually on his way to Heathrow, because the pound was dropping through the floor. A few days beforehand, in an interview with me, he'd explained why the government was now turning to the IMF for a massive loan. 'The alternative to getting help from the IMF would be economic policies so savage I think they would produce riots in the streets, an immediate fall in living standards and unemployment of three million.' Healey, being merely the Chancellor, and not a member of Labour's National Executive, was allowed only a few minutes to tell the conference a few home truths. He laid it on them, to angry shouts, boos and applause from the stunned delegates.

> I am going to negotiate with the IMF on the basis of our existing policies, not changes in policies, and I need your support to do it. But when I say 'existing policies', I mean things we do not like as well as things we do like. It means sticking to the very painful cuts in public expenditure on which the Government has already decided. It means sticking to a pay policy which enables us, as the TUC resolved a week or two ago, to continue the attack on inflation.

Healey stomped back to his seat raising his arms triumphantly as the boos and cheers raised the roof. It was one of the bravest speeches many had heard. Prime Minister Callaghan rammed home the message to the unions queuing up with double figure demands: 'You cannot spend yourself out of recession. Every wage increase that is not paid for out of increased productivity is a ticket to the dole queue.' For Labour it was the moment of truth. The road to electoral defeat lay ahead. But here were a small number of politicians of stature prepared to give a lead and put the national interest first.

It was at that 1976 Labour Party conference in Blackpool that I was called upon to make a speech replying to the Vote of Thanks to the press, the very last item on the conference agenda. The Labour and Industrial Correspondents Group, and the Parliamentary Lobby, took the speech in turns from year to year. Nineteen seventy-six was the Group's turn, and as I was chairman of the Group, it fell to me. Given the love-hate relationship between the Labour Party and the media, the vote of thanks was usually a few well chosen half-jocular insults from a party functionary and the expected reply was a few funny stories from the journalists' representative to send everyone home with a smile. If that didn't happen, then at least delegates were able, for a few moments, to focus their hatred on a representative of the media, rather than on each other.

Three weeks previously, I had done the same thing at the TUC's annual congress in Brighton. The problem was, as I contemplated making the Blackpool speech, I realised I had used up most of my best jokes on the TUC, many of whose delegates were now also in the Blackpool audience. I also had the problem of making a speech that wouldn't be totally inappropriate after one of the most traumatic weeks in Labour's history. Fortunately, I had had the good sense, a few days beforehand, to ask the advice of a real professional – none other than Denis Healey himself. Chatting over a gin and tonic after one of our increasingly frequent interviews, he suggested a sure-fire joke about a fictional Chancellor of the Exchequer. Come the day, at the close of the final morning's business, I mounted the rostrum, with the entire Cabinet sitting grim faced above me, and just a few feet behind. In front were a thousand or more brothers, sisters and comrades, willing someone from the media to fall flat on his face. It was a daunting prospect. I had no policies to argue, points of order to put, composites to propose, or block votes to cast, just jokes to tell. And it had to be done in one take. I pulled it off. I even made a joke about Jack Jones. And I finished with the Healey joke, which brought the house down.

I will not recount it here – my pension fund still depends on making entertaining after-dinner speeches! Subsequently Robin Day described my Blackpool speech as 'brilliantly witty' and one of the best of its kind he had ever heard. However, when I left the rostrum and went back upstairs to the ITN office, they told me that the network had cut away to another programme just as I had started speaking. And most of my colleagues were so busy writing and editing their material for the lunchtime news, that they hadn't seen my moment of triumph anyway, nor had they recorded it. Ah well, not many reporters get to have the undivided attention of the Cabinet and the ruling party in the depths of an economic crisis...

Nineteen seventy-six did have one low point for me – for the first and only time, I threatened to resign. Alastair Burnet had returned to ITN after three years at the BBC and two years editing the *Daily Express*. The ITN slot he returned to initially was a re-launched *News at 5.45*, which, with the great man at the helm, was to be given a new status out of the shadow of *News at Ten*. As the conference season approached, it was decided that, as part of Alastair's wide editorial responsibilities, all party conference and TUC coverage would be edited and written by him, as he watched the proceedings on a monitor at ITN. It meant that on the 5.45 bulletin, during the TUC conference, there would be no role for the Industrial and Labour team, who had effectively been relegated to the functions of fixers and gofers. Their judgement, inside knowledge and wide range of contacts might be asked for – if needed. But such was Alastair's standing, a former Editor, not just of the *Daily Express* but of *The Economist*, that that didn't seem likely. When I arrived in Brighton for the TUC, on the Sunday before it began, the issue was eating away at me and I phoned the then Editor of ITN, Nigel Ryan, at his home.

During the course of a long conversation, I told him that if being his Industrial Editor meant anything, it meant being responsible for ITN's coverage of such conferences. If I wasn't, then I would resign. Nigel agonised, clearly not wanting to alienate his most valued newscaster or to lose me. For a few days there was a messy compromise, with Alastair too busy writing and editing bigger stories to have time to attend to the TUC. Then towards the end of the week the matter was settled once and for all. Very late in the afternoon, a trivial inter-union dispute erupted out of control on the conference floor. It pitted a tiddler of a union, the National Association of Licensed House Managers, against the biggest union of them all, the mighty Transport and General Workers. The issue was TGWU draymen allegedly trying to bully the manager of a Midlands pub, the Fox and Goose, into joining their union. Congress backed the underdog, with many unions taking the opportunity to settle a few old scores against the T&G, by voting for its suspension. Humiliatingly, Jack Jones, one of the most powerful men in the country, had to lead his delegation from the hall. The expulsion was very dramatic, totally unexpected and fairly short-lived. There was no way anyone sitting in London could interpret what was going on, let alone begin to report it. Within ten or fifteen minutes my small team at Brighton were ready to go live into the 5.45, with comprehensive coverage and follow-up live interviews, including Jack Jones. We didn't miss a trick, and there were herograms all round. Nothing more was heard of the arrangement for Alastair's remote control over ITN's TUC coverage.

Nineteen seventy-eight brought a major reshuffle of the pack of ITN newscasters. Andrew Gardner had gone to Thames Television to present its flagship regional news programme – a move from his high-profile national role made easier by a chauffeur-driven car exclusive to him and £100,000 a year – the equivalent of £470,000 today. Andrew, who became the senior *News at Ten* newscaster during Burnet's absence at the BBC, also seemed to have seen the writing on the wall, that now Alastair was back, it would only be a matter of time before he would have to cede that role. With Andrew Gardner gone, Alastair Burnet duly moved – after a decent interval – from the *5.45* to *News at Ten*. Leonard Parkin moved from the lunchtime news to the *5.45*. And Anna Ford joined the company – ITN's response to the BBC's first female newscaster, Angela Rippon. In the middle of all this, I received a call out of the blue to see ITN's new Editor, David Nicholas. I was thrilled to be offered the opportunity to become a full-time newscaster, on the lunchtime news.

I had been presenting regularly for ITN on a part-time basis, combining that, for most of the 1970s, with the demanding industrial portfolio. I was ready for the change and the challenge, and I promised David that I wouldn't let him down. Ten years previously, when he was Deputy Editor, he had given me an enormous boost by trusting me with a stand-in appearance, newscasting on *News at Ten*. Now he expected me, as a full-time ITN presenter on one of its three major daily broadcasts, to deliver on the promise he had seen back then. David Nicholas knew a lot about me – he took a close personal interest in all those who had the good fortune to work for him. But what he didn't know was that, having had no sort of relationship with my father, his interest in my professional development and the friendship and trust that grew around it, was something I appreciated more than I ever could confess. But, to his credit, he was such a great Editor that I wasn't the only one who looked upon him as a father-figure. Eleven years later, that relationship was to be severely tested.

Chapter 7

Into the Presenter's Chair

Without doubt, presenting the news at lunchtime is one of the best slots a newscaster can be asked to fill. Let me explain.

If you are presenting news at breakfast time, you generally have to be in the office by 4 a.m. Getting to bed early – no later than 9 p.m. if you are conscientious – plays havoc with your social life. When you come off-air around 9 a.m., you are shattered. Even if you manage to function for the rest of the morning, you will need a nap in the afternoon. After four consecutive days of this, you will not be good company and you'll need most of the weekend to recover. Your children and your wife will think you are not a lot of fun. And you will age prematurely. The lovely Selina Scott spent five years launching the BBC's breakfast programme from 1983, and it seemed to age her by ten years. Sitting in the make-up chair, morning after morning, short of sleep, trying to make your brain work while assailed by heated rollers, is not natural. And for a country girl like Selina, it took its toll – although the effects were reversed once she stepped off the treadmill.

Presenting news at six in the evening is more civilised. Not being required in the newsroom until lunchtime you can have a lie-in every day if you wish and you'll never have to travel to work in the rush hour. Likewise, if you are presenting at 10 p.m., you can also have a decent lunch before you show up for work – although if you overdo the wine it is bad form to nod off at your desk in the early evening. And, of course, if you are presenting the *News at Ten*, and have young children, you will never be able to tuck them up in bed and read them a story. You will probably also wake the neighbours when you arrive home after midnight, particularly in one of the clapped-out minicabs that ITN provided for your journey home.

But the lunchtime news is something different. Without doubt it is the best of the newscasting shifts, particularly if you have a young family as Sylvia and I did when I made the move – eight-year-old Michael and five-year-old Jonny. Suddenly, my life was transformed. In my previous life as Industrial Editor I went out early, came home late and often didn't come home at all – staked out for all-night crisis talks at Longbridge or the National Coal Board. Now, all was predictable; I left home in an ITN car at the same time early – but not too early – every morning. And I was home with time to spare to pick up the kids from school in the afternoon. In the summer particularly, it was just such a joy to leave London, and put my feet up in my own back garden in Kent while colleagues on other programmes back at ITN were just getting into their stride. I couldn't believe my luck.

Lunchtime news programmes on television today are ten a penny. But it wasn't like that in the early 1970s. The BBC didn't appear interested in daytime TV news and put its major lunchtime effort into radio news. Its flagship was *The World at One*, anchored by a former Editor of the *Daily Mail*, the redoubtable William Hardcastle. Every day he commanded attention by intoning 'This is *The World at One* with William Hardcastle.' The one exception was the day he announced breathlessly 'This is *The World at One* with William Whitelaw', momentarily forgetting his own identity in his pre-occupation with the day's momentous political events.

ITN's TV breakthrough at lunchtime came in 1972, when the ITV companies on the ITN board were persuaded to back a twenty-minute programme at 12.40. Its first Editor, Barrie Sales, was a talented and thoughtful ex-BBC man, quietly passionate about making serious news add up for a wider audience, and who'd been out-putting the *News at Ten*. Barrie thought that ITN could mount a TV challenge to *The World at One*, and he was right. But what to call the ITN programme? *The World at Twelve-Forty* didn't sound right. He wanted something that suggested work in progress, the first stab at the day's big stories. I bumped into Barrie in the ITN bar one night and said it was obvious – the new programme should be called *First Report*. He bought it, and *First Report* it was.

The first presenter of *First Report* was already one of the country's most distinguished journalists, both in print and broadcasting, Robert

Kee – a counterweight to a former *Daily Mail* Editor if ever there was one. Robert was persuaded to do it because the programme was going to depend heavily on live interviews with the big figures in the news. ITN's news machine hadn't yet entered the age of routine satellite and electronic news gathering – indeed that age wasn't yet upon us. Practically everything still depended on film that had to be physically transported to ITN, developed, cut and dubbed with commentary. It was time-consuming – and meant that the amount of filmed material available for lunchtime transmission was severely limited.

So from the beginning, *First Report* depended heavily on interviews and interviewing, and Kee was a very good interviewer, as well as having a wealth of specialist political knowledge, particularly about Ireland – it was the height of the 1970s troubles – on which he was an authority. He'd also been a bomber pilot during the Second World War, been · shot down, and spent three years as a prisoner of war, making constant efforts to escape, which he eventually did. They don't make presenters like that anymore.

Kee had one handicap, if you can call it that: he didn't like the teleprompter, the device that enables the presenter to read the words from a screen directly in front of the camera lens, more often these days called the autocue. I believe his eyesight was not good enough to rely on being able to read it fluently. So from the beginning Robert not only insisted on writing most of the programme himself, he then largely memorised the scripts. In effect, when he addressed the camera, he was ad-libbing around notes he had written himself. Some of his remarks and interjections prompted complaints to ITN and the IBA that he should keep his views to himself. What the complainants didn't know was that it wasn't just the odd remark that was off-the-cuff, but quite often most of the programme.

The combination of Kee and Barrie Sales made *First Report* a ground-breaking programme. Politicians queued up to appear on it, and its interviews were widely quoted. Thus not only did it report the news, it made the news. Making the news is what all producers aim for. For a newly launched programme it gains it valuable publicity. For the team working on an established programme it puts one over on the competition, and reminds the boss of their great value to the organisation. The danger is that they then choose the content of the programme with publicity and ratings in mind, and that they neglect important stories which are not 'sexy' enough to be widely picked up. However, in those early days on *First Report* the calculation was entirely pragmatic: the scarcity of film needn't be a disadvantage, because it left space and time for interviews, which became the programme's lifeblood.

First Report did have one weapon in its armoury that gave it an extra edge – a small outside broadcast unit. This was usually deployed to places where the day's news was still unfolding, giving a sense of real drama. As Industrial Editor I often found myself reporting live into *First Report* from the scene of the latest trade union cliff-hanger, when one of the many strikes of the 1970s was in the balance. On one occasion, during my piece to camera outside Congress House in Bloomsbury, a crisis meeting of the TUC General Council broke up and behind me the union bosses started to leave the building. The programme editor, Barrie Sales, stayed with me as I buttonholed a succession of them. These days, with twenty-four-hour rolling news, that sort of thing is routine. But then it was new, brave even. What with Kee's ad-libs, and intelligent deployment of the OB, *First Report* soon became the programme to watch.

It had its failures, and one of them involved the deployment of the OB. It was thought a great idea to enable Robert Kee, in the studio, to interview members of the public in shopping centres or high streets, often many miles away. Thus he could solicit their views about events in the news – such as measures announced in the Budget. Robert's disembodied voice was played to the OB, and thence to passers-by on the pavement, or in the supermarket, through what became known as the 'magic horn', a small metal loudspeaker held by the OB's floor manager. The reaction of members of the public was often puzzlement and sometimes fright, as the instrument was pointed at them, and a strange voice addressed them. One woman, in a queue at a Brixton supermarket, was said to have run away claiming that the Lord had spoken to her.

First Report's success in building an audience forced the hand of the doubters among the ITV companies, and after a couple of years it was moved to 1 p.m., head-to-head with *The World at One*. Robert Kee left ITN in 1976 having established the programme, which was re-named *The News at One*, and Leonard Parkin took over. Parkin, too, had an impressive pedigree which included a stint as the BBC's Washington correspondent, in which role he broke the news to Britain of the assassination of President Kennedy in 1963.

After two years, when the presenter pack was shuffled again, it fell to me to maintain the reputation that the programme had acquired, and the momentum my two predecessors had given it.

There had been changes on the *News at One* as the production team had gained in confidence and learned from early mistakes. But one thing hadn't changed – the dependence of the programme on intelligent interviewing. My credibility, when I inherited the programme from Leonard Parkin, depended on making the grade as an inquisitor. I hadn't been appointed as a newsreader. I thought I had the skills from the hundreds of interviews I had conducted as Industrial Editor, many of them with tough and experienced players in the long-running political and economic crisis that was the 1970s. But not many of those interviews were performed live. Now was my chance to prove I could deliver as an interviewer day in, day out, in live broadcasts – at the same time as holding the programme together. And it suddenly came to me: this is what I really wanted to do.

Without doubt, when this door opened for me, it was the key point in my career. I had briefly tasted the glamorous life of the foreign correspondent, which had nearly finished me off. I had worked hard as a specialist home-based correspondent, acquiring a range of other skills during testing times. But as I started off as a full-time news anchor, I knew it would never be enough just to be a programme's figurehead; the most important and satisfying aspect of any job I was given was to remain the skill of asking the right questions. That didn't come easily. It was something I had to work on, and as so many interviewers before me had found out, it can take time to find your own style and technique. It also does no aspiring interviewer any harm to have made mistakes – as long as you learn from them – and I had already made my share.

As a general reporter I had been sent to interview Sidney Greene, the General Secretary of the National Union of Railwaymen, whose national executive was deliberating whether to call a national rail strike, an all too frequent event. I asked him a string of what I judged pertinent questions, and proudly brought my filmed interview back to the office, where the news editor grabbed me and enquired whether the strike was on or off. Jesus! It was the one question that I had not put to the NUR boss! From that day to this, I have asked myself this before every interview: what is the single most important question I should be asking this person? It sounds, and is, elementary – but in the bustle and fuss of a TV or radio studio even experienced performers can forget it.

So I settled in to what was to be four formative years as a full-time presenter on ITN's *News at One*.

The most impressive thing about the small production team around me was its enthusiasm. A number of talented young trainees competed with each other to make an impact. They included Mark Damazer, who went on to rise through BBC News, eventually moving to radio and being trusted with the Corporation's jewel in the crown, Radio Four, from where at the age of fifty-five he was appointed to be master of St Peter's College, Oxford. Damazer sharply divided opinion while he was at ITN. Although he had a starred Double First in History at Cambridge, some didn't rate him at all, but others saw great depths of talent. Edward Stourton, another young trainee, was generally thought to be a better bet for eventual stardom, and a more impressive ITN find. Thirty years later Ed was devastated when Mark, who by then was running Radio 4, controversially replaced him as a presenter on the *Today* programme, and in true BBC style the first Ed knew about it was from the newspapers.

Then there were Sarah Cullen and Sue Lloyd Roberts, two young ITN trainees whose drive and enthusiasm were matched only by their rivalry. Nominally on the programme as writers, they fought tooth and claw – figuratively speaking, I hasten to add – to get out on the road and report, volunteering for practically anything that would get them on air. The programme editor could be guaranteed that neither would turn a story down if he so much as hinted that if Sue refused he would give it to Sarah – and vice-versa. Both were incredibly conscientious, and passionate about unfairness and injustice.

Sue Lloyd Roberts went on to make a particular reporting genre her own – often travelling alone into hostile places, carrying a small video camera in her handbag, and taking great risks to bring back stories that oppressive regimes around the world didn't want told. She remains one of the bravest reporters I have ever met – and could have found herself behind bars, or worse, in Zimbabwe, Tibet, Burma, China or the other places where she travelled to expose crimes against humanity. In my book, one Sue Lloyd Roberts is worth a dozen of some of the others who've made it to the reporters' desk and have become household names despite having no discernible talent.

The pushy youngsters on *News at One* were balanced by some older hands, including a new programme editor, Alex Spink. Alex had many strengths, and some weaknesses, which including a predilection for holding most of his editorial meetings in the ITN pub, the Green Man, round the corner. Alex lived a charmed life. One morning, shortly after the pub opened – and not much more than an hour before *News at One* went on air – Alex, feeling a bit thirsty, nipped out of the back door of ITN for a quick refresher. Entering the Green Man, which was so close to ITN House it was almost an extension of it, he found the place deserted; not only were there no other customers, there was no landlord to be seen, although there were noises from the cellar. Short of time, Alex went behind the bar and was pulling himself a pint when in walked the Editor and Deputy Editor of ITN, who'd slipped out for a private, pre-lunch drink themselves. Alex, whom the two men knew full well should have been outputting the lunchtime news, nonchalantly asked them what they'd like to drink, served them and made his exit before his shocked bosses could react.

One of the things I thought about as I settled in to *News at One*, was 'who are we making this programme for?' Every editor or presenter has a mental picture of the people they are addressing. Some imagine that they are talking to three or four reasonably intelligent but under-informed folk gathered round the TV, hoping to find out what's going on in the world. Others personalise it more – imagining they are talking to their own mother, who's sat down with a cup of tea to watch the news. The lunchtime audience for TV news certainly had a serious element – traders at their desks in the City, for example, anxious to know of any news that may affect the markets. And at Westminster it was watched with an eagle eye. For what it's worth, as my typical viewer I imagined a young mother, stuck at home, putting her feet up for a few minutes in the middle of the day, and hoping that the TV news would not just inform, but interest and entertain her. And I always remembered some of the first advice I was given at ITN: 'Never underestimate the intelligence of your viewers, but never overestimate their knowledge.'

I think my view was largely correct – judging by the number of middle-aged women who now come up to me and say what a welcome part I was of their daily routine. But they all add that there was a welcome side-effect: if they plonked the baby in front of the TV when I came on, it was asleep in no time.

I really started to feel my age when the children themselves, now in their thirties, started to approach me, many admitting that two of the first words they learned were 'Peter' and 'Sissons'. I didn't have the heart to enquire when, if at all, they began to associate me with more than a warm bottle and a rusk.

Although I had been a presence on all ITN outlets for more than ten years, the other thing that happened to me when I eventually had my own programme to present was a big increase in the number of letters from viewers. They came in all styles and colours of ink. Most were complimentary, a few offensive or pedantic or both, usually about a pronunciation or a split infinitive. I will never forget one letter which was a real sign of the times. 'Dear Mr Sissons' it read, 'As a teacher I really must give you a lesson in grammar. The other day you said "none was" when of course it should be "none were". I hope I can expect an apology.' I was so angry that I explained to this 'teacher' that it was about time he started teaching that 'none' was simply an elision of the two words 'not' and 'one', and would he care to apologise to me as well as the children he was failing. He didn't reply.

Going through my mailbag I was also surprised to discover that a small number of viewers thought that newscasters could see into their homes, enquiring of me if I liked their new three-piece suite, fitted kitchen or whatever. One woman even accused me of spying on her as she got undressed in front of the TV. I also began to get little gifts from viewers, and some of them not so little. One kind lady knitted me a different sweater or scarf every couple of weeks for two years. The more I begged her to stop, the faster they came in all the colours of the rainbow, in all sizes, most more suited to the figure of some Quasimodo impersonator than to mine. But it's the thought that counts. At Christmas viewers sent boxes of chocolates. It's then than my imagination ran riot – what if one of these boxes were from a homicidal maniac, who had injected them with cyanide? What if the teacher I had offended had decided on a dreadful revenge? They were unworthy thoughts which I put out of my mind as, in true festive spirit, I shared the chocs with my grateful colleagues, selflessly letting them choose and eat the best ones, before I so much as nibbled what was left.

One morning during my time on *News at One* I was sitting at my desk when the phone rang. It was the lady on the ITN reception desk, who told me I had some visitors, and would I come to reception immediately. The sight that met me was of a dozen or more Hare Krishna devotees, in their distinctive saffron robes. They had clearly taken a diversion from their usual route along Oxford Street 500 yards away, where they could be seen on most days chanting and bashing their tambourines. From among them stepped forward a familiar face in unfamiliar garb. It was George Harrison, by then a former Beatle, whom I had long known from our schooldays. Although the Beatles had dabbled in eastern mysticism, notably the Transcendental Meditation of the Maharishi Mahesh Yogi, George had gone further than the others and lent his practical support to the Hare Krishna temple.

Indeed, he and John Lennon had done much to bring the Hare Krishna mantra to a wider audience in some of their lyrics. He had come to ITN House on a mission – to bring their message to the nation. George greeted me warmly, and came quickly to the point. 'Pete,' he said, 'we've got a big news story for you, and we want you to get it on tonight's *News at Ten*. In fact, it has to be their lead story.' Well, you can imagine my reaction. What raced through my mind was that even if it wasn't the lead, ex-Beatles were still big news. After all, hadn't John Lennon and Yoko Ono succeeded in turning the simple act of lying in bed into a political statement? So, my journalistic juices rising, I asked George what *was* this big story? He moved closer to me, took my arm, looked me in the eye, and said one word – 'Peace'. Resisting my instinct to say 'Is that all?' I asked him to go through the Big Story again. He added nothing to the single word 'Peace'. He said it two or three times more as he and his friends drifted towards the door. And then they were back in full happy chant as they headed back towards their familiar Oxford Street territory.

I was to present ITN's lunchtime news for four years. And there was no respite from the pace of events. The Lib-Lab pact kept the Callaghan government on life-support for eighteen months, but after staggering from crisis to crisis, his government was finally swept away by Margaret Thatcher in May 1979.

During the general election campaign I continued to present *News at One* five days a week, and on the day after polling I presented the early segment of the general election coverage itself from first thing until 10 a.m., when Alastair Burnet resumed his overnight marathon.

The election coverage in May 1979 was considerably enhanced and enlivened by ITN's revolutionary computer graphics in the inspired hands of Peter Snow. Indeed, ITN had a terrific election, leaving the BBC looking ponderous and dated. The corporation cried foul, accusing ITN of broadcasting constituency results before they had actually been declared, which in many cases was probably true. Someone at ITN had the simple idea of paying a £50 bonus to every local freelance working for us if they beat the BBC to the result – which was often quietly obtained from a friendly official once the count was complete, but before the Returning Officer had stepped before the microphones. The BBC didn't take long to come up with their response – they poached Peter Snow, offering him a major role on their election unit, and making him the first presenter of *Newsnight*. I had shared an office with Peter, and when he received the BBC offer, I was one of the first at ITN that he told. Over a glass of wine in Wolsey's over the road, he seemed flattered by the BBC's interest, but saddened at the prospect of leaving his journalistic alma mater. But he sensed that the time had come to move on. Little did I know, that ten years later I was to be in exactly the same position myself.

There still being only three TV channels – ITV, BBC1 and BBC2 – and no BBC Breakfast, TV-am, Sky or BBC News Channel, the lunchtime news on television was a far more important point in the schedules than it is today.

Today there is such a call by broadcasters on the time of ministers that it is usually only those from the junior ranks you see at lunchtime. Indeed many junior ministers seem to do little on some days except traipse around TV studios satisfying requests for interviews. Often, paradoxically, the thinner the news day, the greater the demand by broadcasters for media-friendly ministers – it's a cheap way of filling air time. I've seen it done so many times: the editor of a news programme comes to work in the morning to find a real shortage of material. The forward planning has been a joke, and other expected stories haven't materialised. How do you fill the programme? You trawl through the morning papers, find a couple of marginal stories that 'still have legs', and hit the phones requesting interviews either from the relevant government departments, from the political opposition, or some interested pressure group. Preferably, you approach interviewees that you know can be relied on to 'do a turn' – they will keep it brief, even entertaining, and come up with some sound-bites that are picked up by the news agency wires.

Suddenly, from having no news, your programme is making the news. It's even easier to fill if the story you decide to follow up is not political, but a lightweight, vacuous story from the world of entertainment. It becomes an excuse to interview any number of so called 'celebs', not because they have anything to say, but merely out of what I would call zoological interest. This is not just a caricature. It's the reason why on the continuous news channels there is so much entertainment news, and why the line between news and entertainment is so shamelessly, and I believe dangerously, blurred.

Little of this was of concern to me as I began my four years on the lunchtime news. At a time of major domestic and international political change, the TV lunchtime news was a key part of ITN's three-pronged news strategy. The *News at 5.45* was essentially a punchy summary of the day's main news stories that had already happened, or were still breaking at Westminster or abroad. The *News at Ten* was the fuller account of the day, putting it in perspective and able to go live to the Commons for late votes. It could also catch prime-time developments on the east coast of the United States, and preview likely developments in the UK the next day. But the *News at One* was also a key player in the continuum, as it was not only ITN's first response to stories breaking overnight, but its approach and editorial commitments often set the tone for the whole organisation for the rest of the day.

A case in point was the outbreak of hostilities with Argentina over the Falklands. On 2 April 1982, the *News at One* was the first TV broadcast to cut through the fog of conflicting claims, reports and caveats from the South Atlantic and announce that Britain was at war with Argentina. It wasn't a guess, it was a certainty based on all the information we had, and for the rest of the day ITN stayed hours ahead of the competition.

These years were not spent exclusively on the *News at One*. Among the special programmes which I anchored or helped to anchor were those covering the first launches of America's space shuttle. It gave me a break from the daily treadmill of reporting foreign crises, and political and economic news, and re-kindled the kind of fascination I'd felt for the Concorde project. ITN put immense effort and ingenuity into its space programmes, which is not surprising since ITN's Editor, David Nicholas, and his Science Editor Frank Miles were space 'nuts'. Indeed, it was a joy to work with David on any special programme, many of which, although he was the Editor in Chief, he continued to produce himself with an enthusiasm that was quite infectious. It is rare these days to find a senior TV executive who is capable of rolling up his sleeves, and showing the younger people around him how it should be done.

Being involved in the space project, I got to meet two of the twelve men who had walked on the moon, Jim Irwin and Dave Scott of Apollo 15. In fact they went one better than walking – they were the first to drive on the moon. I also worked with Dick Gordon, who was the command module pilot on the second moonshot – Apollo XII. Some years later, I was also to meet and talk to Buzz Aldrin, and I would count meeting those extraordinary men as among the most memorable encounters that my career gave me. Who else was there? Many. But being a Liverpudlian I would have to single out two: Bill Shankly, whom I interviewed a number of times on the *News at One*, and whose charisma and enthusiasm was everything you'd expect from a legend. And David Sheppard, the Bishop of Liverpool and former England cricket captain, who gave so much to his adopted city through some of its most troubled times. He was also one of my boyhood sporting heroes, and giving up the game he loved for the church was a huge sacrifice for him. I asked him once if he ever still played occasionally, perhaps for charity. He looked me in the eye and said that if he'd ever been tempted to pick up a bat again, he might not have been able to put it down. I thought he was a saintly man.

The other role ITN handed me around this time was the one Peter Snow had made his own – the electronic puppeteer behind ITN's increasingly sophisticated computer graphics. I was a regular fixture on the annual Budget specials, explaining the impact of the Chancellor's tax changes, appearances that brought me up to speed for the far more complicated computer graphics operation in the general election coverage of 1983 and 1987. For many of these programmes I was seated next to Alastair Burnet, ITN's star anchor, whose prodigious political, economic and financial knowledge was so effortlessly retrieved on air, and transformed into understandable English.

For three or four years he and I shared an office, and I came to have some understanding of the secret of the success of this private and self-effacing man. Apart from being a hugely experienced journalist and editor, he read widely, even the most obscure publications, and he wrote quickly and economically. He had an extensive range of contacts, evidenced by his disappearance at lunchtime most days to one or other of Charlotte Street's fine restaurants. And his encyclopaedic political knowledge of many of the individual constituencies across the UK was not second-hand. Alastair never went anywhere without taking in the boundaries and the demography, and he filed it all away in that unfailing memory – in which there was also a space reserved for anything that might be useful during a day at the races, the only thing that passed for a hobby.

The other secret ingredient Alastair threw into the mix was kept in the bottom drawer of his filing cabinet. He enjoyed a scotch, and usually kept a small glass just out of sight of the viewer, when he was on air.

Just as a Chancellor delivering a Budget might sip from a weak whisky and soda to improve his flow and stop him from flagging, so it was with Alastair and his wee dram. If I was in the office at the same time as him, he'd offer me one, usually not all that wee. Had I accepted them all, I would again have lost the use of my legs. But I never saw Alastair the worse for drink. Indeed, it seemed to have no effect on him. There are usually tell-tale signs if a news presenter has touched so much as a drop – particularly a difficulty with words containing the letters s and t – but I never, ever, saw Alastair display any of them.

That, of course, was in total contrast to ITN's most popular and charismatic newscaster, Reginald Bosanquet. Reggie had skated on thin ice for years, with ITN loyally making excuses for his eccentricities. The ITN press office once even assured viewers who'd rung in to complain that Reggie was 'pissed again', by explaining that he wasn't drunk, but had a speech impediment. How he'd got to be a leading national newscaster despite having a speech impediment was left to their imagination. He, like Alastair, usually kept a drink by his side while he was on air – in Reggie's case it was red wine in a paper cup. But unlike Alastair, there was often more than a small measure and it showed.

Reggie had many loyal and protective friends at ITN, but his luck ran out at the end of November 1979, when David Nicholas, personally exasperated and under pressure from his board, fired him at a tearful final meeting. Reggie didn't work again – no commercials, no voiceovers, nothing – and he was dead within five years from pancreatic cancer. He was one of the most generous men I ever met. Now and again, when I was feeling a bit low, he'd rummage through his pockets for a five pound note, and march me over to Wolsey's Wine Bar. A bottle of Freixenet and several games of bar billiards later, and the world had changed for the better. Many others also enjoyed his warmth and his hospitality. His was a fine mind, but flawed. However, despite the flaws, more than thirty years after his last broadcast he remains a legend among newscasters, probably the most popular there has ever been, for his sheer ability to address the camera lens as if it were an old friend. There can never be another Reggie Bosanquet, indeed there can never again be a presenter who could get away with behaving like Reggie. In today's politically correct BBC, for example, the drinks cupboard – except in hospitality – is now practically a thing of the past. The notion of a presenter tippling his or her way through a news programme would be regarded as the stuff of fiction.

The four years on *News at One* flew by. The highlight of my personal life was the birth, after our two boys, of a daughter, Kate. The working hours meant that I saw much more of Sylvia and our new baby than I would have done had I been involved with another programme. Professionally, I was fortunate in that much of the domestic news remained economic and industrial, which played to my strengths. I also had firsthand experience of the seemingly perpetual Northern Ireland crisis through the time I had spent there. The turmoil in the Labour Party, and the emergence of the SDP, was meat and drink to me through my union contacts, and the unions pulled the strings in the Labour Party. As a Liverpudlian, I could bring inside knowledge to our response to the Toxteth riots, and as someone who had known John Lennon I was able to bring a personal touch to our coverage of his murder and the assessment of his legacy.

It was harder work getting to grips with complex international issues. During the protracted Lancaster House negotiations that gave independence to Zimbabwe, Robert Mugabe and Joshua Nkomo made many live appearances on the programme. Mugabe in particular, with his pinstripe suits and studied English accent, gave not a hint of the despot behind the mask. The capacity of *News at One* to get major figures into the studio never faltered, and in my four years I conducted more than 2,000 interviews. None of them was particularly long – three, four or five minutes at the most, but I got to grips with the technique of asking no more than the one or two most important questions, with tough supplementaries.

It's one thing having a half hour or forty-minute slot on a programme like *Panorama* or ITV's old flagship *Weekend World* in which to elicit answers from someone – you can hardly fail to get something new or quotable. But there was something satisfying about the short, punchy interview, which often grabbed the attention more and was just as enlightening. The only occasion on which that technique failed me miserably was when I interviewed a young Labour backbencher called

Robert Kilroy-Silk. Robert was an expert on prison reform, or some such topic, and I duly asked him my opening question. He then spoke non-stop for more than four minutes, and try as I could I failed to interrupt the flow. On and on he went, and he would still be going now if the end music hadn't started to play.

Towards the end of 1981, unknown to me, the end music for my stint on *News at One* was being slowly faded up. Preparations were well in hand for the launch the following year of another TV channel – Channel Four – and the centrepiece of its early evening schedule was to be a totally new kind of news programme. It would be just under an hour in length, and cover a range of serious topics in such depth that no other news programme would be like it. There would be no coverage of horrible murders, or the antics of junior members of the royal family or of the rest of the tabloid agenda. The only sport it would cover would be 'Front Page' sport, the only crime would be 'Landmark Crime'. Its bread and butter would be political and economic coverage at home, significant developments abroad, and major science and arts stories. In fact it was to be the first news programme with its own, dedicated arts correspondent. They were fine ambitions, but shared by no other news programme, and for a very good reason – the remorseless march of the celebrity culture and the ascendancy of entertainment as news and news as entertainment. *Channel Four News* today struggles not to be affected. It is a programme that could never be invented now.

Despite the feeling in some quarters that *Channel Four News* as originally envisaged was the type of programme that ITN could not deliver, ITN was eventually the chosen contractor, convincing an initially sceptical Jeremy Isaacs – the first chief executive of Channel Four – that they could be trusted to do the job. But who was going to present it?

David Nicholas believed that the best he could do for the new Channel Four Company would be to entrust the new programme to his most senior newscaster, Alastair Burnet. Alastair was without question ITN's number one – in a pecking order in which I was four or three at most. Pilot programmes were duly commissioned early in 1982, leaving plenty of time before the channel was launched in the November. I saw some of those pilots, and Alastair Burnet looked as if he hated the whole exercise.

There was no sign whatsoever that he wanted the job, which is just as well, because Jeremy Isaacs had already decided that he didn't want Alastair, whom he thought was too closely identified with the existing mainstream news programmes. I am not aware that Alastair has ever said how he felt about the exercise in which he clearly looked so uncomfortable. However the distinguished former ITN reporter Richard Lindley, in his exhaustively researched ITN history *And Finally* observes that Alastair has never had a good word to say about *Channel Four News* from that day to this. A few weeks later David Nicholas sent for me and told me he wanted me to be the first presenter of *Channel Four News* – an appointment made without him having seen me do a pilot programme. By the summer I had presented my last *News at One*, and the team began assembling for a long build-up to the launch of the new venture on 2 November. But our enthusiasm was soon dampened by the realisation that ITN and Channel Four had made one elementary and depressing mistake.

Chapter 8

The Making of *Channel Four News*

Channel Four News is today rightly regarded as one of the most important news programmes on television. It often puts lesser programmes in the shade with the rigour and depth of its reporting, the originality of its presentation and the breadth of its agenda. It, and its reporters, cameramen and presenters, have rightly won a stack of awards. It is feared, admired and loathed – depending on where you are coming from. It is rarely boring and often controversial. It reaches the parts that other news programmes leave behind. Having worked on every major terrestrial TV news broadcast, on the BBC, ITV and Channel Four, it is my view that *Channel Four News* is the one that can make other flagships look pedestrian and predictable.

How is it then, that it came so close to disaster at the very outset? How could it be that two of the most experienced figures in television journalism got the most important and elementary decision so wrong? I haven't a clue, but they did. That decision was not the appointment of who to present it – which was important enough. It was the appointment of the first Editor of *Channel Four News* which was absolutely crucial.

Editing a major television news programme is not an easy job. He or she must know the medium inside out – what can be done technically, how fast it can be done, and the cost of doing it. He or she is the most important journalist on the programme, and she or he must be able to command the respect of the team of technicians and journalists who work on it. Besides organisational and management skills of a high order, being a good writer is important, and it also helps to be a good diplomat and nursemaid.

David Nicholas of ITN and Jeremy Isaacs of Channel Four knew all this. So they appointed to be the first Editor of *Channel Four News* someone who had never before worked in television, freely confessed to knowing nothing about how a news programme was made, and who was unknown to the team he had to lead. The theory was that a new kind of news programme needed a new kind of editorial leader, someone not encumbered with the baggage of all those conventional TV bulletins. Someone who would not only think outside the box, but when it came to TV, had spent all his working life living outside the box. The theory was mad, and so it proved. The man they appointed was a decent enough chap, but from day one it was apparent that in such a pivotal TV role, on which such high expectations were pinned, he was out of his depth.

His name was Derrik Mercer, and he had been recruited from the *Sunday Times* where he was managing editor (news). The grammar of television news was unknown to him, technical terms and acronyms had to be explained to him, and he clearly struggled with the business of re-programming himself from the demands of print to the demands of television. Indeed, I am not so sure he saw that as essential, referring more than once to his vision for *Channel Four News* as 'a quality newspaper of the air'. There was much rolling of eyes behind his back at the first meetings he chaired, and much time was spent putting him in the picture about things that should have been obvious to anyone acquainted with the medium. Despite it all, however, we, the chosen team, decided to give it a go. I myself gave Mercer the benefit of the doubt long after many of my colleagues gave up on him – after all, he was the one anointed by Nicholas and Isaacs, for whom I had deep respect.

It was a talented and experienced group that had been put together under Derrik Mercer's command. I was the lead presenter, with three other senior figures who would present and report as needed. Trevor Macdonald, ITN's first black reporter, had not yet made his name as a presenter, but had made a great impact as a foreign and diplomatic correspondent. Sarah Hogg was one of the UK's foremost economic commentators, but primarily in print. She was married to a Conservative MP, and was the daughter-in-law of Lord Hailsham. And Godfrey Hodgson was a distinguished foreign affairs specialist, but again, his strengths lay as a writer rather than a television presence. The idea was that I would anchor the programme and do most of the major interviews. Trevor would be diplomatic correspondent, concentrating on analysis of the big foreign stories. Sarah would present and report on all matters economic and financial, and display her considerable insider's knowledge of Whitehall and the Treasury. And Godfrey would head off to foreign capitals and trouble spots to give us insights, as needed, into the politics there.

There was also a very good team of other specialists which included Elinor Goodman, as political editor; Stephen Philips, arts correspondent; Lawrence McGinty, science editor and my old industrial opposite number from the BBC, Ian Ross, who was persuaded to join as labour and industrial correspondent. One other great success was Jane Corbin, who joined in a general reporting role. No one was faster on their feet than her when a late story broke, and her energetic professionalism got us out of trouble on many occasions. There were others, also. Two of them had been Presidents of the Oxford Union: one, Damian Green, a business specialist, eventually became a Conservative MP; the other, Michael Crick, now at *Newsnight*, but then in the second year of an ITN traineeship, was seconded to *Channel Four News* and was always going places. As Union President he'd invited me to Oxford to speak in his Presidential Debate, invariably the occasion for a bit of levity. The debate went well, with Michael Palin and myself on the same side, but the social arrangements were a disaster. Crick, instead of the traditional fine dinner afterwards in the Union Library, thought it would be fun if we all ate fish and chips out of newspaper, and drank pale ale out of bottles. The food was cold and congealed, the beer was flat and warm and his two dozen distinguished guests were not appreciative.

His skills as a TV journalist, luckily for him, were in a different league. Indeed, most members of the *Channel Four News* team made a great success of the opportunity they were given, and went on to enhance their reputations in broadcasting. Only Sarah Hogg and Godfrey Hodgson fell by the wayside, returning to pastures more suitable to their talents. Indeed Sarah went on to become the head of John Major's policy unit, where she was later joined by Damian Green.

Sarah was judged – not by me – not to quite fit as a presenter. I thought her contacts and depth of knowledge were worth a place on any team. Godfrey, a thinker and writer of the Old School, never looked comfortable in the fast moving world of a brand-new TV news programme. He liked to deliver his judgements in a considered way and at length, often straight to camera from the roof terrace of a very good hotel in the latest European capital he was visiting, and he didn't seem happy writing to picture. Both Sarah and Godfrey remained friends of the programme when they left.

So, *Channel Four News* had an Editor, and an editorial team. We had our own newsroom, on the floor above the main ITN newsroom and we had fifty minutes of airtime to fill every weeknight at 7 p.m. Eventually we had a Moscow and a Washington bureau, both of which posts were filled with distinction by David Smith, a former Reuters correspondent. We also had our own dedicated technicians in film and graphics, and had access to all the news material brought into the building by ITN. Or at least we did in theory. There were tensions when ITN rightly wanted to hold stuff back from time to time to make an impact on its own flagship, *News at Ten*.

Throughout the summer of 1982, in preparation for the launch of Channel Four in the November, we put in place the organisational and editorial structure of the new programme and made pilot programmes. We also made mistakes. For a start, we got the opening titles and music wrong. The initial idea was for an opening title sequence more like the Antiques Roadshow, with an elegant statuette revolving on a sort of potter's wheel, while some Mozart trilled away. That was put right – there'd be some newsy pictures and the punchy tune you hear to this day. The tune – 'Best Endeavours' by Alan Hawkshaw – chose itself from a disc of film music on which no royalties were payable. Some thought the tune a bit too fast and brash, but money was tight, and that was the deciding factor. It's now been played maybe tens of thousands of times, and has never been re-orchestrated, so poor old Hawkshaw lost out. Quite a contrast to John Malcolm who composed the original ITN theme tune 'Non-Stop', on which ITN paid royalties for more than twenty-five years.

What wasn't put right before the opening night was the studio set. The first set for *Channel Four News* was a vast expanse of beige carpeting with a large and ugly cut out of a world map on the back wall, and in the foreground three or four black leather chairs, each facing a camera. One wag unkindly and correctly said that it looked like the international headquarters of Allied Carpets.

There were no desks for the presenters. That was regarded as The Big

Idea. The thinking was that a desk was old hat. Men at desks was the old way of doing news. Desks came between the presenter and the viewer. So we wouldn't be having desks. Thus, organising your scripts became impossible. From day one scripts had to be balanced on your knee. If one fell off, it was invariably the one you needed next. And they were always falling off. It was a nightmare.

As was the opening night, 2 November 1982.

I co-presented most of the programme with Sarah Hogg and Trevor. Trevor also did a weighty piece on foreign affairs, Sarah did a long read on the economy, and Godfrey did a long think-piece on something or other. The night's big interview was with the former Foreign Secretary Lord Carrington, who had resigned over the Falklands at the beginning of the year. As he sat next to me, patiently waiting for his turn as the rest of the programme ponderously unfolded, he glanced at his watch and – off camera – courteously enquired of me 'How long does all this go on?'

After fifty minutes the programme ended. By the time I signed off, I was alone on the set. It had felt like five hours. The music ended, and I sat there feeling numb. None of the cameramen said a word. The floor manager, normally chatty and cheerful, couldn't think of anything to say, so we gazed at each other in stunned silence.

Then the studio door opened, and in danced a half-naked young lady, calling my name. It was a kissogram girl, or it may have been a strippogram judging by how few clothes she was almost wearing. Whatever she was, she was the last person I wanted to see, let alone be jumped by. Poor girl, she wasn't to know what I had just been through. She plonked her fishnets, frills and suspenders, so amply filled, on my knee and smothered me in wet kisses. My face and collar were covered with bright red lipstick. Just my luck. My first kissogram at forty years of age, and I just didn't have the strength to join in. The press seemed more interested in the girl, who was called Nicky Scicluna, than the programme we had just made, which in a way was a blessing. She told one reporter: 'I've surprised a lot of people but never seen anyone as stunned as Peter.'

Upstairs in the newsroom not much was said. There were ritual congratulations. Our new Editor seemed reasonably satisfied, and I think there was even an encouraging phone call from Liz Forgan, our commissioning editor at Channel Four. Most of the team, however, knew the truth of the matter, but kept their silence. They knew that the programme had been a shapeless mess, and that there had been no sign of anyone having an editorial grip. We all went home.

The next day, to our surprise, there was remarkably little adverse comment in the newspapers. There was plenty about the debut of the new channel, but in general we escaped. We were also helped over the following months by the print media being distracted by the build-up to the launch of TV-am, with its star-studded line-up of Robert Kee, David Frost, Anna Ford, Michael Parkinson and Angela Rippon, and the derision with which it was finally received when it went on air at the beginning of February 1983.

We did start improving *Channel Four News* and making it more watchable, which wasn't difficult because it couldn't get much worse. At the same time there was a lot of soul-searching at Channel Four and ITN, particularly about whether it was on at the right time. Weren't people just too preoccupied at seven in the evening to sit down and watch an hour of news? Was the programme itself so lacking in shape that viewers couldn't easily familiarise themselves with it? This second question was judged to be the most pressing, and the answer that ITN came up with was, with hindsight, quite extraordinary.

Paul McKee, ITN's deputy chief executive, computer specialist and the father of its computer graphics wizardry, was seconded to *Channel Four News* to devise a way to 'signpost' the programme. I am also fairly certain, because McKee had a senior ITN management job, that he had another role – to keep an eye on Derrik Mercer, and to report back to ITN's Editor on how Mercer was faring. What McKee devised was a new opening sequence for the programme, the centrepiece of which was a colourful pie-chart. Each segment of the pie represented a slice of the programme – the first small slice was the opening headlines, then a bigger slice for the main news, some smaller slices for other significant stories, and so on. The idea was for the presenter, reading a script tightly edited to the slices as they were revealed, to guide the viewers as to what they could expect on that night, and where in the programme the different ingredients would be.

Writing this signposting script every night, and co-ordinating with the computer graphics technician was going to be tedious and time-consuming, and I refused to do it. Although as a matter of course I wrote the lead story on every programme, and the opening headlines, I wasn't going to spend my time in the countdown to the programme, 'writing the pie' as it became known.

But someone had to do it, and it landed next on the desk of the individual programme 'editors of the day', who also balked at it, because they had more than enough to do already. The upshot was that on many nights the pie was written by Derrik Mercer himself. Instead of busying himself with taking the big editorial view, and making the crucial pre-transmission checks and interventions, he would often be found for an hour or two before transmission, sitting at a terminal composing words that fitted McKee's pie. I felt sorry for him.

The overriding problem that Mercer had, and for which he alone had to carry the can, was that practically no one was watching our programme. It wasn't enough to say that it was on at the wrong time. There is a core audience for TV programmes beginning at 7 p.m., and we weren't even getting a crumb of it. The ratings were officially zero. This meant you could travel the land at 7 o'clock each night, and find only one or two TV sets tuned to *Channel Four News* in every square mile. At one editorial post-mortem I was so depressed that I suggested that it might be cheaper to visit each viewer in person and hand them a tape of the programme. Mercer held many such brainstorming meetings among his team, and we chipped in with many ideas. But at the end of the day he had to come up with a route out of the mess we were in. We waited in vain for him to tell us The Plan.

There had been one big idea early on. The defeated US President Jimmy Carter had completed his memoirs, and access to him was being hawked around by various middle men. It was decided that *Channel Four News* would buy the rights to an exclusive interview with him for use in the UK. In return for many tens of thousands of pounds we would be able to question him for something like ninety minutes. The interview would then be sliced up and used over three or four nights on *Channel Four News*, bringing it was hoped, prestige and recognition to the programme in its early weeks.

The problem was that Carter, a good and worthy man, had written a dull book and as I was to find out, was ready to add very little to it in the course of an interview. I and a producer travelled to Carter's home town, Plains in Georgia, where he had returned to live and teach Sunday School, and the final arrangements were made. President Carter would meet us and our film crew at his mother's tiny house on the main street. A standing joke about Plains was that if it were hit by an H-bomb, the bomb would do about fifteen dollars' worth of damage. I saw what they meant. There really was little there apart from a lot of dust, a few houses, a railway halt and a filling station run by Carter's brother. And for hundreds of miles around there was nothing but peanut fields. Carter's own modest home stood off the road at the end of the street, surrounded by a massive iron fence – which apparently is erected for all former presidents by the secret service. Quite what or whom they were protecting him from in Plains, Georgia at that time was not clear.

At the appointed hour we waited for him outside the venue, in an empty street in a largely deserted town, if you could call it that. A dozen secret service men appeared at the end of the street, and fanned out towards us. It felt like *High Noon*. Then from their midst appeared President Carter himself, smiling that smile, and looking just a touch embarrassed at the absurdity of it all. We sat him down inside, did the interview and got on well. Afterwards I asked him to autograph my copy of his book. He signed it 'J. Carter'. Apparently he signed the more familiar 'Jimmy Carter' only for friends and family, public bodies, or people willing to buy a book at a substantial premium. Jimmy Carter was not a rich man.

The interview itself was not a great success. Carter's answers were very long, and he objected to being interrupted. Even the most pointed and interesting questions ignited no spark. Perhaps the most revealing moment was when I asked him whether, as a deeply religious man, he would ever have pressed the nuclear button. He replied 'They only had to believe that I might'. The interview was duly run in instalments during the course of a week on *Channel Four News*, and was soon forgotten.

After a few depressing months, some senior figures on the programme urged me to take the lead in a palace revolution. It was clear there was much plotting against our own Editor, and I was drawn into it. We went through all the arguments a number of times, usually over a carafe of the house red in the Monte Bello, a friendly little restaurant round the corner; to this day veterans of those machinations still wryly refer to the Monte Bello's very drinkable house red as Chateau Machiavelli. What eventually persuaded me was the realisation that there was a real possibility of the programme failing – and that would mean thirty or forty people losing their jobs. A general election was imminent, and none of us was confident that the programme could pass such a test under its present leadership. I slept on it all one more time, and the next morning went to see the Editor of ITN, David Nicholas. I explained, with regret, that in my judgement Derrik Mercer no longer had the confidence of most of his editorial team. David said little, but I got the feeling that I was pushing at an open door. Derrik Mercer had gone by the evening.

I was not proud of what I had done, but felt better when I saw how relieved most of my colleagues were. One or two thought I had behaved badly. Ian Ross told me to my face that I had stabbed a decent man in the back. Coming from the BBC I suspect he was more than familiar with the practice, but his judgement hurt. I believe that I did no more than bring forward the inevitable by a month or two.

We put a programme on air that evening without an editor, but under McKee's paternal eye, and afterwards Sarah Hogg and I sat in our office, totally drained. Derrik Mercer was having farewell drinks in the wine bar opposite, and I felt that it would not be right for me to go, and said so. Whereupon Sarah looked me in the eye, said that I would never make a politician, and practically frogmarched me across the road. I am glad I did go. I won't say it wasn't awkward, but if Mercer held a grudge against me, he didn't show it. We wished each other well – which is how things eventually worked out for him. He never returned to print or TV journalism, but went on to write or edit a number of bestselling books, including the encyclopaedic *Chronicle of the 20th Century*, which I should imagine made him far more comfortable than ever *Channel Four News* could have done.

Looking back on the unhappiness of those first months of *Channel Four News*, I think one of the most striking features was the dignity with which Derrik Mercer conducted himself. He could have been forgiven for bad mouthing anyone connected with the hand he had been dealt, and the way it all ended. But even when he had left ITN, he rationalised his predicament as being basically a victim of circumstances – asked to perform miracles with an underfunded and undermanned production team at a time in the evening when the appetite of the TV audience was conditioned not to sitting down and watching serious news, but *Coronation Street* and *This is Your Life*. Three months after he was sacked he wrote a long article in *The Times* about his experience at *Channel Four News*, in which he did pin some of the blame for his departure on me, alleging that I had swung from being the programme's greatest champion to being its greatest critic. Sissons, he said 'had lost confidence in two of the three producers, and when I rejected his request to work only with the other producer, he lost confidence in me'.

Mercer also claimed that I had declared that the only way to save the programme was to make it newsier and go downmarket – which was not true; and he also accused me of thinking that he, Mercer, should be replaced by a television 'professional', which was. The article went on: 'Hour-long news was very much Jeremy Isaacs' baby and he had been frustrated by our apparent inability to match the standards he had once set at *This Week*... Maybe, he asked Nicholas, Sissons was right and it was the editor's fault?' The only new thing I learned from that article was that after the TV-am debacle, Derrik Mercer had wanted to re-recruit Anna Ford to ITN as part of the team on *Channel Four News*, but that David Nicholas had refused to let him approach her.

After Derrik Mercer's sudden departure – which he chose rather than accept the offer of another post inside ITN – *Channel Four News* continued for a few weeks with Paul McKee in charge.

Paul was a popular man, and a shrewd office politician, and it was he who saw that time was running out for the programme unless its assembled talent had a leader who could act fast and decisively with vision and energy. He and David Nicholas decided that that man was Stewart Purvis. Stewart was one of ITN's rising stars. He'd started his career at the BBC, but it was ITN that gave full rein to his talents. By 1983 he was editing *News at Ten*, bringing to it flair, pace and ideas. His coltish enthusiasm had made him friends and enemies, but the exceptional ratings for *News at Ten* spoke for themselves.

Stewart did, of course, make his share of mistakes – including one *News at Ten* that no one, especially him, ever talks about now, when he led with film of a very obvious wardrobe malfunction which afflicted the Princess of Wales as she attended a glittering function in a very revealing evening dress. But Stewart was a fast learner, and I have never met anyone with a journalistic brain allied to such a complete knowledge of what television could achieve technically. He was to go on to be Editor in Chief and Chief Executive of ITN, and to be awarded the Royal Television Society's Gold Medal for outstanding contribution to television. In 1983 he wasn't the finished article, but he was what *Channel Four News* needed, and Nicholas reluctantly decided that *News at Ten* would have to manage without him.

Selling him to Channel Four was another matter. It would mean them eating many of their fine words about breaking the mould and producing a new kind of news, because Stewart was another of those with ITN through him like a stick of rock. In the event, Stewart sold himself to Channel Four at a lunch with the chief executive Jeremy Isaacs and the chairman Sir Edmund Dell, at which another board member, Sir Dickie Attenborough, was also present. Isaacs and Dell reminded him of the heavy burden he would have to bear, meeting all the requirements of a weighty news programme dedicated to serious analysis. But as they parted Sir Dickie, who'd been largely quiet, gave him the advice that I suspect he really wanted to hear, and took some of the pressure off – 'Never forget darling, you're in entertainment!' Nonetheless, Purvis was warned by Isaacs that he had six months to turn the programme round.

When Stewart arrived in the Editor's office at *Channel Four News*, we – and I mean most of the team that was in place – did wonder about him. What of the guiding principles of the programme? *News at Ten*, whence he came, never shirked serious news at home or abroad, but it also thrived on stories about royalty, major crime, and sports and showbiz personalities, and liked to lighten the mix with the occasional 'And Finally' about cats stuck up trees. Few stories were ruled out of *News at Ten* if they were judged to be of interest to a mass audience.

So how would Purvis adapt to the *Channel Four News* founding principles, the Tablets of Stone – no royals, no horrible murders, no salacious society or showbiz scandals, no cats, no froth? Unwittingly, I happened to put my finger on a way out which served the programme well for many years.

It happened quite by accident, but at one of our many daily editorial discussions about the shape and content of the programme, the Tablets of Stone became a matter for heated argument among the team. I forget the precise issue, but there was a story which interested us all, and would clearly be of great interest to our audience, but which appeared to be more *News at Ten* than *Channel Four News*. The argument went to the root of the kind of programme we wanted to make. Everyone let off steam and some became rather angry, and then Stewart asked for my view. I said simply 'What's the issue here?' It was blindingly obvious: *Channel Four News* was intended to deal with the issues of the day. Whatever the story, provided we could identify an issue, and deal with it intelligently, then we were right to cover it. On both sides of the argument, honour was satisfied.

That approach gave *Channel Four News* a new purpose. Major stories of all kinds could now get the *Channel Four News* treatment. Crime would be covered, if it were 'landmark crime' – the sort of crime that led to a change in the law, or took the offence into a new dimension. Royalty were covered intelligently, with recognition given to how their behaviour might undermine their standing with the public, and so on. It still gave us every reason to avoid stories that were totally vacuous – there was nothing that we would want to follow up from *Hello* magazine – but *Channel Four News* had a new guiding principle. Allied to intelligent interviewing and debate it was, and remains, a potent mix. And nothing helped to focus the programme on issues more than one of its great innovations – commissioning short films setting out the arguments for and against a position from two of the protagonists. That approach had its greatest success in 1984, when, at the height of the bitter coal strike, the NUM's Arthur Scargill and the NCB's Ian MacGregor were each equipped with a film crew and set out their stalls in compelling fashion.

So, under Stewart Purvis, *Channel Four News* began to build an audience and to win critical acclaim. Central to its success in both regards was its coverage of that 1984 miners' strike.

The year-long NUM strike in 1984, called by the union's president Arthur Scargill without a national ballot, was the most bitter and divisive industrial dispute since the war. It was also the longest national stoppage ever. The immediate issue was the determination of the National Coal Board to close twenty pits. The underlying cause was the determination of Margaret Thatcher, who had backed down in the face of an NUM strike threat in 1981, to break the ability of the NUM to bring the economy to a standstill – or indeed bring down the government, as it had in 1974. In 1984, with mountains of coal stockpiled at the power stations, she was ready to take the miners on, and Arthur Scargill's critics believe he walked into her trap. As the dispute became more desperate for the miners, scenes of violence were commonplace, as flying pickets tried to close vital links in the nation's fuel supply. At the Orgreave Coking Plant in Yorkshire, where thousands of miners fought running battles with mounted police, industrial confrontation took on a shocking new dimension. The onset of winter brought great hardship to communities where miners were on strike, while the rest of the country went about business as usual. Deprived of official Labour Party support, and with key pits in the industry, particularly in Nottinghamshire, still working, the NUM was eventually broken. The dispute was a tragedy for the coal industry, and shattered the solidarity that had long been the hallmark of the people who worked in it.

Covering such a complicated and bitter series of events in a measured and responsible way would be a massive challenge to every news organisation, and *Channel Four News* came out with its reputation considerably enhanced. The balance struck, and the depth and breadth of the coverage, made it the only programme to earn the respect of both sides in the dispute. As a result, *Channel Four News* film crews and reporters were able to gain access to communities where other organisations dared not show their faces. Indeed, there was some evidence that rival film crews, on occasion, had used *Channel Four News* stickers on their cameras and camera cars to immunise themselves from the striking miners' hatred of the media. Looking back, you might be forgiven for thinking that *Channel Four News* sacrificed its obligation to impartiality to win the grudging confidence of striking miners that their case would be fairly reported. Nothing could be further from the truth. I believe that it was simply a model for how to cover a painful and protracted industrial dispute.

The high point, and certainly the most dramatic part of that coverage, was the evening we persuaded the NUM firebrand Scargill and NCB hatchet man MacGregor to talk to each other on television, something which by all accounts they hadn't managed anywhere else. It took weeks of negotiations. They certainly weren't going to sit in the same studio together. Scargill would be in Yorkshire, and MacGregor at the Coal Board HQ in London. There was no agreement on who would have the first word and who would have the final word. And they couldn't even agree on how long their joint appearance would last. MacGregor dug in his heels and said he'd take part for no more than ten minutes.

Scargill, a much slicker performer than MacGregor, was much more keen on the debate however long it ran, and it was obvious to me that if it happened, I was going to have to ensure that both got a fair crack of the whip.

On the evening in question, when we went on air none of these issues had been resolved. All I knew was that there was still a chance the debate might not happen. It was the only time that I have started a news broadcast without the faintest idea of what was coming next. So, I decided just to busk it, and to level with the viewers. I told them that, as of a couple of minutes ago, it was still not certain that the debate we hoped to broadcast would take place. Half of me was talking to my camera. The other half was watching the two monitors, one giving me the Yorkshire picture, and the other the NCB feed. The only thing to be seen in both was an empty chair. Then, as I spoke, I saw Arthur Scargill sit down in the Yorkshire chair. Still I couldn't promise the debate that had been so widely anticipated. Then I saw the bulky figure of Ian MacGregor lower himself into the chair at the NCB. I thought we'd better get cracking before either had a change of heart, so I improvised an introduction, and dived right in. There was little point in those in the control room trying to direct me – I knew as much about what was going on as they did.

You could cut the atmosphere between the two men with a knife, even though they were 200 miles apart. Scargill loosed off a torrent of invective, and I had to interrupt to let MacGregor reply. The contrast between the practised rhetoric of the dedicated union activist and MacGregor's curt, matter-of-fact managerial responses in which the contempt for his opponent was scarcely concealed, was the stuff of high drama. It was mesmerising, not so much for its content – for nothing was said that changed a thing – but for the stark illustration it gave of how intractable the dispute had now become. There was not an inch of common ground. Then, ten minutes into the exchange, a shadowy figure tapped MacGregor on the shoulder. It was his press officer, reminding him that ten minutes had passed, and MacGregor began to leave his seat while Scargill was still speaking. I was amazed – and put it to MacGregor whether he really wanted to end it there and leave the field to Mr Scargill. Whereupon MacGregor slumped down again, and we went on for another ten minutes. That debate put *Channel Four News* on the map. The two men had never spoken before that day, and they never spoke again – ever.

I think the distinguishing feature of those days was the willingness of the programme to take risks. During the miners' strike, I and a small production team left one morning for the Nottinghamshire coalfield, determined to present the programme from a suitable location. In fact we didn't have the faintest idea where we would present the programme from. At four in the afternoon we were still driving around, gathering material, garnering interviewees, and trying to find the ideal pit-gate location from where to present the programme at seven. That done, we took over the saloon bar in an adjacent pub as our makeshift newsroom. From there we arranged for other guests to be interviewed 'down the line' from London, and scripts to be written and faxed to base. All the while the technical lines and links were put in place. At seven we put out a programme packed with atmosphere and embellished by some fine contributions by our reporters. Then we drove home. All in a day's work.

On a smaller scale, but still quite a risk in production terms, someone had the bright idea one evening for me to interview a dozen or more unemployed people. The unemployment figures had been particularly bad, and it was thought it would be effective – and put the interviewees at their ease – if I went to a pub to interview them.

The chosen venue was a pub next door to Central Hall at Westminster, a couple of miles away, where there'd been a lobby of Parliament. The plan, which for some reason I went along with, was for me to close part two of the programme, just before half past seven, by trailing ahead to the event in the pub. Then, during the commercial break, I was to rush from the building, pull on a crash helmet, jump onto the back of an ITN despatch rider's motorbike, and whizz off through the West End traffic to Westminster. The commercial break was two minutes long, but I was going to be given an extra three or four minutes by the second presenter in the studio reading a summary of the foreign news that day. All this duly happened. My knuckles were white, and my hair was starting to go white, when I arrived at the pub, jumped off and tried to stroll nonchalantly inside, with only thirty seconds to spare. It worked, but we didn't tempt fate by ever trying it again.

By far the most dramatic moment I experienced on air during an edition of *Channel Four News* was in the first few minutes of the broadcast on 12 October 1984. I and a small production team were in Brighton for the Conservative Party Conference. Just before 3 a.m., an IRA bomb had practically blown apart the main conference hotel, the Grand. I myself had been in the crowded bar of the hotel until just before midnight. The bomb was an attempt to assassinate Margaret Thatcher and her Cabinet. No Cabinet minister was killed, but five others were. At 7 p.m. that evening I began *Channel Four News* with the wrecked hotel in shot a couple of hundred yards behind me. As I began to speak, a large part of the front of the hotel collapsed. It was an awful moment, bringing home the enormity of the crime. I let the scene speak for itself, before we took our viewers through the day's shocking events, and Margaret Thatcher's defiant reaction to them. My colleagues, especially Elinor Goodman our political editor, performed brilliantly that day and the programme they produced was among our best.

The enthusiasm and commitment of everyone who worked for *Channel Four News* at that time was remarkable. In fact, I would go so far as to say that no news programme I subsequently worked on came anywhere near it in the ability to get the best out of its people. A lot of it involved basic instincts of self-preservation. If the programme went up the spout, we all knew that *we* went up the spout. But the main ethos came from the top – it was the ITN way to try harder because no one owed ITN a living. And both ITN and its *Channel Four News* division were run by journalists who had the ability to roll up their sleeves and do the job themselves.

As a programme it was also, when it mattered, very fast on its feet. During the time I was the main presenter, its reflexes were tested as never before on a Wednesday evening just before Christmas in 1988. It was not a particularly busy news day, and in the moments before transmission our news editor Garron Baines was on the phone to a contact in the press office of the Ministry of Defence. It was a routine check call. Garron, incidentally, for some inexplicable reason was nicknamed 'Garbled Brains', but on his day he was one of the sharpest tools in the box. As he spoke, his contact at the MOD broke off, to tell him that they were getting a report that an airliner had disappeared from radar screens over Scotland. We learned later that it was Pan Am 103, with 259 passengers and crew that had taken off from Heathrow at 6.25 p.m. Garron's contact was known to be reliable, so within minutes of *Channel Four News* going on air at seven, I was alerted to the possibility of there being a major air disaster over Scotland, and was able to tell our viewers that we were getting such reports. Shortly afterwards, the phones were red-hot from Lockerbie, where the aircraft had come down, killing another eleven people on the ground. For the next forty or fifty minutes *Channel Four News* reported the breaking story quickly and in growing detail.

A Glasgow cameraman had jumped into his car when we got the first alerts, skirted the crash scene, and raced back to the local TV station in time for us to show the fires raging on the ground, less than an hour after the crash, before we closed the programme. They were scenes from a nightmare, a massive crater gouged out of the earth where the 747's engines had fallen, and the surrounding area on fire. The shock of it all brought out the best in the editorial team, no one went home, and we ran updates on the channel throughout the evening.

So, under Stewart Purvis, *Channel Four News* at last began to fulfil its potential. He ratcheted up the ratings to levels very similar to those of today, and gained the programme the acclaim and recognition by broadcasting professionals that Channel Four craved.

The bonus for me and senior colleagues during my seven years on the programme was an annual night out at the BAFTA awards, rubbing shoulders with the legends of TV and film. After the shaky beginning, we had to pinch ourselves when we carried off BAFTAs in three successive years, and were nominated in two other years. That was unprecedented for a news programme. In 1984 I was voted Best Front of Camera Performer by the Guild of Broadcasting Journalists, a prize I particularly appreciated because it was awarded by some of the hardest-nosed critics in the business.

Another accolade of a different kind also came my way. The producers of the famous Westminster sitcom *Yes, Minister* approached me, asking if I would appear as myself, the storyline being that *Channel Four News* was one of those programmes that really got up Jim Hacker's nose. I was given the impression that it might develop into something more than a 'one-off' appearance, a regular piece of grit in the Hacker oyster. I was bound to ask permission to do this, but when I went to see ITN's Editor David Nicholas about it, he was quite firm: out of the question, because it would damage the credibility of me and of *Channel Four News*. I thought he was wrong, and that *Channel Four News* would have garnered great publicity from such an appearance. And watching the way those brilliant episodes have endured, the repeat fees would have come in handy today!

When I later left ITN, I must confess that I was less assiduous in asking permission when anything similar came up, and which I thought would be fun, in case it was refused. But my cameo appearances in *The Spice Girls Movie* and the *Basil Brush Show* were approved by the BBC on the grounds that it was all harmless publicity for the news and for me – showing that I did know how to smile.

I would always, however, draw the line at playing myself in a serious context. It must be wrong for a well-known newscaster to appear in a drama, to give impact to a storyline that might leave some people confused as to whether it was real or not. The BBC has allowed that to happen with a number of presenters, notably in their spy series *Spooks*, and whoever authorised it should have known better. I would go as far as to say that it is unethical to use a familiar presenter who has built up trust in news programmes, where facts are supposed to be sacred, to enhance the credibility of fiction. No one is suggesting that we could have another 'War of the Worlds' panic, the hysteria that gripped America in 1938 after a series of simulated newsflashes in an Orson Welles drama, announcing that the Martians had landed. But the standing of its newscasters and current affairs presenters, especially during times of crisis, is a priceless asset to a broadcaster. It's good to see that most of the BBC's first division presenters know which side of the line to be on.

Although a cameo in *Yes, Minister* might have been harmless enough, and could never have been mistaken for the real thing, David Nicholas's refusal to let me appear was reflecting a view widely shared at ITN that *Channel Four News* could not afford to be seen as lightweight. Certainly among the editorial team on the programme itself, enthusiastic and motivated as they were, there was a constant striving to be taken seriously and not to let the side down. That spirit was severely tested on only one occasion that I can recall – indeed it came close to falling apart.

It happened one evening in 1986, when the former Defence Secretary Michael Heseltine was sitting next to me as I read the opening headlines at 7 p.m. There was to be an interview with him later in the programme, and the studio director cut away to Heseltine as I mentioned him in the programme 'menu'.

I also mentioned that later in the programme there was to be a film report featuring a recorded interview with a former official from Heseltine's old ministry, a middle-ranking civil servant called Clive Ponting. Ponting had been acquitted of leaking official secrets, but we were interviewing him on a totally different matter to the Heseltine topic. When I mentioned Ponting's name, Heseltine bridled, tore off his microphone and walked out of the studio. Normally, that would have been the end of the matter, but to entice Heseltine back Stewart Purvis grabbed him before he left the building, and assured him that the Ponting clip would be dropped. Heseltine came back, and I did the planned interview with him. It was only afterwards that we all realised the price that we had paid – we had bought off a walkout by a senior politician by letting him dictate the content of the programme. Most members of the team were shocked, and Stewart was in the dog-house. Mutiny was in the air. But to his credit, he stayed up all night sending out individual letters of explanation and apology to his editorial colleagues. Nonetheless, it took some weeks for the atmosphere to get back to normal.

It was an isolated upset. Suddenly, from being the poor relation of ITN, *Channel Four News* became the programme to work on, and there was no shortage of applications when jobs became available. Generally, I found it tremendously fulfilling, and often great fun. But what I didn't want to admit to myself was just how stressful it had become. We'd been through the fire at the beginning and we'd got it sorted out. But there was constant pressure to maintain standards, to do better, to come up with new ideas. I am sure that others felt it too, but presenting that kind of programme four or five nights a week did begin to affect me. I have never taken a drink in my life before or during a TV programme, but after a long day with *Channel Four News*, I found I needed one. I am reminded of Laurence Olivier's reply when someone asked him what was the best thing about acting – 'The drink after the performance dear boy!'

Later in 1986, after three years of Purvis, *Channel Four News* was secure.

It was in that year that I had my first approach from the BBC. The phone rang one day, and someone I didn't know introduced himself as Richard Tait, the editor of *Newsnight*. He came straight to the point: his principal presenter, John Tusa, was leaving *Newsnight*, and would I like to take his place? I was very flattered. No one had ever approached me like that before. Every time I had changed my job it had been inside ITN, and just seemed to happen. Now someone who really seemed to want me was offering me a complete career change.

There are two reasons I turned Richard down: I knew in my bones that I still had work to do at *Channel Four News*, and just two weeks previously I had signed a new contract at ITN. Although I was on the staff at ITN, it was one of those contracts that gave me security of employment for two years, instead of the usual three months. I never got as far as discussing money with Richard Tait. I just knew that I owed ITN, where I had been for twenty-two years, a bit more of my life.

Less than a year later, the Editor of ITN David Nicholas decided that Stewart Purvis's time on *Channel Four News* was up. He had done the job he was put in to do, and was now needed back in the ITN mainstream. David told me that it was his intention to appoint a new Editor of *Channel Four News* from inside ITN. He mentioned a number of names to me, each of whom had his strengths, but none of whom measured up to Purvis. I suggested to David that the job be advertised externally.

That was a tricky one, because ITN had never before appointed at that level from outside – except for *Channel Four News*'s first Editor, who was not judged a success. I said that nothing could be lost by trawling through some outside candidates, just to see what came up in the net. So, with the agreement of Channel Four, the job was advertised. Before the advertisement appeared, I thought I might do Richard Tait of *Newsnight* a return favour, and tipped him off. He was very interested, and duly applied. But he had competition from the BBC. Tim Gardam, another of the top talents in BBC Current Affairs, also applied. David Nicholas subsequently told me that he had never interviewed two such outstanding candidates for a job. And although he hired Tait, he regretted not creating another senior position just to get Gardam on the payroll. Tim Gardam was not disadvantaged by missing out. A glittering career took him to senior jobs at the BBC, Channel Four and Channel Five, and he now heads an Oxford College.

Tait very nearly walked away from the job before he had even started. He rang me to say that he thought that ITN had in some way diminished the status of the editorship of *Channel Four News*. Previous editors of *Channel Four News* had also been members of the board of management of ITN, which had responsibility for the strategic direction of the whole company. Such membership also carried perks like a company car. Tait told me that what he was being offered was membership only of the editorial management, which wasn't quite the same thing. The car didn't matter to him, but his position inside ITN did. I got the impression that he really would be prepared to walk away over the issue. I picked up the phone to Jeremy Isaacs, the Chief Executive of Channel Four, and told him that the editorship of his news programme appeared to have been downgraded in status by ITN, and that as a result he was about to lose an outstanding candidate for the job. Within a day Tait had got all he wanted from ITN.

In truth, I hadn't the faintest idea how good an Editor Richard Tait would be. But he was brilliant. A PhD in Medieval History may not be the usual qualification for editing a daily news programme, but he brought the intellectual rigour of his days as an academic to every aspect of the job. Not everyone liked that approach. The ITN way was more visceral, more emotional.

At the BBC, it is plain that he'd had his fill of his decisions being unpicked and second guessed. At *Channel Four News* he made it plain from the outset that when he had thought a thing through, that was the way things were going to be done. He never spelt it out – he was too much of a gentleman for that – but you would ignore the boss at your peril.

From my point of view, and I am sure that others involved in presenting the programme agreed, Richard Tait was a presenter's ideal Editor. He realised that without your presenter, you didn't have a programme and there was never a moment when I didn't feel reassured that he was sitting in the Editor's chair. However busy he was, he would always come out of his office and put his hand on my shoulder in the last few minutes before I went on air. And he always had a suggestion or a thought that, even at that stage, was going to improve the programme or make an interview even more effective.

Tait's first big challenge was our coverage of the general election in June 1987. It was meat and drink to him – he had already produced the BBC's marathon results programme in 1983.

We had a good campaign, arranging separate pre-recorded debates between each individual party leader and large groups drawn from generally non-committed voters. At those debates, several days apart, there were confident performances by the Labour leader Neil Kinnock and the joint leader of the SDP/Liberal alliance, David Steel. Margaret Thatcher's date with our group of citizens was the last of the three, and I am told she came close to cancelling. There was an anxious wait until she turned up, and when she did she was clearly under a lot of stress. We now know that on that day, behind closed doors at party headquarters, she had thrown the most astonishing tantrum. The day became known as 'Wobbly Thursday', and the author Michael Dobbs, who was in the room when it happened, described her as 'more than furious, almost frothing'. The trigger had been a rogue opinion poll showing her lead slipping, and she convinced herself that she might lose.

She arrived not only upset, but as we found out later in great pain because of toothache. Anyone watching the recording when it was transmitted would not have known. In the event, her majority was reduced – to 102. The afternoon after the election, I went to Downing Street to interview her, an interview granted at short notice. She was calm, and sat patiently while my film crew set up their gear. I apologised for the delay, but said that if we had been allowed to set up our cameras in Number 10 the previous day, we wouldn't have had to keep her waiting. She looked me in the eye. 'Mr Sissons,' she said, 'I didn't know yesterday that I would be here today.' I wonder now if she knew then, in her bones, that the iron lady would never fight another election.

One bit of history I made at *Channel Four News* came out of a meeting I had with the Director of Public Relations at the Sellafield nuclear facility, who in his previous job had been a member of the Industrial Correspondents Group when I was the Group's chairman. Sellafield had just received yet another damaging mauling in the media for its safety record, after it had been forced to admit yet another radioactive leak. I suggested that Sellafield would always be on the receiving end of bad publicity, so long as it remained one of the most secretive and mysterious places in the country. Shortly afterwards he telephoned me, offering a facility to tour the plant, something that no journalist had ever been allowed to do. The invitation at first was just for me – no cameras. We made it clear that wasn't acceptable, and pushed for unconditional and unrestricted access with cameras. To my amazement, that was conceded. Just to be sure, I made it plain that our visit would take place only on the express condition that we would have access to any part of the plant that we chose. One of the programme's senior producers, Howard Anderson, fixed a day, assigned a crew and sealed the deal with a Sellafield management apparently ready to change the habits of a lifetime and open the doors of one of the most secretive sites in Europe. He also recruited someone to accompany us who would ensure that Sellafield wasn't trying to pull any wool over our eyes, the Canadian nuclear analyst Walt Patterson.

That visit was one of the most extraordinary experiences of my life. Our hosts were as good as their word. I stood on top of Sellafield's repository of high level nuclear waste – containing every drop of the most toxic, unstable and dangerous by products that Britain's nuclear plants had ever produced. Although thirty feet of concrete separated me from the vast tank of nuclear waste below me, the concrete was quite warm underneath my feet. I was told that what kept the waste stable and contained was a huge refrigeration system, with double and triple back-ups and safety locks. It was designed never to fail. Failure of that cooling system would have meant catastrophe. It has never failed.

I explained all this to camera. As part of the tour I also asked to be shown the location of the latest low level radioactive leak, which had nonetheless provoked something near hysteria among Green groups. We were taken to the building where it had happened, the sort of light industrial area you might find in any factory.

We looked down through a window into a work area, and our guide pinpointed for us the exact location, where gallons of fluid had spilled and been cleaned up some days beforehand. 'Is it safe now down there?' I asked. 'Quite safe' came the reply. 'Then let's go down,' I said, and we did. After which, if Sellafield's critics were to have been believed, I would have been glowing in the dark. It was of course possible that I had been deliberately shown a totally different location, but that could not possibly have been the case with the last place we inspected.

It had been a long day, and I thought we had done all we came to do. Then Walt Patterson whispered in my ear 'Ask to see the plutonium store'. Which I did, and for the first time that day our guides hesitated. They didn't, they said, think that would be possible. At which I gently reminded them that there had been no conditions for our visit. After a few minutes of consultation, and a telephone call, they agreed.

The plutonium store at Sellafield was in a nondescript building in the heart of the complex. Unless intruders knew in advance exactly where it was, they wouldn't find it. There was no sign, no indication of any kind, telling what its function was or what its deadly contents were. It housed, so I was told, Britain's store of plutonium. I wasn't told how much plutonium that was, or what types of plutonium were stored there. Plutonium is an element practically unknown in nature; it is a by-product of the nuclear industry, out of which nuclear weapons can be made, and which can also fuel types of nuclear reactor. It is not, I was informed, radioactive – in the sense that a lump of plutonium on the table in front of you would do you harm, because its radiation does not penetrate the skin. But it is a very toxic substance. If you ingest or inhale a particle, the radiation kills you from the inside.

Well, in for a penny, in for a pound. I asked them to bring me a flask of plutonium so that I could hold it and record a piece to camera. After a few minutes, a trolley was wheeled into the room, with a steel flask upon it – about twice as big as a large Thermos – which was carefully handed to me. This was the serious bit. In my hands, gently warm despite the insulation of the flask, was more than a kilogram of plutonium. There was no time to be awestruck, just to get my piece to camera in the can, in one take, and to hand back the plutonium flask. As I handed it over, the smooth steel flask slipped slightly in my grasp. For less than a second I thought it might fall to the floor. I swear that in that second most people in that room went white. The flask was quickly steadied and taken away, and our visit was over. A couple of days later we ran a twenty-two minute report on *Channel Four News*, lifting part of the veil in which Sellafield was cloaked. I consider it one of the most memorable things I did at *Channel Four News*. I still don't glow in the dark.

Chapter 9

Incredible Offer,
Credible Threat

By the time *Channel Four News* was five years old on 2 November 1987, the programme was on the crest of a wave – taking my career with it. The early disasters were forgotten, and the awards for the programme and its reporters had started to stack up. On practically every big story it had touched, it had performed well, usually with flair and imagination and often to critical acclaim. The changes needed to transform the programme, after the initially disastrous six months, had been identified and pushed through by Stewart Purvis and it was under Stewart that my status on the programme received formal recognition; in addition to my duties anchoring *C4N*, I was appointed Associate Editor. There were few practical implications in that, indeed it was largely symbolic. But it is something that would never happen in today's BBC, where news presenters are rarely allowed even a nominal role outside their box.

When we raised our glasses celebrating the first five years of *C4N*, it was under the new Editor Richard Tait. Why was such a talent, who was probably destined for great things at the BBC, ready to join us? One of the things that had hastened Richard's departure from the BBC, I firmly believe, was the way things were going with the Corporation's journalism.

In July that year, John Birt had been appointed Deputy Director General of the BBC. He was to be in charge of all the BBC's journalism, News and Current Affairs, and his expertise was judged essential to counterbalance the appointment of Michael Checkland as Director General. Checkland was not a journalist, but an accountant. But far more than being nominally in charge of the BBC's thousands of journalists, Birt had a remit to shake up the BBC's journalism, root and branch. He took to the task with relish, in the process making himself deeply unpopular, feared even, among most of the BBC's journalists, especially the old guard.

Although his own programme pedigree in ITV was impressive – *World in Action, Weekend World*, producer of the Frost/Nixon interviews – they gave only a partial clue to the type of journalism he admired. What he appeared determined to do at the BBC was to push further ahead with the journalistic philosophy that he and Peter Jay had set out in three short articles in *The Times* in 1974. In those articles, they accused television news of 'a bias against understanding'. They argued that the obsession of TV news with pictures and images, and the paucity of analysis, made the case for what they famously called their 'mission to explain'.

So when Birt got his hands on the levers of BBC journalism, BBC journalists didn't know what had hit them. There wasn't a nose that Birt wasn't prepared to put out of joint, as he systematically rubbished the work of some of the BBC's most prominent reporters and correspondents, in the name of this Birtist revolution. I was not to know it at the time, but the appointment of John Birt was to be another crucial moment for my own career.

ITN's headquarters at that time was in Wells Street, in the heart of the West End, and only a two minute walk from Broadcasting House, the headquarters of the BBC. One day, early in 1988, six months after the Birt appointment, I was walking past Broadcasting House when I bumped into him leaving the building. I knew him a little from various social encounters at TV events, but he stopped and we had a brief conversation. It was small talk – I said he looked on good form, clearly enjoying his new job; he remarked how well *C4N* was going. We went our separate ways and I thought nothing more of it.

However, I must have given him an idea, because a week or so later I had a telephone call at home from his secretary. Could I go to see Mr Birt? I said that wouldn't be too difficult; when convenient, I could walk over from ITN House to Broadcasting House. She said that he didn't want to meet me at the BBC, so would I mind going to see him at his home? Intrigued, I jotted down his address, just off Wandsworth Common in south London, and arranged to go round to meet him a couple of days later.

In those days, as a result of my Biafra injuries, ITN used to provide transport for me to and from work and I had a regular driver. It sounds impressive, but the reality was that the mini-cab company concerned had secured the ITN contract on price, not on the quality of the cars. On the morning in question I directed the driver to take me to John Birt's house in Wandsworth and wait round the corner. I didn't want the Deputy Director General of the BBC to see the principal anchor of *Channel Four News* arrive in a car that more resembled a skip.

The house was an elegant Victorian villa in a quiet, leafy street. The door was opened by Birt's attractive wife Jane, who sat me down with a cup of coffee and explained that John was busy taking calls. Jane disappeared, and I could hear his voice from the back room. After a few minutes he appeared, and got straight to the point: he wanted me to be the Political Editor of the BBC. Then, before I could reply, he set out what the job would entail.

He wanted me not only to be Political Editor, the on-air authority guiding BBC viewers through the complexities of Westminster and Whitehall, but I would be the Managing Editor of the entire BBC political operation, based at Westminster. Some eighty or ninety staff would be under my control, and I would have powers of hire and fire.

I said nothing – not because I had nothing to say, but because I was speechless. But there was more – I was also to be the BBC's main political interviewer on all major occasions. All the BBC's big set-piece interviews with the leading members of the government or Opposition, whatever the programme, would be done by me. In addition, as if that wasn't enough, I would present a major hour-long Sunday lunchtime political programme on BBC1. Bloody Hell! I couldn't believe what I was hearing – and all said to me in even, unemotional language, friendly but without a smile.

When I spoke, I asked some questions. First, what of the big beasts who were already doing these jobs for the BBC? The BBC's Political Editor at the time was the widely impersonated but respected and popular Ulsterman John Cole. His popularity, however, clearly didn't extend to the Deputy Director General. John Birt's only reply to my query was to wave a hand dismissively. And what, I asked, of David Dimbleby? I had always regarded David, whom I did not know personally, as the doyen of political front-men. He, too, got the dismissive hand-wave treatment. I was left in no doubt that if I accepted this job, both John

Cole and David Dimbleby would not have a particularly rosy future at the BBC. I couldn't believe this, so for the devil of it I had another go, another shake of the tree. If I accepted, I asked, would I have the total authority of John Birt behind me in making any changes in the BBC operation at Westminster that I thought necessary, and would my word there be law? He indicated that was his intention.

I lapsed again into a shocked silence. It never occurred to me to mention the topic of money. Then he stood up, shook my hand, and asked me to think it over – but let him know soon. I walked back to the rusting minicab, waited in bemusement while it refused to start and the driver yanked at the wires under the bonnet, and eventually was noisily driven back to start a day's work at *C4N*. Throughout that day it was difficult to concentrate. Even more difficult to keep quiet about what I had spent an hour that morning doing. I have kept quiet about it publicly until now.

I had the next day off. I talked to my wife Sylvia about it, and went through with her what I recalled about the Birt offer. She was as amazed as I was, not so much that Birt should have offered me a job, but the responsibility that went with it, presumably because he calculated that I wouldn't be able to resist.

The reality is that I was flattered by the attention, but not for one moment did I did consider accepting. I was not prepared to live with the reputation of the man who elbowed out Cole and Dimbleby to do John Birt's bidding. I admired both men. They also, rightly, had many admirers and friends at the BBC and in other high places. Overnight I would have become the enemy within. But there were other huge minuses – I did not believe the amount of work expected of me was realistically do-able. To do it all conscientiously, and put in the long hours at Westminster as well, could have driven me to an early grave, or the divorce courts, or both. I had no management expertise or skills, and being seen as Birt's presence on earth I risked being eaten alive by what would be a hugely disgruntled and hostile BBC Westminster team of which I was supposed to be in charge. Some of those people, many of whom I knew very well, were past-masters in the black arts of office assassination.

This, then, was not a job I could even conceive of doing – so why had John Birt offered it to me? With hindsight I think, whether I took the job or not, I was being used by Birt to send a signal to those resisting him at the top of the BBC. Basically, I believe he was saying to them 'don't mess with me – I can do anything I like'.

Before I put pen to paper refusing this extraordinary proposition, I confided in one other person, my *C4N* Editor, Richard Tait. It was the weekend by now, and after I spoke to him on the phone he shot round to see me and we sat in the sunshine in our garden in Kent. Even though I assured him I wouldn't be tempted, and that I was enjoying myself at *C4N*, he spent several hours telling me what a mistake I would be making if indeed I took the Birt shilling.

I don't think he believed me when I said we hadn't got as far as talking money. But Richard, who had intimate knowledge of how the BBC worked, made my hair curl with lurid tales of how expert the BBC's world-class back-stabbers were at picking people to pieces, even if they had the backing of the Deputy Director General. Still, we had an enjoyable afternoon, it had cleared my mind, and after Richard had left, I penned a brief, polite note to John Birt declining his offer and explaining that I still had work to do at *C4N*. I walked to the end of the road, and dropped it in the pillar box with a certain sense of relief.

It wasn't the end of the matter. A couple of days later, I had got home from ITN after that evening's *C4N*, and in the middle of dinner the doorbell rang. It was a BBC despatch rider in his helmet and leathers, and before roaring off into the night, he handed me an envelope. Inside was a typewritten note from Ron Neil, the Deputy Director, News and Current Affairs, effectively number two to John Birt. It's as well I kept this note, because I have a feeling that, without it, some people may doubt my account of the Birt offer.

Dear Peter,

I was saddened to read your note to John. I do strongly believe the proposition that we were discussing is probably one of the most exciting in broadcast journalism today. I think you would prove an outstanding political editor of the BBC, and I think you would reap enormous enjoyment and reward from presenting your own hour long programme every week. That, together with your presence on many of the major occasions of the year, is, I believe, a journalistic offer of enormous attraction. It comes at a time when the Governors of the BBC (despite what the papers say) are dedicated to investing many more millions in our journalism. In the course of the next few weeks we will begin to build our specialist units and start our timetable for opening more foreign bureaux. We will be spending a six figure sum on enhancing the quality of the *Nine O'Clock News*. We are determined to reorganise our political reporting to gain it the respect it ought to have...

The senior management team were all excited at the prospect of you joining us to help spearhead what I think is going to be the most exciting step forward in broadcast journalism. Is the whole question of you coming to the BBC now closed in your mind, or could we profitably have a lunch in a week's time to see whether your interest in the project is still alive?

With every good wish, Ron Neil.

We never had that lunch. But inside a year we would be having a congenial dinner, under conditions of the utmost secrecy, to discuss an offer from the BBC that *was* of interest.

Although I had assured Richard Tait that I had no intention of accepting John Birt's offer, my conversation with him clearly rang alarm bells. David Nicholas, ITN's Editor, suggested that we meet, and the next weekend he and his wife came round to Sunday lunch at my home. After lunch we went for a walk in the woods at the bottom of our garden and I told David no more than I had told Richard Tait – because there was no more to tell. Later in the year, the most fanciful accounts of this walk began to appear in the press. One version, given prominence by Eddie Shah's *Today* newspaper, was headlined: 'Sissons rejects £100,000 for Sir Alastair's title.' It claimed that I was at the centre of a tug-of-war between ITN and the BBC, and had 'finally cracked' when the BBC upped the salary to 'over £100,000'. Hearing of this, the report went on, 'Wily ITN Editor David Nicholas with another senior executive whisked Sissons away for a weekend's hill walking. On the desolate moors, Nicholas revealed ITN's cunning counterbid – the heirdom to Sir Alastair's kingdom. "And money, my boy," he was told yet again, "will be no object."'

The report added that Sissons had returned from the moors with his mind made up to stay at ITN – 'He may, however, have quite a wait before he collects the offered prize: Burnet likes him not and shows no signs of planning early retirement.'

The really interesting invention in that story, from my point of view, was that I had been offered the prospect, sooner or later, of succeeding Sir Alastair Burnet as ITN's senior newscaster. Alastair was a towering figure at ITN, of enormous influence. He established the position of

ITN's senior front-man at a level that has never been matched before or since. Anyone who knew David Nicholas, who was and is one of Alastair's closest friends and admirers, would realise that David would never have promised Alastair's position to anybody. Indeed, David was the sort of editor who just didn't make any promises to anybody that changing circumstances might make it impossible to keep.

Although I was highly regarded inside ITN at the time, and others might have wondered what would happen had Sir Alastair stepped under a bus, it was never mentioned to me at any time that Sir Alastair's mantle could be mine. It was never on offer, and I never asked for it. I can also honestly say that at that stage in my career I didn't even covet it – which is more than I can say for one or two of my then colleagues. But what if? Well, you can play that game; I couldn't possibly comment.

If what I got from ITN was the nice warm feeling that comes from being wanted, Channel Four's response to the BBC's attempt to lure me away was more pragmatic. By now Channel Four had a new chief executive, Michael Grade. Grade asked to see me, and we met for a drink after the programme one night at the Waldorf Hotel at London's Aldwych. It was a very friendly chat. Grade, coming from a family of impresarios, has always struck me as being more like a theatrical agent than a manager. He enjoys spotting the talent and putting a price on it.

He obviously had done his homework about the deal I was getting from ITN and I don't think he believed me when I said that the BBC hadn't mentioned money. With immediate effect, he said, Channel Four itself would be paying me a one-off loyalty bonus. The money was very welcome, especially as it would be paid in a lump sum, and I was in the process of moving house. But also very attractive was his promise that in addition to my duties on *Channel Four News*, I would be asked to chair a number of special debates on Channel Four on topical issues. I had already presided over a small number, which had been very successful, but he had ambitious plans to build on that. He also told me that he believed that ITN would be renewing my contract immediately, on improved terms. I was more than happy with the outcome of the evening, and went home musing to myself that, impressed by the supportiveness of Grade and Tait, I would have actually settled for a lot less.

So it was back to work. And 1988 went by. *Channel Four News* went from strength to strength, and so did my reputation. One commentator wrote:

> More than any other bulletin, *Channel Four News* is identified by its presenter. Whisper it within Alastair Burnet's earshot, but the superb Peter Sissons is now the country's premier newsreader ... ITN colleagues who have sat in on the decision-making processes there confirm that it is Sissons' analysis of what makes a *Channel Four News* story that is the most astute.

The programme picked up yet another major award, for its backgrounder on the King's Cross fire at the end of the previous year. Two years previously it had won a similar award for its coverage of the disaster at Manchester Airport, when a British Airtours flight to Corfu had to abort its take-off due to an engine fire, and fifty-five people died. *Channel Four News* was getting something of a reputation for the considered way it reacted to such disaster stories, never jumping to conclusions about the causes. Indeed, I think such coverage is the hallmark of a good news programme – always asking the right questions while keeping pointless speculation to the minimum.

The Manchester disaster, incidentally, was a day I put my foot down about presenting the programme from the place the disaster occurred. I have always had doubts about the value of anchoring a news broadcast 'from the scene'. In your own studio you are in control, and have access to all the tapes and newswires. You may find yourself at a location for one story, and find it has been superseded by developments at another. You may not even be able to get close to where the incident happened, and it may be much easier for people you want to interview to get to your studio, than find their way to another strange location. In addition there are technical risks – if generators fail or lines go down, then your broadcast can fall apart.

Of course there are times and events when it is obvious you have to take the programme to the news – much of ITN's Gulf War coverage was a case in point. But I was right about the Manchester plane disaster. It happened early in the morning, and by the evening there was little or nothing to see.

Programmes that presented from the scene that evening – and they included *News at Ten* – did so in darkness against a meaningless backdrop and the constant intrusive background noise of planes taking off and

My mother in 1933, just before she was married. She was seventeen when this photo was taken by one of Liverpool's leading photographers, Fred Ash. The black and white doesn't do justice to her striking red hair.

On the beach in the Isle of Man in 1951, with Dovedale Road School's annual summer camp. I am on the far left, with John Lennon next to me, and Jimmy Tarbuck with the clenched fists.

An early picture from the Liverpool Institute High School for boys, of me (L) and Ivan Vaughan – whose place in history is secure for introducing Paul McCartney to John Lennon. Ivan was one of my closest friends.

The four Sissons brothers in September 1952. L–R: Clifford, who was eighteen; David whose third birthday it was, and who was the only son born when his father was not at sea; me, ten; and John, fifteen. Unknown to him, our parents had been told that John had only six months to live after developing thyroid cancer, a disease he eventually beat.

Acting at the Oxford Playhouse – I'm the one with the beard. The play was *A Man Has Two Fathers* by John McGrath. The male actor standing is Michael Emrys Jones, one of Oxford's finest at the time, who went on to a successful stage and TV career as Michael Elwyn.

I've made it! Just weeks after being made a reporter in early 1967, I am outside Number 10 interviewing the Leader of the Opposition and the shadow Foreign Secretary. Edward Heath and Alec Douglas-Home had been to see Prime Minister Harold Wilson to express their concern about the deteriorating situation in the Middle East. Note that I had one of those overcoats long before the BBC's legendary John Cole!

The Six-Day War in the Middle East. As the fighting died down, UN observers appeared. I interviewed one of the first to take up station overlooking the Suez Canal.

Mad dogs and Englishmen ... totally exhausted after a gruelling day driving through the Sinai, I flake out in the desert near an Israeli base.

Another piece to camera on the road through the Sinai. I was getting a taste for the life of the foreign correspondent.

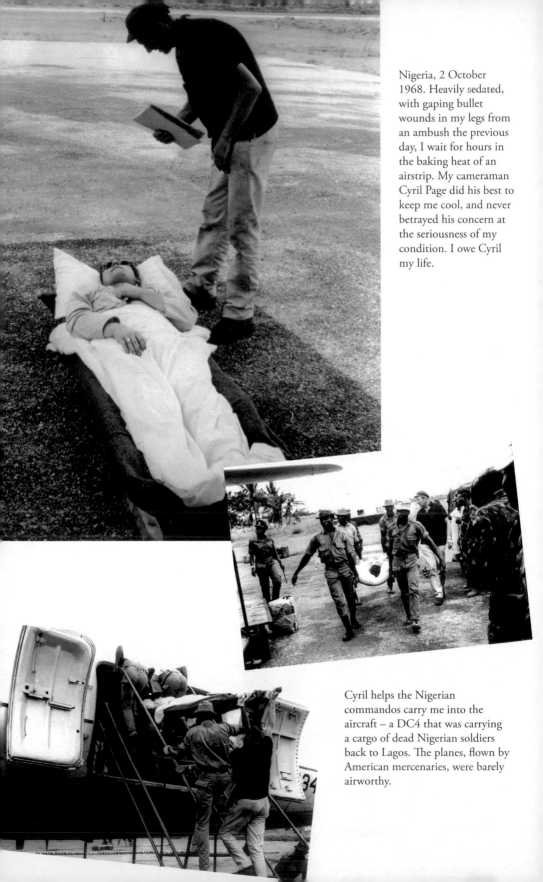

Nigeria, 2 October 1968. Heavily sedated, with gaping bullet wounds in my legs from an ambush the previous day, I wait for hours in the baking heat of an airstrip. My cameraman Cyril Page did his best to keep me cool, and never betrayed his concern at the seriousness of my condition. I owe Cyril my life.

Cyril helps the Nigerian commandos carry me into the aircraft – a DC4 that was carrying a cargo of dead Nigerian soldiers back to Lagos. The planes, flown by American mercenaries, were barely airworthy.

Just before Christmas 1968, they let me leave the Royal National Orthopaedic Hospital in central London. Sylvia and I thank the ward sister, who'd had to cope not just with me, but a procession of friends from ITN a few blocks away. I'd lost nearly three stone in weight and was wearing a calliper on my left foot.

Wedding pic, taken in Liverpool on 24 July 1965. I had been at ITN just under a year. Sylvia was about to start her first teaching job, at a junior school in north London.

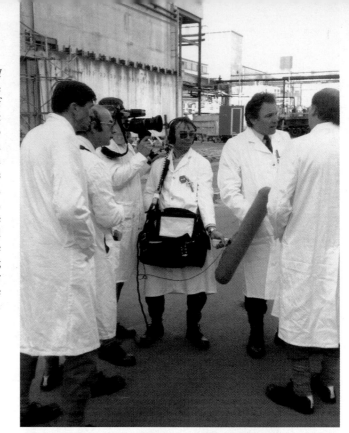

Reporting for *Channel Four News* inside Sellafield, one of Britain's most secret establishments. No reporter, let alone with a film crew, had been granted such access before. My producer, Howard Anderson, is second from the left. Note the special footwear, which we surrendered on leaving so no traces of nuclear material could be carried off the site.

Dick Gordon explains the intricacies of the space shuttle. All the landmarks in the American space programme were marked by special programmes from ITN, which were notable for the enthusiasm of the producers and the originality of the coverage.

The first *Channel Four News*. I'm flanked by Trevor McDonald and Sarah Hogg. No desks, acres of carpet, and a wall map that had Australia suspended from Indonesia by a length of wire. Everything designed to make the presenter uncomfortable and to distract the viewer. It was all scrapped within six months.

Holiday snap taken in Crete in 1988, the year before I left ITN for the BBC.
L–R: Michael, seventeen; me; Sylvia; Kate, eight; and Jonathan, fifteen.

Outside Liverpool's Anglican Cathedral with a proud wife, after being made an Honorary Fellow of Liverpool John Moores University. Not long afterwards I was awarded an Honorary Doctorate at Liverpool University. These awards from my home city I will always treasure.

Question Time 1991, my second year in the chair. Michael Heseltine, Paddy Ashdown, Julia Neuberger and Tony Blair. We'd just abandoned the first desk – a large plastic Q that developed a mind of its own under studio lights.

The 1984 miners' strike. Arthur Scargill, the NUM national president, with me in the *Channel Four News* studio. If he had any doubts about winning the dispute, he never showed them. The programme made its name with even-handed reporting.

Interviewing Margaret Thatcher early in 1989, a few weeks after I, like Salman Rushdie, had received a death threat. It was after that interview, when she took me to one side and told me of her concern, that I was finally convinced the threat had to be taken seriously.

landing. *Channel Four News* did more to enlighten the viewer by sticking to the studio.

But back to 1988. It was the year that the government, rattled by the intensifying IRA campaign of murder and bombings, made it illegal for viewers and listeners to hear the voices of IRA spokesmen and apologists. So we had the nonsense of seeing people like Gerry Adams on screen while their words were dubbed by an actor. It was the year of the Piper Alpha disaster, the year of the Soviet withdrawal from Afghanistan, the year that the elder George Bush was elected President, and, of course the year of Lockerbie.

It was also the year in which Salman Rushdie published his novel *The Satanic Verses*, a book that gave such offence to Muslims and resulted in a wave of violence and threats worldwide against publishers and bookstores. Reaction to Rushdie's book took an even more sinister turn in February the next year, when the Ayatollah Khomeini, Iran's supreme ruler, urged Muslims to kill the author. When the Fatwa became known, there was widespread outrage, and I was despatched to interview the Iranian ambassador Mr Akundzedeh Basti at their Kensington embassy. I must confess that I was as shocked as anyone that someone in the modern age could be sentenced to death for something that he had written and I let my feelings show in the interview.

Among the questions I put to him was 'Do you understand that we don't regard it as civilised to kill people for their opinions? Do you understand that people in this country fought a world war to protect themselves and others from being murdered for their beliefs and what they write?' Mr Basti was defensive, but polite. He said that the command of Ayatollah Khomeini to faithful Muslims to kill Salman Rushdie did not imply any political gesture by Iran, nor did it imply any interference in Britain's internal affairs. He repeated the mantra that it was 'the purely religious-based opinion of a religious head' and that it was 'very unfortunate' if it was going to be interpreted politically – although he must have known that it was more than political. As was widely pointed out at the time, it was at the very least an affront to international law.

I found it very hard at one point in the interview to prevent my anger showing, when Mr Basti reminded the British people that they also had their fanatics – football hooligans. Nonetheless I believe we parted on good terms, and that evening *Channel Four News* ran every frame of the twelve-minute interview.

A few days later I arrived at ITN as usual around 10.30 a.m., and before I had taken my coat off I was summoned to the office of the Editor in Chief, David Nicholas. He had with him the Editor of *Channel Four News*, Richard Tait, and a number of other men whom I had never seen before, all wearing dark suits. David came to the point: as a result of my interview with Mr Basti, it was believed that my life was now in danger. A series of four telephone calls had been received by the UPI press agency.

They'd all been made by apparently the same unidentified man, not only escalating the threat against Salman Rushdie, but now widening it to include other targets – including me. One of the strangers in the Editor's office, who identified himself as being from the Special Branch, handed me the UPI transcript of the last call, which I read:

> In the name of Allah and Iman Khomeini. So far we have regarded the British as friends of the Islamic struggle against the Shah of Iran. From now on this is not the case. From now on we have no respect for the British monarch, governments and law, and we regard them as conspirators against Islam. If Rushdie does not come from hiding we will regard the British police as conspirators in blasphemy. Geoffrey Howe [Foreign Secretary] and Douglas Hurd [Home Secretary] should remember we will do to them what we have done to Sadat of Egypt when he gave sanctuary to the criminal Shah. If Rushdie does not come out of hiding, British embassies abroad, British airlines abroad and inside the country, the pubs and disco and other government offices will become our targets. A message for Peter Sessons [sic] of Channel 4, he will pay the price for being rude and insulting to the representative of Iman Khomeini.

The caller signed off in the name of a group calling itself The Guardians of the Islamic Revolution, which was incidentally one of the first groups to claim responsibility for the Lockerbie bombing. The men in the dark suits didn't mince their words. They told me that they had reason to take the threat very seriously.

My initial reaction was to thank them for letting me know. I didn't for a moment expect, or welcome, what they said next – I and my family were to have twenty-four hour personal protection until further notice. ITN had already made the arrangements, on the recommendation of the security services, with a discreet private firm which specialised in protecting public figures from high level threats. Shortly afterwards I was introduced to the two men who were to be my and my family's constant companions for what was predicted to be at least a couple of months.

They were two youngish men, clearly ex soldiers, and they knew their business. The last big job that one of them had been assigned to was three years previously, protecting Andrew Neil, the then Editor of the *Sunday Times*. Neil took the brunt of the anger of the print unions when Rupert Murdoch sacked 6,000 printers, replaced them with members of the electricians union, and moved his titles to Wapping. Andrew, who had many death threats, needed protection for fourteen months.

So, back I went to Kent, with my two new friends. And I got a taste of things to come as we left the ITN building that evening, as one went out first and checked the car and the surrounding area before the other escorted me out. One bonus was that my transport was no longer a dodgy minicab, but a newish black Mercedes.

Sylvia and I and our young family had not long moved into a large Edwardian house on a leafy road, and the house still needed a lot of work doing to it. Word soon got out that I had been threatened, and for a few days the press were camped outside. *The Sun* wrote of me being shut away in my 'mansion' while 'a new security fence' was erected round it. Another newspaper described my house as a historic building set in its own grounds.

There were references to 'teams of workmen' making the place more secure. In fact the main addition was a new four-foot high wooden fence, to replace the old garden fence that had been blown down in the great storm. It was more chaotic inside – there was no room to accommodate my protection team, unless they were prepared to rough it in the attic. Although they had little choice, they were perfectly happy and soon set up camp at the top of the house. In many ways, they pointed out, it had advantages because the windows overlooked the surroundings on all sides. They also had interior plans of my property, presumably obtained from the local authority, and a panic number for the local police, whose superintendent arrived to make his own assessment of the vulnerability of the house. It was after that visit that we had a high-tech alarm system installed.

My security detail didn't talk much about their backgrounds, although I suspected they were former SAS men. I never asked them how they would protect me in an emergency; I presumed they didn't carry weapons, but they always carried important looking briefcases.

So, we got into a routine. In the morning, one would check the car parked in our drive, especially underneath it, and walk round the block checking other cars in the road. He and I would then leave for ITN. My other custodian stayed at home to keep an eye on my wife and kids. When we arrived at ITN my guard went everywhere with me. If I went out to lunch he would follow a few steps behind, then go ahead into the restaurant to have a look around before I could enter. He always booked himself an adjacent table, presumably for which ITN was billed. And if I went to the toilet, he would enter the gents ahead of me and gesture for me to enter only when he was satisfied that there was no one lurking there ready to pounce.

The professionalism of my two protectors was very impressive. A case in point was when we were being driven home from ITN one night. On a fast stretch of the A21, some miles from my home, the electrics on our car failed completely. I was in the back; my guard in the front passenger seat, when the dashboard instruments went black. My man told the driver to pull onto the hard shoulder, where we stopped. A few seconds later a police car pulled onto the hard shoulder fifty yards in front of us. My man got out, carrying his briefcase, at the same time as one of the officers left the police car and walked towards us.

What happened next was extraordinary. My protection officer shouted to the police officer 'Stay where you are'. The policeman stopped, and my man walked towards him. A few feet from him, although the officer was in uniform, my new friend demanded to see his police identification card. Only when this was produced did the encounter assume any sense of normality. The police were friendly and helpful, and drove us home. My man said little. I suppose he was just carrying out the drill for situations where a man in uniform may not be all he appears. After a few weeks of this, I had an important overseas appointment to keep.

I had been booked to compère a major international marketing conference in Monte Carlo. The flight was from Heathrow to Nice in an Air France Caravelle. Sylvia, I, and our protector arrived at the airport to find all the passengers having to open and identify every item of their baggage. Most were very cross, and the flight was going to be delayed for at least a couple of hours. I asked what the fuss was. Someone angrily told me that there was some kind of security scare. What he didn't know was that he was talking to the security scare. I kept quiet.

In Monaco, if anything, my man intensified the precautions. He shadowed me constantly. He searched our hotel room before Sylvia and I retired for the night. There wasn't a toilet in the hotel or the conference centre of which he didn't know the architecture. Wherever we went, even trying to escape for an evening walk, his footfall was just behind us. It was unreal.

While I was in Monaco there was one very pleasant surprise. Sir Paul Fox, at the time Managing Director of BBC Network Television and also an official of the Royal Television Society, interrupted me on the conference platform and presented me with the highest award of the RTS – The Judges' Award – for my work on *Channel Four News*. It was one of the proudest moments of my career.

On my return from Monaco, I had occasion to interview the Prime Minister, Margaret Thatcher, after a major conference at Westminster. After the interview she took me to one side, in a most maternal way. She knew all about the threat to me, she said, and assured me that everything possible was being done to keep me safe. I was quite touched.

But I was also beginning to think the security business had gone too far. And I had another reason for wanting to have some privacy – the BBC had again started putting out feelers in my direction. Through a mutual friend the message came through to me that they wanted to make me another offer. It was far more attractive to me than the minefield of a job which I had discussed with John Birt, although he had clearly endorsed this second approach. It was obvious that I couldn't talk face to face with anyone from the BBC as long as I had ITN's security detail in tow. In another week or two, however, that problem was resolved. After six weeks of being my constant companions, it was decided that they had done their job.

They packed up their stuff in the attic and left me and the family. They went with our thanks, but not before giving me a thorough briefing on how to remain vigilant against possible threats, and assuring me that the local police were still on my case. The Kent police demonstrated that several weeks later. My younger son had come home from school to find no one in and that he'd forgotten his key, so he left his schoolbag on the doorstep and went off to a friend's house. When my wife returned from shopping, she found three police cars in our drive, and concerned officers contemplating blowing open my son's bag.

Chapter 10

Seduced by Auntie

In those surreal early weeks of 1989 ITN may have saved my life from the random impetuosity of some fanatic – but I will never know. They'd certainly saved my legs, if not my life, by the speed with which they'd reacted to my Biafra misadventure. I owed them professionally as well, for the chances given to me and the trust put in me by successive editors. ITN had taken me in and taught me everything I knew about broadcasting, and the ITN way of doing things ran deep in my veins. Indeed, as far as I was concerned there was *only* the ITN way of doing things. Most of my closest friends worked there, and I was judged to have a good future ahead of me. Without ITN, I would have been nothing. So why, in the spring of 1989, in my twenty-fifth year with ITN, did I decide to walk out?

It's a question I have asked myself many times since, and which many people have asked me. In no particular order, then, I will try to explain.

It was flattering to be asked, and to be offered a big job, by an organisation with a world brand as impressive as the BBC. I was nearly forty-seven. The BBC had offered me a job once before, albeit one which might have entailed signing not so much a contract, as a suicide note. But if I turned down their second approach, which had much more appeal, would I ever be asked again? I doubted it.

If I stayed at ITN, what were my prospects? I would be expected to carry on anchoring *Channel Four News*, probably the most fulfilling job that ITN can offer any presenter. Then at some stage, when Sir Alastair Burnet retired, I might be considered for his role as ITN's senior newscaster, and presenter of special programmes. But I wasn't inclined to take that for granted, since it had never been suggested to me.

(In the event, when Alastair stepped aside at the ridiculously young age of sixty-two, it came down to a choice between Alastair Stewart and Trevor MacDonald, and Alastair Stewart walked away when he didn't get it.) Another less tangible factor was that I tended to tire of a job after six or seven years and although I was enjoying fronting *Channel Four News*, I was getting the first twinges of that seven-year itch. It had also afflicted me when I was Industrial Editor, making the move to the lunchtime news that more welcome.

Later, at the BBC, I was to find that for the ruthlessly ambitious, those determined to claw their way up the hierarchy, even three years in the same job was regarded as too long – with the next move being planned almost as soon as they'd got their feet under the latest desk. Anyway, those weren't my motives: quite simply I had begun to get itchy feet and deep inside me I knew I needed a new challenge. The BBC spelled that challenge out for me. But I had absolutely no idea what might eventually be on offer if I stayed at ITN. Another thought kept nagging at me: did I want to finish my career at ITN in twenty years' time, without ever knowing whether I could have succeeded at the BBC? Could I cut it at the world's greatest name in broadcast journalism?

I know that many people will read all that and dismiss it as sanctimonious self-justification. Sissons, they will say, was offered a shed-load of money and that was that. It's not true. ITN and Channel Four offered to more than match every penny on offer from the BBC. It was a career move. I believed at the time it was the right one for me, but I'd be lying if I said I never had doubts – it depends what day you caught me on, but those days were few and far between.

The second approach from the BBC came through a *Channel Four News* colleague who had also been poached by the BBC, in a senior production role. We had kept in touch, and he asked me casually over lunch one day – and a commemorative bottle of Chateau Machiavelli – if I would be interested in joining BBC News. And not just BBC News. What made me sit up was the possibility of combining news presentation with the chairmanship of *Question Time*, the mother of all studio debate programmes.

Now that *did* appeal. I had watched *Question Time* for many years. I was a fan of the format, and of Robin Day. Indeed, to a large extent Robin had become the format. At his best, he was quite superb, driving the programme along, emboldening the audience and turning *Question*

Time into the programme you had to crack before you could consider yourself a serious politician. But in the last few years I had watched a growing number of editions of *Question Time* that had lost their edge, and sometimes Robin looked as if some of the old zest had deserted him.

I wasn't to know, but there were two reasons for that: tensions with his editor whose management of the programme, especially the choice of panellists, wasn't always to his liking; and Robin's vulnerability to ill health, not improved by chronic chestiness and a liking for large cigars. The message conveyed to me was that Robin was almost certainly doing his last series of *Question Time*, and the next one was mine for the taking. I told my friend who was acting as BBC emissary to take back the message that I would regard succeeding Robin Day in the *Question Time* chair as a proposition I could not turn down. But I also said something that I was to repeat ad nauseam in negotiations over the following weeks – if they were going to sack Robin Day to make room for me, they could forget it. Only when he had decided to go of his own volition would I start talking about it.

The message was duly relayed to TV Centre.

A short time later I had a phone call at home from John Birt's deputy, Ron Neil (he who had pleaded with me to reconsider when I turned down the political editorship). I didn't know Ron, but I knew of his reputation – in the BBC's world of grey men and earnest women, he was one apart. He was, as they say, a fully paid up member of the human race, in his case the Scottish race: popular, widely liked and respected, tough and realistic, and with an engaging sense of humour. Ron suggested we meet, and named the ideal place – one of the best restaurants in Kent, Honor's Mill in Edenbridge. He had clearly done his homework – it was not too far from my home, and it was the sort of discreet place where we were unlikely to attract attention.

We duly met there one cold winter's night and I liked him at once. There was a certain furtiveness about our meeting, with us both tucked up in a quiet corner. Every time the door opened we wondered if the restaurant might by ill chance be the country watering hole of one or two of Fleet Street's finest who might see us and put two and two together. At that first meeting we talked only in generalities and gossiped thoroughly indiscreetly about the many acquaintances we had in common. The meal was almost as good as the company. After the final course Ron suggested we round things off with a nice dessert wine, and as the waiter poured out two small glasses of Beaumes de Venise, Ron grabbed the waiter's hand and rasped 'Just leave the bottle'. By then I don't think either of us could remember if we'd made any progress in determining whether I would join the BBC, but as we parted Ron made it clear that we would soon meet again, and that next time there would be a third at the table – Tony Hall.

It was only then that I learned that Tony would shortly be taking over from Ron Neil at the top of the news directorship. Ron was moving on to be Head of Regional Broadcasting.

The morning after my dinner with Ron Neil, although I had a sore head, I was still able to think straight – with the assistance of some barely legible notes I had taken. But I needed impartial advice from someone who knew me, knew the BBC and ITN, who could be relied upon to be discreet and whom I could trust implicitly. I turned to the veteran broadcaster and writer Robert Kee, who had been the first presenter of ITN's lunchtime news. Robert listened to my account of what appeared to be on offer from the BBC and unhesitatingly said that I should go for it. Robert Kee had never flinched from a challenge. Some you win – he escaped, after a number of attempts, from a Nazi prisoner-of-war camp; some you lose – his involvement with 'the famous five' who launched TV-am was a disaster. But Robert thought that it was time for me to see what I could do on a different stage to ITN.

A few days later I met the BBC's Ron Neil again, at the same place, this time with Tony Hall. But Ron was still in the driving seat, and this meeting although very congenial was much more businesslike. Ron laid out the basic proposition: they wanted me to take over the chairmanship of *Question Time* from Robin Day, and combine that with anchoring the *Nine O'Clock News*, which I would share with one of the two incumbents, Michael Buerk. The other *Nine O'Clock News* presenter, Martyn Lewis, would be moved to the *Six O'Clock News*. I had two comments – I needed from them an absolute assurance that they had Robin's voluntary resignation, which they said they had received in writing. And I wondered whether it might not be better for me to start newscasting for the BBC on the *Six O'Clock News*. I thought that it would initially be a better fit with *Question Time*, which it probably wasn't. But Ron Neil had been the founding Editor of the extended half-hour *Six*, a programme to which he had a special link, and I think my suggestion appealed to him. I also think that at the back of my mind was the thought that I didn't want to be seen to be elbowing out Martyn Lewis as well as Robin Day. They agreed to all that, and then we talked money.

On the back of a menu, Ron sketched the basis of a contract – number of days on the news, number of editions of *Question Time*. Then he wrote down half a million pounds over three years – the equivalent, at the time of writing, of well over a million.

It was twice what I was getting at *Channel Four News*, and a huge amount of money for anyone working in news at that time. The then Director General of the BBC, Michael Checkland, was paid an annual salary of about £100,000. Since then, the growth of some BBC salaries makes half a million, even a million, over three years seem positively puny. But in 1989 it made me the highest paid newscaster in the country. There was little more to be said. Provided other aspects of the contract were settled satisfactorily, I gave them my word that I would join the BBC, and went home to tell my wife.

Sylvia's reaction was totally unexpected. She was not pleased. She thought I was mad to consider leaving ITN, where she had as many friends as I did. She thought I would not be anywhere near as happy at the BBC, and she remembered vividly Richard Tait's chilling warning – given with all the authority of a former senior BBC insider – that I would go nowhere at the BBC once they had taken me from ITN, which was the main object of the exercise. But Sylvia knew that my heart was by now set on making the change, and that it was something to which I had given a great deal of thought.

From that point on she backed me. It was only during those spasmodic rocky periods that were to come in my later years at the BBC that she would gently suggest that it might have been a big mistake to go there in the first place. That sentiment sounded fine, except when I considered what had happened at ITN not long after I left. By all accounts, for some time it became a very unhappy place. Placed under huge pressure by its board, and reeling from the discovery of a big financial shortfall, ITN adopted a tough policy of retrenchment which involved hundreds of redundancies. Two years after I left, the ITN board appointed a new chief executive, Bob Phillis. With the departure of Sir David Nicholas, who'd been knighted two years earlier, the ITN that I knew and loved became a totally different place. Phillis halved the staff in two years, and his legacy, when he eventually moved on to be John Birt's deputy at the

BBC, may have been an organisation on a sounder financial footing, but there was much bitterness among the hundreds who were shown the door after many years of loyal service.

I was in no doubt that I was one of those fortunate to have been there for ITN's best days. Indeed, during the twenty years that I was to spend at the BBC, whenever I met former ITN colleagues, most thought I had made the right move at just the right time. If the old ITN had still been in existence during my years at the BBC, then there were times when I might just have been persuaded that it was a mistake to leave. But it wasn't. Along with most news organisations in the world, the accountants now called the shots and cut the journalistic cloth accordingly. On the few occasions that I subsequently entered the huge new ITN headquarters in the Gray's Inn Road – the construction of which nearly bankrupted ITN – I felt like a total stranger. The news family had become the news factory.

There was one more social meeting with senior BBC people after I had given them my word to join. Under conditions of great secrecy, we met at a country hotel in Sussex and it was at that meeting that I was pressed to set the date on which I would tell ITN that I was leaving. Before doing that, however, I took the precaution of putting the detailed construction of my new contract into the hands of one of Britain's best media lawyers. It was money well spent and the provisions he insisted on, together with the modifications to the existing BBC template for such contracts, stood me in good stead for many years.

I also consulted him about my contractual situation with ITN. I was only a year into a three contract with ITN, but I explained that the principal reason I was happy to bind myself to ITN was as a result of that meeting a year previously with Michael Grade, the boss of Channel Four. It was his assurance that I would anchor a string of special Channel Four debates if I stayed with *Channel Four News* that made me inclined to renew my commitment to the maker of *Channel Four News*, ITN. My legal advice was that without the Channel Four programmes the ITN contract was weakened, and I could be justified in breaking it.

My lawyer made a very interesting point: if a broadcasting company promises a certain amount of programme exposure to a 'contract artiste' it is not enough for them to say 'we're sorry, we haven't been able to make the programmes – but we have paid you for them, so we are not in breach of contract'. For a performer, exposure is everything – the money without the exposure is, it has been argued successfully at law, not the whole deal.

But putting aside such legal niceties, the expert advice I received was that these sort of contracts are usually seen by both sides as principally a protection for the employee. In broadcasting, if individuals are unhappy and ask to be released from a contract, their employers usually let him go. I believe that was the case when ITN poached Julia Somerville from the BBC two years previously. The practice was summed up by Geoffrey Levy in the *Daily Mail*: 'When their mind is made up beyond recall, they are usually allowed to go in moderate grace, rather than shackle them unhappily to the general debilitation of a department or an organisation.' Moderate grace? Some hope!

While all this was going on, I was asked by ITV to do the commentary for the network on the occasion of the first Hillsborough Memorial Service at Liverpool's Anglican Cathedral. On 15 April 1989, ninety-six Liverpool fans attending the FA Cup semi-final against Nottingham Forest had been killed in a deadly crush at the Hillsborough stadium outside Sheffield. It was one of the most shocking disasters in sport, and a terrible tragedy for Liverpool which has left deep and searing emotional scars to this day – scars made worse by a widespread feeling that the full truth about the disaster, and whether so many had to die, has never been told.

On that Saturday there had been no *Channel Four News*, since we were only a five-day operation, but our broadcasts the next week began to report the city's grief and to ask searching questions, many of which after more than twenty years are still to be answered. A fortnight after the nightmare, on Saturday 29 April, the bereaved and the survivors came together with many other stunned and grieving Liverpudlians in the city's great Anglican Cathedral. I suppose I was the obvious person to describe the occasion for ITV – I had been born and bred in the city, been a regular at Anfield with my brother Cliff, and had gone to school in the shadow of the great sandstone cathedral where the city was now coming together to mourn. The BBC's commentator was Desmond Lynam, then the host of *Match of the Day* – reflecting I suppose the

BBC's judgement at the time that this was primarily a sporting tragedy, a view shared by nobody in Liverpool.

Early on the morning of the service I met the Bishop of Liverpool David Sheppard for breakfast at the mobile food wagon that the broadcasters had set up for their crews in the Cathedral grounds. We talked through the order of service, and how he would conduct it with the Catholic Archbishop, Derek Warlock. The Archbishop of York and Cardinal Basil Hume would also be there, as would the Prime Minister Margaret Thatcher and the Leader of the Opposition, Neil Kinnock. But David Sheppard knew that the most important people attending were those whose lives were going to be changed forever by Hillsborough. He appreciated instinctively that Hillsborough was a wound that time alone would not heal. This was a bishop showing why he was a bishop, at a time when his flock needed him more than ever before.

That day was the most moving and emotional that I have ever experienced. Any script that I might have prepared in advance – I had armed myself only with some notes – would have been totally inadequate. Indeed, from the moment that I installed myself in my commentary position, high up overlooking the nave, I simply found there were moments of such emotional intensity that I could not speak. With hindsight, that was probably exactly the right thing to do, as any words would have been intrusive. In particular, there was one moment in that service that reduced me, and I suspect everyone else in that cathedral, to tears.

It was the breaking of a long silence in which you could hear the dropping of a pin, by the unaccompanied voice of a lone boy treble singing the Kop's adopted anthem 'You'll never walk alone'. To this day it makes me catch my breath just to think of it.

Twenty years later I had no hesitation in accepting when the Home Secretary Alan Johnson asked me to be a member of a new body, the Hillsborough Independent Panel, under the chairmanship of David Sheppard's successor as Bishop of Liverpool, James Jones. The Panel was not a new inquiry, but a response to the continued sense of injustice of the Hillsborough families, both of the bereaved and of the many traumatised survivors. The task, which is still in hand at the time of writing, is to get into the public domain every last scrap of information about what happened on that dreadful day. There are hundreds of boxes of documents and reports written at the time by the police and other emergency services, by medical teams and other officials, which have never seen the light of day. The first members of the public to see them will be the families who were rightly convinced they have never been allowed to see the complete picture. I did not bring to the task the expert knowledge of others on the panel, but I did bring the commitment of a Liverpudlian who will never forget those terrible weeks in 1989.

That first Hillsborough memorial service put into perspective the other things that were happening in my life, and for a time completely eclipsed my thoughts about the BBC move. But I had given my word that I would join the BBC, and they gently but firmly insisted on a date. They had even prepared a press statement, which they would release once they heard from me that I had resigned from ITN. So it was that one morning in May, after *Channel Four News*'s editorial conference, I walked up a couple of flights of stairs in ITN house, and asked to see ITN's Editor, David Nicholas.

David was by then a close friend as well as a mentor. Two years previously he had asked if my seven-year-old daughter Kate would be the only bridesmaid at the wedding of his only daughter Helen. In a profession like broadcast journalism you don't get much closer than that. It had been a quite beautiful day, Sir Alastair Burnet read the lesson, and the casual observer might have been forgiven for thinking that we were all part of the same big family.

I thought I knew David as well as most, and as I waited to see him that morning I rehearsed what I was going to say. I expected him to be surprised, even saddened, but to understand my reasons for leaving and the attractiveness of the BBC offer. I had given ITN the best years of my life and I thought that he would say that he wouldn't stand in my way. There might then, I thought, be a friendly, maybe even tearful handshake as David wished me well in the new phase of my career. I couldn't have been more wrong. I had misjudged the man totally.

He went ballistic. Talk about shaking my hand – he very nearly shook me by the throat. I have never seen David more angry, before or since. It was cold anger, spat out. There was anger at me, but he reserved his real invective – and David has one of the most impressive vocabularies in that regard – for the BBC. What he said about the BBC in those few moments can't, as the saying goes, be printed in a family newspaper. I sat there speechless – because there was nothing to talk about. This wasn't how it was supposed to be. Shell-shocked, I went back to the Channel Four newsroom and tried to get on with my day's work.

Less than an hour later I was summoned back to David Nicholas' office. Also there was Richard Tait, my Editor on *Channel Four News*. David, who had come down from the ceiling, did most of the talking. He said that there was no question of ITN accepting my resignation. They both reminded me that I was under contract to ITN and urged me to reconsider. If it was a question of money, they were sure they could do something about that. David then asked me what the BBC were offering, and I told him. He exhaled through clenched teeth. I was physically shaken by the reaction I was seeing, but my resolve was not. I went back to my desk, and tried, not very successfully, to concentrate on that evening's broadcast. As I sat there, a secretary came into the room and pinned a management memo on the notice board.

The memo informed everyone that I had been approached by the BBC, that ITN was taking advice about the matter and made it abundantly clear that they were not prepared to let me go. It was effectively a declaration of war on the BBC, and it suddenly hit me that this wasn't going to be easy. I was right. In the middle of the afternoon I was asked to walk round to the headquarters of Channel Four in nearby Charlotte Street, to see Michael Grade. From Michael, I got the 'good cop' treatment. He was sympathetic, and he dropped into his theatrical agent mode. He put the equivalent of all the BBC money on the table, and more. I dug in my heels and went back to ITN to front that night's edition of *Channel Four News*, but when I left the building after the broadcast, I had become the news. Reporters and photographers were waiting on the steps outside, and I had to struggle to get to my waiting car. I'd often seen or indeed been part of, a press pack in full cry. I was shocked at how destabilising it is to be on the receiving end.

The next day Michael Grade sent for me again. With him was Liz Forgan, our commissioning editor at Channel Four. Michael's attitude had changed: Channel Four would join ITN in legal action to prevent me leaving. It was hardball, or at least it was from Michael. Liz said little, and I felt very guilty about sitting in the same room as her at that moment. No one had been more supportive of me during the evolution of *Channel Four News*, and I still treasure some of the handwritten notes she sent me. But Michael Grade was now in overdrive, and after I left he put out a statement saying 'Peter is not leaving. He's under contract to ITN. The contract won't be broken.' He added, 'It is up to the BBC how they spend the licence payers' money. But I think it is very dangerous for them to offer such large sums.' The BBC replied with a statement – more of an understatement really – of their own: 'Peter has agreed to join us, but he hasn't yet negotiated his release from ITN.' Too bloody right I hadn't.

While I believe that David Nicholas's anger was genuine, I believe there was more than a touch with Michael Grade of the synthetic affront of the poacher turned gamekeeper. Two and a half years previously, when he was Director of Programmes at the BBC, he himself had staged a raid on ITN's talent – luring away Martyn Lewis and Pamela Armstrong. At the time it was speculated that he'd also made offers for me and for Leonard Parkin, which was not true. On that occasion David Nicholas was rueful, but more relaxed, telling the *Sunday Express*: 'It's a new twist on the old theme – if you can't beat 'em, buy them!' He went on: 'I find it staggering that out of 30,000 employees the BBC can't rustle up any talent of their own.' But he warned: 'It's a fact that quite often talent, like fine wine, does not travel very well. Whether it will survive the four miles from here to BBC Television Centre remains to be seen.' Also at that time Alastair Burnet – who was never a fan of Martyn Lewis – dropped his usual courtly demeanour to put in the stiletto: 'There are only two television news teams – ITN and ITN Reserves. And now ITN Reserves are going to play for the BBC.'

When the *Sunday Times* examined that poaching spat between ITN and the BBC back in 1986, it concluded that 'though the BBC is very good at luring talent, it is also very good at burying it'. It was exactly the warning given to me at various times by both the Editor of ITN and the Editor of *Channel Four News*. But when it came to my turn to be poached, my mind was made up and at no time during the acrimony of the ensuing months, as ITN and the BBC exchanged blows over my defection, did I feel that I had done the wrong thing.

For the next four or five days the press ran with the story, and I came to work each day trying to concentrate on doing a professional job, which became more and more difficult. It had its lighter moments – pre-recording a 'down the line' interview with the Foreign Secretary, Sir Geoffrey Howe, I enquired if he could hear me OK. He replied that he could hear my 'very expensive mellifluous voice' very well. I was more famous than I had ever been, but for all the wrong reasons.

I made one final attempt to mend my fences with ITN. Sylvia and I went round to have a drink with David Nicholas and his wife Juliet at their home in Blackheath. Despite the cloud over our relationship, we all had a convivial – and at times emotional – evening over a bottle or two of cold white wine, and went through it all again. Then I asked the big question – why not just let me go, on friendly terms? The wine had not affected David's resolve: I had a legal fight on my hands.

A day or two later, becoming more and more stressed, I had privately made up my mind that things couldn't go on in this way. I signed off as usual at the end of *Channel Four News*, told no one but my Editor that it was my last broadcast for ITN, went home and never came back. One or two colleagues telephoned to wish me luck. One in particular tried to talk me out of it in person: Garron Baines, our news editor, who was particularly upset. Garron had been in China when my news broke, and on his arrival at Heathrow came straight round to my home in his ITN minicab. For most of the day and into the evening he begged me to reconsider. He got so carried away that he forgot about the minicab waiting outside. An hour's waiting time was usually frowned on at ITN, but nine hours was one for the record books.

For most of the spring and summer of 1989 I sat at home while the BBC and ITN lawyers slugged it out. ITN served the BBC with a writ alleging all sorts of things, including enticement to break a contract, and seeking huge damages. Most unusually, I received a personal writ accusing me of damaging *Channel Four News* by leaving it in violation of the terms of my contract with ITN. I and my legal team sought counsel's opinion, and went to see a top QC. I thought I had a good case, citing the failure of Channel Four to come up with the special programmes it had promised me, and which made signing my new contract with ITN more attractive. The QC, as they do, counselled caution, advising that I had probably a 50 per cent chance of success with this argument. Eventually a date was set for a hearing before a judge.

As the days ticked by it looked increasingly likely that I would have to brace myself for the prospect of being just another minor celebrity causing a media ripple as I arrived at the Royal Courts of Justice in the Strand. But at the eleventh hour I was told that the lawyers had reached an out-of-court settlement. ITN would let me go and I could start

Question Time as planned in September. But I could not work for BBC News until November, a full seven months after I walked out of ITN.

The BBC also agreed to pay a transfer fee of £40,000, all ITN's costs, and all of mine. There was some comment in the press about the transfer fee. There'd never been one before in circumstances like this, nor has there been one since. Some reports said that Michael Grade had demanded a £200,000 transfer fee for agreeing to release me to his old employers. If he did, then, given his record poaching for the BBC, I'd be surprised if he was able to do it with a straight face. But of course there was another factor in play here, Grade's deep animosity at the time to John Birt, who once had to take orders from him at London Weekend Television, and had subsequently pipped him to the Director Generalship of the BBC. None of this was of concern to me at the time. I just had a sense of total relief that we weren't all going to end up in front of a judge.

During those stressful months I had no official contact with ITN. It was a matter of great sadness to me that I had never had an opportunity to say goodbye to everyone; after all, ITN were hardly going to push the boat out with a leaving party. So I had a party of my own. Towards the end of the summer, on one glorious Sunday, many of my longest and closest friends from ITN gathered in our garden and much food and drink was consumed until the shadows lengthened. I was among friends, and still count most of those people among my friends today. Only one friend from ITN management came, but at that stage with feelings still raw I didn't feel that I could invite many others.

The one who did come made it plain to me as soon as he got a glass of pink champagne in his hand that he thought ITN had greatly overreacted to my departure, and that I deserved better from them. I was grateful for that lone declaration of support from inside the ITN hierarchy. However, it wasn't many months before the wounds began to heal, and I am glad to say that all the old friendships were fully restored within a year or two. Later, Sir David Nicholas, as he had become, told me that none of his reaction was aimed at me personally; he was doing what he saw as his duty to protect ITN, and I accept that. I still don't think he's ever forgiven the BBC, or ever will, but for the rest of my career he continued to send to me the occasional note of congratulation or encouragement, as he did when I worked for him.

While I was in that no-man's land during the hostilities between

ITN and the BBC, I realised just how much I missed being at work in a newsroom, especially when big stories were running. I had lived off adrenalin for so long, now here I was lazing around and getting depressed at being out of the game. The BBC tried to cheer me up – John Birt himself and his wife Jane took Sylvia and me out for a quiet congenial dinner. I wouldn't have been human if I didn't begin to wonder whether the BBC's enthusiasm for recruiting me might have diminished. John put my mind at ease.

So the summer slipped by into autumn, and my mind turned to how I was going to justify the BBC's big investment in me. I never doubted my own ability. I had got to the top at ITN because I could hold my own with some of the best broadcast journalists that television has produced. Two things always irritated me: being asked by strangers if I'd ever been in journalism, and being sneered at by others in the public eye who insisted that I was only an autocue reader – an occupation that needed no ability at all.

However, the great unknown for me at that stage was the mighty BBC itself. What sort of reception awaited me there? Would there be resentment at the amount I was being paid, especially as they were in the middle of a prolonged dispute over pay with their 28,000 staff, whose union representatives were calling my expensive contract 'an absolute disgrace'? Whom would I be able to trust? Who would watch my back? It wasn't the news that was my principal concern – I could do that standing on my head. It was the day I had to step into the shoes of a legend. It was my appointment with *Question Time*.

Chapter 11

Question Time

The interior of the building was deserted and dark, and it took my eyes a few seconds to get accustomed to the gloom. I was standing in a small but rather nondescript modern theatre – except that this one was dressed in all the familiar clutter of a TV studio – cameras, microphone booms, cables, autocue. I'd entered by a side door, and the stage was masked from me by a screen of black curtain. I pushed past it, and there on a modest rostrum was a plain, wooden, oval table, about eight feet long, with five black leather chairs arranged behind it. I'd seen it so many times sitting at home. But here it was, the most famous table on television, the *Question Time* table. I slowly walked over and stood before it, taking it in. If all the famous people who had sat round it had signed it, it would be worth a place in the British Museum. As I ran my fingers along it, the thought hit me. What on earth had I taken on? This arena was a national institution, and for ten years it had been chaired *by* a national institution.

Until this moment I had entertained no doubts that I could fill Sir Robin's shoes. I hadn't failed at any job I'd undertaken in my TV career so far. But suddenly it hit me – this could be a lot more difficult than any of them. Gingerly, I walked round the back of the table and pushed back the centre chair – his chair – and lowered myself into it. For the next four and a half years my occupancy of that chair was to dominate my life, provoke great controversy and involve a significant amount of personal stress. But I never regretted accepting the challenge and am proud of the popularity and status that the programme continued to enjoy under my chairmanship. When I finally left after 150 editions to concentrate again full-time on my core job in the newsroom, the programme was in good shape and watched by more people than ever.

At the outset I suspected it wouldn't be easy, and it wasn't. But the main reason for that was one I hadn't anticipated. During my tenure of the *Question Time* chair, the team producing the programme was constantly being changed. Robin Day had one editor for ten years – I had three editors in four years. The first two of mine were on the staff of the BBC, producing the programme 'in house'. Each left the editorship unwillingly after a year with me, but for totally different reasons. Each time there was an upheaval – the biggest of all coming at the end of my second year when the programme was put out to tender among independent producers and everything was changed again. Whenever a new production team takes over in television, they like to put their own mark on it, or 'freshen things up' to use a favourite phrase. For me, it has always been important to have a settled, loyal and trusted team around me, so that I can concentrate on the 'on screen' work and not have to be concerned with the internal politics of a programme. But for the whole of my time on *Question Time* there was an internal issue of some kind that was very destabilising; indeed there were few times that I, and other members of the team, didn't feel a lot of pressure.

When any of these distractions leaked into the public domain it was usually because someone who was, or had been, close to the programme had an agenda to promote. But as the public face of *Question Time* it was invariably my future that became a source of speculation and rumour.

In all candour, I never got used to it, but I learned to live with it. It was the price of trying to fill the shoes of a legend.

Question Time was ten years old when I took over. It had begun, back in 1979, almost by accident. There had been a temporary gap in the schedules, Current Affairs was asked to fill it and Robin Day had nothing to do – indeed, in the BBC it was felt that his great days were behind him, at the age of only fifty-six. Despite all the taunts in the BBC about it being *Any Questions* with pictures, Robin turned the programme into a BBC flagship. He was made for it and *Question Time* was a superb vehicle for him. From the beginning he had a strong editor, with whom he didn't always get on. She was Barbara Maxwell, who'd originally joined the BBC as a secretary, but was soon a current affairs producer. *Question Time* was her first editorship and she ruled the roost. She was also not averse to using her considerable feminine charms – she was a striking redhead – to get her own way. She had a wide circle of contacts in political circles and Robin used to refer to her mockingly as 'the flame-haired temptress'.

When I was secretly negotiating with the BBC, prior to leaving *Channel Four News*, our main topic of conversation was not Maxwell, but Robin Day. I made it plain that under no circumstances was I going to be the person who pushed Robin aside. Only when he had decided for himself that he would leave *Question Time*, and the BBC had his intentions in writing, would I be prepared to talk about taking his job. To the best of my knowledge this is exactly what occurred. Sometime later there was a suggestion that Robin changed his mind. He may well have been egged on by his friends in the Garrick Club to reconsider, but if he did, his initial wishes had already been acted upon and it was too late. In any event, there was no mention of such a change of heart in a very cordial letter he wrote to me five weeks before my debut.

Those hoping that Robin could have gone on for ever chairing *Question Time* also overlook the fact that he was not in the best of health. During his ten years with the programme he missed a number of editions because he was unwell. At various times, Sue Lawley, Robert Mackenzie, Bernard Levin, Ludovic Kennedy and Donald McCormick deputised for him. Indeed, the year before I entered the frame, the *Daily Express* put my name forward as a possible replacement for him, its columnist observing 'that Robin appears to be fighting against the natural mellowing process of his advancing avuncular years'. Under a headline, 'Has Sir Robin had his day?' the *Express* remarked favourably on my qualities as an interviewer and concluded that although I didn't have Sir Robin's bow tie and mischievous demeanour, 'this inquisitor deserves a bigger stage'. Although the *Express* was pressing the case for me, the real significance of the article was its perception that Robin may have been struggling to maintain the seemingly effortless mastery of the programme that had made him such a legend. I think the truth had nothing to do with Robin being over the hill or losing his touch. It was quite simply that coping with a big, networked and widely watched programme like *Question Time* is made much more difficult if the presenter is not on top physical form. And Robin no longer was.

Throughout my career, I count myself lucky never to have missed any programme, *Question Time* included, because I was unwell – except at ITN when I was recovering from gunshot wounds. My successor on

Question Time, David Dimbleby, has to date missed only one programme, as a result of tangling with a bullock on his farm – an incident that added John Humphrys' name to the list of *Question Time* stand-ins.

Robin's health, however, never came up in my discussions with the BBC, and I have no idea whether or not they considered it an issue. My total preoccupation was ensuring that I knew as much as possible about his intentions before I signed on the dotted line. But in doing so I took my eye off the other figure on the programme with whom I would have to work.

I was not privy to the saga that was Robin's professional relationship with Barbara Maxwell, but I know it was often stormy. Mine wasn't stormy. There were no stand-up rows. There was just no kind of trusting relationship or mutual respect. It began badly. The first that Barbara knew that I was going to be Robin Day's successor, and her new presenter, was when she read it in the newspapers. In typical BBC fashion, she was not formally consulted, indeed she was deliberately kept in the dark. Her favoured candidate was Brian Redhead, who was at the height of his considerable powers anchoring the *Today* programme on Radio Four. With hindsight, it is impossible not to sympathise with the way she reacted – she was furious, and rightly so. But at the time I was unaware of how she had been treated and how deep her resentment ran. I was soon to find out.

The name of Barbara Maxwell only came up when I was about to put pen to paper with the BBC. The Head of Current Affairs, Samir Shah, asked me if I wanted to start on *Question Time* with a new editor. I was in a strong position and at that moment I was left in no doubt that they would have removed Barbara had I expressed a wish for a totally fresh team. I could think of no good reason, nor did they give me one, why the woman who had presided over ten years of success with the programme should be replaced, and said I would be happy to work with her. If those that knew her well thought I was making a mistake, they kept their thoughts to themselves, and let me – who didn't know her at all – get on with it.

Soon after, I met her for the first time, at her invitation, at a Soho restaurant. She was superficially pleasant to me, but I detected great bitterness over the way the BBC had treated her, and her total contempt for the people in charge of News and Current Affairs. I didn't tell her that I had ensured she kept her job. I also had a glimpse of what Robin had meant by the 'flame-haired temptress' remark, and realised how much she appeared to enjoy the sobriquet, and the status and influence among opinion-formers that the editorship of the programme gave her. We parted to go off on our summer holidays, knowing the real test would be in September, when the programme returned to the screen. What I didn't know was, following our lunch, Barbara Maxwell's long list of people held in contempt now included me.

A few weeks later, I had a letter from Robin Day. At the top of the first of five handwritten pages, next to the date, 9 August 1989, and his address in Great Peter Street, a stone's throw from the Palace of Westminster, he had written in big capital letters CONFIDENTIAL. YOUR EYES ONLY. Until now I have kept that letter private, but I think it is an important insight into how even the great presenters sometimes struggle to impose themselves on a programme, and have to fight off efforts to teach them their job. Even in his memoir *Grand Inquisitor* there's nothing quite as frank as Robin Day's advice to me. I make no apology for publishing parts of it now, twenty years on. I don't think Robin would have objected.

He came straight to the point: 'Some advice for you' he wrote, then added in brackets 'strictly between us, and not to be mentioned to she who thinks she should be obeyed'.

He then set out seven numbered paragraphs.

1: Insist on your having the right to be consulted as to the panellists. If that right has not been spelt out – demand it. I tried to get it, but too late. In the end I didn't fight, because of other pre-occupations Even though they may decline to give you that right, the fact of you having demanded it will show them that you are not to be ignored.

2: The only strain in QT comes when there are inexperienced inadequate panellists who have never proved themselves as debaters in the public arena – such as B Maxwell's 'discoveries'.

3: Do not stand for frequent instructions from her in your earpiece. Show your distaste for this from the outset. You must be left to conduct the programme. QT cannot be well chaired by a committee of two.

4: Do not let her force you to have more than four subjects. The net programme time for panel-talk is about fifty-five minutes. If you have five subjects that means only eleven minutes on average for each. (That's a paltry time for four panellists and audience participation.) Or it means one or two subjects getting ten minutes or less, which is trivialisation run mad.

5: Do not obey BM when she says (on your bloody earpiece as she will) – 'Move on now'. You are handling the argument. You know, unlike her, whether you have another point to cover, another contribution to include. Retain control. If she rabbits on 'Move on now', take the ear-piece out. I did frequently. This always had a salutary effect, for a time.

6: Do not compose long intros. The problem is that witty jokes are OK when each of the panellists can be made fun of, but when you have people about whom there is no conceivable humorous reference to be made, the introduction is liable to look unbalanced, or else contrived jokes have to be created about the dull panellists – (as happens on Any Questions with Jonathan Dimbleby, whose intros are embarrassing).

7: Do it your own way. Forget the Day prototype. You have your own style, your own wit and your own personality. I remember the brilliantly witty speech you made at a Labour Party Conference on behalf of the hacks. So it's all yours. Don't stand for any nonsense from B. Maxwell. Have any arguments at the start. You are in a very strong position. (When QT started in '79, I was 'finished', thought 'very difficult' and was in a weak position.) And when having your arguments, go above B. Maxwell to Hargreaves (the new head of Current Affairs) or Birt, if necessary.

You'll be brilliant.

Yours ever, Robin.

Well, I can't say I wasn't warned! The trouble is, the warning came a couple of months too late. The next twelve months were to be a crash course in all the dark arts of surviving at the BBC.

The principal difference I was to find, after so many years being an insider at ITN, was that I had become an outsider at the BBC. At ITN I was always on the staff, but when I joined the BBC, like many presenters, I became self-employed, which had certain tax advantages. I was not allowed to broadcast for anyone else, but a variety of corporate and other non-broadcast work that came along established my freelance status with the Inland Revenue, and it was never questioned. Indeed, during an average year, I might work for a dozen or more other organisations. I make the point because it was another of those things that set me apart from BBC staffers, many of whom had known no other employer. And it wasn't just me. Other presenters whom I knew well, and who had been poached by the BBC, invariably experienced the feeling of never quite being part of the culture. There was also a certain amount of resentment at the money I was being paid, not least among one or two of my team on *Question Time*. Ten weeks before my first programme, Maxwell wrote to a viewer, a Mr Goldstone of Forest Gate, agreeing with his complaint that I was overpaid. 'I agree with you' she wrote, 'that it is a ludicrous sum of money which is resented by everyone here very much.' What was also resented by key individuals in Maxwell's small team, and their disquiet grew, was her penning letters like that. The more she showed disloyalty to me, so she herself began to lose the loyalty of some of her closest friends who leaked to me specimens of the correspondence. I reacted with disbelief, but decided that it was not worth a confrontation and got on with the job.

It's against that background that on 14 September 1989 I finally recorded my first broadcast edition of *Question Time* and it was transmitted, as was the routine, an hour or so after the recording ended. The previous week I had taken part in a 'pilot' edition. In all respects the 'pilot' was an authentic *Question Time*, with a panel of politicians, a studio audience and full technical rig. Everything about the 'pilot' was real – except that it was not transmitted. Immediately afterwards Barbara Maxwell, from her seat in the control gallery, rang my wife and assured her in the most glowing terms that I had done very well. She then put down the phone, put her head in her hands, and sobbed to everyone around her in the gallery that I was a total disaster. Within the space of a few minutes she had been two different people. The continuing difficulty I had during our working relationship was wondering which Barbara was going to turn up. Even worse than that, was the realisation that her bitterly trenchant views were not being kept 'in house'. Many print journalists were sympathetic to her and she was a world-class gossip.

Nicholas Hellen, by far the best of the media correspondents at the time, was later to write in the London *Evening Standard* that my real crime in the Maxwell camp was not just that they thought me not up to the job intellectually, but, worse, I was not clubbable and not an insider. In some media circles it is judged essential to be a member of the Garrick, the Reform or the Savile. But whether one was actually a member of a club or not, there were those who judged their lives to be enriched by insider gossip and social intrigue, and I was not one of them. In my journalistic career thus far, that had been a positive advantage.

The home of *Question Time*, for its first ten years, had been the Greenwood Theatre in Weston Street near London Bridge in south east London. It was originally built as a lecture theatre on the Guy's Hospital campus, but the hospital made extra money by letting it to the BBC. For many years, few editions of *Question Time* came from anywhere else, as indeed was the case with the Greenwood's other big show, *Parkinson*. For *Question Time* to travel beyond the Greenwood ramped up the cost. There were a few excursions to big cities outside London, and also to the main party conferences, although Robin Day's last programme, as a treat for him, had come from Paris, and, amazingly, he got to choose the guest list.

My routine became fixed quite quickly. Panel guests were booked weeks in advance – so much for me having any influence over who they were. Indeed, control over the choice of guests was the one thing that all my editors on *Question Time* jealously guarded. It was how they put their mark on the programme and it was where their power lay. I was usually given the final line-up on the Monday or Tuesday before Thursday's transmission. I wrote the introductions – thumb-nail sketches of each panellist – on the Wednesday, and faxed or handed them to the Editor at her office in Lime Grove, a short walk from Television Centre where I spent most of my time. It became increasingly difficult to think of new things to say in these introductions, especially for guests who appeared on the programme regularly, and David Dimbleby has wisely discontinued the practice. My editors, however, insisted on it. Usually I did a good job, but on one programme I forgot Robin Day's wise advice not to make jokes unless you can say something amusing about each of the panel.

The guest in question was Tony Benn, who appeared on the programme so regularly it was difficult to think of anything original by way of introduction. When Benn's turn came, I began: 'The Rt Hon Tony Benn was once described as a mad Marxist werewolf...' Mr Benn sat stony faced, in big close-up, and then interrupted me: 'You could have said forty-one years in Parliament, eleven years in the Cabinet, chairman of the Party. But you just brought out the abuse. You ought to be factual when you introduce someone.' I'd left myself wide open to that, but it didn't cross my mind for a moment that my embarrassment should be edited out of the programme. It gave an edge to the proceedings that was worth having.

I did make a more successful joke, however, on another occasion when Gordon Brown first appeared on the panel, which was quite prescient, given allegations about the chaotic state of his office when he made it to Number 10. I informed the *Question Time* audience that when Gordon Brown was a student, his room was such a tip that vandals broke in and decorated the place.

I was later to find out that my joke held an element of truth, when an acquaintance of Brown told me that someone once called the police to his university room, suspecting that he had been burgled. But apparently the place always looked like that.

On Thursday, the day of transmission, I would arrive at the Greenwood about 4 p.m., and sit in my dressing room reading the day's newspapers and any other cuttings that might be useful. In effect I was second-guessing the audience about what questions they would submit. Usually it is not difficult to anticipate the matters of greatest current controversy and with experience I found that it was best not to be over-briefed – better to rely on background knowledge and judgement.

Around 6.30 the panel would arrive, and then followed a curious ritual – they sat down to quite a substantial dinner, even though I suspected the politicians may not long have finished lunch. The idea was to put the panel at ease and promote conversation, although bizarrely they were discouraged by Barbara Maxwell from talking about any issue that might come up later. I found it all very strange. It wasn't a satisfactory way of starting the evening and a lot of food was left on the plates. I certainly never finished the meal, nor did Maxwell, because by 7 p.m. our audience had arrived and were submitting questions, which we had to go through.

The audience was usually seated by 7.30, and then they were 'warmed up'. This was sometimes done by quite a senior figure from the BBC including at one time John Birt himself, who tried to get a discussion going while the director lined up the cameras for the various shots. By eight, Maxwell and I had selected the questions, which also meant selecting the members of the audience who would ask them and seating them within easy camera range. Next, I would be introduced to the audience. I'd tell them a few jokes – always the same ones – and then

I'd bring in the panel to a round of applause. By 8.30 we were usually recording.

There were two golden rules. The panel were never given advance warning of the questions, and the programme was always recorded 'as live' – in other words it was never edited. What the viewer saw, when it was transmitted at 10.30 or 11 p.m., was what happened. During my four and a half years on *Question Time*, there were only two exceptions to that. One was for a libellous comment, which we edited out. The other was when a member of the audience collapsed and died. As I recall, Robin Cook was in full flow when suddenly a gentleman seated in the middle of the audience appeared to have a heart attack and fell forward onto the floor. Members of the production team had been worried about him when he arrived. Agitated and ashen faced, he'd fretted so much about putting in a question for the panel, that they asked his wife if he was on medication. As it happens, he was – for angina. As soon as he hit the floor we stopped the recording while he was given help by an off duty paramedic who was in the audience, but there was nothing that could be done even though Guy's hospital was only yards away.

After about twenty minutes we re-started the recording, with Robin Cook taking up precisely where he had left off. The join in the tape was totally undetectable even though we were all quite shaken.

My introduction to *Question Time* was generally well received by the press, one critic calling it 'a splendid debut' and adding that all that was missing, perhaps, was a bow tie. Another TV critic, Jaci Stephen, wrote that I 'handled the proceedings with considerable quick-witted ease'. She went on: 'When any journalist shows willing and able to do the same, *then* I'll start listening to what they have to say on the subject of Sissons's pay packet.'

However, over the months there was a steady drip of adverse comment and I suspected that it was being fed from inside the production team. Another copy of a letter written by my Editor to a viewer was leaked to me – 'I'm sorry you found Mr Sissons so inept, and this clearly marred our programme completely.'

All in all, that first twelve months on *Question Time* was by far the most challenging and difficult time I have had in broadcasting. Six weeks into my tenure, and alongside my *Question Time* duties, I started news casting three days a week on the *Six O'Clock News*, which I had been forced to delay under the terms of the agreement between ITN and the

BBC. But despite all the setbacks, in a funny way I began to enjoy my predicament. My education in BBC internal politics continued apace, at *Question Time* and in the newsroom, and I made far more friends than enemies. When you take over a programme so completely identified with your predecessor, who was a broadcasting legend with a large and influential fan base, you are bound to be on a hiding to nothing. Indeed, my advice to anyone placed in a similar position in the future would be 'don't do it!' But I walked into it with my eyes open, because above all I was doing what I wanted to do – chair one of the most important political programmes on television.

It helps, of course, if you develop a thick skin. This sort of challenge is not for sensitive souls, but I never felt I didn't have the strength to see it through. Well, almost never.

The one thing that matters, of course, in today's television, is the ratings, which our public service broadcaster scrutinises just as closely as ITV. In fact, during the whole of my twenty-five years at ITN and twenty at the BBC, I detected no difference in approach whatsoever to programme ratings; the BBC is as obsessed with them as the most dedicated commercial operator. The average rating for *Question Time* for its first ten years, under Robin Day, was 4.5 million. At the end of my first year it was 4.6. The Audience Appreciation Index, which reflects the public's enjoyment of a programme, was seventy-seven out of 100 before I arrived. Under me it was seventy-six, at or above the average for current affairs programmes.

At the end of my first year in the *Question Time* chair, Barbara Maxwell was moved from the editorship to take charge of the BBC's coverage of the party conferences.

Losing a flagship programme for a month or two's work in the conference season was not a sideways move, although it was presented as such. I had stuck with her, but people other than me had noticed that *Question Time* needed a new editor with fresh ideas.

Her admirers, and there remained one or two, conceded that she could be an inspired editor, spotting early on, for instance, that the young Tony Blair and Gordon Brown were destined for great things, and installing them as *Question Time* regulars. But she became her own worst enemy, doing herself no favours with the outspoken way she voiced her views of the top BBC management to anyone who would listen, and inevitably her outbursts got back to the offices on the sixth floor of Television

Centre. Her old friends on the production team were initially prepared to cover up for her, but that didn't stop her becoming more indiscreet and disloyal, not just concerning me, but about her BBC bosses. Her views about them were unprintable.

Most of her own team who'd worked with her for years dismissed these anti-management tirades as 'Barbara being Barbara', but what really tested the loyalties of some of them was her treatment of me. One of her longest serving colleagues told her to her face that she had behaved disgracefully towards me. Accordingly the only person who seemed surprised when she was told she was no longer Editor of *Question Time* was Barbara herself, and she took it very badly. I was about to go on air with the *Six O'Clock News* when she phoned me in a very emotional state, and asked me to intercede to save her job. I told her, truthfully, that the decision had already been taken at high level. What I didn't tell her, until we met socially some years later, was that management wanted to remove her when I joined the programme, but that I had ensured she carried on as Editor for another twelve months. The great mystery, still, is why Barbara Maxwell, an intelligent woman capable of brilliance as a programme editor, didn't see from the outset that the BBC had invested heavily in me, and that it was in her best interests – whatever her personal feelings – to make our relationship work.

My second twelve months on *Question Time* were a total departure from the stressful and depressing experience of the first year. The BBC appointed James Hogan as editor, one of its brightest and most original political producers.

James was no stranger to controversy. He had been the producer six years previously of an edition of *Panorama* called 'Maggie's Militant Tendency', which led to one of the biggest rows ever between a government and the BBC. The BBC had stood by the programme, which accused two Conservative MPs of right wing links but balked at a lengthy libel action and eventually agreed to settle out of court. When I met James for the first time, I thought we could enjoy working together, and I was right. The word 'cool' was coined for James, but his well-groomed laid-back approach in his designer suits was a stylish front. Behind it lay a shrewd political brain, a wicked sense of humour, and an ability to make things happen despite the dead hand of BBC bureaucracy.

James was well connected politically – his wife is Neil Kinnock's cousin – yet I never detected any party bias. He made up his mind quickly, but not dogmatically. Together we discussed the changes he wanted to make. If I thought he was wrong and won the argument, he would change his mind. Even the lowliest member of the production team, if he or she made a valuable point, could affect the outcome.

Many of the principal changes he made have lasted to this day. But from my point of view the best thing about James was his total loyalty to me and the rest of his team. If things went wrong, he saw it as the editor's job to take the bullet. That was not the BBC way – the old saying 'Deputy Heads must roll' still raises a smile, but only because of the truth it contains.

The team James assembled was totally new – except for two survivors from the Maxwell era whom I urged James to keep on and whom I knew he would like and come to depend on. They were the long-serving programme director Ann Morley, whose skills Robin Day rightly summed up as 'superlative'. Ann was a quite brilliant and intuitive programme director, listening intently to the way an argument was going and calling the next shot even before a panellist had decided to react. The other was Audrey Bradley, who had been Robin's 'minder' for ten years and mine for one. Occasionally, she became so exasperated with Robin that she would refer to herself as not so much his minder, as his nanny. Audrey was an old-style BBC hand – discreet, loyal, fair minded yet tough. On the night, Audrey was everywhere, making things run smoothly, and calming nerves, not least among the *Question Time* panellists – of which she kept a meticulous record, the only complete one in existence. I was very comfortable with Ann and Audrey on board, as well as with James's lively team of newcomers.

The most obvious change he made was to the set. Out went the plain oval table against a neutral cyclorama and a few square pillars. I never did find out what happened to that old table. I would have loved to have owned it. But I suspect it found its way onto a skip in SE1, along with the rest of the original scenery. The new set was a deep blue, emblazoned with the title of the programme, and the location from which it was being broadcast. It was portable, and designed to be easily dismantled and to fit inside a truck. It had cost a small fortune to build. The new table was a large Perspex Q, lit from inside. As the series progressed the table developed a life of its own – as the lights inside heated the Perspex it softened and buckled, occasionally making weird noises to the consternation of many a panellist and the puzzlement of the sound mixer.

James secured a budget for thirty-four programmes, of which well over half would come from outside London, and he insisted on a new London base. His approach to spending the BBC's money was to sign the cheques and argue with the bean-counters afterwards – but it was all justified in his mind by the imperative of revitalising one of the BBC's most important programmes. Instead of the rather dowdy Greenwood Theatre tucked away in a South Bank side street, we were to broadcast – when we weren't on the road – from a plush theatre at the Barbican Centre on the other side of the river in the heart of the City of London.

Out went the ritual of the dinner that no one wanted to eat; in came a smart Barbican Green Room with canapés and waitresses.

Instead of a dingy dressing room, I was given the use of the stylish flat, high in the Shakespeare Tower, belonging to the Barbican's managing director, Detta O'Cathain.

Once or twice I bumped into her next door neighbour, the retired Master of the Rolls, Lord Donaldson, in cardigan and slippers, putting out his rubbish. Sometimes Detta herself would appear with a calming cup of tea.

There were two other huge changes – James wanted most programmes to be transmitted live, a total departure from previous practice; and the method of selecting the audience was to become more scientific. Under the old production regime, the search for political balance took the form of distributing *Question Time* tickets in blocks which were sent out to the main political parties, rotary clubs, women's institutes and other pressure groups. Of course, the BBC always said publicly that the *Question Time* audience was balanced, but it had no way of knowing until they actually turned up on the night. On one occasion a block of tickets was sent to a gardening club, and after the programme one elderly lady was heard to complain that the only reason she came was that she thought she'd been given a ticket to *Gardeners' Question Time*.

What James introduced was a system that allocated tickets to individuals, but not to everyone who applied for one. Applicants were sent a form, on which they were invited to tell us about themselves, which social group they would put themselves in, their ethnic origin, gender, and which political party if any, they voted for. On this basis a *Question Time* audience was selected which, as far as possible, represented the make-up of the nation as a whole, based on the latest general election result and other current data. The important thing was that if anyone wrote in complaining that a *Question Time* audience was unbalanced, or packed with supporters of one particular party or faction, we could say with a high degree of confidence that that was not the case. The system generally worked well and I believe it is largely the same to this day.

Such care is needed because the audience is at the core of *Question Time*. Intelligent, informed and balanced *Question Time* audiences provide the unexpected, and politicians generally hate the unexpected. The well timed verbal stun grenade, tossed by a member of the audience, is an ever-present hazard for a *Question Time* panellist, however experienced. If he or she is a politician, they know the party machine will be watching to see if they keep the party line intact, with all that means for their career prospects.

If the panellist is a member of the government, one unguarded word can mean damage limitation for days to come. Ignorance of your own party's manifesto can make you a laughing stock. And while an audience member can be rude to a panellist, for a politician to be rude back is to lose it completely. For the non-politicians, there is the certain knowledge that their peers are watching with critical eyes. And serious gaffes now have a worldwide audience, thanks to YouTube.

Worst of all, if you blow it under pressure on *Question Time*, the BBC's flagship discussion programme, then your status and prestige comes under scrutiny. Although the pressure comes principally from the audience, who are the great unknown, a well-timed intervention or request for clarification from the Chairman can also be enlightening, or damaging, or both. Edward Heath, the Prime Minister who took Britain into the European Community, had sold it to the public at the time as above all an economic move. But he let the cat out of the bag on *Question Time* on November 1 1990 when I intervened to ask him 'The single currency, a United States of Europe, was all that in your mind when you took Britain in?' To which, without hesitation he replied 'Of course, yes'.

Apart from successfully reforming the system of audience selection, the other major innovation did not work well – the decision to broadcast the programme live. For added immediacy, James also decided to pre-book only two guests some time in advance, leaving the casting of the remaining two, for maximum topicality, right up to the last minute. As insurance against one of these last-minute guests being too last minute for comfort, James booked a fifth standby guest, who came in on the night ready to appear, but on the understanding he or she might not be needed. A surprising number of top people agreed to be booked on that basis. The thing that caused some grumbling was James's decision, on economy grounds, to halve the appearance fee for everyone, which wasn't much anyway.

But it was the decision to broadcast live that got us into trouble. I was up for it – any anchorman worth his salt gets an added buzz from the knowledge that what he or she is doing cannot be undone. Indeed, until I joined the BBC I had never known anything but live television. But the old hands, our programme director Ann Morley, and our 'minder' Audrey Bradley said it wouldn't work, and they were right.

The first few live shows at the Barbican went off smoothly enough, but we should have heeded the warning signs when we attempted a live programme from Heriot-Watt University in Edinburgh. It was a mid-October night when *Question Time* sailed closest to the wind without quite hitting the rocks. The booked panel was Margaret Ewing, Malcolm Rifkind, Tony Benn and Andrew Neil – then the Editor of the *Sunday Times*. When Ewing and Rifkind turned up for the live transmission, Benn and Neil were still sitting on the tarmac at Heathrow Airport, their flight from London having been delayed.

After frantic phone calls, two prominent Edinburgh residents, Menzies Campbell and the Editor of *The Scotsman*, Magnus Linklater, agreed to rush to the campus and join the panel instead. Twenty minutes into the live programme there were sirens and flashing blue lights outside. Benn and Neil had arrived at Edinburgh airport, dashed from the plane, been given a police escort to join us, and walked onto the stage.

Two extra chairs were hurriedly found, and so for the first and, up to then, only time, *Question Time* proceeded with a panel of six. Apart from that everything was fine, except for a sit-down protest by Heriot-Watt students over some student grievance. And the students also thought it was a great joke to set the fire alarm off halfway through.

But the going live experiment wasn't abandoned yet – thanks almost certainly to a night a month later, on which *Question Time* went live AND acquitted itself with great distinction.

On 22 November 1990, Margaret Thatcher resigned after ten years as Prime Minister and two weeks of high drama. She had changed the face of Britain, and her going was a political earthquake, polarising loyalties beyond Westminster, and obliterating any other news story.

It was a Thursday, and *Question Time* was scheduled live from the Barbican Centre with Paddy Ashdown, Roy Hattersley, Michael Howard and Nigel Lawson. Everything was in place to go on air at 10 p.m. What we didn't know, when the team gathered at the Barbican in the late afternoon, was that across town at Television Centre there was the most almighty panic. The BBC programme entrusted with the definitive coverage of the Thatcher resignation was *Panorama*, whose producers – the cream of BBC Current Affairs – had been asked to provide a special programme. During the early evening the word came through to us at the Barbican that the *Panorama* team were struggling. *Panorama* wasn't a programme that liked to be rushed, often requiring six weeks to get a major report ready for air, and six hours seemed to have led to a collective nervous breakdown. The upshot was that the *Question Time* team were asked to fill the gap. They rose to the challenge magnificently.

Within an hour James Hogan and his team had booked yet another panel, and got them on the way to the Barbican, to take part in a sixty-minute discussion – quite apart from the evening's scheduled *Question Time* – specifically about the Thatcher years. And we are not just talking about a 'B' team here – James Callaghan, Enoch Powell, Dr David Owen, and the Editor of *The Times* Simon Jenkins, who all dropped what they were doing to come to the Barbican to evaluate the legacy of Britain's first woman Prime Minister. Before them sat a bemused studio audience, who'd only just turned up for the later programme and scarcely had time to get their coats off. It was a great success, saved the BBC's bacon, but didn't spare *Panorama*'s blushes.

When that live special programme ended, there was only an hour or so before we were ready to go with the scheduled live *Question Time* – with Ashdown, Hattersley, Howard and Lawson. Their agenda included the Thatcher resignation, but ranged wider, and the two programmes complemented each other very well. The evening was plainly a notable editorial, organisational and technical success.

The icing on the cake for me and my production team was that on that November night in 1990, *Question Time* was watched by the biggest audience since it began, 7 million viewers – a record broken only by the 7.8 million who tuned in nineteen years later to watch the appearance by the leader of the British National Party. And what was the reaction of BBC management? I don't recall them telling us.

As to why *Panorama* freaked out that night, leaving the BBC to be saved by *Question Time*, we could only guess. The most plausible explanation I have heard is that morale on *Panorama* had been shot to pieces by the determination of John Birt to bring its journalists into line with his controversial theories about how to make current affairs programmes. The then Deputy Director General's obsession with what he famously called TV journalism's 'bias against understanding', and his insistence on endless preparation and analysis in advance of filming, had led to near paralysis on *Panorama*. One of *Panorama*'s most distinguished reporters, Richard Lindley, who eventually couldn't take any more, wrote about it in his book '*Panorama* – 50 years of Pride and Paranoia': 'As Birt, through his appointees, got a grip on *Panorama*, a suffocating blanket of fear wrapped itself around the programme team. It led to self censorship. *Panorama* journalists saw what happened to reporters and producers whose films failed to satisfy the new regime; they became cautious, no longer confident that editors could protect their backs if they undertook difficult or sensitive missions.' Assessing the career of Margaret Thatcher at short notice certainly came into that category.

The two programmes that *Question Time* produced that night had added immediacy because they were transmitted live. We should have quit the live experiment while we were ahead.

At that time in the early '90s, London was on high alert for IRA bombs, and one night we paid the price. On 21 February 1991, with a live *Question Time* in full swing, I was told in my earpiece that we had received a credible bomb threat, and that the programme had to come off the air. I interrupted the speaker – I think it was the then Home Secretary Kenneth Baker – and handed back to the continuity announcer at Television Centre. Then, panel, audience and production team all trooped into the cold street outside. We stayed off air. Exactly a month later we lost another *Question Time* completely, the power supply to the entire area mysteriously being cut off a few minutes before transmission. With no emergency generator to fall back on, and without the cushion that an earlier recording would have given us, we were horribly exposed.

The resulting hole in the evening's viewing on BBC1 did not go down well at the top. There was no shortage of people pointing out that in both instances, if the programmes were being recorded, as was the usual practice, they could almost certainly have been saved – the first by resuming after a safe interval, and the second by rushing in an emergency generator. The live experiment was finally abandoned. The upside was that *Question Time* was getting buoyant ratings and was making news.

But inside the BBC the knives were out for the programme, and for James Hogan. Outside the BBC, they started again to have a go at me.

One theory I have heard is that James Hogan was never meant to succeed as Editor of *Question Time* – that he was appointed as no more than a useful stop-gap. BBC Kremlinologists who subscribe to that view say that after a year with Hogan, *Question Time* would be ready for one of two things: to be taken off the air completely or to be put out to tender among independent producers. There were strong internal lobbies for both courses of action. According to this conspiracy theory, it just wasn't envisaged that James Hogan would make a success of the programme. So the sniping went on, with his enemies making much play of his failed attempt to turn *Question Time* into a live event. Those occasions when the programme had to be abandoned led to whispers about his judgement being suspect. James had also tried to add immediacy to some debates by bringing in major figures such as Henry Kissinger and Casper Weinberger by satellite link, an experiment that was worth trying but failed mainly because of the ponderousness of the personalities involved and the delay on the satellite sound. There was no shortage of ammunition for the rumour-mongers who were trying to undermine him and the programme, and if that particular vein of ammo did run out they resurrected gossip about how his career had been blighted by his role in the 'Maggie's Militant Tendency' controversy.

This knife-sharpening for James, for me and for the programme generally was manifested in a succession of hostile newspaper columns. Barbara Maxwell was quoted in one as saying she didn't watch the programme anymore because it was 'too distressing'. And she went on, 'I can't bear to watch. I definitely think it's lost its danger and its sparkle.' Those quotes were widely picked up. There were even articles suggesting that Robin Day could be approached to return to the *Question Time* chair, much to his bemusement. 'I wish they had discovered their support when it could have helped my remuneration' was all he would say. The only other public quote I can find from him about *Question Time* was when he told the *Daily Mail* 'I refuse to discuss *Question Time*. It would be unfair.' That was the true professional – whatever his personal views, he was not going to help those who had it in for the programme and its new team.

But it didn't stop the gossip factory. It seems that whenever diarists had a dull day, they'd suggest another name who was about to be parachuted in to save the programme. One columnist detected 'a scramble' for the *Question Time* chair, with Jeremy Paxman, Jeremy Isaacs, and even Kate Adie in the frame.

And so it went on, with even Sir Paul Fox, the departing managing director of BBC Television speaking out publicly against the show – *Question Time*, he said, was a mess. Gillian Reynolds, the doyenne of broadcasting correspondents, found this odd – observing that his comments about *Question Time* at each week's internal BBC programme review board were always warm and favourable.

Edward Pearce in *The Guardian* also reflected this schizophrenic attitude. *Question Time*, he wrote, was 'unwatchable ... Awful'. In his view what was killing *Question Time* were the guests on the panels – 'big names flying on the auto-pilot of reputation, without actually managing interest, wit, flair or flavour.' But he exonerated my chairmanship – 'it is no good blaming Mr Sissons for not being Robin Day; nobody else is either. His own style of sensible restraint is perfectly acceptable.' It seemed we couldn't win – if it wasn't me, it was James's selection of panellists – even though he regularly enticed leading political gladiators onto to the show using criteria entirely dictated by news values and topicality.

Sometime later, when I had left *Question Time*, I learned just how long the knives were that were being wielded against us during that second year. By chance I met Brian Walden, who told me that he'd been eagerly approached by a national newspaper to review the programme, and write an extended piece about it.

The deal was that he would watch three or four editions, then pass judgement. This he did, and came to the view that there was little wrong with the programme, that it was as good a watch as ever, and that he could not fault my chairmanship. When the newspaper concerned learned of his conclusions, they withdrew the invitation to him to write the review, although Brian ensured they did pay his fee. I also found out that the newly appointed TV critic of a national newspaper was asked, as one of her first assignments, to write a piece designed from the outset as a hatchet job on *Question Time* and on my chairmanship. She refused, and when pressed to do as she was told, resigned. Fortunately, she was such a talent that she wasn't out of work for long. Indeed, she claimed later that she'd walked straight into another job at twice the salary. Her name is Jaci Stephen. At such times you find out who your friends are.

Against this background we produced thirty-four editions of *Question Time* in my second year, with ratings as healthy as they'd ever been. We took it up and down the country, and produced many programmes of which I was very proud. The achievement was the greater, because of the pressure of not knowing what we were going to find each time we opened the newspapers. For instance, one of the most successful 'discoveries' we introduced to *Question Time* was Stephen Fry – probably one of the most intelligent and articulate people in the entertainment industry. He acquitted himself well – but all we got was armchair critics and columnists sniping that *Question Time* was dumbing down by including 'a comedian' on the panel. Since then, however, there's been a string of well-informed showbiz people on *Question Time* – it's almost routine to include one – whose views on current issues are accepted as colouring and enlivening the public debate.

We were only two thirds of the way through that year, when the BBC announced the biggest change in the history of *Question Time*.

Far from scrapping the programme, as had been rumoured, it was to be put out to tender among independent producers, in line with the new policy of commissioning 25 per cent of programme strands from independents. *Question Time* was an obvious candidate for being put into the independent sector. At an hour in length, it was a large proportion of the current affairs output and its 'privatisation' would ensure that other core programmes could be kept 'in house'.

Putting a flagship programme like this in the hands of an independent production company, even though the BBC would retain final editorial control, was controversial.

Sir Paul Fox, the retiring Director of Television, called it 'barmy'. But the die had been cast. Tenders were duly invited, so at the very least I was in for my second re-launch within two years. It was, incidentally, a condition of the tendering process that I would continue to be the *Question Time* Chairman. Indeed, the Head of Current Affairs went out of his way, in a *Guardian* article, to express his satisfaction with the show, and with me, underpinned by excellent ratings and surveys of audience opinion – 'Sissons' he wrote 'has successfully run with the baton handed to him by the brilliant and original Sir Robin Day.'

Thirty-five independent producers tendered for *Question Time*, and they were pared down to a shortlist of nine. The list had some distinguished names on it. Carole Stone, the Editor of radio's *Any Questions* was associated with a bid. And Barbara Maxwell was resurrected as the preferred new editor of another independent hopeful. How could he not have known that, as soon as the BBC Current Affairs management saw Maxwell's name on his tender, it was dead in the water? Extraordinary.

All the tender documents setting out the various ambitious plans for the show had involved substantial expenditure and effort by hopeful independent producers, some spending twenty or thirty thousand pounds on glossy documents and detailed brochures. The reason I hoped I would not have a third editor was that James Hogan saw his opportunity, resigned from the BBC and put together a company to join the race. I thought he had done enough to carry on producing *Question Time* as an independent, and I made it quite plain to the heads of News and of Current Affairs that James was my preferred choice. I argued that *Question Time*, and I, needed a period of stability, and that James had done nothing to merit losing the programme. I began to suspect, however, that I was wasting my time.

I then had an idea. If James was regarded on his own as unsuitable, what if he had a formidable backer with an international name? That Easter we had a family holiday in Florida, and on the Virgin flight to Miami, had met Richard Branson, the owner of the airline. As was Richard's habit at the time, if he was on board he liked to do a turn pushing the drinks trolley and chatting up the passengers. When he came to me, we got talking, and found that he was booked to stay for a week at the same hotel as us.

Indeed, at the hotel in question he had the room above us, as I discovered when the familiar bearded face hailed me from the balcony. Within hours my daughter Kate and his daughter Holly became friends, and the Sissonses and the Bransons spent some happy, relaxing hours dining out and exploring the Everglades.

The upshot was that I was impressed with Richard Branson, and felt I knew him well enough when we were all back in the UK, to ask if he would see James Hogan and me. At his magnificent home in Holland

Park, I and James made the case for Virgin backing our bid for *Question Time*. But after a few days of consideration the message came back: the numbers didn't add up sufficiently for Branson to make a commitment. Richard Branson didn't become rich through sentiment, but by aiming at healthy returns on his capital. *Question Time* did not pass his test. But it was worth a try.

On the day, early in June 1991, that the winning tender for the show was announced, I learned the outcome from a Press Association wire story. It was late in the afternoon, and I had the *Six O'Clock News* to do. As soon as I came off-air I phoned the Head of News to express my disappointment. Unusually, he couldn't be found – nor could any of the other people who'd been involved in taking the decision, and it appeared to me that they'd gone to ground and didn't want to face me. I made a call to James Hogan, who had also just heard the result. He was disappointed, and briefly angry, but not surprised.

The contract to produce *Question Time* had gone to Brian Lapping Associates. I had never met Brian Lapping, a prize winning producer of many acclaimed documentaries, but I had heard of him, and his work. Before setting up as an independent, he had been part of the success story at Granada Television's *World in Action* – and one of his greatest admirers was John Birt, another *World in Action* protégé, and now the man whose will was law across the BBC's journalistic output. It is tempting to believe that, with Lapping in the field, and Birt the Deputy Director General, the BBC was just going through the motions with the other independent hopefuls. But I was subsequently assured by the Lapping team that this was not true, and I have no reason to disbelieve them. By all accounts they performed very well at the selection board. But what seems to have swung it was that three of the four Lapping people at the board – the exception was Lapping himself – had worked closely with me on *Channel Four News*. They were friends of mine, we'd worked well together in the past, and they felt they were just the people to support me on *Question Time*. That was their winning card, and when it sank in, I was completely torn.

It would be great to work with friends from the *Channel Four News* team again. But I'd had a good year building a relationship with a different group of people, who had given me their total backing, and rebuilt the confidence that had taken such a battering under my first *Question Time* editor. So there was sadness when I bade farewell to the

Hogan team at a splendid lunchtime party in the conservatory of an expensive Kensington restaurant. Much wine was consumed, and we were still going strong as the shadows lengthened.

One consolation was that James, true to form, had managed to extract the substantial cost of the event from the BBC. On my way home that evening I reflected that things could have been worse – for me it was, after all, a win-win situation. That feeling didn't last long.

I opened a copy of *The Independent* a day or two later, to find that Brian Lapping, whom I still hadn't met, had given an interview to Michael Leapman. By any standards it was patronising towards me and dismissive of the achievements of the previous team – who had, in the series just ended, achieved average ratings of 4.8 million, the same as in Robin Day's final year. Lapping's verdict on me was that I was often badly briefed and needed coaxing into shape. He thought I'd been brilliant at *Channel Four News*, but had not fulfilled my promise on *Question Time*, principally because of the failings of the outgoing production team. 'At the end of *our* first year' he said, 'I am sure the BBC will want him to stay on.'

The stuff about being badly briefed particularly annoyed me. During my twenty-five years at ITN the company never employed researchers. I remember Nigel Ryan, the distinguished former Reuters man who became Editor after Geoffrey Cox, saying that a reporter's best researcher was the reporter himself. He was right. On the rare occasions when I had to rely upon someone else's research I was unhappy about it – once being embarrassed by being fed inaccurate information before interviewing a Cabinet minister. At other times I have simply not used research because I felt I could not trust it. It's not nice quoting as fact to any interviewee, let alone a member of the government, something that turns out to be untrue. As a rule, since then, my practice has been if I haven't checked it, I don't use it. Lapping had also, besides criticising the editorial team I had worked with, implicitly criticised the director, the brilliant Ann Morley, for the use of her camera angles, something at which she excelled.

I first spoke to the head of Current Affairs about Brian Lapping's remarks. I told him that whatever I felt personally – and I was pretty brassed off – the most damaging thing about them was that they undermined my credibility in the *Question Time* chair. I then wrote to Brian Lapping, accusing him of rubbishing the team with which I had just spent a happy and fulfilling twelve months. He wrote back, saying he was sorry that we had fallen out, and that he had no intention of hurting me personally. We subsequently had lunch, which was not the warmest of occasions, and I went away not much happier, but determined to see things through in my third *Question Time* series.

As I have indicated, Brian Lapping's strongest card was not so much his ideas for the programme, which were similar to those put forward by other independents, but the team he recruited to work on it. At its core were three women with whom I had worked closely on *Channel Four News*. I counted them all among my friends, and they were friends with each other. The Editor was to be Alexandra Henderson, a woman of strong will and great organisational skills, who didn't suffer fools gladly. Her father was a distinguished diplomat, the late Nicko Henderson, Mrs Thatcher's first ambassador to Washington. Alexandra's husband is the photographer Derry Moore, who also happens to be the twelfth Earl of Drogheda.

That made Alexandra a real-life Countess, although for some reason we always called her The Duchess.

The studio director was to be Sue Judd, a gifted pianist as well as a talented director of news programmes. I had mixed feelings about Sue's appointment, despite our friendship. Much as I liked and admired Sue, Ann Morley had done nothing to merit being cast aside, something I regretted very much. The other woman new to the team was Lea Sellers, who was to be Alexandra's producer, a role she'd had at *Channel Four News*. Lea's calm temperament and easy manner were a huge asset. When she eventually left the team, she was replaced by another old friend of mine, and ITN veteran, Prue Keely. Prue is married to the former Deputy Governor of the Bank of England and now head of the LSE, Howard Davies. The combined experience of these women, their background and their connections, would have been a great strength to any programme. And so it turned out.

There was one other member of the team I insisted should be included, and that was Audrey Bradley. She had been with the show since the very beginning and was absolutely indispensable. Loyal and wise, diplomatic yet firm, a better fixer and minder I have yet to meet.

Incidentally, Audrey agreed to join the new team on one condition – that no outside journalist should ever be allowed in our Green Room. What went on there was totally private and Audrey kept it that way. We had politicians on *Question Time* who said one thing in the privacy of the

Green Room and the exact opposite on the programme itself. But during my time I am not aware of any Green Room confidence being broken on *Question Time*. It's an important rule on any show, but especially one where public figures, before and after they have appeared, expect to be able to relax. It's also a rule that the BBC has recently not done enough to protect.

So, a new series, and a new team. And new teams want to make their mark with *change*. Some of the changes were entirely predictable. For a start we got yet another new set. This one was all wood panelling, and the team quickly nicknamed it The Rovers Return.

And we got yet another new London location. When we weren't travelling the country, we were now to be based in the grand Queen Elizabeth II Conference Centre opposite Westminster Abbey. What I should also have seen coming, was that an all-woman production team would have strong ideas about the alleged male bias of *Question Time* panels. The composition of the panels, how frequently you could introduce totally inexperienced new panellists, and how many should be women, inevitably became a matter of disagreement between me and Alexandra, although with nothing like the friction that existed between Robin Day and Barbara Maxwell. I felt she didn't quite appreciate how difficult it was to chair a discussion between people totally new to the show, whether they were men or women.

The reality is that an edition of *Question Time* is only as good as its panel. If the panel won't engage with each other, there's little the chairman can do to rev the thing up – and you can sense the audience becoming bored and impatient. We set out to discover new women, something Lapping had promised in his prospectus, and on which the BBC had insisted, but I quickly found that anything I said publicly about the topic was misrepresented by the newspapers as either patronising or chauvinistic, or both. Nonetheless, the new team got on with it, and soon produced the first ever all-women *Question Time* panel, which achieved an audience of six million viewers, with a little help from a documentary about the Queen which preceded the broadcast. Indeed, then as now, *Question Time* never ceased to make news. But the default reaction of the print media was to interpret any changes as changes for the worst. After the storm that had greeted Stephen Fry's *Question Time* debut under her predecessor, Alexandra trod carefully, but had some notable 'discoveries' of her own. The historian Niall Ferguson was one of them, going on to great success as a documentary maker for Channel Four.

So *Question Time*, as an independent production, settled down, although, astonishingly, it still hadn't become established at a fixed time in the schedules. It is very important, if you are building audience loyalty, to have a regular slot. But the BBC continued to shunt it around – sometimes starting at 10.30 p.m., at others 11 p.m. or 11.15. But against all the odds, and despite some very late starts at times when the nation starts going to bed, the ratings remained excellent.

Making a programme like *Question Time*, week in, week out, will expose any latent tensions in a team, and over the two and a half years with the Lapping team we had our share. But Brian Lapping himself was sensible enough to stay out of the way, and let us get on with it. Sometimes the issue was the mix of panellists, but by now I accepted – as Robin Day had warned – how disagreements about that went with the job. There were also one or two panellists I simply objected to on personal grounds, indeed whom I came to actively dislike. I got the feeling that the individuals concerned were deliberately trying to make my job as difficult as possible, and even in private they were unfriendly. I got a sinking feeling when told any of them was going to appear, despite having made known my feelings about them. Gradually, it began to cross my mind that *Question Time* might not be something I wanted to do indefinitely.

There were, however, some memorable programmes. I met the Lord Chief Justice, Lord Taylor, at a party, and discussed the possibility of him appearing on *Question Time*. Alexandra followed it up, set Lord Taylor's mind at rest on the few doubts he had, and the appearance duly took place.

No holder of that office had ever appeared on such a programme, taking questions from the public, and none has since. It worked well, he was positive about it, and between five and six million people watched it. I don't recall any acknowledgement by BBC management of the programme's success – or if there was, it wasn't passed on to any of the production team.

As well as travelling around Britain, we also took the programme to Washington DC, the furthest afield it had been since Robin Day's farewell expedition to Paris.

We had our share of gladiatorial panels, of the type that made the name of the show, and our editions either side of the 1992 general election attracted big audiences. It was always encouraging that the political big guns still queued up to appear. I had an extra workload at the time, having been assigned a prominent role as studio interviewer on the BBC's general election results programme, and also anchoring the daily Election Call, the flagship election phone-in that was simulcast throughout the campaign on BBC1 and Radio 4. But it was an invitation to a place on the *Question Time* panel that the political big hitters really coveted, whether or not there was an election in the offing. Incidentally, on the night of the 1992 election, Robin Day, with no role at the BBC, had returned to his broadcasting roots with a role on the ITN results programme. It was ITN's gain, but a disgrace that the BBC could find him nothing to do. At least *Question Time* lent him Audrey Bradley for the night, to make sure all went smoothly, and keep him out of mischief.

After the election, *Question Time*'s continuing popularity didn't stop the sniping. The production team suspected that Barbara Maxwell was still at work feeding hostile comment to the press, and we all felt that the BBC could have given us more public support. In fact, the Lapping honeymoon hadn't lasted long at all, with Jonathan Miller writing in the *Sunday Times* at the end of 1991, that 'The Show had had its Day!' His main complaint was the predictability of the programme and the same old faces on the panel – which was quite unfair considering the effort that had gone into finding new ones. Predictably, I was criticised for not being Robin Day: 'Sissons is smart, intellectually nimble and professional. But the job calls for more than a journalist; it demands a ringmaster.' His other criticism was one with which I had more sympathy, and the point he made remains valid for all political programmes: 'The politicians,' he wrote, 'who at first were reluctant to appear on *QT* for fear of being made to look like fools when asked questions outside their brief, have learnt to steer well clear of danger. They arrive armed with crib sheets, stuffed with briefings and fresh from media training courses where they are taught to look sincere and stick to the party line.'

There was, and remains, a large element of truth in that. Some panellists, in my time, even had their crib sheets in front of them during the programme. I used to try to wrong-foot them by going to them first, after the question was asked, so they didn't have time to glance at their notes. There were really two types of panellists – those that were so happy in their own skin that they came along ready to handle anything thrown at them – the prime example being Michael Heseltine. For all I know, as a minister he *had* spent all afternoon doing his homework, but he would never bring it with him. The other type is personified – or was in programmes I chaired – by John Prescott. Before the show he would sit in a corner with a stack of notes, beetle browed, reading them and scribbling away right until the last moment.

He rarely joined in Green Room small-talk, indeed it seemed that there were some guests on *QT* to whom, in principle, he would not talk at all. They were called Tories. By contrast, Alan Clark would talk to anybody, including the QE2's attractive waitresses, although I suspect that was his way of calming his nerves.

Of course, success as a *Question Time* panellist isn't just a matter of being well briefed, and reciting position papers. Nor will success be achieved by spending months on media training courses. The ultimate performers are those that are willing to engage with the audience, as well as with the others round the table. They also, invariably, are good public speakers anyway, whose pattern of speech has an easy rhythm, tying their best points into attractive bundles that just trigger applause – however little they may stand up to close examination. In his prime, Arthur Scargill knew exactly how these applause triggers work, and could induce audiences to cheer even the most outrageous and extreme propositions. In the mainstream, the names of Tony Benn, Paddy Ashdown and of course Michael Heseltine come to mind as performers who know all the right buttons to press. There are many more, but not as many as those who don't have the gift.

I worked with the team that Brian Lapping selected for two years, and at the end of the second in the summer of 1993 I began to think that I had done as much as I wanted to do. My initial three year contract with the BBC had been renewed a year earlier, and we had deliberately kept the *Question Time* element vague. The Head of News wanted to move me to the day's main bulletin, the *Nine O'Clock News*, which I would present jointly with Michael Buerk. The other incumbent on the *Nine*, Martyn Lewis, was to be moved to the 6 p.m. bulletin. For all of those four years I had had to live with speculation about my future on *Question Time*, and hostile comment from a dedicated band of bashers who ignored the fact that the programme was as popular as ever.

Never in my career had I had such a long period of having my morale eaten away. I am not a sensitive flower professionally, but it had finally all got to me. The worry was, when I went to the *Nine*, a more demanding proposition than the *Six*, would the unfriendly speculation over *Question Time* be a distraction from my core work on news? News was what I had built my reputation on. It was decided that I would stay with *Question Time* up until Christmas 1993, and my successor, whoever that might be, would take over in January. I was relieved when the decision was taken.

There was one final critical swipe. At the end of November, the veteran political correspondent Ian Aitken wrote from the deep armchairs of the Garrick Club – where Robin Day was still the most famous member – calling for the great man's return to *Question Time*. On a full page of the London *Evening Standard* all the usual stuff was churned out – he even used an earlier headline practically word for word – 'The show that's had its Day'. It wasn't so much the comment that riled, but his claim that the audience for *Question Time* before I arrived could be counted in tens of millions – a total fiction. And he rattled off a list of names whom, he claimed were being canvassed within the BBC to succeed me – 'Jeremy Paxman, the obsequious David Frost, the two humourless Dimblebys, LWT's over-talkative Brian Walden, and even the newly arrived Kirsty Wark.' Aitken's own preference was for James Naughtie, then presenting *The World at One* – if Sir Robin could not be persuaded to return.

I was genuinely angered by this article. The BBC stayed silent, so often its reflex when its presenters are attacked. So I wrote in person rebutting it – something I hardly ever did. In a letter given some prominence by the *Standard*, I corrected his nonsense about the ratings and the levels of audience appreciation, which were as high as any in the past. I concluded that these were matters of fact and that I lost no sleep because they cut no ice in the Garrick.

But I had already made up my mind: I didn't need any more of this.

Soon afterwards I signed off from my last *Question Time*, having completed 150 editions.

My team gave me a surprise leaving party a few days later in Alexandra Henderson's home in Notting Hill and, amid all the warmth, I admit that I shed a tear. All the vexations of the past seemed to fade, and we were again just a group of old friends with more in common than ever we disagreed about.

Among the BBC managers, the preferred candidate to succeed me was Jeremy Paxman. But Brian Lapping leaned towards David Dimbleby, and there was a strong lobby for Sue Lawley. Samir Shah, the Head of Current Affairs, decided to settle it with three auditions. When told of this, Sue Lawley dug her high heels in. She told the BBC they already knew all about her, since she had previously deputised for Sir Robin (when she had affectionately parodied him by wearing a large floppy bow tie) and there was no way she was going to audition. So, under conditions of great secrecy, a two-way run-off was arranged at the QE2 Conference Centre – two audiences, two panels, Paxman in the morning, Dimbleby in the afternoon. According to a trusted source, who was there, it was no contest – 'Jeremy chewed up the audience, and chewed up the panel.' He also chewed up his chances. David Dimbleby was the clear winner. The tapes, sadly, were then destroyed.

David Dimbleby has now been chairing *Question Time* for longer than Sir Robin and I put together. He's seen other independent producers come and go. The programme, as it did with Robin Day, keeps him in work, since the BBC seem to have eased him out of much of what he used to do so well for them, particularly commentaries on the big national or royal events. But Dimbleby likes *Question Time*, and it shows – every presenter is the stronger for having a good, strong, tested format around him, or her.

It's a format that you tinker with at your peril. One new producer tried to get David Dimbleby walking around in the audience and chairing the programme at the same time. Then they sat him, not in the middle of the panel, but at the end – all changes just for the sake of change, which were soon abandoned. The one major change they have persevered with is the introduction of a fifth panellist. I don't think that works – it slows proceedings down and often makes for a series of individual statements rather than the cut and thrust of debate.

But *Question Time* is now part of the furniture of national broadcasting, and I am proud to have played a part in its history. I've still got some bruises, but I don't regret a moment of it.

Chapter 12

Ins and Outs of BBC News

Two months after starting on *Question Time*, under the terms of the legal settlement between ITN and the BBC, I was able to start newscasting. Given the choice, I had opted for the BBC *Six O'Clock News*. I had always rather liked the *Six*, which had been given status and appeal by a good partnership between Sue Lawley and Nicholas Witchell. The *Nine* carried greater prestige, but had become rather stuffy. In any event, my old friend Anna Ford was now installed on the *Six*, and I looked forward to working with her again. In addition, I thought that I would probably fit in more quickly at the BBC if I eased my way into the *Six*, rather than risk any ill-feeling if I was seen to be the reason Martyn Lewis was removed from the *Nine*. While I had been chairing my first few editions of *Question Time*, I had not visited the TV newsroom at Television Centre in West London. *Question Time's* offices were half a mile away in Lime Grove, the iconic former film studios where early Hitchcock films and Ealing comedies were made. But as the day approached when I would be free to newscast for the BBC, I decided to put in an appearance at TV Centre. The BBC TV newsroom was not as big then as it is today, but I found the set-up impressive and I was given a warm welcome. There were a number of friendly faces who used to be at ITN, and the curiosity of most of my new team now that I had arrived, soon broke the ice.

The *Six O'Clock News* was at that time presented by two newscasters, and it would be the first time I had co-presented for more than ten years. Moira Stuart was the third regular presenter, in addition to Anna who, after her disastrous involvement in the launch of TV-am, from which she was sacked, had found her way back to newscasting at the BBC three years previously. She had been widowed the year before, when the cartoonist Mark Boxer died of a brain tumour. Mark was the love of her life. I had been a bit player in her love life while she was at ITN, when she became engaged to Jon Snow for a few days. Realising it was a mistake, she rang me and asked what to do. I advised her to put out a statement saying it was over, make no other comment about it, and the fuss would die down in about a week. It did. (I must admit I had had some practice in the Agony Aunt department. The ITN newscaster Gordon Honeycombe, who was also a close friend, rang me one Sunday morning, evidently distraught. He'd proposed to a girl, been accepted, but she changed her mind within hours. The problem was that he'd already announced their engagement to the press. I gave him the same advice I was to give Anna, and all was soon forgotten.)

I hadn't met Moira before, but instantly took to her and her wicked laugh and sense of humour. What I didn't know about her, until I had it from an impeccable source many years later, was how little she was paid. She was by a long way the worst paid of the newscasters. Indeed, it has always puzzled me what a poor hand Moira Stuart was dealt by the BBC for many years – her remuneration never coming remotely near her popularity. Status and popularity in a news organisation are often two totally different things. However popular you are, your status can change overnight, most often with a change in the management who have your job in their gift. I was advised to do something I had never done before – get my status written into my contract, where it was duly laid down that if I was on duty in the BBC newsroom I was the senior presenter. Anna told me that I was the only presenter in the BBC to whom she would agree to be number two. She didn't know that, strictly speaking, if we were rostered together she would have no choice in the matter. But throughout my time at the BBC I kept that clause in my contract under wraps – it was my safety net for the unknown world of the BBC. I never had to invoke it, never told anyone about it, and status never became an issue with any fellow presenter.

As well as working amicably with Anna Ford and Moira Stuart, I would also occasionally co-present on the *Six* with Jill Dando.

Jill, who was one of the most versatile presenters, was regarded as the BBC's golden girl, but like Anna and Moira she had her feet firmly on the ground. I was particularly impressed, at a showbiz party, when she spent a lot of time with my young daughter Kate, whom she put at her ease and steered towards other people that Kate wanted to meet. The three women were a joy to work with. My relationship with Jill Dando, however, was eventually wrecked when she took personally some light-hearted remarks I'd made about blonde presenters. More on that later.

The production team on the *Six* was also to my liking. The programme editor, Dave Stanford, was, like me, a Liverpudlian. Dave's career path was impressive. He had been to the same school as I, started his journalism on a local newspaper in south Liverpool, and while still relatively young had risen to edit one of the BBC's most important news programmes. He had an easygoing manner – but that was deceptive. It concealed a very shrewd editorial brain, he knew what he wanted and expected the editor's decision to be final. Dave was not only very popular with his team, but he also impressed the news directorate – two things that don't always go together at the BBC.

When after three or four years he moved on from the *Six* to a senior BBC post in Manchester, someone had the idea of making a special, light-hearted video about him. It was only a long shot, but they approached Ken Dodd to feature in it. Would Ken be interviewed down the line by Peter Sissons about a Liverpudlian called Dave? Doddy didn't know Dave Stanford from Adam, but he knew of me, and amazingly agreed to do it. Up he came in vision from a Liverpool studio, I fed him various lines, and Doddy did ten minutes or more of one-liners about a fictional Scouser called Dave. It was very funny, a very generous thing for Ken Dodd to do, and an affectionate leaving gift to the Editor of the *Six*.

So, on that first day I shook a lot of hands, kissed one or two cheeks and looked forward to starting on the programme in a few days' time. I was more than looking forward to it. I itched to get back to the news, the more so as I had been forced to sit at home during one of the most momentous peacetime events of the twentieth century – the fall of the Berlin Wall. Watching those scenes being reported by others while I had to twiddle my thumbs made me realise why news had become my life. It had really hurt to be simply a bystander. But now I was back.

Before I left TV Centre on that day I was invited to go and have a drink with Paul Fox, the managing director of BBC Network Television. Paul, during twenty-five years at the BBC one of the most successful and respected figures in television, had left to spend ten years in ITV as managing director of Yorkshire Television, two of those as chairman of ITN, where I had first met him. But he had now come back home to the BBC. In his office, high above TV centre, we shared a bottle of wine and he made me very welcome – although I found out later that he had serious reservations about me getting the *Question Time* job. As I left, and he led me to the lift, he gave me a little insight into the way things are done at the BBC – he reminded me not to mention our meeting to anyone.

The clear inference was that it was not done at the BBC to go over the heads of your immediate superiors, even for such an informal meeting as the one we'd just had, and that it might be resented if it became known that I had been having a private chat with the managing director of Network Television.

At the time I found his comment puzzling. Later, when I'd found my way around the BBC, I was to understand fully: in the arcane and crafty world of BBC politics there would always be those ready to believe that the most innocent of meetings had some hidden agenda.

There was one other extraordinary ritual before I started work on the News. An appointment was made for me to attend an office in TV Centre to meet a rather formidable woman, whose precise job title was never relayed to me, but I was told that it was essential for me to attend. When I was shown into her presence, she was accompanied by a rather serious looking gentleman, carrying a tape-measure. He looked and dressed like a funeral director, and did indeed measure me up – for a suit. He was a tailor from Savile Row, and the formidable woman explained that every presenter had to have a sombre suit, the sole purpose of which was to ensure that the presenter could be dressed appropriately in the event that he had to announce the death of a senior member of the royal family.

A week or so later the suit had been made, and I went back to try it on. It was very old fashioned and definitely not the kind of suit I would have bought for myself. Indeed, I was amazed to find that it was double-breasted, and in a rather heavy worsted. The last thing you want as a news presenter is a double-breasted suit tangling up your microphone cable, made of material in which you would bake under the studio lights, and as far as I was concerned it was many hundreds of pounds down the drain. The suit was then placed in a zip-up bag on a clothes hanger, and placed in a locked cupboard in a room used by the make-up artists. I think I was actually given a key to the cupboard, which I eventually lost. From time to time I would visit my suit, still hanging there, alongside other bagged suits, each carrying the name of a news presenter, some of whom I noticed had long since retired or even passed away. When I lost the key my visits stopped, but I should imagine that those suits – none of which as far as I know was ever worn – are still hanging up somewhere in TV Centre, like ghosts from the past.

Having made a social visit to the newsroom and gone through the ritual of the suit, at last the day came for me to report for duty on the *Six O'Clock News*. My co-presenter on my first day as a BBC newscaster was Moira Stuart.

As was expected, and as was my practice on all the news programmes I have presented, my task was to write the headlines of the programme, the lead story and possibly another main story. I also re-wrote scripts prepared by the programme's six or seven producers, each of whom would be in charge of one or more stories in the running order. Such re-writes were usually no reflection on their writing, simply me imposing a style with which I was comfortable. However good other writers may be, they invariably write prose intended to be read; I always wrote scripts intended to be spoken, and that led to my first disagreement on the programme.

At *Channel Four News*, and before that on the ITN News, I had always written in a style that never avoided a colloquial, or semi-colloquial phrase, if I believed it added to the viewers' understanding of what I was talking about. We are not talking about slang here, simply viewer-friendly prose – I just didn't think you should address viewers as if you were from the ministry of information. I also attempted, as was my practice at *Channel Four News*, to insert the occasional 'aside' – a fairly neutral type of comment that gave context.

It was the ITN way of writing, but after I had written my first few scripts it was made clear to me that it was not the BBC way. It is the BBC way now, of course – indeed in some regards it has now gone too far, with accusations of 'dumbing down', sloppy grammar and pronunciation and other sins against the English language. That's quite apart from the subliminal expressions of personal opinion that have started to creep into the observations of presenters and reporters alike. But at the time I joined the BBC, my attempts to tell the news, rather than read it, went against the grain.

The procedure with news scripts, after they were written, was for them to be given final approval by the programme editor and the newscaster – each signing off the script on the computerised newsroom system, when it was complete. But occasionally I would find scripts to which I thought I had given final approval for broadcast, coming back to me changed yet again. Sometimes the changes would not be made until I was sitting in the studio, which made it difficult to re-instate what I had originally written. This was not something that usually happened at *Channel Four News*, without someone having a word with me.

Then it dawned on me: on the ITN bulletins and on ITN's *News at One* and *News at Ten* I had been expected to do more than newscast. At *Channel Four News* I was the 'anchor' of the programme – the editor's representative on air. This role was recognised by my appointment as Associate Editor of *Channel Four News*. It was also commented on by Sir Robin Day in *Grand Inquisitor*, the memoir he penned in the year I joined the BBC.

'Peter Sissons,' he wrote, 'as anchorman of ITN's *Channel Four News*, has shown us the newscaster system in its highest form.' He went on:

> The ideal newscaster-anchorman is very hard to find. There are few, very few, who have the personality, the skill, the experience, the authority and the presence to hold a news and current affairs programme together, to share in the editorial planning, to interpret the news, to conduct interviews, to chair discussions and to be the viewer's guide, philosopher and friend. If Sissons is one of the few, Sir Alastair Burnet is, of course, another. Sissons should give freer rein to his sense of humour. Sir Alastair's forte is not interviewing. But Sissons and Burnet are the nearest we've had to a Walter Cronkite in Britain.

In those first weeks at the BBC it slowly dawned on me: I was now a newsreader, full stop.

That change was manifested in other ways: at the BBC, although I took part in editorial discussions about content, I never had the feeling I was helping to shape the broadcast. Having my say was a formality, part of the ritual. But most of the important decisions had already been taken. This demarcation between production and presentation appeared to me to be deeply ingrained in BBC News. Presenters were kept in their place, and for one of them to attain the status that Alastair Burnet and I had at ITN – where in addition to everything else Alastair was a member of the Board of Directors – would have been unthinkable. Indeed I never detected in those early days in the BBC TV newsroom any sense that the people who ran the BBC operation felt they had anything at all to learn from ITN, which was such an innovator in TV news and was watched by far more people. At ITN we would avidly watch the BBC bulletins to see how we compared. Every BBC bulletin was monitored by ITN's cuttings department, and the monitoring sheets were distributed and pored over throughout the building.

I saw little of that kind of competitiveness in the BBC newsroom, where the attitude to their main rival, ITN, was manifested in a sense of superiority allied to studied complacency. Accordingly I decided early on that it would make me no friends to draw comparisons with ITN. I kept my own counsel and got on with the job that they wanted me to do, in the way they wanted me to do it. I was not going to pick an unwinnable fight.

Moira and I had a good first programme. There wasn't a lot of news about, and with each of us reading perhaps eight or nine brief stories or introductions to film reports, I suppose that neither was speaking for more than three or four minutes. It wasn't very taxing but I had broken my duck, and we all made off to the BBC Club where I bought a round of drinks. Thus did I settle into a routine: Monday and Tuesday on the News, Wednesday researching the likely topics for Thursday's *Question Time* and writing the introductions for the panel; Thursday in the chair for *Question Time*, and Friday back on the News.

Frankly, I found the *Six O'Clock News* very predictable, but perhaps that familiarity was what made it so popular and easy on the eye. The format was set in stone. The two presenters read alternate stories – there was no attempt, say, to cluster two or more foreign stories together and have them read in succession by the same presenter; then to change gear by having two or three stories of a different texture read by the second presenter. That seemed to me to be the logical thing to do. No, it was 'one for me, one for her', regardless of the news logic. Stories that I had written for myself to read were often never read by me at all, when the 'turn and turn about' got out of sync. But they stuck with the system, because it was safe and everyone in the control gallery could be certain what was going to happen next.

I also found enormous reluctance among the editors of the day to take risks. At ITN they thought nothing of changing the lead at five, or sometimes two, minutes to transmission. I lost count of the times at ITN that we scrapped the top of a programme, going on air with words like 'In the last couple of minutes we've learned that...', and then re-structuring the broadcast as we went along. Somehow the BBC system seemed so inflexible, and I found that frustrating. At ITN they'd go for it; at BBC News caution seemed inbred. What so many news producers seemed not to realise was how much viewers love the unexpected. It makes the news seem more human when things come off the rails.

That's the reason one of my early six o'clock broadcasts is still talked about. It was the day in November 1990 that Margaret Thatcher, holed up in the British Embassy in Paris, heard how much trouble she was in after the first round of voting in the challenge to her leadership of the Conservative Party. On the *Six* we went over live to the BBC's political correspondent, John Sergeant, who was in the embassy courtyard, and he assured viewers that there was no sign of her emerging. As Sergeant spoke, I saw the Prime Minister come through the door behind him accompanied by her press secretary Bernard Ingham, and shouted the words that have enlivened many a pantomime 'She's behind you!' John didn't hear, because his earpiece had failed, and the first he knew he had an exclusive was when Ingham and Thatcher commandeered his microphone to assert that she would 'fight on'. The moment not only electrified a staid BBC bulletin, it became one of the defining moments of John Sergeant's career... until the nation discovered he could dance.

Generally though, I missed the danger and unpredictability that was part of the last job I'd done in news, on Channel Four. There was one notable occasion on the *Six O'Clock News* however, when for half an hour it felt as if I was back in the old routine. One Tuesday at the height of the Bosnian War in early April 1993, I was sitting in the newsroom as usual, with about an hour to go to the 6 p.m. transmission. A phone rang and someone answered it and passed it to me saying it was Lady Thatcher's office. A male voice at the other end established he was talking to me, and said that Lady Thatcher would like a word. The former Prime Minister came on the line, and came straight to the point: she had something strongly critical to say about the government's Bosnia policy, and she wanted to say it on the *Six O'Clock News*. I kept her on the line, told my editor what I was doing, and then asked her to get to TV Centre as quickly as possible.

There would be no time to pre-record; she would have to go live. Talk about a flutter in the dovecote! This wasn't the way things were done at the BBC! A former Prime Minister grabbing prime airtime? There had to be meetings! The Director General and the Director of News had to be informed! Perhaps one or both might wish to greet her personally. A hospitality room would have to be prepared. The Perrier would have to be hidden and the Malvern brought out. There was time for none of that. She was on her way.

At five to six I was sitting with my co-presenter in the studio when Lady Thatcher bustled in. She sat down, was miked up and we went on air. The lead story was a BBC report on the latest atrocity perpetrated by the Bosnian Serbs in Srebrenica, in which many Muslim children had been maimed and killed. Lady Thatcher watched intently and, when it ended, launched into an astonishing attack on the policy supported by the government of her successor John Major, which was not to intervene militarily but to provide humanitarian aid while encouraging negotiations. She accused Britain and the other western governments of effectively being complicit in the massacres, and called for the arming of the Bosnian Muslims. 'We can't go on,' she said, 'feeding people but leaving the innocent to be massacred.' I asked her about the Foreign Secretary's opposition to arming the Muslims – Douglas Hurd had said it would give everyone 'a level killing field'. That, she said, was 'a terrible and disgraceful phrase'. It was the old Margaret Thatcher, and she was on fire. Having said her piece, and said it at length, she departed as quickly as she had arrived. Her remarks caused an international row, and the rest of the evening saw other programmes playing catch-up. Oddly, in the full transcript of the interview, which appears on the website of the Margaret Thatcher Foundation, the interviewer is named as Martyn Lewis. It won't do him any harm.

But there is a serious point to be made. BBC TV News is a leading world brand in news broadcasting. There was no reason why BBC news bulletins shouldn't have been able to interview like that more often. In their prime, the American networks could beam all the international big hitters, often live, into their flagship evening bulletins, to be interviewed by their big anchors, Murrow, Cronkite, Rather, Brokaw and Jennings. But perhaps the moment has gone for BBC News. The bulletins, each of which was for so long a distinct fixture in a set part of the schedule, are now effectively incorporated into the twenty-four hour rolling news machine. Their clout, prestige and distinctiveness has been diminished, and diminished as an act of policy driven by the need to control costs and harmonise the BBC news output.

One effect is that the main bulletins and the News Channel often run the same reports by the same people throughout the day. The element of competition and creative tension between the news outlets, which at its best led to sharper journalism, has gone. The journalistic edge has also been dulled by the increasing frequency with which the BBC interviews its own correspondents. Instead of spending more time interviewing the leading players in a story, or spreading the net wide for a range of views, they frequently choose to use the time interviewing their own correspondents in a format intended to help clarify the facts, but which often invites the expression of opinion. When that happens, instead of hearing both sides of a story, the audience gets what is in effect the BBC's view presented as fact. The people doing it have a range of titles: there are 'correspondents', there are 'news correspondents', 'special correspondents', 'chief news correspondents' and even 'analysts'. One of the noblest titles in journalism – 'reporter' – seems to have gone out of fashion.

The writing, too, has begun to suffer. Under the pressures of continuous news programming – pressures of time and staffing – producers handling a story throughout the day often don't have time to re-write or freshen up a text from one end of the day to the other. You could be forgiven on some days for thinking that if you've seen one BBC news bulletin, you've seen them all – especially as all the studio sets for news are identical across the BBC.

At the time I was presenting the *Six O'Clock News*, however, the *Six* and the *Nine* were very distinctive broadcasts in tone, content and presentation and there was a real competitive edge between them. But it's a matter of some regret to me that for much of the time I wasn't totally focused on news. It was *Question Time*, and the goings-on behind the scenes of *Question Time*, around which my life revolved. It suited me to fit in with the news operation and, strange though it may sound, enjoy it as some light relief from the internal politics of *Question Time*. I had enough on my plate with the continuous changes taking place at *Question Time*, without picking pointless fights I couldn't win on the News. In any case, for all the shortcomings I perceived in the newsroom production system, my colleagues on the *Six* were fun to work with, and during the most stressful periods of my association with *Question Time*, kept me sane.

I also valued during that time the easy access I enjoyed to the recently installed new Director of News, Tony Hall – the same Tony Hall who went on to become chief executive of the Royal Opera House and Baron Hall of Birkenhead. Tony must have had a fiendishly difficult job being in charge of News and Current Affairs while John Birt, for whom it was an obsession, was Director General. But he was a good communicator and a good listener, and his door was always open to me. We also got along well because we were both Merseysiders. I think that the reason I never lost heart during some of the *Question Time* upheavals was that I had Tony's support. But as with any top job at the BBC his powers were limited because of all the other internal politics in play. When he left the BBC in 2001 I saw nothing like as much of his successors or their deputies. Indeed, in a couple of cases not only were their doors not open to me, I hardly knew where their doors were.

In April 1992 I took part in my only general election results programme at the BBC. It was in my contract that on election night I should occupy the interviewer's chair which was traditionally the property of Robin Day, although I knew full well that handing that job to an outsider was resented by a strong lobby that felt it should have gone to Jeremy Paxman who'd spent his entire working life at the BBC.

The BBC's election operation, with its massive results studio, was impressive, far outstripping anything I had seen at ITN. As polling day approached, the scores of people involved were gathered together for a briefing, and I was gently prodded to share my inside knowledge of the rival ITN operation.

ITN had the reputation, on election nights, of being faster on its feet, more innovative and more entertaining, despite having nothing like the resources of the BBC. What, I was asked, could the BBC learn from my experience of ITN election results programmes? My reply was that ITN had nothing like the firepower of the BBC, but could say to the viewers that if they stuck with ITN they were going to have a better election night party. This went down well, and I subsequently heard David Dimbleby trailing the BBC's 1992 election night coverage as the best party in town.

At that 1992 election the BBC was desperate not to repeat the fiasco of the exit poll it conducted on the day of the 1987 general election.

Early returns from that, believed to have been leaked to the Labour Party, gave Neil Kinnock – who had been narrowly ahead in the polls before the election – some hope that he might win. In the event it was another big majority for Margaret Thatcher. In 1992 I suggested to the BBC that they hire Paul McKee, the father of ITN's election graphics, who by then had left ITN. Paul came on board – incidentally renewing his partnership with Peter Snow – and on polling day I watched him scrutinise the highly confidential exit poll findings as they came in.

He wasn't happy with what he was seeing, feeling in his bones that it was going to be better for the Conservatives than the exit poll numbers were suggesting. I don't know exactly what he did, but I saw him take a pencil to those numbers. The adjustment he made, which I am certain Paul made on a hunch, still had the BBC announcing that the election was too close to call, but I believe his caution saved the BBC from making a bigger error. In the event, as soon as the first marginal declared – Basildon – the former Conservative Party chairman Cecil Parkinson told me on air that the Tories would win with a majority of twenty. He was wrong – it was twenty-one. It was an extraordinary win for John Major's government and one of the biggest post-war upsets, with the Tories polling a record number of votes for any party in a British general election.

In the run up to that 1992 election I had another part to play for the BBC – I was assigned to preside over Election Call. Pioneered, like *Question Time*, by Robin Day, Election Call was a phone-in programme that was simulcast on television and on Radio 4 every morning at 9 a.m. throughout the campaign. Each morning a leading spokesman or woman from one of the main parties would sit with me in the BBC's Westminster studio, and take calls, live, from viewers and listeners. When the lines opened, anything could happen. An invitation to appear on Election Call was an offer that no politician could refuse, but it was high risk. Politicians can be rude or dismissive to interviewers, but it's not wise to insult or brush off a persistent pensioner from Peterborough.

All the senior figures of the major parties, including the leaders, passed through my Election Call studio in three general elections. The programme made news, often setting the campaign agenda for the rest of the day, and was widely judged to be one of the jewels in the crown of the BBC's election coverage. I anchored Election Call in the general election campaigns of 1992, 1997 and 2001, but played no part in the overnight results programmes after 1992. That saddened me.

I'd played a part in eight general election results programmes at ITN, mostly in quite a major role. But the overnight 1992 general election results programme at the BBC was my last of that kind, and thereafter Jeremy Paxman was duly installed as the election night interviewer. From then on I was just another viewer on general election nights.

But there was no suggestion – or if there was I never heard it – that the BBC was having second thoughts about my value to the corporation. After my initial three-year contract had expired it was renewed on even more favourable terms – as it was for some years. Also, during those early years at the BBC I continued to enjoy 'trophy' status, being invited with my wife to major events which were in the BBC's gift – Wimbledon, the Cup Final, racing at Goodwood and the Proms. The invitations were greatly appreciated, and of them all, I would say that a seat in the Director General's box at the Last Night of the Proms was the best. But the longer I worked at the BBC, the rarer such invitations became.

What struck me about such events was the lavishness of the BBC hospitality – and that such a large proportion of the beneficiaries of such hospitality appeared to be BBC executives themselves. There were many corporate and individual guests from outside the BBC, but always a big BBC contingent, very few of them with faces I recognised and many with arcane management titles. On one occasion at Wimbledon in the early '90s I made some discreet enquiries about how much it cost the BBC per head to entertain an individual for the day, BBC personnel included – centre court tickets, champagne, marquee, lunch, tea and all the overheads. The answer was a staggering £1,400 each!

It was at just such an event, during the years I was occupying the *Question Time* chair, that I had my only meeting after his retirement with Sir Robin Day. We'd both been invited to a BBC box at the Proms. Robin was very friendly and on good form – but neither of us spoke about *Question Time*. I think he missed it very much. He loved the spotlight, grew under its warmth but was diminished when it was switched off. But that evening the old mischievous Robin was back on display. The entire first half of the Proms programme was a long and demanding – some would say interminable – piece by the composer Sir Harrison Birtwistle. Neither I, nor Robin, nor I suspect many others were among Birtwistle's most devoted fans, but that evening we had to sit through a long atonal Harrison masterwork as the price of listening to some magnificent Beethoven after the interval. As the Birtwistle unfolded, the dissonance subsided for a few bars and the Albert Hall fell quiet – a quietness broken not by the BBC Symphony Orchestra, but by the distinctive voice of Sir Robin, who enquired loudly, looking at his wristwatch 'How much longer does this go on?'

During my early years at the BBC I saw at close hand the two John Birts. The John Birt, who as Deputy Director General and then as the boss, gained the reputation of being almost the Pol Pot of BBC journalism – a humourless automaton who questioned every aspect of the old BBC culture and, for many who had grown up with it, became a hate figure. Then there was the John Birt who could be the perfect host, spending hours, or so it seemed, perfecting guest lists to events that were in his gift, such as the Last Night of the Proms and the Cup Final, where no expense was spared on food and drink. But one of the more bizarre but thoroughly enjoyable events to which my wife and I were invited certainly didn't bankrupt the BBC. It was John Birt's Scouse Lunch. This was held at his home, and the guest list was confined to people who'd broadcast or otherwise worked for the BBC and who, like Birt himself, were born on Merseyside. I was able to take my wife because she, too, was a Liverpudlian. But the likes of Bel Mooney had to leave her then husband, Jonathan Dimbleby, at home. Also among the guests were Cilla Black and her husband Bobby Willis, Beryl Bainbridge, Tony Hall, the 102nd Archbishop of Canterbury Robert Runcie, Roger and Thelma McGough, Gillian Reynolds, Anne Robinson, Laurie Taylor and Colette Bowe. John Birt's mum and dad had come down especially from Liverpool to do the catering.

For starters we had chip butties. The main course was scouse – the legendary Liverpool stew – with choice of HP sauce, beetroot, pickled red cabbage and piccalilli. The dessert was jelly with evaporated milk. The neatly typed menu also listed the drinks – Typhoo tea and Tizer. Guinness and Vimto were also available – the latter a purple carbonated drink with deeply evocative northern overtones, which had last passed my lips at the VE Day party in our street fifty years previously. The limited drinks menu led to a minor but good humoured revolt, and the Birts soon produced some decent wine. But it's the thought that counts, and many memories of Liverpool life were re-lived.

My association with the *Six O'Clock News* ended at the beginning of

1994, when I left *Question Time*. Martyn Lewis moved to the *Six*, and I joined the *Nine O'Clock News* to share the presentation with Michael Buerk. That seemed to please Michael. He hadn't got on with Martyn, whom he constantly accused of organising their joint rota around Martyn's social life and charity work, to his, Michael's, disadvantage. It was in fact a demanding schedule for two presenters. Although we were given the flexibility to decide the precise rota, it was mandatory that one or the other of us had to present the *Nine* every weekday, and we were also expected to present the late evening bulletin on Saturdays and Sundays. We were the faces of the BBC's flagship bulletins, expected to give them continuity and credibility. That survives only partly today, with practically anyone getting the chance to present at weekends.

Working around our social diaries and scheduled holidays required a lot of give and take between Michael and me, and from time to time there was no alternative to one of us working day after day while the other was away. During this time I set a record of sorts, presenting the BBC's main evening bulletin on twenty-one consecutive days. Adrenalin kept me going, but I was totally bushed when that three weeks came to an end.

Soon after I joined the *Nine*, I had my first run-in with the BBC's Health and Safety bureaucracy, when I received a memo asking me to attend a 'Studio Safety' course – which was to take half a day. I ignored it. I had never been on a course in my life, and this one didn't seem likely to add to my store of useful knowledge. I thought that would be the end of it, but I couldn't have been more mistaken. Directives to go on any kind of BBC course are just that, but have extra weight if they concern Health and Safety. Memo after memo followed, each one more threatening in tone. From being an 'ask' it became an instruction, then an order. When I ignored that, I was called in to see my line manager.

He was clearly embarrassed by the whole thing, because he was a friend of mine. Nonetheless he explained that I just had to go, and would I stop being awkward. I then enquired as to the purpose and content of this course that was judged so vital. To cut a long story short, it was explained to me that the modern news studio was a complicated place technically (I'd never have guessed) and that there were a number of potential hazards. Prompted by me, my friend went further: the main hazards were judged to be the robotic cameras which were operated from the control gallery, and glasses of water on the newscasters' desk. Apparently, although it had never happened (and never has) the robotic cameras had the potential to go out of control, like some crazed Daleks, and could inflict a nasty injury if the news presenter couldn't get out of the way. The glassware on the desk was also seen as life-threatening, because if it was broken it might just cut the wrists of an unaware presenter with potentially lethal consequences.

Curious, I asked what was being done about these dangers. I was told that there was a red emergency switch in the studio that immobilised the cameras, and that glassware was being replaced with plastic cups, which were to be kept out of vision. Proper water glasses would be available only for discussion programmes, when it might be aesthetically pleasing to have them in shot – but on such occasions the floor manager would receive a special payment for handling them. Thus briefed, I asked what was the point of me going on the course, when I now knew all that I was going to learn from it. Answer came there none and I heard no more of the matter.

I had another run-in with the BBC Health and Safety establishment three years later, during the 1997 general election campaign. As part of the campaign coverage it was decided that Michael Buerk and I would contribute three or four reports to the *Nine O'Clock News* from key marginal constituencies. My first assignment was a day out in Gravesend, where I would do some filming and talk to the main candidates and some of the floating voters. The day before, I was minding my own business in the newsroom when I was approached by a clipboard-carrier who asked if it was me who was going to Gravesend the following day. When I confirmed this, there was much sucking of teeth, and I was asked if I had been on the Operational Hazards course. No course, no Gravesend.

Now, my wife and I used to go shopping in Gravesend. We'd pushed prams around Gravesend. We'd never felt in danger in Gravesend, or been a danger to others. Ah, I was told, but you've never been to Gravesend with a film crew. All those trailing wires. And had I ever tried to park a loaded camera car in Gravesend? The list of hazards that made Gravesend sound like Gaza City went on. The clipboard-carrier went away. The next morning I drove to Gravesend straight from home, met up with my crew and did the job.

I mentioned my Health and Safety encounter to the cameraman, who pulled out of his pocket a three page Hazard Assessment form that he had had to fill in before he could leave the building – scores of boxes to tick identifying ways in which our trip to Gravesend might end in disaster, for us and for its citizens. Hazards which we had to be on the look-out for included Diving Operations, Hydraulic Hoists, Animals, Children, Derelict Buildings, Excavations, Glass, Physical Exertion, Abnormal Stress, Manual Lifting, Falling Objects and Inexperienced Performer. The thought went through my mind that no one asked us to fill in one of those forms before my life-changing assignment in Biafra – nor would it have made any difference if we had.

Most BBC employees know the value of working in a safe environment, and most also think the BBC Health and Safety culture, born of the best intentions, has become an expensive joke. Google records 1,300,000 hits if you enter 'BBC Health and Safety'. If you enter 'Ministry of Defence Health and Safety' it gives you 693,000; and if you enter ITV Health and Safety the number of references is 105,000.

I anchored the *Nine O'Clock News* with Michael Buerk until it was moved to ten o'clock at the end of 2000. The programme had been a fixture for thirty years, and I presented the last edition on 15 October of that year. Buerk and I then presented the *Ten O'Clock News* for a further two years. I remember my nine years on both programmes not so much for the major events with which they were packed, but for the friendship of colleagues who never let the eccentricities and occasional provocations of BBC management take the shine off their professionalism.

Part of my learning curve working for BBC News was discovering what a deeply political organisation it is. The office politics can be byzantine: you'd expect that in any big organisation, but at the BBC office politics have been refined into an art form. What was also new to me was the BBC's sensitivity to external politics and how they might impact on its ability to maintain support for the licence fee. What the BBC wants the public to believe is that it has independence woven into its fabric, running through its veins and concreted into its foundations. The reality, it began to dawn on me, was that for the BBC, independence is not a banner it carries principally on behalf of the listener or viewer. Rather it is the name it gives to its ability to act at all times in its own best interest.

Accordingly, at any given time there is a BBC line on everything of importance, a line usually adopted in the light of which way its senior echelons believe the political wind is blowing. This 'line' is rarely spelled out explicitly, but percolates subtly throughout the organisation, most potently through the process of promotions and appraisals which ensures that the careers of those who set themselves at odds with the corporation's perceived wisdom do not advance.

Take the issue of climate change, to which I will return later: there was never the slightest chance of the BBC running any serious scientific enquiry or debate that challenged the slogan 'The Science is Settled'. The entire proposition that warming was being caused by man was accepted without question, and, in my view, accepted because it had become an article of widespread political faith. It was also judged to be beyond challenge because it was the gospel according to the United Nations, an organisation regarded with reverence at Television Centre. Another figure treated reverentially for a time was Al Gore, the high priest of global warming alarmism. On one of the former vice-president's visits to London, senior editorial figures were practically eating out of his hand in his suite at the Dorchester.

Only when the political consensus started to look shaky after the abortive Copenhagen climate summit and the Climategate scandal, was a questioning note injected into some BBC reports. Even then, leading 'sceptics' were still generally regarded with disdain and kept at arm's length. As for the BBC's feared interviewers, most seemed to lose the powers of enquiry which they were so ready to parade when dealing with lesser topics.

The BBC's ability to position itself, to decide for itself on which side its bread is buttered is what it calls its independence. It's a flexible and sophisticated kind of independence, and one acutely sensitive to which way the wind is blowing politically. Complaints from viewers may invariably be met with the BBC's stock response 'We don't accept that, so get lost'. But complaints from ministers, though they may be rejected publicly, usually cause consternation – particularly if there is a licence fee settlement in the offing. And not just ministers, if a change of government is thought likely. Take what happened on 3 October 1995, a year and a half after I joined the *Nine*. It was a Tuesday during the Labour Party Conference, and the Leader of the Opposition, Tony Blair, was making his big speech as party leader, a position to which he'd been elected fifteen months previously. The Major government was deeply unpopular, and the betting was that Blair would walk the next general election. Labour's problem was that there was enormous interest in the outcome of the trial of O. J. Simpson, and the verdict was due at 6 p.m. UK time. Half the population of the United States was tuned in for the verdict, and after a sensational trial there was massive interest in the UK as well. Indeed, at the Labour Conference itself delegates crowded round TV sets in anticipation of the *Six O'Clock News*, and it wasn't to see a rerun of Tony Blair.

Alastair Campbell, Tony Blair's Press Secretary, was having none of it. He faxed the BBC and ITN: 'I would implore you not to lose sight both of the news value and of the importance to the country of Mr Blair's speech.' It wasn't as if either news organisation was planning to ignore the speech. It would clearly be given thorough coverage.

But Campbell wanted it to lead the news. ITN ignored his letter. The BBC made sure the *Six O'Clock News* complied. As someone who has worked for many years for both organisations, that spoke volumes. Such a letter from a spin doctor to ITN would almost certainly have been binned on principle by the great editors I worked for. At the BBC the instinct, faced with such a plea from a party of the left, standing on the brink of power, was to do as requested.

The story became public almost immediately, not least because some people in the BBC newsroom were so outraged that they phoned their friends in the press. The BBC rushed out a statement: 'To suggest that the running order of BBC news programmes was influenced under pressure is defamatory.' It clearly wasn't defamatory, but a reasonable inference given the sequence of events, and the volume of complaints after the *Six* clearly hit a raw nerve. The *Nine O'Clock News*, which I was presenting, led on OJ. Our brief editorial meeting beforehand was livelier than usual, with more than one producer venturing the view that the *Six* had taken leave of its senses. All governments work hard on influencing the news agenda – Whitehall doesn't employ hundreds of press officers to collect newspaper cuttings. But what I found quite uncomfortable during my years on the *Nine* and the *Ten* was how blatant those attempts to pressurise the BBC became, particularly at general election time. You'd have thought that the party machines – both government and opposition – would operate discreetly. But they all had the internal BBC telephone numbers of the editors of the major news programmes, whom they would try to bully in person both before and after programmes. The scene was always the same: the duty editor of the programme, either trying to get a bulletin on air or trying to get home after it, had a phone clamped to his ear and would be trying above the hubbub of the newsroom to be polite to someone from a political party who was telling them how to do their job. On one such night, after an edition of the *Nine*, when we all got back to the newsroom, the programme editor's phone was ringing. It was a direct call from Number 10, questioning her judgement and complaining about our political coverage that night. Remember, this wasn't a call to the Director General, or to the Head of News, but to a harassed and tired programme editor who had been on duty for fourteen hours. As I was putting on my coat, I realised what was going on. 'Tell him to get stuffed' I said. She looked away and pushed the phone closer to her ear. 'Well, transfer the call to the duty officer' I suggested. She rolled her eyes, knowing better than I the row that would cause.

Government attempts to manipulate news broadcasters are, of course, as old as broadcasting itself. Indeed, at the outset, the BBC didn't need any persuading – Lord Reith believed that BBC News broadcasts should carry nothing of controversy, and told ministers as such. When I joined ITN in the early 1960s, Britain had the fourteen-day rule, designed to prevent the discussion by broadcasters of any controversial matter likely to be raised in Parliament during the next fourteen days. ITN ignored it. Today we have the dark arts of 'spin': politicians' attempts to persuade the media to see it their way, regardless of the facts of the matter. There have always been people employed in Whitehall to put the best possible face on what governments are doing. The first of them that I met regularly, back in the 1960s, was Bernard Ingham, a former industrial correspondent, who worked for Barbara Castle and then Tony Benn. He was fiercely loyal to all his ministers, but carried that loyalty into the realm of personal devotion with Margaret Thatcher. He became, as Thatcher would put it 'One of Us'. Ingham was the first person I ever heard utter the phrase 'You might say that ... I couldn't possibly comment', made famous years later in a TV drama. It wasn't so much his way of telling you what to think, as indicating that you were thinking along the right lines. In the 1980s I had little direct contact with Peter Mandelson, the man credited with taking spin into a new dimension, but I did see him in action. At one Labour Party conference, ITN was short of a reporter to doorstep Neil Kinnock, then the party leader. The person they sent was not a reporter at all, but a news desk assistant, Joy

Johnson (who later went on to work for the BBC, and for the Labour Party). Anyway, Joy threw a question at Kinnock which caught him off guard, and made for a minor damaging headline. When I bumped into Mandelson soon after, I jokingly suggested that his man had been caught out by a rookie reporter. 'No,' said Mandelson without cracking a smile, 'she was a very experienced and senior reporter.' It was his ability to look a reporter in the eye and swear that black was white that set him apart. On such occasions the words of my old headmaster J. R. Edwards came back to me: 'Never give up what you do know for what you don't know.'

Early in 1995 I was shaken out of my preoccupation with BBC News by the death of my mother. It was the saddest day of my life. She had battled stomach cancer for many months, and my brothers and I had ensured she was looked after in a loving care home not far from Wrexham, in easy reach of the homes of Cliff and David, her eldest and youngest sons. I was at home in Kent when my eldest brother Cliff telephoned to say that mum was dying. It was early evening, and I was in the car within minutes, arriving in north Wales in record time. She was deeply unconscious, and I was the last of the family to arrive. I held her hand and spoke to her, and thought I detected some response, a sign that she knew that I had arrived, which comforted me greatly. Soon her nurses asked us all to leave the room, so that they could turn her and make her more comfortable, but within minutes they called us back. She was dead. I have missed her every day since. She was a brilliant, selfless mother. But more than that, she knew that if we were to succeed in life, we had to have a good education, the education that she never had. We could never repay her for that.

During my years on the *Nine* and the *Ten* (Greg Dyke moved the evening news to ten o'clock in October 2000) there were very few occasions on which I presented the programme from the location of a major story. I'd always taken the view that there was an element of risk involved technically if you left TV Centre without proper production backup, and I had mixed experiences when I did leave the studio. The first occasion was on 13 March 1996. On my way to work that day, about lunchtime, I had intended to have a brief look around the Ideal Home Exhibition at Earl's Court. As I was going up the steps my mobile rang, and the Editor of the *Nine O'Clock News* told me the dreadful news from Dunblane, a small town in Perthshire. A man, later identified as Thomas Hamilton, armed with four guns, had walked into Dunblane's little primary school and opened fire on a class of five- and six-year-olds. Sixteen children and their teacher died. Hamilton then shot himself.

I hailed a taxi and went straight to Heathrow. Nine years previously, I had been in the Channel Four newsroom when the first reports came through of Michael Ryan's lethal rampage at Hungerford, in which he shot sixteen people. Because early reports from Hungerford were so sketchy and fragmented I was slow to grasp the significance of what was going on, much to my shame and the annoyance of some colleagues. But I needed no urging to go to Dunblane. Key production personnel were also on their way, and I sat on the plane next to Kate Adie, a reassuring presence as the BBC's senior reporter.

I presented the *Nine* live from a car park next to the church in Dunblane, conducting a couple of live interviews, and Kate produced a sensitive and thorough report on the tragedy and its immediate aftermath. Earlier, I hadn't been able to get close to the school itself, but just to gaze upon it from a few hundred yards away was to experience almost physical pain at the thought of the bodies still inside.

In the town the grief was everywhere: groups of bereaved and bereft people numb and speechless at the atrocity for which they'd been singled out. There were few residential streets in Dunblane in which the curtains weren't drawn. And the media had arrived in force, just as the people wanted to be left alone. I felt like an intruder, but I and Kate had done what we had come to do. The most difficult part of my day was closing the News, with a few lines that did justice to the awfulness of what had happened. It's on occasions like this that a presenter *has* to get it right. I left it until the last moment, standing in the dark scribbling a few words on my notepad. This is how I signed off the news that night: 'Dunblane tonight is a bitterly cold and bitterly sad place. A place not of anger but of incomprehension. I stood across the playing fields from the gymnasium in which these innocents were murdered. The outside could have been any one of similar schools throughout Britain. But the senselessness and brutality of what happened here today will long set it apart. And as for the emotional scars – who can blame those for whom they may never heal?'

The next morning a taxi picked me up to take me back to Glasgow Airport and my flight to London. As we drove out of Dunblane my mobile phone rang, and it was the Editor of the *Nine*. He asked me if I would go back, and spend the day in Dunblane knocking on doors and getting reaction. I had no hesitation in refusing. I had seen enough to know that those people wanted, and needed, to be left alone. I don't believe any reporter who did stay in Dunblane that day got close to anyone who'd been directly affected, let alone got them to talk.

Waiting for me when I returned to London was a letter from a Catholic priest in Cornwall, which concluded: 'I simply want to thank you for not being intrusive into people's grief, and for presenting this ghastly story in the traditional BBC way, that is, with utter dignity. We do notice and appreciate your efforts.' I have rarely treasured a letter more.

The next time I anchored, or attempted to anchor, the news from an outside location was more than two years later. The President of the United States, Bill Clinton, was in deep trouble over his relationship with Monica Lewinsky, and the Independent Counsel Kenneth Starr was about to produce the report that led to his impeachment for allegedly perjuring himself. It was thought possible, however, that Clinton might suddenly resign, rather than face such a trial. Early on the morning of 11 September 1998, learning that the Starr report was to be published that day, the news desk decided, without giving me any early warning, to send me to Washington to anchor that evening's main news.

The night before, I had been with my wife to a rather jolly party at Broadcasting House, for the BBC's former aviation correspondent Reg Turnill, and his wife Margaret. We had not gone home to Kent, but instead had stayed in London – fortunately. Lying in bed, my phone rang at just before 8 a.m., and I was told that I'd been booked on the Concorde to New York leaving Heathrow at 10 a.m. To be certain of catching the flight I had to check in no later than 9.30. I had an hour and a half to dress, pack and travel from our pied-à-terre in SE1 across London to Heathrow at the height of the rush hour. The news desk told me that a car would be outside in fifteen minutes. I rushed out of the door fifteen minutes later to find, not a fast car, but one of the oldest black cabs I have ever seen driven by a man who had clearly been born without a sense of urgency.

By 9.00 a.m. we were stuck in a gridlocked Fulham, having been forced to take a detour because the main route out of town was blocked at Hammersmith. We reached the motorway at 9.30, and I told the driver to put his foot down. In his clapped out cab it didn't make any difference. On my mobile, the news desk told me to keep going – British Airways would hold the gate for me. In the event, they held it until my arrival just after ten, and as I shoehorned myself into a seat, the Concorde pushed back. I was totally frazzled and emotionally drained – a condition considerably assuaged by the sound of a stewardess opening a bottle of champagne. A glass or two later my pulse rate had returned to normal, and I looked around me. I was the only one drinking alcohol. Without exception my fellow passengers were businessmen in suits hunched over laptops and refusing any drink except mineral water. One suit had his secretary with him, crouched in the aisle beside his seat, endlessly taking dictation. He didn't even make sure she had a glass of champagne. What a waste! Was this what we built Concorde for? I realised why I was more at home in journalism, where we saw Concorde, Britain's Apollo, as a thing of beauty and of national pride, not a fast desk.

Concorde being Concorde, I arrived in New York a few minutes before I left London. Next I had to catch a shuttle flight to Washington, and because I had just missed one, and the internal flights departed from a totally different part of the airport, I lost another two hours. It didn't get any easier. Arriving in Washington DC I jumped into a cab and asked the driver to take me to the BBC office. He didn't know where it was, and I realised to my horror a) that although I'd been there before, I couldn't remember the address, and b) that my mobile battery was now flat and I couldn't phone London to ask them. We drove up and down a few roads that looked familiar until I saw the building and rushed inside.

It was 1.30 p.m. local time, but 6.30 p.m. back in the UK – two and a half hours to my transmission time, when I had to stand on Capitol Hill to open the *Nine O'Clock News*. The BBC Washington Bureau was a hive of activity, with producers and presenters from practically every BBC news or current affairs outlet fighting for the few desks available. There was a producer from the *Nine* waiting for me, and fortunately he was one of the very best. He'd already organised somewhere to sit and much of what I had to do. Two and a quarter hours later we stepped out of a taxi behind the Capitol near to where a local camera crew had set up the position for our broadcast. I put my jacket on, straightened my tie, and plugged in my earpiece.

Relief – I could hear the control gallery. Despair – they couldn't hear me. The freelance crew shrugged – and assured me that everything was leaving them OK. They checked everything and still London couldn't hear me. I heard the studio director at TV Centre in London tell the standby presenter, George Alagiah, that he would be doing the programme. My contribution would be an interview with a US senator that I had pre-recorded on the way to our camera position and which had already been played down the line to London from the BBC bureau. That apart, my day had been a very expensive waste of time, as well as probably taking a year off my life.

I stayed on Capitol Hill listening to the *Nine* in my earpiece, and when it came off-air my American crew started to pack up their gear. At which point one of the two guys noticed that a wire in the back of his control box for the camera and sound equipment was slightly out of its socket. He pushed it home, and suddenly they could hear me in London. Without a word of apology he and his mate packed up their gear and left. If they'd been paid to sabotage the *Nine* that night, they couldn't have done a better job.

Some presenters, I am sure, will go through their professional lives and have no trouble with presenting their programmes live from a distant location. But two years later I became convinced that in that regard, I was jinxed. And Concorde was involved then also, but in the most tragic circumstances. It was the morning in July 2000 that the aircraft was involved in its first and last air disaster – an Air France Concorde, taking off from Charles De Gaulle airport, bursting into flames and crashing on the village of Gonesse. I was sent to Paris to present the *Nine O'Clock News* from the location, and arrived in the early afternoon.

By then the press and other media had been corralled by the police well away from the crash scene, and well out of sight of it. I never saw so much as a wisp of smoke, just the occasional police car heading up the road. There was no indication whatever that one of the world's most iconic aircraft, and its 109 passengers and crew, were scattered over a field less than half a mile away. Nonetheless, it was a sunny day, and I set about writing my links for the main evening news. The programme editor in London was particularly keen that at the end of the bulletin I should do an extended pay-off to camera, drawing all the threads of the story together, putting it into the context of the Concorde achievement and underlining that this was more than just another air crash. By early evening I had written this piece – all in longhand on a notepad – and gave it to our autocue operator to put into the portable prompter.

The *Nine O'Clock News* went well, until half way through there was a clap of thunder followed by a torrential downpour. Our camera position was in the open, but underneath a tarpaulin stretched between four poles. In between the segments of our report from Gonesse and background material assembled in London, I watched with concern as the rain began to fill the tarpaulin, which sagged alarmingly under the weight of the water. Then, just as the time came for me to begin my sign-off, the tarpaulin gave way. To my horror several gallons of water cascaded straight onto the autocue operator, drenching her, shorting out all her equipment, and washing my notebook off her portable table and into the gutter. I had the best part of two minutes to fill. Michael Buerk – who was in the London studio that night doing 'the rest of the news' – remarked a few days later that I closed the programme in a very thoughtful manner. Too true. I was thinking hard to recall what I had written – but it did help that I had been familiar with the Concorde story since I had been ITN's aviation correspondent nearly thirty years previously.

Although we were not close friends, there was much mutual respect between Buerk and me, based on the long experience each of us had at the frontline of news. Indeed, to many people watching we *were* BBC News. Both of us knew, however, that that was not the view of our BBC bosses, who only eighteen months previously had hung us out to dry, letting speculation about our futures – and that of other senior presenters – run riot. They wouldn't even deny rumours that they were planning to replace us with Trevor McDonald.

We were kept in the dark, most of all about the debate going on at the top of the BBC about, yes, 'freshening up' and 'reshaping' BBC News, to make it more understandable for, and accessible to, younger viewers. And what we didn't realise was that our prospects were in the hands not of those who ran the news operation, but of our new masters – the Focus Groups.

Chapter 13

The Dreaded 'Freshening Up'

In February 1997 I had been at BBC News for just under eight years. I had packed a lot into that time, chairing *Question Time*, presenting the major news bulletins, doing some well received radio and generally establishing myself, or so I believed, as an asset to the BBC's news operation. But I still knew very little about the BBC. What I was totally unaware of was the inherent tension between the executives who ran BBC Television and those who ran BBC News. This meant that news was always under pressure, often quite subtly, to justify the place it occupied in primetime by producing programmes that fitted in, not with any grand BBC vision to inform and educate, but with the requirements of the Controller of BBC1 to entertain and to keep the ratings buoyant.

Particularly important in the evenings was an obligation placed on news not to throw away an audience that had been built by scheduling earlier in the evening. The biggest crime for news was to be so worthy that large swathes of the audience switched channels. In recent years that pressure has intensified. Despite all the fine words about Public Service Broadcasting, there hasn't been a BBC channel controller who hasn't been as obsessed with ratings as any counterpart in commercial television. This pursuit of mass audiences manifests itself as almost an obsession with never being seen to stand still. Accordingly, established programmes like the news are always at risk, as controllers search for ways to stop audiences tiring of them, even though the only evidence that such programmes have lost, or may lose, their appeal may have come from asking a dozen people in a focus group. Above all there is the Holy Grail – that somewhere out there is a massive but elusive new audience for News, the under twenty-fives. These sought-after viewers, the thinking goes, have a low boredom threshold when it comes to serious news. The challenge is to feed them such news, but presented in new ways dictated by their attention span. The target audience are also perceived to want more showbiz and entertainment news, and to have an aversion to too many middle-aged presenters. A senior BBC executive, who defected to Channel 5 to establish a new populist strand, soon saw the flaws in that approach. News organisations all over the world, he said, were obsessed with how to attract and hold younger people, but 16-24 year-olds had better things to do. 'They go out to the pub, they go clubbing, they'll do anything rather than sit waiting about for the nightly news. They pick up news as and when they find it.' Nonetheless, established BBC programmes, those generally with an appeal to older age groups – and that includes the news – can be guaranteed some sort of makeover as an incoming channel controller invariably turns his or her attention to 'freshening them up', in a way designed to widen the channel's appeal particularly among 'the yoof', and regardless of the tastes of the BBC's most loyal viewers, the over-fifties.

Controllers always want to stamp their distinctive mark on their channel and want to be remembered for the changes they made, not for keeping things the way they were. What I detected at the BBC, and my view was shared widely by colleagues with whom I worked, was that many changes appeared to have little rationale apart from being a personal statement by the executive who ordered them.

So it was that early in 1997 the relatively new controller of BBC1, Michael Jackson, anxious to remodel the schedules, began looking at the News, particularly in the early evening. The response of the Head of News, Tony Hall was to order a root and branch review of all its news programmes – billed as the biggest overhaul of the BBC's News output for ten years. It was a shrewd move by Hall, because it kept him in the driving seat and kept Jackson at arm's length. Hall promised conclusions by the autumn of that year. In the event the review took a year longer.

What wasn't so clever was that for the whole of that time BBC News was destabilised by constant speculation and rumour about what would be the outcome of the review. And as is the practice of much of the press, they personalised it. The conventional wisdom became that the days of comfortable and familiar middle class and middle aged broadcasters were numbered. For eighteen months hardly a week went by without stories appearing saying that either Peter Sissons or Michael Buerk or Martyn

Lewis or Anna Ford or Edward Stourton or Justin Webb was going to be sacked (all at that time being regular presenters of one or other of the BBC's main bulletins).

I lost count of the number of times that the press confidently predicted that Trevor McDonald (that well-known youngster) or Kirsty Young or any one of half a dozen young blonde female presenters had been approached to take over from us. I was buttonholed by one reporter at a social event, and suggested to him that I was thinking of getting my hair dyed blond, that being the only way to ensure that I held on to my job. Most people saw the joke, but it is a matter of great regret to me that one of my female colleagues didn't. Jill Dando, the BBC's most famous blonde, took great offence, and stopped speaking to me. Jill was part-time on the *Six*, and was hoping that the review would establish her as its full-time principal presenter. As the review dragged on and it became obvious that she wasn't in the running, she decided to leave news altogether, and concentrate on her current affairs and lifestyle programmes. I don't know whether she blamed me in some way, but I was pointedly the only presenter colleague not invited to her drinks party on the day she said goodbye to the *Six*. A year later, when Jill was murdered, we still hadn't spoken. I announced her death on the *Nine* that night – 26 April 1999 – feeling doubly anguished: at the brutal and atrocious way the life of such a special colleague had been snuffed out, and at my own negligence of her feelings a year previously. I am not proud of that, and I haven't forgiven myself.

So it was a long wait – a year and a half – for the outcome of Tony Hall's review. Why did the rumours go on for that long? And why was there no statement from the BBC that was convincing enough to put an end to them?

Looking back now, it seemed to those of us who were affected that there was an orchestrated whispering campaign against us from inside the BBC. We waited in vain for the management of BBC News to issue some categorical denials – but there was none. I also suspect that agents pushing the claims of outside presenters saw advantage in keeping the pot on the boil by constantly suggesting that a deal was as good as done for one of their clients to take over from me or Michael Buerk, or any of the others. And so the speculation and uncertainty dragged on, as did the review – interrupted first by the 1997 election campaign and then, out of the blue, by yet another change of BBC1 controller.

In the autumn of 1997 Michael Jackson left suddenly after only a year in the job, and was succeeded by Peter Salmon. The rumours flew that Salmon had different views about what should happen to News, centred particularly on the presenters. If the internal debate had been solely about the direction and shape of our programmes, it might have been a good idea to consult the more experienced presenters, but the fact that that never happened confirmed suspicions that there was some truth in the constant stream of rumour being picked up by the press about the personalities involved.

There was, of course, another interruption to the review, one that actually tested BBC News, the competence of its presenters and its credibility with the viewing public. It was an event that should have told BBC executives more about the news and the good health it was in, than a hundred focus groups. It was the shocking death of Princess Diana.

Practically since I joined BBC News I had been involved in rehearsals for the coverage of a royal death. Every six months or so, usually on a Saturday morning, a news studio would be set aside for what was essentially a run-through of BBC procedure in the event of the death of a senior member of the royal family. The actual drill and protocol was laid down according to the seniority of the deceased. At the very highest level, all BBC channels would interrupt their programmes, and come together for the announcement. The national anthem would be played over the fluttering royal standard, and the news would be solemnly intoned. Even the form of words was strictly laid down. A succession of pre-recorded interviews and obituaries would follow – which were stored in a locked cabinet in the newsroom – and there would be a list of phone numbers of suitable interviewees who would drop everything, if asked, and come into the studio to pay tribute. Essentially, the system didn't appear to have changed all that much since the death of the King in 1953, but of course then the BBC had only one channel and was our only broadcaster.

No one liked these rehearsals, and it was generally felt that the only thing worse than being involved with a royal death rehearsal was the prospect of actually being on duty when the real thing happened. A former BBC News editor, Tim Luckhurst wrote an article in *The Guardian*, some months before the Queen Mother died, entitled 'Please God, not on my shift'. 'BBC editors,' he wrote 'all share the same certainty – whoever is the editor responsible for output when it happens will be deemed to have made a mistake of tone, content or timing. If the nation rebels in horror at the antediluvian nature of the broadcast, following the guidelines to the letter will be no excuse. Some poor hack, probably someone who has covered wars, revolutions, general elections and natural disasters without putting a foot wrong and simply by following good journalistic instincts, will be declared an un-person. That blameless scapegoat will take lifelong responsibility for paper clip supplies to outlying local radio stations.' In the fullness of time I was to find out exactly what he meant, although I managed to avoid the paper clips.

The rehearsals I was involved with were mainly technical, their purpose being to ensure that everyone on duty knew what to do, and to identify any snags and pitfalls. On the day of the rehearsal we always worked to a fictional scenario, scripted by a news producer, and at one time or another we simulated the BBC's response to the demise of most senior members of the royal family. In theory, these rehearsals should have been shared equally by the senior presenters, Michael Buerk and myself. In practice I seemed to get most of them, since a number coincided with Michael's holidays, for which he considered himself very fortunate. As the years went by the rehearsal invariably focused on one possible royal death in particular, that of Queen Elizabeth the Queen Mother. We usually pretended that she'd expired at her Caithness home, the Castle of Mey, after choking on a fish bone – something for which she had form, although so far with less dramatic consequences. The fictional scenario for the Queen Mother also had attractions because the remoteness of the location posed particular technical challenges which our rehearsal was expected to help identify.

However, on one occasion we varied the subject and the made-up circumstances in which she had expired. The Princess of Wales had become probably the most famous woman in the world. What would we do if *she* died? A producer was delegated to come up with a scenario around which the rehearsal could proceed. His skeleton script for the circumstances of her 'death' took the form of what he imagined might be the first accounts of it that were flashed on the wire services of the main news agencies. With uncanny prescience, the story we worked to on the day we rehearsed was that Princess Diana had been killed in a car crash on the M4, returning to central London from Windsor Castle. I broke the 'news', reporters reported from the 'scene' and from outside Buckingham Palace, and other reporters played the parts of the great and the good who were queuing up to pay tribute.

It tested our systems, honed up the planning, and most people involved thought nothing more of it. We could forget Diana. After all, wouldn't the Queen Mother die first? The old lady, as we know, had other ideas.

Early on the morning of 31 August 1997, just another Sunday morning, I was awakened at home by the bedside telephone. I looked blearily at the clock. It was just after six. The caller was a senior BBC producer who told me that the Princess of Wales and Dodi Fayed had been killed in a car crash in Paris. I've never woken up so fast. He wanted me in the office by 10 a.m., to take over on air from Martyn Lewis who'd been on duty since the early hours. I put on the TV, and like millions of others who were jolted into consciousness, tried to take in the shocking details.

This was an event for which no rehearsal could equip a presenter, but it was good to have some warning and some time to think about the implications. I drove the forty miles to Television Centre, listening to updates on the radio, and in the newsroom I watched the TV output and read every word coming off the wires. It was by far the most compelling and multi-faceted news story I had ever been called upon to handle. The violent and sudden death of the young and beautiful Princess who had been virtually ostracised by the royal family, was followed almost immediately by a rising tide of popular emotion. A sombre Prime Minister, Tony Blair, instantly caught what he sensed to be the national mood, calling her 'the People's Princess'. Blair may subsequently have acquired a reputation for being a good actor, but that phrase and the way it was delivered touched millions. It certainly worked with Martyn Lewis in the studio, who was close to tears. I was told that I would take over from him at 1 p.m., for the rest of the day.

At a few minutes to one I was ready to go into the studio when the editor assigned to the BBC's Diana coverage that day took me briefly to one side. Some years previously we'd worked together at *Channel Four News*, and he knew that I was not a 'soft' presenter. I had a reputation for asking searching questions and pressing for answers. He wished me luck, and added: 'Go easy. Leave the awkward questions until tomorrow.' It wasn't the sort of approach we'd have endorsed when we worked together on *Channel Four News*. In any event it was the first and only time that day that I was given any kind of editorial guidance or advice.

Just before one, Martyn Lewis signed off, clearly emotionally drained. During a brief break I shook his hand, congratulated him on his stint holding the programme together, then slipped into his seat. The handshake was significant because we'd hardly been on speaking terms for nearly four years – he'd taken offence because I had ridiculed an article he'd written urging the coverage of more 'good' news, something close to his heart, but which I subsequently learned had done his credibility great damage at the higher levels of the BBC.

So far that day, the story, though shocking, had been reasonably straightforward: beautiful Princess, in royal family's bad books, dies in car crash with playboy lover. Shortly after I went on air everything changed. Diana's brother Earl Spencer came out of his home in a Capetown suburb and said that far from being an accident that had killed his sister, it was murder. 'I always believed the press would kill her in the end,' he said. 'But not even I could believe they would take such a direct hand in her death as seems to be the case.' And he went on: 'It would appear that every proprietor and every editor of every publication that has paid for intrusive and exploitative photographs of her, encouraging greedy and ruthless individuals to risk everything in pursuit of Diana's image, has blood on his hands today.' It was a sensational moment.

As I watched, the advice to play it safe and avoid any awkward questions passed through my mind and straight out of the window.

For the rest of the afternoon, without a break, I anchored the BBC coverage. And during those hours I missed no opportunity to try to take the story forward. Everyone who had a view about Diana – and people were queuing up to be interviewed – had a view also about the role her pursuit by the paparazzi may have played in her death. It was obvious to me that it would have been negligent not to continue the debate there and then which Earl Spencer had so dramatically ignited. Tony Blair's reference to her as the People's Princess had also struck a nerve, and I thought it right to fan the discussion that was already heating up nationally as the news sank in: what will this death mean to the royal family? How will they react? Will they continue to distance themselves from her, even in death? How will that play with the grieving public? Will Diana now have an impact greater than when she was alive? Did taking away her royal status – and with it her protection officers – contribute to her death? There was no shortage of similar questions which were to dominate in the days ahead.

I make these points because it illustrates the absurdity of anyone at the BBC thinking they could be avoided once a story has picked up momentum. The BBC has a policy on everything, yet I don't know any senior presenters who, when the chips are down, don't just make editorial policy up as they go along. That is when they earn their money. Certainly, on that day, every nuance, every question, was mine and mine alone, and editorial policy was what I thought fit. I was to learn subsequently that if you get it right the BBC will take the credit; if you get it wrong, you are on your own. But none of that weighed with me on the day: like many before me, I considered it a privilege to be sitting in front of a BBC microphone and camera – the BBC with its worldwide reputation, the trusted source to which the vast majority of the public turned at times like this.

Early in the evening I also got the rare chance to influence not just the editorial content of the BBC's output, but its production.

My first break from the non-stop coverage was scheduled for 6.30, when the regular Sunday Evensong at St Paul's Cathedral was hastily converted into a service in memory of the Princess. It was a truly emotional event and it was broadcast by the BBC. The problem we had was that the Princess's coffin was on its way back from Paris, and due at RAF Northolt in north London between 6.30 and 7. So I had to sit in the studio, ready to break off from St Paul's and hand to our reporter, Brian Hanrahan, who was at the airfield. As it happened, evensong that night, after some prayers, consisted almost entirely of some of the most beautiful and haunting choral music that I have ever heard, and the choir of St Paul's was in wonderful voice. In the studio, alone except for my floor manager, I sat watching them and listening and for the first time that day felt like crying myself.

Then someone said in my earpiece that the BAe 146 of the Queen's Flight was only a couple of minutes from landing at Northolt, and that I should stand by to hand to Brian. It occurred to me that we shouldn't cut away from St Paul's, as if it were just any old outside broadcast. So I spoke over the studio foldback to the director in the news control gallery, and suggested to him that we take the pictures from RAF Northolt and the sound from Wren's great cathedral. It was a simple thing to do, and he did it straight away. The effect was mesmerising and deeply moving. The sky over Northolt was leaden, and our camera there searched in vain for the incoming aircraft. Meantime the choir sang on, the sound soaring and subsiding beautifully. And just as they reached one particularly moving passage, the clouds parted and the aircraft could be clearly seen. But that wasn't all. As it began its final approach, the sun burst through, catching its fuselage almost as if some hidden hand were guiding it, bathing it in light. A Hollywood director could have worked for years trying to get that shot, and to find the right music, but everything came together in that moment. The sun followed the aircraft onto the runway, appearing almost to caress it as it braked and turned in the far distance; and then as it taxied back towards the reception party, the clouds parted just a little more. Even to think about it now brings a lump to my throat. With the aircraft on the ground, and evensong at St Paul's finished, Brian Hanrahan took over with a sensitive commentary on the scenes as the coffin was taken from the aircraft, watched by a sombre group including the Prince of Wales. Brian got it absolutely right, as one would expect. No surplus of words, and not one wasted.

For the rest of that evening I linked to various other special BBC programmes, including a major obituary which had been hurriedly updated, and concluded with a news bulletin at 11 p.m. for which I'd written a brief summary of the main events of the day. As I signed off I felt drained – not so much tired, but affected more than I'd realised by the emotions of the day. I walked to the car park and drove home, making a short detour close to Kensington Palace, the Princess's London home, where a steady stream of people were starting to build what was to become a mountain of flowers.

The tide of sentiment was practically turning Diana into a saint, and over the next few days it would come close to casting some members of the royal family as sinners. Yet, as I waited to go on air earlier that day, I had leafed through the Sunday newspapers, all of which had gone to press before the news from Paris. I happened to glance at a column in the *Sunday Mirror*, by its star writer, Carole Malone. Malone's words remind us that Diana, in the days before her death had forfeited a massive amount of popular support. By her antics with the Al Fayed family, and particularly the way she appeared to relish embarrassing the royals by cavorting with a man caricatured as a Muslim playboy, she'd done herself no favours. In her column, which was rolling off the presses even as Diana's life blood was draining away in that Paris underpass, Malone wrote: 'The Princess, I fear, suffers from the "Open Gob before Brain Engages" syndrome – a condition which affects the trivial and the brain dead ... what we have here is a woman who has little common sense, even less judgement, and a very convenient persecution complex, which she drags out as a defence when her little publicity plots go belly-up.' Columnists like to reflect the mood of their readers. There can't have been many instances when public sentiment towards a prominent figure changed so fast and so far, as it did on that day. In death, the newly beatified Diana was suddenly beyond reproach – bringing bewilderment to the royal family, and danger too.

Three weeks later the top brass of the BBC took themselves off to a luxury hotel in Cambridge to discuss the Diana coverage, from the first newsflash through the whole extraordinary week of mass grieving, to the funeral at Westminster Abbey and the journey of the hearse to Althorp. This was the BBC's post mortem on its own coverage. There was no hint subsequently of any dissatisfaction with what had been achieved on that opening day, or indeed during the rest of the week – the internal rumour mill would been in overdrive if there had been. But what was really puzzling was that neither I, nor any other presenter, or any producer or editor working on that first day was invited to join the discussion or submit their views in any other form. Nor were any conclusions that were reached in Cambridge conveyed officially to the people who'd actually done the work. As I was to find out when I drew the short straw on the next royal death, the editorial guidelines and policies for royal deaths *were* subsequently reviewed and changed. But no one passed them on to the foot soldiers in the newsroom, or discussed them at any stage with any of the newsroom presenters who might be involved next time there was a death in the royal family.

When the nation emerged from its prolonged spasm of grief at Diana's death, the BBC resumed where it had left off – letting all its main TV News presenters remain the subject of prolonged speculation about whether one or more of them would be sacked, cast aside in favour of the latest outsider being tipped as the salvation of BBC News. In fact, the more the speculation intensified, the less the BBC said to deny it.

Astonishingly, the BBC justified the treatment they were meting out to us, in a statement they issued to one of the media correspondents. 'I can understand,' said the BBC spokesman, 'that it is frustrating and unsettling ... but it is the trade-off for their high wages ... insecurity is the price they pay. That's how the system works.' It took the BBC more than another twelve months to end the uncertainty.

The speculation didn't even take a summer holiday. I came back from a break in Portugal to find a note from Michael Buerk on my desk. 'Welcome back to the madhouse' it began, and went on: 'The last three weeks have been ridiculous. Nothing new, but the howl-round in the papers has got worse and the management is paralysed.' He added that the papers were full of stories about Trevor McDonald being offered a million pounds a year to do our jobs, and not a single management figure – 'and God knows there are plenty of them' – bothering to say a word about it.

It was getting past a joke, and I had had enough. Practically the last straw was when my wife was out shopping near our home, and she bumped into a friend who remarked 'I see your husband is going to lose his job'. So I did two things. I gave an interview, more in anger than in sorrow, to one of the leading media correspondents, which was widely picked up by other publications. In it, I accused the BBC of inflicting damage on the professional status of its presenters: 'By refusing to make any convincing public defence of its TV presenting team, it's practically invited the public to conclude that it has no confidence in them ... If the BBC appears to lack confidence in its presenters, why should the public believe in them? We give the BBC credibility. But its managers have been undermining our stature by giving the impression to viewers that we're dispensable.' Elsewhere, I expressed the view that corporation bosses 'were more interested in holding a beauty contest to find viewer-friendly faces than increasing the credibility of their news operation'.

The second thing I did was to speak to the lawyer who had advised me on my original contract negotiations. Although he counselled caution, I believe he may, informally, have marked a few cards in the BBC's legal and contracts departments. Anna Ford was also reported to have taken legal advice. She was particularly incensed by the constant leaks from the BBC that focus groups had presented management with a 'love list' of presenters, who had found certain presenters, her among them, 'aloof, snooty and out of touch'. Anna demanded to see the evidence against her, but met a brick wall. My rating on the 'love list', by the way, was said to be well down in the relegation zone. What I found puzzling was that the BBC set so much store by focus groups, rather than trusting the judgement of their own people. Has the BBC ever made a great programme in response to a focus group?

The way Anna and I reacted made us no new friends among the top echelons of the BBC. Come to think of it, of the six presenters whose futures were constantly being questioned and undermined while the BBC stayed silent, Anna and I were the only ones who actually spoke out publicly. The others, who probably knew the BBC a bit better than we did, were just as unhappy but kept their counsel.

They may have been right – one of the biggest offences at the BBC is rocking the boat, far bigger than attempting to devalue a broadcasting career with a steady drip of rumour. However, many of the points with which I went public stimulated some debate, and earned me the backing of an unlikely ally, the *Daily Express*. In an editorial it said the BBC roster of senior newsreaders was one of its strongest assets, and that the corporation should remember that 'whilst beauty fades, substance remains'. *The Guardian*, however, said I was wrong, that I came over as self-important, and that the BBC was right to ask the viewers what they wanted, even in what it called the 'dreaded focus groups': 'If journalism is forced to become less pompous and more accessible then that should be welcomed. To ignore the problem is to decide news is a commodity best kept pure for the elite, and "the People" might as well turn over and watch *Changing Rooms*.' *The Guardian* isn't the BBC's favourite newspaper for nothing.

There was one person among the BBC's top management who was clearly deeply unhappy at the way the News Review was being handled, and that was Ron Neil. Ron had brought me to the BBC when he was Head of News. Now he was detached from it all in a new job of Chief Executive, BBC Production. He couldn't say so publicly, but he wrote privately to me saying that my sense of upset was entirely justified. He called it a public débâcle that he found distressing, and offered his support and good wishes. It was typical of the man.

At long last the BBC published the results of its labours. But it did it in two parts. At the beginning of October 1998 it announced some organisational and editorial changes. The organisational changes were bad enough for those affected, with some good middle-ranking people forced to re-apply for their own jobs, most of them unsuccessfully. The presenters however were kept in suspense for another seven weeks. The editorial changes were greeted thus by Raymond Snoddy of *The Times*, the doyen of media correspondents: 'The sensible bits are so commonplace as to be risible. The parts that are new are potentially alarming. In future, the BBC insists, the news should be brought to you in clear, simple sentences that explain why a story matters. Really? What have BBC journalists been doing for the last fifty years?'

Snoddy went on to examine the new plans for the *Nine* – which would be mandated to consist of 50 per cent foreign news; and the *Six* – which would focus on UK and regional events. He saw a common thread, which he judged to be 'the BBC's mania for grandiose reports produced after never-ending meetings and reviews, which are then implemented in an arrogant top-down manner that ignores the views of the staff who have to implement the policies'. Snoddy had rightly detected that unhappiness at the much vaunted News Review wasn't confined to highly paid presenters who feared for their jobs. He'd spoken to a BBC journalist who had observed that the BBC's grand strategy 'seemed to be the work of an Eastern European dictator who had been to a Western management school', and he concluded: 'ITN will surely be rubbing its hands together with glee.'

Apart from the editorial wish-list, which was widely interpreted as making the *Six* more cuddly and the *Nine* more accessible, there were two other big operational changes: a new digital newsroom production system would be introduced (which was already triggering some embarrassing technical glitches) and the staff of the hitherto separate television and radio newsrooms would be combined in one giant newsroom. The thinking behind that was that when they were sitting cheek by jowl, there would be much creative interaction between the two sets of journalists. It was a total, expensive misjudgement. I sat for four years at the *Nine / Ten* production desk, which had two radio desks within touching distance, and I hadn't the faintest idea what they did, let alone what radio programmes they belonged to.

Just before Christmas, the news presenters learned the outcome of the second part of the Review, which was the only part that most of the press and the public was interested in. Martyn Lewis was the main loser – he was removed from the *Six O'Clock News* and replaced by Huw Edwards, who had been chief political correspondent on the News 24 channel. The *Six* subsequently abandoned the two-presenter format. Martyn's consolation prize was the offer of work presenting on BBC World. With great dignity, he told them what they could do with their job and decided to leave the BBC. It had taken him twelve years to go from being flavour of the month when poached from ITN by Michael Grade to being surplus to requirements under Peter Salmon. Ed Stourton lost the

One O'Clock News to Anna Ford, who moved from the *Six* team, and Ed himself moved to the *Today* programme on Radio Four. Michael Buerk and I stayed on the *Nine O'Clock News*, and were described in the press statement as 'the most established and trusted duo in broadcast news'. Well, at least we were for now. Two reporters, Fiona Bruce and George Alagiah joined the presenters' roster, filling in on the *One* and the *Six*. And that was it – the result of just under two years work!

The overall impact of the Review seemed little more than a facelift. Despite the promises about programme content, and about how the *Nine* would contain more foreign news, in the months that followed little change was discernible in any of the programmes except in presentation. To me it looked, in the power struggle between the Director of News Tony Hall and the controller of BBC1 Peter Salmon, that it was a score draw. Just over eighteen months later, however, Salmon had gone, to be replaced by Lorraine Heggessy who had her own ideas, and six months after that Tony Hall departed to become Chief Executive of the Royal Opera House. It was soon to be 'all change' again – the wearying story of so much that passes for BBC management. I have never understood why they can't see that people only do their best work when things are not in a state of constant flux.

By far the biggest change affecting BBC News didn't take two years to decide. Early in 2000, Greg Dyke succeeded John Birt as Director General. On a wave of popularity he nailed the slogan 'Cut the Crap' to his masthead and told the news managers to move the *Nine O'Clock News* to ten o'clock.

A year earlier, ITV had scored a spectacular own goal by axing ITN's *News at Ten*, the better – it hoped – to reorganise its schedules round entertainment programmes. The BBC had dithered about grabbing the slot, which wiser heads in ITV and ITN had always known was a much better time for news than nine o'clock, and as soon as he had established his authority, Greg Dyke seized the moment. The *Nine O'Clock News* became the BBC's *News at Ten* on 16 October 2000. There were a few grumbles about the change in working hours, but generally there was great excitement on the programme and a lot of effort went in to commissioning some special reports for the first few weeks that would make as much impact as possible.

The day of the re-launch was a Monday, and we all thought that the BBC would do its best to talk it up, and arrange some pre-publicity for myself and Michael Buerk – it was Michael who was presenting the first programme at the new time. I couldn't believe my eyes, sitting at home a day or two beforehand, watching the Parkinson show, which was again a popular fixture in the BBC schedules. Among Michael Parkinson's guests was ITN's Trevor McDonald, trailed all evening beforehand by the continuity announcer on BBC1 as 'the nation's favourite newsreader'. If the BBC had tried to undermine the re-launch of its own flagship news programme, it couldn't have done better. People in the BBC newsroom also queried why BBC continuity described Trevor as the nation's favourite, when the programme that he was then presenting for ITV – the ITV evening news at 6.30 p.m. on weeknights – was regularly watched by fewer people than tuned to the BBC's main news bulletins. But Trevor had benefited from ITN's clever PR which never allowed that soubriquet to be weakened.

There've been many big stories for which I was on duty during my forty-five years in News. The death of Diana was shocking, but it was put in the shade by the terrorist attacks on the United States on September 11th 2001. Indeed, the world is still reverberating to the consequences of those hijacked aircraft turning the World Trade Centre in New York into twin towering infernos. I first heard the news when I was telephoned at home at just before 2 p.m. that day as I was about to leave for the BBC. The first hi-jacked aircraft had crashed into the North Tower about ten minutes previously. I switched on the TV just in time to see the second aircraft hit the South Tower. Like millions around the world, contemplating the enormity of the crime, I couldn't believe my eyes. I got into my car, switched on the radio and drove to TV Centre.

By the time I arrived, both towers had collapsed, and the speculation was that more than 7,000 people had been killed. The eventual number of confirmed fatalities in New York was just over 2,600, with deaths at the Pentagon, which a third aircraft had targeted, and in Pennsylvania where a fourth had come down, bringing the total to nearly 3,000. The performance that day of BBC News, its reporters and correspondents, was outstanding.

The *Ten O'Clock News* had the difficult task of drawing all the many strands together without underplaying or overdramatising either the scale of the atrocity, its devastating human cost or its profound international consequences. I think we did justice to what had occurred on all counts, with BBC reporters and specialist correspondents showing why many of them are the best in the world. The rolling News 24 channel also came of age, but I believe the main bulletins played a key role by sticking to the core strengths of good broadcast journalism – accurate reporting, economical yet powerful writing to picture, and the minimum of speculation and opinion. There was, however, in a confusing and fast moving day one moment which gave the BBC's many enemies something to bite on – a reporter stating that a third building, the 7 World Trade Centre, or Salomon Building, had collapsed. The problem was that she had reported the collapse *before* the building actually came down. Conspiracy theorists will never be convinced that the BBC was not part of the plot...

I don't believe for a moment that an absurd allegation of that kind was damaging to the BBC. What was surprising was that there were so few mistakes made by BBC reporters and correspondents under those testing and distressing circumstances.

But seven weeks later the BBC made a serious mistake of basic journalism that *was* extremely damaging and that disturbed me greatly. As a result of it, I was the presenter who had to read out on air a grovelling apology. In fact, I believe it was the longest apology ever made by BBC News. And it could have been avoided by someone taking the time to make a couple of phone calls. But the story was too good to check: an international diamond firm was channelling money to the world's most wanted man and his terrorist network. Wow! And a shareholder in one of their diamond mines in the Congo had just been jailed for his part in the attacks on American embassies in Africa three years earlier. Double Wow! Gotcha! Except that he hadn't – they'd got the wrong man. Easy enough to confuse them? Well, they shared half a name and one was thirty-five years older than the other, but what a story! The apology, which took me nearly two minutes to read in my best BBC deadpan style, speaks for itself:

> On the 31 October, we broadcast a special report about the funding of Osama bin Laden's terrorist network, al-Qaeda, and its links to the diamond trade. In the course of that report, we stated that front-men for Osama bin Laden owned shares in an international mining company called Oryx Natural Resources. We also stated that Mohammed Khalfan, who is in jail for the 1998 bombings of the American Embassies in Africa, was the same man as Mr Kamal Khalfan, a shareholder in the company.

It went on with the devastating admission:

> We were wrong about both Oryx and Mr Khalfan. Oryx Natural Resources is part of the Oryx Group, which has interests in banking, hotels and construction. Neither Oryx nor Mr Khalfan has any connection with bin Laden, the al-Qaeda network or the American Embassy bombings in Africa. One of its shareholders, His Excellency Kamal Khalfan, is a respected Omani businessman and an Honorary Consul of the Sultanate of Oman. He is not the convicted terrorist. We apologise unreservedly to Mr Kamal Khalfan, Oryx Natural Resources and its directors.

There can be no excuse. No excuse for running with the story without giving Oryx, and the individual accused, the opportunity to comment. The BBC, it was revealed, made only one attempt to contact Oryx – by email – on the day of transmission, and then wouldn't disclose what the story was about, even though they were about to link the company to the world's most wanted terrorist. I believe there could be no excuse either for the BBC taking three weeks to apologise. The way I was taught was if you feel you've got someone bang to rights, you tell them and report what they've got to say. Not doing that simple thing cost the BBC a lot of money in an out of court settlement, but it cost them more in the damage inflicted on its journalism. The Director General, Greg Dyke, let it be known that if highly paid people miss elementary mistakes and damage the reputation of the BBC, they should pay for it.

That didn't happen and, as is the BBC way, even the DG was second-guessed by Suits on the management floors who thought they knew better. The then Editor of the *Ten O'Clock News*, Mark Popescu, was moved sideways to a succession of other editorial jobs. His defenders, and they went high up in the BBC, took the view that you had to live with the occasional Oryx fiasco – and even have a war chest – as the price of doing big investigative stories on the main bulletins. And wasn't firing people just one more admission of guilt that the BBC didn't have to make? The reporter on the Oryx story, David Shukman, whose friends thought he couldn't possibly survive, still works for the BBC specialising in stories about climate change.

Popescu and Shukman were friends and colleagues of mine, and I took no pleasure in their plight. They were under pressure to produce scoops – especially with a foreign angle – for the new, re-launched BBC TV *News at Ten O'Clock*. It was something the vaunted News Review was very keen on. But I think that what went wrong ran deeper than that. Modern TV journalism is a deeply competitive business, and also a highly technical and expensive one. Getting a story on air is a complex process, and producers and reporters have to master many other skills besides journalistic ones. Under the pressures of a newsroom you can cut journalistic corners and still get on air – indeed it may be the only way you *can* get on air. That's when the rot can really set in.

At around this time, BBC TV News was making another massive leap forward technically, with newsroom desks that twenty years before might have had nothing on them but a typewriter and a telephone, starting to groan under the weight of new machines for accessing, writing, producing and processing news – the whole apparatus of the digital revolution. A procedure that once was 90 per cent journalism and 10 per cent technical process is now more and more dominated by technical process, leaving the reporter and producer less time for the journalistic basics.

I largely exempt radio from these criticisms – it's not called Steam Radio for nothing – but for TV News the name of the game, given extra urgency by the advent of rolling twenty-four hour news, is getting the story on air. Under those sort of pressures, the checking and the writing are the first things that suffer. Later, when I moved to News 24, I was sometimes shocked at the way no attempt would be made to re-write news agency wire copy, and at how easy it was for government departments or organised lobby groups to get their press releases on air virtually intact. That was particularly true of the environmental groups and their advocacy of the theory of anthropogenic global warming – a subject area in which the BBC actually discouraged its reporters from seeking alternative and credible views.

It seems to have taken the BBC some time to wake up to some of these dangers. At the time of the Oryx story, the BBC's internal 'gospel' on editorial standards was the Guidelines for Factual Programmes, which was very thin on the need for reporters and producers to check and double check material destined for broadcast. There was clearly once no need to remind BBC journalists of how they should do their job. But although it was recognised that the guidance may have needed bringing up to date, it needed another shock, a much bigger shock to the BBC, before it was tightened significantly. That was the Hutton report, published at the beginning of 2004, which was deeply critical of the BBC's editorial processes. Hutton's inquiry had been set up to examine the circumstances surrounding the death of Dr David Kelly. He had been found dead in July 2003, after being exposed as the source of the BBC's story, authored by Andrew Gilligan, that the government had 'sexed up' its dossier on Saddam Hussein's capacity to strike with 'weapons of mass destruction'. Hutton put the government in the clear, but heavily criticised the BBC, whose Chairman and Director General resigned – even though there was subsequently widespread acknowledgment that Gilligan had got far more right than he got wrong.

The post-Hutton turmoil at the BBC, described by the new Director General Mark Thompson, as the biggest crisis BBC journalism had ever faced, resulted in a major internal review. It was led by Ron Neil, the same Ron Neil who had recruited me to the BBC fifteen years earlier. Its recommendations aimed at improving BBC journalism were little more that a restatement of what one of my colleagues called the 'bleeding obvious' – such as the requirement that serious allegations must always be put to those concerned in time for a considered response before transmission. But the biggest change was to establish a BBC College of Journalism to improve training and standards. COJO, as it became known, started with a handful of people in a room making simple training videos on dilemmas reporters and producers might face – such as how much the camera should dwell on explicit scenes of violent death and carnage when reporting wars or terrorist atrocities. But COJO, like Topsy, grew and grew, as anyone who visits its website, with its pathways to scores of courses, can discover. Indeed, it is probably the BBC's fastest growing empire, freely available now to anyone and everyone in the UK. As for its original, core purpose, to improve journalistic standards at the BBC, during my time on the BBC's continuous news channel I was not alone in discerning little difference between the BBC pre-COJO and post COJO, except that an awful lot of people went on courses.

Despite COJO's hyperactivity, the BBC got into another pickle over standards three years after COJO was founded, with a series of fakery scandals on radio and television which came to light when an edited TV trailer of the Queen falsely suggested she'd stormed out of a photo-session in a huff. In all, ten programmes were accused of deceiving viewers, including Blue Peter which rigged an online poll to name its cat. COJO was ordered to produce yet another course – Safeguarding Trust – which was compulsory for all staff. One of the first to go on the course was the Director General himself; the last of the BBC's 17,000 editorial staff to be put through it was me, under circumstances which I will explain in due course.

So, by the end of 2007, the BBC was awash with new guidelines for accuracy and for the ethical conduct of its editorial staff. The Oryx blunder, the Hutton criticism and the Fakery scandals had all had their effect, and no one could be unaware of the changes. A blizzard of internal emails, and the fervour with which everyone in the BBC was dragooned onto the Safeguarding Trust course, saw to that. There couldn't be any guidelines affecting the BBC's journalism that people didn't know about. Or could there? Well, yes. Six years earlier, in the aftermath of the terrorist attacks of 9/11, presenters and the programme editors with whom they worked closely were unaware of the introduction of new guidelines for our old friend Reporting a Royal Death. Realistically, there was only one of those on the horizon that the BBC could plan for, that of the Queen Mother, and the changed plans made it quite plain that the old lady was nothing like as popular inside the BBC as she was in the country – or at least in the columns of the popular press.

Changing the plans for a royal death was the result of a heated internal debate in the BBC. The Director General Greg Dyke hated the way the press turned on him when the BBC refused to broadcast live the Queen Mother's 100th birthday pageant in the summer of 2000. ITV seized the moment after a *Daily Mail* campaign excoriating the BBC, and there are those that believe that it was one of the reasons that shortly afterwards Dyke replaced Peter Salmon with Lorraine Heggessey as controller of BBC1. Greg Dyke liked to be liked, even at Buckingham Palace, but there was high level opposition among his senior managers to going overboard when the Queen Mother died, and it was their views that prevailed.

The deciding factor was the terrorist attacks of 9/11 in the United States and it was, significantly, the controller of BBC1 Lorraine Heggessey, not the Head of News who made the announcement in a little noticed discussion at the Broadcasting Press Guild. She claimed the corporation's plans for dealing with what she called the 'much anticipated' death were under review before 9/11, but spoke of the BBC's concern that coverage of the one royal death, when it came, did not seem excessive compared with the thousands who died in America. She made it plain that plans for the old style wall to wall deferential coverage had been abandoned, and went on: 'The Queen Mother has lived a fantastically full life and is now 101. The way you mark that is different from the way you would mark a premature death. It's still a significant event and she's still a much loved figure. But the coverage needs to be in tune with the times.' Heggessy then added an extraordinary statement, that the amount of coverage would be decided only after assessing the depth of public mourning – 'We will take the temperature on the day.'

Instead of giving a lead to the nation, the BBC had apparently decided that it would see which way the wind was blowing before responding fully to the death of the former Queen. Lorraine Heggessy's remarks were not widely reported, and certainly not circulated to the journalistic infantry at the BBC. My reaction when I read them was that if there was anything in them, they would have to be followed up with emails to all those who might be affected by them, or at the very least they would be taken up by the Head of News who would pass them down the line. Neither happened.

The problem with the new BBC policy was two-fold. Not only had it not been discussed at any stage with any of the senior presenters, editors or producers – who were mostly unaware of it. But even if we had known, there was not a word about how the new policy would be put into practice when the Queen Mother passed away. What would we actually DO?

She died at 3.15 in the afternoon on Saturday 30 March 2002. And I was on duty.

Chapter 14

Queen Mother and all that

The last Saturday in March, 2002, Easter Saturday, looked like being just another day in the BBC newsroom at Television Centre. There wasn't much news around and, apart from the Saturday sport, and not a lot was expected to happen. There certainly was no hint of a suggestion that twenty-five miles away, six weeks after her last public appearance, the 101-year-old Queen Mother was fading fast. Not for her the weeks of daily medical bulletins that preceded the death of Winston Churchill, each one awaited by anxious crowds. Over at Royal Lodge in Windsor Great Park the Queen Mother's time had come privately and quietly, and only the closest members of her family had been alerted.

I was the newscaster that day, and it was my sixth successive day on duty. Michael Buerk was on holiday, as he had been when the Princess of Wales died (I never heard him curse his luck). I had arrived in the newsroom at about 10.30 a.m., and read a six minute bulletin at midday. There then wasn't much to do until the next scheduled bulletin, at 5.15 p.m. I got myself a sandwich, put my feet up on the desk and occupied myself with the newswires, the morning papers and catching up on the gossip with the weekend team.

I mean no disrespect to my colleagues on that day, but the resources that the BBC put into its weekend operation at that time were quite stretched. Most of the effort went into the weekday operation, when bulletins were longer and there was usually much more news. Not to put too fine a point on it, the weekend production team was not the most senior, and those that were on duty often complained about how short staffed they were. This put extra pressure on the editor of the day. But there were some advantages to working the weekend shift. It was quieter, none of the management was ever to be seen, and it was an opportunity for the less experienced producers to take responsibility and show what they could do when there was not too much at stake. After the lunchtime news that day, most of the early evening bulletin was fairly predictable. Indeed the time began to drag a little.

The Queen Mother died at 3.15, an event for which the BBC had long prepared. But how prepared was it? The established procedures for *announcing* the death of what was designated a 'category A' royal remained set in stone, and everyone knew the drill. What no one on duty that day knew was where we went from there. The controller of BBC1 had promised that the BBC's response would be determined when they had assessed the public mood, whatever that meant in practice. The only policy that had filtered down to the newsroom was that for the 101-year-old Queen Mother the whole panoply of black-edged mourning might not be appropriate.

But there had been no change to the protocol for the announcement, which had long been agreed with Buckingham Palace. It stated explicitly that even if the BBC was aware of such a high profile royal death, it would be embargoed until a formal announcement was made by the Palace. Clearly laid down in the days when the BBC had a monopoly of news broadcasting, this procedure was binding on the corporation and had never been rescinded.

What I believe to have happened is that the first BBC person to be informed by Buckingham Palace, on an embargoed basis, was the royal correspondent, Jenny Bond, who was driving home to the West Country.

Having taken the call, Jenny immediately phoned the Head of News, who in turn contacted as many of the BBC's top tier as he could. Jenny Bond then set off, through the Easter Saturday traffic, back to London. It was emphasised to everyone who could be contacted that Buckingham Palace would not make the formal announcement until 5.45, which meant that the BBC could not broadcast the news before then.

Now, any reasonable person would have thought that the editor of the day's bulletin team and the duty newscaster would also have been let in on the secret, so that they could begin preparing for the broadcast they would have to make when Buckingham Palace gave the green light. Astonishingly, we were kept in the dark. I thought that it was odd when I glimpsed a few of the BBC's editorial bigwigs flit across the newsroom in the distance, a weekend rarity. It crossed my mind that they were probably having a meeting of some kind, which they couldn't have at any other time. But it didn't occur to me that if something important was happening that affected the bulletin, they would keep it from me and the production team. We carried on with the preparation of a normal Saturday early evening bulletin, which went out uneventfully at a quarter past five and lasted twelve minutes.

What greeted me when I left the studio and went back to my desk in the newsroom, was a flurry of activity. The weekend editor – a middle ranking editorial supervisor who usually kept out of the way – calmly told us that the Queen Mother had died, although I thought I detected a look of panic in his eyes: Buckingham Palace were making the announcement at a quarter to six, and we would go on air five minutes after that. Looking back, I still can't believe that we were given only twenty minutes notice of such a broadcast, when the BBC had been privy to the knowledge of the Queen Mother's death for more than an hour and a half. At the time I was mystified as to why, in the 5.15 bulletin we'd just broadcast, we didn't at the very least hint that the Queen Mother was ill, and that a statement was expected shortly from the Palace. Were we in the news business or weren't we?

The atmosphere became electric. This was the moment that the BBC had talked about and rehearsed for, for the best part of a decade. And those of us on the sharp end that afternoon knew we'd drawn the short straw. We had to move fast.

I spent a few minutes bringing myself up to speed, although we had very little in the way of detail. The senior producer on the team was assigned to write the announcement. The TV News bulletin editor of the day went into a huddle with the studio director, cross checking with each other the procedures laid down. The few people manning the News Intake desk, the news gathering arm of the operation, started bashing the phones to potential interviewees, and scrambling the few reporters and video crews at their disposal. The locked box containing pre-recorded obituary material was opened.

We were quickly reminded of the drill: BBC1 would come together with the continuous news channel BBC News 24 – whose production team also had no early warning – and BBC2 would join us for the announcement, but only for fifteen minutes before it resumed its planned programmes.

I went to the make-up room a few yards away, was done and dusted in record time, and on the way back, with the clock counting down to our transmission, I opened my locker in the adjacent corridor. Inside were four ties. One was a normal striped tie for everyday use which I kept there in case I spilt something on the tie I came to work in. There was also a black tie, and two 'sombre' ties which would be more fitting if I had come to work wearing a colourful tie that turned out to be inappropriate for announcing some awful disaster. Of the sombre ties, one was dark blue, the other a deep burgundy. In the office lighting the burgundy tie looked darker than the blue one, so I took that and the black tie into the newsroom. There I encountered the head of TV News. I was aware of that one policy change that had been floated after 9/11: that the only time a black tie would be worn would be for the death of the monarch, but I needed to be sure. I asked which of my two ties I should wear. There was no hesitation. The most senior figure in the newsroom at that moment indicated the burgundy tie.

Jacket on, tie on. But where's the script? It was still being written. By now, everyone, myself included, was feeling the stress. If only we'd had that extra hour, I could have written the announcement myself. I was being called to the studio, but I still hadn't seen the text I was expected to read. I hate going into a studio without some paper copy at the best of times, and this was one announcement – given that the format had the status at the BBC of holy writ – that I didn't want to adlib. As I walked towards the newsroom door, the weekend editor, whom I hardly knew, caught me up. 'Don't go overboard' he said, 'she's a very old woman who had to go sometime.' The sentiment, when I thought about it later, was a distillation of the new approach signalled by the controller of BBC1 six months earlier. Well, at least someone had been told.

I went into the studio and was counted on air. Still no hard copy of a script – the first time I was going to see it was when it appeared on autocue, the electronic prompter that projects the words in front of the camera lens. Three, two, one. On air. The autocue screen lit up, and I read what was on it. It was not my finest hour, I freely admit. I looked uncomfortable, and I was. The text had a number of minor errors, the product of the haste in which it was written. I failed to read it fluently, but I blame no one but myself for that. Still, we'd got on air, and things could only get better. A long pause while the national anthem was played, over a fluttering royal standard in close-up. Then we were away.

But with what? After we'd run an eight or nine-minute potted obituary, it began to dawn on me that we had very little other pre-prepared material to work with.

Thank God for Jenny Bond, who arrived still glowing from the haste with which she'd hurried back to London. Jenny immediately dropped into Queen Mum autopilot and filled minute after minute with background and anecdote. But where were the top-drawer interviewees we'd been led to believe would be on standby?

At last, in my earpiece, the control gallery told me that we had on the line – not in vision – one of the people closest to the late Queen Mother, her niece who was also a lady-in-waiting. Her name, they told me, was Lady Margaret Rhodes. That was all I knew, and they put her on air immediately. I did not know at that stage that they'd got her name wrong, and compounded the mistake on the caption we used. (It should have been *Mrs* Margaret Rhodes – she'd never been graced with the title we gave her – but she didn't correct me.) In the following days, this interview caused a storm in certain sections of the press, who accused me of showing no human feeling, and of being intrusive and insensitive.

Here's the transcript, so you can judge for yourself:

PS: I believe we have on the phone the Queen Mother's niece, Lady Margaret Rhodes. Lady Margaret, a very sad day for the whole nation.

MR: It is indeed. I think that there has really never been anybody who has been held in such a huge amount of affection by such an enormous number of people as Queen Elizabeth. She was deeply loved by all age groups and all kinds of people. And I think that there's a hole now that will be very difficult to fill.

PS: When did you last see her?

MR: I left at half past three this afternoon.

At this point it dawned on me that Mrs Rhodes may actually have been at the Queen Mother's deathbed.

PS: Oh I see. Were you...

MR: I was there all day, yes.

PS: You were at her bedside?

MR: Yes...

It took me a second or two to take this in. What on earth can I ask now that will *not* be intrusive or give offence?

PS: It must have been...

MR: ... but she will be greatly missed by everybody. She was a wonderful, wonderful person.

PS: It must have been a very private moment.

MR: Sorry, I didn't hear that.

PS: It must have been a very private moment, Lady Margaret.

MR: Yes, it was a very moving and very, very sad moment, but luckily it was wonderfully peaceful.

PS: And without wishing to intrude too much, who was there?

MR: No, I won't go into that. It was just a few members of the family, but the great thing was that the Queen was there.

Pause. I knew that I could be treading on eggshells, but there must be a way of just keeping her talking. I sensed that there was more she wanted to say.

PS: And after you all came out, what happened then?

MR: No, I'm sorry, I really don't want to go into those sort of details. I just want to say how much she'll be missed, and how much she was loved.

PS: I appreciate that. Thank you very much. But can you just stay with us a moment and tell us a little more about what sort of gap there will be in our national life?

MR: Well, I think there will be a huge gap, because she was interested in so many things and was patron of hundreds and hundreds of organisations, all of whom she helped with her work and all of whom she gave a devoted ... a great deal of attention to. So all these people will miss her hugely.

PS: And how will her passing affect the royal family and the way it's perceived – or is it too early to tell?

MR: Well I think that any family is sad when their mother and grandmother dies. It's just a sadness for any family, particularly so for them.

PS: It was a tremendous life.

MR: It was a wonderful life spanning a whole... more than a hundred years, and one can hardly believe that someone who grew up in the horse age has seen people landing on the moon and all the things that happen now.

PS: And as we celebrate the life, Lady Margaret, what will ... what when you recall it ... what will give you most joy?

MR: Just her as a person. She was just a wonderful, wonderful person to know that we'll almost never see the like of again. She just was wonderful.

PS: Lady Margaret Rhodes...

MR: I think that's really all I need to say. Thank you.

PS: ... we're very grateful to you to come on the line like this. Thank you.

And that was it. In my days at ITN I'm pretty certain that would have been regarded as a scoop – the first interview with someone who had been with the Queen Mother when she died. There was, in truth, little of substance in it, except for the disclosure that, at the end, the Queen was at her mother's bedside. Mrs Rhodes was dry-eyed and matter-of-fact throughout. Had she not been, then obviously I would have ended the interview. I also have it on good authority that when, later that day, she encountered the Duke of Edinburgh at Windsor Castle he congratulated her on her performance, saying she 'did well'. But the rumours flew that the Palace was furious, not just with the Margaret Rhodes interview, but with my burgundy tie – which under the bright lights of the studio looked less subdued than it did under the fluorescent tubes of the newsroom. I found out later that my friend Nicholas Owen, who was on air that day for ITN, had chosen a navy blue tie, which on television looked quite black. My bad luck was to leave my navy blue tie in my locker, and plump for the burgundy.

Little of this seemed to worry the next day's Sunday newspapers, who devoted acres of space to the Queen Mother herself. But on the Monday morning, a small number of newspapers focused on the TV coverage, and went for me and for the BBC. One called my interview with Mrs Rhodes 'brutish'. The *Daily Mail* accused the BBC of 'slovenliness, insensitivity and downright tastelessness'. On a lighter note, there were cartoons in friendlier newspapers of me reading the news in the Tower of London, and the Queen Mother at the pearly gates ordering 'a plague of locusts, pestilence and a long famine at Peter Sissons's house'. But the dominant feature of the immediate coverage by newspapers who are no friends of the BBC was how vicious it was towards me and towards the corporation.

In fact when I read those Monday morning papers I was quite shocked. Never in my career had I been the target of anything like this. I knew the shortcomings of my Queen Mother broadcast – I've always been my own most severe critic, and one of the truest sayings in television is that you are only as good as the last thing you've done. Suddenly it was as if all the successes, all the awards, all the good times never happened. I was now the man who insulted the memory of the Queen Mother by being inappropriately dressed and who trampled on the feelings of the niece who watched her die.

But as I thought about it that Monday morning, the words of my old headmaster came back to me yet again: 'Never give up what you do know for what you don't know.' I knew in my bones that it wasn't the way it was being described. I had no reason to question my own ability. Nonetheless, I felt quite lonely.

There was one more shock to come. As I sipped my coffee at home, the phone rang. It was the BBC press office. A female voice enquired, solicitously, had I seen the morning papers? I said I was reading them at that very moment and asked what the press office were saying in reply to enquiries about the Queen Mother broadcast. 'We are saying,' she said, 'that the choice of tie was a decision made by the presenter'. I can't remember precisely what I said, but it was far from polite and contained a threat that included the name of my lawyer. To their credit, from that moment the BBC made no attempt to dodge their responsibility for the tie that I wore. A day or two later the deputy director of News, Mark Damazer, called the coverage of the Queen Mother's death 'excellent and absolutely commensurate with the BBC's standards'.

Some newspapers tried to keep up the pressure on me and the BBC. When, the following week, Prince Charles chose to give a major interview about the Queen Mother to ITN, it was suggested that it was because he was so incensed about the lack of a black tie on the BBC and the way the interview with Mrs Rhodes had been handled. This brought a firm denial from Buckingham Palace: the royals had no complaints about the BBC coverage, and ITN got the interview because it was their turn – the BBC having filmed the tribute to Princess Margaret who'd died six weeks previously.

In the immediate aftermath of the BBC broadcast, while Fleet Street's finest were fulminating on behalf of the nation, the BBC released some interesting figures. The corporation revealed that only 130 people had called to express their anger at the BBC's 'insensitivity'. This compared with 1,500 who rang in either complaining that too much attention had been paid to the death of the Queen Mother, or objecting to their favourite programme *Casualty* being moved to make way for the coverage. Ipsos Mori found that, asked about the BBC's response to her death, 8 per cent of the public said it was too respectful, 11 per cent said it was not respectful enough, and 64 per cent said it was about right.

There were sixteen complaints to the Broadcasting Standards Commission about my Margaret Rhodes interview. Rejecting them, the watchdog said the interview had been 'conducted with due reverence and respect and would have been unlikely to have offended the majority of the audience'.

As for Mrs Rhodes, in an interview she gave to the *Daily Telegraph* about the fuss, she said she didn't even know she was going out live on BBC Television. She said she thought that, although Mr Sissons probably 'meant no harm' I should have worn a black tie: 'When someone of that magnitude dies, one goes automatically into black.' Of the interview itself, she thought I did ask too many questions. And she added, generously: 'Poor Mr Sissons no doubt had a horrible day.'

Well, I've had better.

Six months later I was invited to lunch by the Director of News, Richard Sambrook, who had succeeded Tony Hall the previous year. His secretary explained to me that he was also having lunch separately with Michael Buerk. Although I wasn't as close to Richard as I had been to Tony, I had a good relationship with him. After many years at the BBC he had all the survival skills needed, but was a newsman through and through, and was approachable and popular. Over a very expensive lunch he came straight to the point: it had been decided to move Michael Buerk and me from our position as the BBC's senior news presenters. It wouldn't happen until the middle of the following year, so there would be no immediate announcement.

I wasn't upset or shocked, but intrigued. After all, nothing is forever, and I had been presenting the BBC's main news bulletins for longer than I had done any other job. But why would two experienced and popular television newscasters, presiding over the most-watched news programme in the land and both in their prime, be moved aside? The answer was predictable – BBC1 was judged to be in need of 'freshening up'. The controller of BBC1, Lorraine Heggessey was going through the place putting her mark on every department, and her plans for the news didn't include Sissons and Buerk. I put it to Sambrook directly – whose decision was it? He said it wasn't his. I asked another question – would it be true to say that the Director of News at the BBC no longer had the final say over who presented his news programmes? Sambrook looked uncomfortable and agreed that that was now the case.

I have no reason to believe that Sambrook was not telling me the truth: it meant that the status of the presenters of BBC News was no longer determined by their experience, seniority or credibility as judged by the News Directorate, but about what they contributed to the 'look' and the 'feel' of the channel as judged by a channel controller who may be here today and gone tomorrow, as most of the recent ones had been. Such a shift, in effect, turned news presenters into fashion goods. It didn't happen overnight, indeed the writing had been on the wall for some time. But the latest generation of news presenters who had arrived on the scene – no better or worse than the old guard – had to face a new reality: as soon as their faces don't fit – and there is ample evidence that at the BBC getting older accelerates the process – having years of experience and a safe pair of hands will not be enough to keep their jobs safe. And the new reality is particularly harsh for women. There've been lots of male presenters who are not oil paintings – I worked alongside a few at ITN. But there hasn't been a woman news presenter yet – however impressive intellectually – who hasn't been hired in the first place because she looks good on screen. Sad to say, the moment they stop looking good they are vulnerable, and that usually goes with age. The Anna Fords of this world, who improve like a good wine and can step down voluntarily at the age of sixty-three are very rare birds. Indeed, I'm not sure there'll be another one.

Just before Christmas that year, Richard Sambrook announced a change of plan – Buerk and I would not, after all, survive until the middle of the next year.

Suddenly there was a rush to get us out much sooner, and re-launch the evening BBC News with its new presenter early in the new year. I appeared as a regular presenter on BBC1 for the last time on Saturday 18 January, and Michael the following day. Huw Edwards became the sole presenter of the BBC's *News at Ten* starting on Monday 20th, with Fiona Bruce deputising for him on Fridays. Michael Buerk and I went our separate ways. He had chosen to leave BBC News, and concentrate on his radio work, which included the long-running *Moral Maze*. I took up the offer of transferring to the BBC's continuous news channel – BBC News 24. I did so with enthusiasm. At one time or another I had anchored every major news programme on the terrestrial channels – BBC1, ITV and Channel Four, but continuous news was the one branch of news I had never attempted, and I regarded it as a challenge.

Long before I left the *Ten*, I had also begun to deputise for Sir David Frost on Sunday mornings, and in fact I became his regular stand-in. During one summer I presented fourteen consecutive editions of *Breakfast with Frost*, which was a great experience. I loved the format, and there was impressive back-up from the small but talented production team led by the experienced Barney Jones. Barney, a BBC veteran, loved his job and it showed, combing through the Sunday newspapers and rarely getting much sleep the night before the programme. Always well briefed, he thought deeply about the content of the programme, and cosseted his presenter. When it came to the live interviews, Barney liked to exercise a measure of control through the presenter's earpiece, with suggestions for questions and instructions on when to move on to the next topic. On one occasion, so the story goes, he kneeled down and beat the control gallery floor with his fists in frustration, because Sir David was taking no notice of him. But he never, ever, left his presenter exposed through an inadequate or poor brief. Barney also ensured that the breakfast that followed the programme was something of an occasion, with guests often staying afterwards for an hour or more to gossip over the sausages, bacon, eggs, black pudding and lots of coffee. He was the sort of editor that presenters like working with, and Andrew Marr is lucky to have inherited him.

It was a privilege to be involved with *Breakfast with Frost*, and to get to know Sir David himself, whose abilities I had admired for many years. You don't have a CV like David's unless you are a huge talent. And the Frost sofa, as many politicians will testify, was a dangerous place, as week after week David relaxed them into saying much more than they intended when they sank into what they mistakenly believed to be its comforting velour. What was – and is – David's secret? I'm sure it had something to do with being scrupulously polite, and never having a bad word to say about anyone. After I parted company with the BBC's *News at Ten* my association with the Frost programme continued for more than two years, until its last edition on 29 May 2005. I was among an invited studio audience that morning – the only one it had ever had –

when a glittering array of friends and former guests gathered for what turned into a memorable *Champagne Breakfast with Frost*.

My immediate thought as I signed off on my last *Ten*, and that door closed, was to get started on News 24. Half way through January a second Iraq war was looking increasingly likely and I thought it would be just the time to switch to the continuous news channel. I was taken aback when I was told that they didn't want me to start until the end of March, and that I could take two and a half months off. To my great frustration, although I was available for work, I missed the entire build-up to the second Gulf War, and worked my first shift on News 24 on 29 March – the tenth day of the invasion. I was told by a friend high in editorial management that one of the principal reasons I was kept off the screen was to give Huw Edwards a clear run, and not invite comparisons with the old presentation line-up by having me involved in any way. I hope that wasn't true. Huw was more than capable of looking after himself, and quickly took to his new role. I, meanwhile, acquired a decent tan in Barbados and a very neat garden in Kent.

So began, belatedly, what was to be the final stage of my career, in my thirty-ninth year in television news. It was agreed that I would not work full-time on News 24. I would work a long shift, the longest done by anyone on News 24 – 1 p.m. until 7 p.m. – on Saturdays; and a short shift – 5 p.m. until 7 p.m. on Sundays. I would also be expected to do occasional shifts during the week, mainly covering holidays and absences, and occasionally to stay on at the weekend as required to read the main evening bulletin on BBC1. The pattern of work suited me well.

One thing had been worrying me, but it was quickly resolved. For my first broadcast on News 24 it was arranged that I would co-present – in other words, in common with most of News 24's output, I would be one of two presenters. I had nothing against my female co-host, but I quickly decided that it did not suit me. I found that instead of concentrating on the journalism – the texts and the interviews – I was constantly distracted by presentational trivia. For me, it became a real diversion from the journalistic job in hand, thinking about whose turn it was next, where to look when the other one was speaking, and manufacturing some smiley chemistry in those moments before the sport or the weather. My co-host was one of the least pushy of the female presenters, and couldn't have been more kind to me, but I decided that under no circumstances would I co-present again except in an emergency. If I was going to anchor six hours of news, there was only going to be one person in the driving seat. To my great relief, this was accepted, and I settled in to my new routine.

My first impression of continuous news was mixed. On days when there was no developing news story it became boring and repetitive. On such days writers became lazy, sometimes not bothering to re-write their material from one end of the day to the other. Indeed, there seemed little interest in the quality of the writing. On one occasion I complained about some elementary spelling mistake, to be told that it didn't matter because it was being read, and there was no way the viewer could be aware of it. When I suggested that a story that had been around for half a day might benefit from a re-write, just to refresh it, it was almost never acted upon.

But the most fulfilling days, days on which continuous news came into its own, were those when a big story broke on air and kept moving. The biggest that I had to deal with was the Boxing Day tsunami of December 2004, caused by a powerful earthquake in the Indian Ocean. Shortly after I started my shift, the first reports coming in spoke of maybe a few hundred fatalities. When I signed off six hours later we were reporting deaths running to perhaps a quarter of a million in more than a dozen countries, caused by one of the earth's greatest natural disasters.

The terrorist attack on Glasgow Airport in June 2007 was another case in point. Two men, one of whom died in the attack, drove a Cherokee Jeep loaded with gas canisters through the airport's glass doors, where it burst into flames. It happened at 3.15, and the whole thing was captured on CCTV. The initial statement from the police said it was an accident, the driver simply having lost control of the vehicle. Our coverage made it plain it was nothing of the sort, and it was only after I stated that it had all the hallmarks of a terrorist attack that the police changed their story. One of the first eyewitness accounts that we put on air came from the BBC's Head of News, Helen Boaden, who happened to be at Glasgow Airport, and phoned in. A former award-winning radio reporter, she gave a graphic account of the chaos. I took the precaution of referring to her on air as a BBC executive. If she'd cocked things up it wouldn't have done to tell people she was in charge of all the BBC's broadcast news, but I needn't have worried. It was, incidentally, the first and last time I spoke to her. As a senior presenter I spoke regularly to her predecessors, but in the five years Helen Boaden was in post before I left the BBC, we never met.

For the most part I found my time on News 24 – which was re-launched as simply the BBC News Channel in April 2008 – enjoyable and fulfilling. My best days on shift were like an extended *Channel Four News*, having to think on my feet, do a lot of ad-libbing and handle a succession of interviews. I was in regular demand for other occasional shifts during the week, and there was also a gap to be filled when *The Andrew Marr Show* replaced *Breakfast with Frost*. For six or seven weeks in the summer, when Marr's show was on vacation, we filled the slot at the same time on a Sunday morning with an edition of what we called *News 24 Sunday*. This was a fast-moving hour with major interviews and a lively paper review, but done on a shoestring from the News 24 studio and put on air by people who were on duty anyway. I think the biggest expense was the traditional breakfast that was provided afterwards, and to my great satisfaction *News 24 Sunday* achieved audience ratings as good as, or better, than the show it was temporarily replacing.

It was during this time, however, that a number of developments at BBC News began to disturb and depress me. I was having more and more moments when I felt that things were not right with the organisation. But why? Could it be that I was becoming a Grumpy Old Man? I was by far the oldest person in the newsroom, but most of my views were shared by much younger colleagues, many of whom were also far from happy. They, however, had their careers to think of.

So they talked to me, and I found myself reflecting their views, as well as my own, in occasional indiscreet public outbursts. I didn't set out to be disloyal, but to speak as a candid friend of a unique organisation, which I believed to be losing its way in its core activity, news. Any damage to the reputation of BBC News inflicts disproportionate damage on the organisation as a whole, and things were happening in the news division, particularly television news, that were undermining and weakening that reputation.

I began to notice more and more the lack of leadership in the newsroom. My earliest memories of working in news, as a graduate trainee at ITN, were of the editor or his deputy, making their presence felt throughout the day – sleeves rolled up, in and out of their offices, constantly involved in what was going on, their fingers on the pulse. On a day to day basis the people in charge of BBC News were rarely seen on the shop floor. Harassed programme editors would be summoned to routine editorial meetings on the management floors above, and the sentiment most often expressed when they returned was that they had wasted valuable time reading lists to each other and explaining the day's news to the man or woman notionally at the helm. As a presenter on the BBC's nine and ten o'clock news bulletins, I stopped going to the editorial meetings because my time could be better spent. Too many senior executives were just playing out their roles, oblivious to how irrelevant they had become to what was actually being done in the news factory below. If a visitor to the BBC's huge newsroom at Television Centre were to ask who was in charge, you wouldn't be able to point to any individual in the room.

The place was crying out for leadership, and not just in news. To his credit, the Director General Greg Dyke saw this and early in 2003 launched his blueprint for internal change. 1,500 managers a year for five years would go through an intensive leadership programme at the Ashridge Business School in Hertfordshire, a five-fold increase in management and leadership training. But little seemed to change, with most people seeing an eight-day residential course in the country as an excuse for some well-deserved R & R at the corporation's expense, At the grand internal event launching all this, which Dyke called The Big Conversation, BBC staff were invited to put forward their own ideas for change in the way the place was run. Many people to whom I spoke saw this as the management asking the staff how they wanted to be managed – in reality an abdication of management.

Hand in hand with weak leadership went the steady growth of political correctness. In fact, it was almost certainly the unchallengeable PC culture at the BBC that was beginning to make strong leadership impossible. Leadership itself, one person being in charge, trusting his or her own judgement, taking a decision and telling others what to do, was shied away from. More and more one saw taking place, through the glass partitions of conference rooms, endless meetings of a dozen or more people trying to arrive at some sort of consensus. Some elements of political correctness can be quite harmless, indeed provide a lively source of entertainment. But I saw it beginning to spill over into influencing the BBC's journalism.

At the newsroom level it became impossible to discipline someone for basic journalistic mistakes – wrong dates, times and numbers, inaccurate on-screen captions and basic political or geographical facts – for fear of giving offence. You'd never see anyone, to use a technical term, get a bollocking. There'd be whispers about them. They might even get a black mark at the annual appraisal with their line manager. Sometimes, they might even be promoted to a position in which they could do less harm.

This culture of political correctness was bound to have an influence on what appeared on the screen, and over time it began to do just that, in all sorts of ways. For example, soon after I started News 24, in the middle of May, the aircraft carrier *Ark Royal*, the navy's flagship, returned from the Gulf. At Portsmouth she was given the traditional greeting by thousands of well wishers and relatives of the crew. TV reporters closed in to interview crew members, the vast majority of whom are men. Of the five vox pops that featured in the BBC News, four were with women sailors. During my stint on News 24 that day I complained about this and asked if we could have some more balanced vox-pops, but in vain. I have always been in two minds about vox-pops: they can give texture and interest to a story, but unless they are selected with scrupulous impartiality by a conscientious producer they are worse than a waste of time – they amount to a deception of the viewer.

I was also very unhappy about aspects of the BBC's reporting of the Hutton enquiry into David Kelly's death, in August that year. On the 28th, Tony Blair gave evidence before Hutton, and I watched both the BBC coverage and the ITN coverage at home. I was so angry at the contrast that, with this book in mind I wrote myself an aide memoire, in particular about the early evening news on each channel. On BBC1, BBC correspondents queued up with their opinions, unanimously agreeing that Blair was very impressive. On ITV, ITN's reporters gave no opinions; the only judgement on Blair that ITN aired was that of members of the public who'd watched his performance. ITN also interviewed the leaders of the Opposition parties, Iain Duncan Smith and Charles Kennedy. Neither was given space on the BBC's *News at Six*. ITN's star was Nick Robinson, who had joined ITN from the BBC in 2002, but was enticed back three years later. ITN also brought back Michael Brunson, their former political editor, to put the Blair predicament into a historical perspective – was this as damaging to Blair as Suez had been to Eden, or Profumo to Macmillan? I noted at the time 'the BBC really has lost it. Early news just a joke. Is the Beeb sucking up to Blair as part of the deal to mend fences?' It needed someone to get hold of a programme on a day like that by the scruff of the neck.

It was obvious to me that the backbone of any successful TV news operation – quite apart from a team of editors who are not afraid to lead from the front – has to be its senior correspondents and presenters. In total contrast to the flaccid management structure, the BBC has been fortunate in maintaining the loyalty of a select cadre of on-screen men and women, most of mature years, who can be depended on, who are respected throughout the world and whose loyalty to the BBC, despite all its imperfections, can be relied upon to keep the flag of broadcast journalism flying.

They don't do it for money – you'd be surprised at how little some get paid for the responsibility they carry. Their overseas assignments are often taxing or downright dangerous, and those that staff foreign bureaux are not only BBC employees but unofficial ambassadors, with all the exposure that brings. *You* know who they are and *they* know who they are. If I have a criticism of them, and it doesn't extend to all of them, it is that they are increasingly drawn into not just reporting and assessing the significance of events, but giving the viewer their opinions. Inexperienced studio presenters often don't help them, by explicitly asking for their opinion, and it's easy after a long and testing day to fall into the trap. I've actually heard a presenter, after prime minister's questions, ask a correspondent 'who won?' All the evidence is that viewers don't like it, and rightly. They are perfectly capable of making up their own minds. They appreciate facts; they've had enough of spin.

One story, or type of story, that recurred with increasing frequency during the last ten years of my time at the BBC, was the issue, in some form or another, of global warming, which became climate change when temperatures appeared to level off or fall slightly after 1998. From the beginning I was unhappy at how one-sided the BBC's coverage of this issue was, and how much more complicated the climate system was than the over-simplified two minute reports that were the stock-in-trade of the BBC's environment correspondents. These, without exception, accepted the UN's assurance that 'the science is settled' and that human emissions of carbon dioxide threatened the world with catastrophic climate change.

Environmental pressure groups could be guaranteed that their press releases, usually beginning with the words 'scientists say...' would get on air unchallenged. On one famous occasion, after the 2009 inauguration, the science correspondent of *Newsnight* actually informed viewers that 'scientists calculate that President Obama has just four years to save the world'. What she didn't tell them was that only one alarmist scientist, NASA's James Hansen, had said that.

My interest in climate change grew out of my concern for the failings of BBC journalism in reporting the subject. I have written previously about what was expected of a journalist in my early days at ITN: you have an obligation to report both sides of a story. It is not journalism if you don't. It is close to propaganda. The BBC's editorial policy was spelled out in a report in June 2007 by the BBC Trust, which disclosed that the BBC had held 'a high-level seminar with some of the best scientific experts, and has come to the view that the weight of evidence no longer justifies equal space being given to the opponents of the consensus'.

The error here, of course, is that the BBC *never at any stage* gave equal space to the opponents of the consensus.

But the Trust continued its pretence that climate change dissenters had been, and still would be, heard on its airwaves: 'Impartiality always requires a breadth of view: for as long as minority opinions are coherently and honestly expressed, the BBC must give them appropriate space.' Such a statement showed how detached the Trust was from what the BBC was actually doing – the 'appropriate space' given to minority views on climate change being practically zero. The policy was underlined a year later in another statement: 'BBC News currently takes the view that their reporting needs to be calibrated to take into account the scientific consensus that global warming is man-made.' Those scientists outside the 'consensus' waited in vain for the phone to ring.

My principal concern was that this policy represented a dereliction of journalistic duty by the BBC, which damages the BBC's reputation among people whose support it should be able to take for granted. One of the things I do from time to time, as a freelance, is to chair business conferences, often involving senior entrepreneurs, financiers and industrialists. In private conversation I find that almost none of them can tell me how much of the atmosphere consists of carbon dioxide. Some would say as much as 20 per cent, others 3 or 4 per cent. When

I tell them it's 0.039 per cent, most of which is natural, the invariable reply is why has the BBC never told us that?

As for the top-level BBC seminar which I mentioned above, we know practically nothing about it. Despite a Freedom of Information request, they wouldn't even make the guest list public. There is one brief account of the proceedings, written by a conservative commentator who was there. Richard D. North was a former environment correspondent at *The Independent* who had morphed into one of the more moderate climate change sceptics, and somehow got under the radar for the event. He wrote subsequently that he was far from impressed with the thirty key BBC staff who attended. None of them, he said 'had shown even a modicum of professional journalistic curiosity on the subject'. He also said that none of them appeared to read anything on the subject other than *The Guardian*. That was also my experience from observing at close hand the pervading influence that newspaper and its soulmate *The Independent* have in the BBC newsroom – a mindset, incidentally, that goes far beyond attitudes to climate change.

It's this lack of simple curiosity about one of the great issues of our time that I find so puzzling about the BBC. As a presenter, when the topic came to prominence, the first thing I did was trawl the internet to find out as much as possible about it. Anyone who does this with a mind not closed by religious fervour will find a mass of material by respectable scientists – yes, who are in the minority – who question the orthodoxy. Even I, who had a classical education, could understand what Albert Einstein was getting at when he said that it didn't matter how many scientists agreed with him, it took only one to prove him wrong. If scepticism should be the natural instinct of scientists, it should certainly be the default setting of journalists. Yet the cream of the BBC's inquisitors, during my time at the BBC, never laid a glove on those who repeated the mantra 'the science is settled'. On one occasion, the MP Denis MacShane, himself a former President of the National Union of Journalists, used BBC airtime to link climate change doubters with perverts and Holocaust deniers and his famous interviewer didn't bat an eyelid.

All this wasn't just down to the proselytising of *The Guardian* and the hold that it has on the BBC.

Al Gore, who had entertained the BBC's editorial elite in his suite at the Dorchester, and been given a free run to make his case to an admiring internal audience at Television Centre, had done his work well. His views were never subjected to journalistic scrutiny, even when a British High Court judge, Mr Justice Burton, ruled that Gore's film *An Inconvenient Truth* contained at least nine scientific errors, and that ministers must send new guidance to teachers before it was screened in schools. From the BBC's standpoint, Mr Justice Burton's judgment was the real inconvenience and its environment correspondents downplayed its significance.

At the end of November 2007 I was on duty on News 24, when the UN's Intergovernmental Panel on Climate Change produced its fourth Assessment Report at a conference in Valencia. To be fair, reporters at the time couldn't have known that it contained significant inaccuracies, many stemming from its reliance on non-peer reviewed sources and best-guesses by environmental activists. But the way the BBC's reporter treated the story was as if it was, beyond a vestige of doubt, the last word on the catastrophe awaiting mankind. The most challenging questions addressed to a succession of UN employees and climate activists were 'How urgent is it?' and 'How much danger are we in?' Sceptical scientists were referred to as if they were some kind of oddballs. Back in the studio I tried to redress the balance in an interview with the environment minister, Phil Woolas. I put to him, not questions of mine, but questions emailed by viewers to the BBC website, where sceptics were often in the majority.

It was a lively exchange, but the problem was that it began at about twenty-six minutes past the hour. After a short time I was told in my earpiece to wrap it up and hand to the weather, which is a News 24 fixture just before the top of the hour and at half past. I was frustrated and annoyed. It was quite obvious that no one in the control gallery was even listening to the interview I was doing. Mr Woolas could have confessed to me that he had just murdered his wife and I would still have been told to hand to the weather. Subsequently I suggested that we line up one or two sceptics to react to the IPPC's report, but received a totally negative response, as if I was some kind of lunatic. I went home and wrote another aide memoire: 'What happened to the journalism? The BBC has completely lost it. Don't we have a duty to challenge any position that is put forward for public support, to test it in the public interest – especially when there is so much at stake, should the analysis be mistaken? Do these reporters even realise what their job is? Have they completely lost their critical faculties?'

A damaging episode illustrating the BBC's supine attitude in the climate change debate, came in April 2008, when a Green activist, Jo Abbess, emailed the BBC's 'environment analyst' Roger Harrabin, complaining about a piece he'd written on the BBC's website reporting some work by the World Meteorological Organization that questioned whether the warming would continue as projected by the IPCC – both organisations being arms of the UN.

Abbess complained; Harrabin at first resisted. Abbess berated him: 'It would be better if you did not quote the sceptics (something Harrabin had not actually done) ... please reserve the main BBC online channel for emerging truth... Otherwise I would have to conclude that you are insufficiently educated to be able to know when you have been psychologically manipulated.'

Did Harrabin tell her to get lost? He tweaked the story – albeit not as radically as she demanded – and emailed back: 'Have a look in ten minutes and tell me you are happier.' This exchange went round the world in no time, spread by a jubilant Abbess. Later, Harrabin defended himself, saying they were only minor changes – but the sense of the changes (as specifically sought by Ms Abbess) was plainly to harden the piece against the sceptics. Many people wouldn't call that minor, but Harrabin's BBC bosses accepted his explanation.

The sense of entitlement with which Green groups regard the BBC was brought home to me later that year, when what was billed as a major climate change rally was held in London. It was a miserable, wintry, wet day, and turnout was much less than the organisers hoped for. I was on duty that Saturday afternoon, on News 24. It had been pre-arranged that the leader of the Green Party, Caroline Lucas, would go into our Westminster Studio to be interviewed by me. She clearly expected, as do most environmental activists, what I call a 'free hit' – to be allowed to say her piece without challenge.

I began, good naturedly, by observing that the climate didn't seem to be playing ball at the moment, and that we were having a particularly cold winter while carbon emissions were powering ahead. Miss Lucas reacted as if I'd physically molested her. She was outraged; it was no job of the BBC – the BBC! – to ask questions like that. Didn't I realise that there could be no argument over the science? I persisted with a few simple observations of fact, such as there appeared to have been no warming for ten years, in contradiction of all the alarmist computer models. I don't have a transcript, but remarks about the interview did make it onto the most respected and mainstream of the sceptical websites, Anthony Watts' 'Watts Up With That?' Here's an excerpt of what a viewer posted on WUWT :

> Today I watched an interview on the BBC News channel here in the UK where a leading Green campaigner was challenged by a BBC correspondent as to the veracity of Anthropogenic Climate Change. I was floored by this novel and totally unexpected treatment from a BBC correspondent. [Lucas] went immediately into a save the world monologue including the tipping point is nigh and other related phrases ... Sissons when he got back in injected no warming since 1998 and made the point that contrary to the 'consensus' an increasing number of scientists are coming out against the consensus. By this time Lucas was virtually apoplectic, mixing words and demanding to know how the BBC could be coming out and making such comments ... Sissons came back that his role as a journalist is always to investigate and review all sides and he would continue to do so. Lucas finished with a further attack and a somewhat veiled warning to which Sissons replied with an 'oohh'.

Later that afternoon I interviewed the Liberal Democrat leader Nick Clegg, on the same topic, and put the same points. He seemed a bit surprised by my line of questioning, replying only that he didn't think what I was saying was true. It was obvious that, like Lucas, he was quite thrown by the novelty of this line of enquiry by a BBC reporter, indeed any reporter, and had never given serious thought about what answers he might give if challenged in this way. What was undeniably true is that at the time no other interviewers on the BBC – or indeed on ITV News or *Channel Four News* – had asked questions about climate change which didn't start from the assumption that the science was settled. In my lonely position I was eventually joined by Andrew Neil, who skilfully eviscerated the then environment secretary Hilary Benn on his show *The Daily Politics*.

But it was the scandal over the Climategate emails that was a real game changer, and more recently a number of other colleagues have started to tiptoe onto the territory that was for so long off-limits. The BBC Trust has also finally responded to the damage being inflicted on the BBC's credibility in numerous respectable internet forums, where its climate change coverage has long been regarded as a joke. What is billed as a 'major review' will examine whether the BBC's science coverage, particularly of climate change, is biased. Don't hold your breath.

A week after the Saturday on which I interviewed the leader of the Green Party, I went into work as usual, and picked up my mail from my pigeon hole. Among the envelopes was a small jiffy-bag, which I opened. It contained a dollop of faeces wrapped in several sheets of toilet paper.

About this time I gave up trying to persuade the head of the newsroom that there was something wrong with the BBC's climate change coverage, and became involved in another argument with him. This was over a mandatory course for all 17,000 of the BBC's production and content staff, called 'Safeguarding Trust'. The course had been devised in response to a series of scandals that involved the deception of BBC viewers and listeners in various competitions, by the misuse of telephone voting including the rigged naming of the Blue Peter kitten, and most embarrassingly, a TV trailer that was edited in a way that misrepresented the behaviour of the Queen. The course was produced by COJO, the BBC's new College of Journalism, and involved a two-hour seminar at which groups of BBC personnel would be lectured about, and discuss, what conduct was acceptable and what was unacceptable for BBC programme makers, journalists and presenters.

I resisted taking part in the course, arguing that I had been hired by the BBC for reasons that certainly included being able to judge what was acceptable conduct editorially and what was not. I pointed out that it was written into my contract that I would do nothing that could bring the BBC into disrepute, and that if I let the BBC down they could always show me the door. In truth, I found it so demoralising, after all those years in the business, to be lectured about journalistic ethics. I delayed and prevaricated for many months, and ignored deadline after deadline for attending the course.

At the beginning of April 2008, I returned from an overseas holiday to find a letter on the mat at home from the head of the newsroom. He told me that until I had completed the Safeguarding Trust course, I was suspended from news presenting. In effect it was an ultimatum: attend the course, or you're sacked. As a sweetener he had arranged for it to be a one to one session, although it wasn't such a concession as I was the only one left. Not being ready to retire just yet, I drove up to London to comply. When I walked into the office at TV Centre where my session would take place, with my tutor for the afternoon, there was a stir of interest among other training staff who were present. I was told later that it was because their work was now done – I was indeed the very last to tick the box. I was astonished to be told that even such experienced and respected BBC figures as John Humphrys and Jeremy Paxman had been dragooned into taking it. Oh, and also Andrew Neil, whose experience editing the *Sunday Times* was judged to be no substitute for a lecture on how to do his job from the BBC. My mentor for the course, a fine journalist who was actually a good friend of mine, was apologetic about the content, much of which said things that were blindingly obvious, and we got through it in record time. To this day I can't remember a thing about it. It was the first and last course I had ever been on, but it meant I could resume doing my job. Indeed, there were so few hard feelings that I was offered another year on my contract. I was coming up to sixty-six years of age, and my inclination was to do one more year if the terms were right.

The deal we arrived at for that last year was that I would stop doing the Sunday shift – I was having to cut short too many enjoyable Sunday lunches at home with my family. But I would continue with my long shift on a Saturday, and would also be available during the week for the newshour on the news channel between 5 and 6 p.m. All BBC news presenters had suddenly been told they weren't doing enough to earn their money, and Huw Edwards, who was now the BBC's senior presenter, was no exception. I believe that in a number of cases not only were presenters expected to do more work, they were told that when their contracts came up for renewal they would be doing it for less. Huw was told that, in addition to presenting the *News at Ten*, he would also have to present the hour on the news channel that preceded the *Six O'Clock News*, and I was contracted to do a number of such broadcasts when Huw wasn't available, which was usually on a Friday. It suited me fine.

But there was one condition I insisted on before I signed on the dotted line. For the last couple of years, the BBC1 bulletins at weekends had all originated from the studio used by the news channel, and were simulcast on it. It knitted the two operations together and it was done principally to save money. It meant that the presenter of the output on the news channel, just before the transmission of the BBC1 bulletin, had to move out of his or her seat to make way for the person who was presenting the news on BBC1. I found this 'musical chairs' situation unsatisfactory, and it was agreed that it would stop, with the BBC1 early evening bulletin being done by me if it fell within my six hour shift on the news channel. I am not sure it went down too well with some of the younger presenters, who coveted their Saturday peak-time exposure on BBC1 and were now being deprived of it by me.

The new contract arrangement worked well for a while, and I was kept busy not just on Saturdays, but during the week. In Huw's absences I rediscovered my enthusiasm – and probably talent – for anchoring a fast moving hour of news and interviews, doing what I always did best. But I had forgotten the extent to which, on BBC news, the notion of a presenter exercising a degree of control over the output, runs totally against the grain. It came to a head a week before the 2009 local and European elections in which, as time started to run out for the Brown government, there was a massive amount at stake. I arrived at Television Centre at about 2.30 to start preparing for the 5 to 6 p.m. news hour on the news channel. As expected, when I was taken through the likely running order, there was a high political content, the centrepiece of which was to be an extended interview that I would conduct with Labour's deputy leader, Harriet Harman. I then did what I have always done before thousands of interviews: I drew up a list of the most important current issues that I felt she needed to be asked about, drafted a few core questions, and scoured the newswires and morning papers for any issues that I'd missed.

Then it started – a steady stream of email messages from producers telling me what to ask. No one person was in charge of this segment of the programme, but three or four producers all wanted to have their say. They seemed particularly twitchy about Harriet Harman being interviewed by me, unsupervised. And most seemed to be fully paid up members of the Harman fan club, which has a strong following at the BBC. News producers at the BBC have a perfect right to try to ensure that a news presenter sticks to their agenda – it is the BBC way. But what the BBC does to many of them is to make them constantly concerned not about what will be the best journalistically, but about what will best please the news executives on the floors above. The two are not necessarily the same thing. I think it was Michael Grade who once said that second-guessing programme makers after the event was the BBC's corporate pastime. It doesn't encourage enterprise and risk taking among producers when they know they are going to be picked apart the next day.

I managed to bat away most of the stuff my producers suggested to me, and the way the interview might go took shape in my mind. Then, half an hour before transmission, a producer arrived with a list of questions for Harriet Harman which had been emailed in by viewers. This was news to me, but I had no choice in the matter because they had already been set up with captions, and it was my job simply to put them to her. After that, if there was time – and the interview was to run to no more than eight minutes – I could put some questions of my own. I was asked what did I have in mind? Well, having looked through the morning papers, I said it was clear to me that a row was brewing about Gordon Brown not inviting the Queen to the sixty-fifth anniversary commemoration of D Day, and that I would close the interview with a question about that. The response shocked me. It was suggested to me that it was not a topic worth raising with Labour's deputy leader because it was 'only a campaign being run by the *Daily Mail*'.

I have no doubt that if it had been the lead in *The Guardian* or *The Independent*, the most read papers in the newsroom, I would have been instructed to nail Ms Harman to the wall. I did ask the question, and Harman, clearly uncomfortable, promised a statement when she had found out all the facts. As I drove home an hour later I asked myself a question: did I want to go on working for the BBC? By the time I arrived home I had decided to leave.

I worked out my contract, which expired three months later. A few weeks before I went I had a brief meeting with the new head of the newsroom, who'd been recently appointed, and she made no attempt to talk me out of going. I said I didn't want any fuss, or any kind of leaving party, and my wishes were observed. No one in the newsroom knew that Saturday 27 June 2009 was my last day. I wondered whether I should indulge myself by clutching an onion and saying a tearful goodbye to the adoring fans, and thought better of it. Instead, just before 7 p.m. I handed to the weather presenter, pulled out my earpiece, gathered up my bits and pieces and left the studio for the last time. After cleaning off my make-up I walked into the newsroom as I usually did to say goodnight. Everyone in the control gallery was busy, and took no notice of me. I walked to the car park and went home. It was just under forty-five years since I had turned up at ITN in my three-wheeler van. Another door had closed.

Chapter 15

Reflections

What else do you want to know? You know where I came from, who I worked for, who I admired, and what got up my nose from time to time. It's the perspective of someone whose career path is unlikely to be repeated – forty-five years in the news business with only two employers is not something that today's graduate trainees can look forward to. And it wasn't forty-five years spent examining my navel about the nature of broadcast news, but taking what opportunities were offered and learning from my mistakes. Accordingly, my views about broadcast journalism are scattered throughout the narrative, and that was deliberate. But I'll now attempt to fill in some of the gaps.

You must remember that these are the personal views of someone who has worked for a long time only in television news. I have done very little radio, but some of my observations are no less valid for sound only. At the very least they may be of value to someone contemplating a career in broadcasting, or just to satisfy the curiosity of the casual viewer who wonders whether reading the news is as simple as it looks.

Of course 'reading the news' is as simple or as difficult as the programme you are working for. I've been fortunate to have been involved continuously at the top end, where you need a few more skills than remembering not to smile when reading the sad bits. So let's deconstruct some of what it takes to be a successful news presenter in today's fast-moving world of communication. To start with, you'll get nowhere without the ability to interview.

I've called interviewing a skill. But is it an art? To do it properly certainly takes a great amount of skill; done badly it is usually immediately apparent what a mess the interviewer is making of it. But I think art could be the right word. Because to see or hear a really good interviewer at work, you are aware that something more is needed than forensic skill. You are aware of the good interviewer using the medium in which he or she is working, to try to reveal something, to shed some light, not just to demonstrate what a clever interviewer he or she is.

The shorter *Oxford Dictionary* gives two main meanings for the word 'interview': to have a personal meeting with; and to conduct an interview with a person, especially someone whose views are sought for publication or broadcasting. A broadcast interview should be both of those things. But as someone whose entire working life has been in broadcast journalism, I believe that the word has another meaning wrapped into it: intervening on behalf of the viewer or listener. An interviewer who loses sight of the fact that he or she is a representative of the informed viewer or listener is not doing his or her job. And not just the informed viewer. Lots of people are not informed, but they want to be. Above all, the best interviewers maintain their detachment; they never allow the interview to become an argument.

On New Year's Eve 2009, an 89-year-old woman, given the freedom of the BBC's flagship *Today* programme, gave a masterclass in interviewing. Baroness P. D. James, a former BBC governor, made her name as a best-selling crime writer. She was not a professional interviewer. Yet her performance on that day put in the shade some of the most vaunted interrogators on the BBC's generous payroll.

Once a year, *Today* gives selected outsiders the chance to guest-edit the programme. It usually works well, bringing a fresh perspective to topical events, while enabling the *Today* production team to stay in the background – although never relinquishing ultimate control over what goes on air. No one would have called it high risk for anyone involved – until P. D. James got her teeth into the Director General of the BBC.

The next day's headlines tell the story: 'PD James handbags BBC Chief'. 'BBC DG reduced to a stuttering wreck', 'How PD skewered the DG' ... and so on. For the Director General of the BBC, Mark Thompson, it was an event which did massive damage to his credibility, just at a time when the future of the BBC and its right to exist and take our money, was becoming a bigger political issue than ever before. How come Mark Thompson blew it? Was he browbeaten, interrupted or sneered at? Was he confronted with some new revelation that wrong footed him? Was he taken into territory with which he wasn't completely familiar, or couldn't be expected to know the answers? No, no and no. He was confronted with an amateur interviewer who had done her homework, wouldn't be fobbed off, had a fistful of damning references to use in evidence, and was disarmingly polite and civil.

I have to confess I was lying in bed at the time the *Today* interview began, a luxury I allow myself now I no longer work in broadcasting. But I was soon sitting on the edge of it, punching the air – not at the discomfiture of the DG, but at the fact that someone was asking the questions that, more and more, are being asked by ordinary viewers and listeners. P. D. James was acting for them – not having a private argument, or making clever points, or trying to look tough, but getting on with the job of asking the core questions that were troubling the public. Most important of all, every major point she made she was able to back up with meticulously researched examples – listing a number of the BBC's most awful programmes, and having in her hand chapter and verse on how bloated the BBC's overpaid bureaucracy had become.

This was forensic interviewing at its best, and Thompson had no answer to it. For me, the clearest sign that an interviewee is floundering is the 'Y'know' count. As the DG started to flannel, the 'Y'knows' came tumbling out – at times three or four in a sentence. The man had lost it. P. D. James may not have done Mark Thompson any favours that chilly December morning, but she did a service – firstly to the art of interviewing and secondly, most importantly, to the listener.

For years the sort of interview that producers and editors have favoured, as making for good television or radio, has been the interview laced with acrimony, cynicism and point-scoring. What Baroness James did was remind us that there is a far more effective way of conducting an interview – tough questions meticulously researched, and politely but tenaciously pursued. Questions, moreover, that accurately reflected the views being widely expressed among the informed public.

What made this interview particularly effective was that, though Mark Thompson and Baroness James knew each other well, she was clearly not going to let that get in the way of the job in hand. She addressed him as Director General, in contrast to his attempts to engage her more informally by calling her Phyllis. She was having none of it. She had a job to do.

The interview that Baroness James conducted with the Director General of the BBC, was a timely reminder that there are better ways of conducting important interviews than those that are now in vogue – whether they are confrontational and aggressive, or too cosy by half and characterised on both sides by the use of first names. P. D. James took us back to basics.

Interviews today account for a prodigious amount of time on radio and television, and are often planned and carried out as a relatively cheap way of filling airtime while remaining as entertaining as the interviewer and interviewee can make them. In addition, the advent of continuous news and sofa-based formats, has increased the pressure on producers to find interviewees on specialist topics that may not be the most expert in their field, but can be relied on to entertain.

Political interviewees have caught on to this, and know what the form is. Backbenchers on both sides of the House, with time on their hands, appreciate that they are often only invited into the studio to 'do a turn'. Producers will openly plot how to contrive a punch-up or a row, seeing the interview or discussion essentially as entertainment. I once chaired a major studio debate on Channel Four about education, with a studio full of parents, politicians and various experts. The script devised by an independent production company was divided into segments – not entitled part one, part two etc., but row one, row two, row three: And most of the principal figures were happy to oblige.

The development of the interview as entertainment has led to the establishment of a first division of interviewees across politics, the economy and practically any other area or topic that is regularly in the news. Many of them have become household names, not because of what they do at their place of work, but because of the frequency with which they appear on television. Some expect, and even relish, the prospect of being given a tough time, because they can be seen to cope, and so enhance their public standing. The encounter between interviewer and interviewee becomes a kind of ritual dance – interviewer talking tough, interviewee showing they can handle it.

Recent years have, particularly on the BBC, seen the development of yet another kind of treatment for interviewees – the kind meted out to the spokesmen and women of the principal environmental organisations. On any environmental issue, these spokespersons expect to be interviewed uncritically, and broadcasters have been unusually obliging. Invariably, ministers who appear on mainstream TV programmes can expect none of the indulgence routinely extended to representatives from Greenpeace, WWF or Friends of the Earth.

For government ministers, the advent of continuous news has brought problems as well as opportunities. Some could, and sometimes do, spend whole days doing the rounds of radio and TV studios, because if they don't fill the news vacuum someone else will. Dare they risk getting some work done in their department, when their opponents, with more time on their hands, are given a free run on the news channels? They might think twice if they were to see some of the morning editorial conferences across all news broadcasters, where producers go through the morning papers looking for the issues which are not necessarily the most pressing for the country, but the most fertile ground for a lively and intellectually undemanding discussion, or with luck a studio punch-up.

I've seen an issue dropped from the news agenda when a government department, in response to an interview request, has offered to the broadcaster a junior minister rather than the secretary of state. What concerned the producers was the status of the programme itself, which would be seen to be diminished if it could only merit a minister of state. We live in the age of the celebrity interviewer, so the thinking goes, so we can't have them interviewing nobodies. At the very least it helps if there's someone worth them getting their teeth into. And that's where things start to diverge from the interests of the viewer or listener.

Some years ago, Brian Walden addressed the issue, reviewing Michael Cockerell's book about Prime Ministers and television, *Live from Number 10*. Said Walden:

> Confrontational interviewing is the easiest, most elementary and least rewarding of all the methods available. The single most important function of an interview is not to prove anything, but to reveal something. An interview is neither a debate, nor the case for the prosecution. It can be incisive or discursive, but its point is to persuade interviewees to admit what they would prefer to conceal and to expose their real motivations. Interviewers who want to take part in a debate, to heckle, contradict, and push their own opinions, should become politicians, and run for office.

And Walden, perhaps because he was himself a politician for so long, has some sympathy for politicians in the television age: 'It is a cruel medium, more suited to the diversions of show business than the propagation of ideas. Serious television broadcasting is always in jeopardy, not because of anything politicians do, but because of the nature of the medium.'

Walden was writing more than twenty years ago, and in those twenty years has anything changed? Have interviewing techniques become better or worse? Are we better equipped as a democracy because of our interviewers? Has the interview become just another way of refining politics into entertainment?

Essentially, in news, there are three basic reasons that people are interviewed. The first is what I call the information-seeking interview, the purpose of which is to find out the facts of a situation: what happened in the bomb blast? How many casualties are there? What did you see? Describe to us the atmosphere in the City. How many robbers were there? Would you expect to make an arrest? How fast can these aeroplanes fly?

Then there's the analytical interview, with an expert, and if you are asking the questions you don't for a moment pretend to know more than him. What are the underlying causes of the war? How long can the enemy hold out? What are the prospects for peace? Why are the markets so jittery? How long till the stock market picks up again?

You may be surprised that these are the sort of interviews that I am often most sceptical about. In my experience, producers don't often examine the credentials of potential interviewees of this kind too closely. There may be more qualified people, but not as entertaining. But, again, the chosen expert can be relied on to do a good turn, and to keep it brief and entertaining. The world is full of dull experts, who know ten times more but who never get a look in, because they are not judged to have the entertainment skills.

The third type of interview is the interview of challenge. Such interviews are invariably the most interesting and the most controversial, because they are with people – usually politicians in or out of government – who only want to say a limited amount. They agree to be interviewed because it is in their interests to be seen to be willing to answer questions, but in reality, they have come to say their piece. Many are skilled in doing that, and media training courses teach them how to resist saying more even under robust interrogation. The interviewer invariably wants to take them further than they want to go – indeed that is his job. But to persist aggressively when a politician repeatedly evades a question and is clearly not going to give a straight answer may make for good television or radio, but it can waste time better spent on other pressing topics.

Viewers and listeners, by and large, are not fools. They want to hear politicians explain their motives, and be examined closely about vague promises and policies. Faced with a shifty and evasive interviewee, the good interviewer takes the viewer or listener right up to the conclusion that this man or woman is an untrustworthy public liability – but lets the audience take the decision for themselves.

A new development is for the interviewer to produce a sheaf of emails from concerned viewers, and rattle off some hostile comments from them in the hope of getting his interviewee's guard to drop. It can make for 'good television' but the temptation for the producer is to equip the interviewer with only the hostile emails – whereas a more representative selection would make for a less entertaining interview. The increasing reliance on emails from viewers or listeners also disenfranchises those – usually of the older generation – who don't care to join the internet age, or can't afford to.

The reward for the interviewer, if the interviewee does drop his guard in an interview of challenge, is that his interview makes news in itself. It will be widely quoted, or clips of it used, by other programmes.

It will reflect well on the interviewer and his programme, and may even be seen as an important part of the democratic process. These are the interviews around which controversy flies, with everyone having strong views about whether the interviewee has been treated badly, got off scot-free, won hands down, appeared shifty or dishonest; or whether the interviewer had interrupted too much, been too rude or too deferential, been badly briefed or well briefed. Or about who, quite simply, won.

I believe that the viewer or listener has two rights when an interview is being conducted. The first is to know if any deal has been done as to the structure or content of the interview. Broadcasters routinely negotiate with potential interviewees about the terms on which they will appear. Some ministers refuse to join in a discussion with their shadows, so although they might be sitting next to each other in the studio, they are interviewed separately. Others say they'll take part in a discussion only if they have the last word. Some may insist that certain topics are off-limits. I believe that the viewer or listener is entitled to know if such a deal has been done. The BBC's insistence on 'Safeguarding Trust' shouldn't just be about the procedure for naming the Blue Peter kitten; it should extend to complete transparency about any agreement governing the terms on which an interview is being done.

The second entitlement of the viewer or listener is to have confidence that it is his or her concerns that will be put to the interviewee, and not any hobby horse of the interviewer. Leading questions and smug point-scoring designed to make the interviewer look good and diminish the interviewee are a fraud perpetrated on the viewers and listeners who expect interviewers to fight their corner for them. An interview is not an ego trip, it is a mission on behalf of the interested viewer or listener.

On both the above counts, the P. D. James interview with Mark Thompson was a model.

I am glad to see that the website of the BBC College of Journalism contains a lot of sense about interviewing. You will find there what I consider to be the best set of guidelines for an interviewer ever written. They were written by Sir Robin Day in 1961, and they will never be out of date.

1. The television interviewer must do his duty as a journalist, probing for facts and opinions.

2. He should not allow himself to be overawed in the presence of a powerful person.

3. He should not compromise the honesty of the interview, by omitting awkward topics or rigging questions in advance.

4. He should resist any inclination in those employing him to soften or rig an interview so as to secure a 'prestige' appearance, or to please Authority. If, after making his protest the interviewer feels he cannot honestly accept the arrangements, he should withdraw.

5. He should not submit his questions in advance, but it is reasonable to state the main areas of questioning. If he submits specific questions beforehand he is powerless to put any supplementary questions which may be vitally needed to clarify or challenge an answer.

6. He should give fair opportunity to answer questions subject to the time-limits imposed by television.

7. He should never take advantage of his professional experience to trap or embarrass someone unused to television appearances.

8. He should press his questions firmly but persistently but not tediously, offensively, or merely in order to sound tough.

9. He should remember that a television interviewer is not employed as a debater, prosecutor, inquisitor, psychiatrist or third-degree expert, but as a journalist seeking information on behalf of the viewer.

Looking at those Robin Day guidelines today, I wouldn't alter a word – indeed other interviewers have tried and they haven't been improved. But the depressing fact is that one or more of them is routinely ignored every day in the hundreds of interviews conducted across all broadcast outlets. The reason is that old fashioned journalistic values like the Day precepts are no longer enough: the interviewer, with the collusion of editors and producers, has become a player in a branch of entertainment in which it has become fashionable to be aggressive or even rude. When Frankie Howerd referred to Robin Day's 'cruel glasses' he couldn't have been more wrong. Robin was many things – pompous, tetchy, witty, avuncular – but never cruel. He never flinched from asking the tough question, but it was generally put with the detachment of the lawyer, and far more effective for that. More than anything he revered the democratic process; even if he disliked his interviewees – and he would never show it – he had deep respect for the offices they had been elected to. He would have been mortified if a good person had decided against a career in public life, or curtailed one, because he was not prepared to be treated like a criminal in a television studio.

In too many interviews, conducted on the smallest local radio stations to networked television flagships it's plain that the interviewer considers the most important person in front of the microphone to be himself – and so does the adoring editorial team. However, there may be some hope: the BBC has an award for interviewing, and it is named after a broadcaster whose high standards were never compromised, while commanding widespread affection and respect, the late Nick Clarke. He'd have been pleased that the first two winners, not drawn from among the Rottweilers of the airwaves, were Carrie Gracie and Victoria Derbyshire.

I think the BBC interview series 'Hardtalk', which is transmitted on BBC World News and the BBC News Channel, also deserves a mention. Currently presented by Stephen Sackur it generally interviews to a high standard. And then, in my view, it undoes everything by concluding each and every interview with the interviewer shaking hands with the interviewee.

The message it sends to the viewers is that there's more to this interview than meets the eye. The viewers might be entitled to ask what's going on between these two people that they don't know about. Was the hard talking all a game? I may have felt like shaking hands with someone after an interview, but I never did so. And there've been far more that I've interviewed whose hands I wouldn't have shaken if you'd put a gun to my head. Stephen Sackur justified the handshake to me as 'adding a useful element of theatre to the end of the show – otherwise we'd just sit there staring awkwardly at each other as the credits roll and the lights go down … the ubiquity of the gesture ensures it carries no message of complicity or approbation'. So in the interests of 'theatre' – or 'entertainment' to you and me – he'd presumably shake the hand of any old monster or crook. In my book, that meaningless handshake may be seen around the world as a mark of approval of the BBC. It's a mistake.

I wasn't going to write about presenting. I think you've either got it or you haven't. There are some things that you *need* – particularly a good broadcasting voice. There must also be the ability to speak to the viewers or listeners as if they were an acquaintance, rather than address them like a public meeting. In the radio work – too little of it – that I did with the BBC, I worked with some very good radio producers who educated me in how to talk to a listener. After twenty-five years in television I thought I knew most things about presenting, but I was wrong and radio completed my education. On television you can hold the attention of the viewer by how you look and your body language, as much as by what you are saying. On radio you have to be able, by voice alone, to give someone a reason not to switch you off. If you can, by going into her home with only your voice, hold the attention of a harassed housewife trying to get the tea for the kids, you can begin to think you are a reasonably good presenter. And such radio skills can only make you a better presenter on television.

On TV, however, how you look is everything, particularly for the woman presenter. A man can look like he's slept in his clothes, and have a face that looks like a worn tyre, but still be trusted and credible. The female presenter with a hair out of place, or inappropriate earrings, is judged to be a distraction. She may be the brainiest person on the box, but go on TV looking like a baggage and she'll never make it past the snide comments on the fashion pages. At the BBC the men get two minutes in make-up if they are lucky. The women routinely get ten times that – or more. Some insist on it; but the main reason is that a skilful and experienced make-up artist, like the BBC's Jenny Binsted, will simply not let one of them go on air looking less than very presentable, because to do so risks making them the story, and not the news they are paid to present.

Sounding good, looking presentable – it's a piece of cake isn't it? After all, we have it on the authority of the BBC's John Humphrys, that newscasting isn't work, requires no brain and could be done by his four-year-old son.

While senior BBC newscasters may wince, I have a feeling that Humphrys was taking aim, not at them, but at the rise of the airhead presenter, the female variety of which is generally referred to as an 'autocutie'. There are, of course, autocuties of both sexes, whose principal value is as an adornment and who are generally confined to summaries or short bulletins which make no demands on presenter or viewer. An additional attraction for their employers is that they can be cheap (as in price) as well as being cheerful, unable to stop smiling however bad the news, and in seemingly endless supply across the countless channels we now have. They are a natural consequence of the boundaries between news and entertainment being eroded, they clearly have a fan base and they aren't going to go away.

But Humphrys knows more than anyone that there is nothing more damaging to the credibility of a serious news organisation than a newscaster or anchor who clearly doesn't know what she or he is talking about. This can betray itself in many ways, but most usually by ignorance of past events that have a direct bearing on today's news. That's why the best presenters are those that have had a substantial background in reporting, often in print as well as broadcasting. Without such a background the presenter will be very exposed, particularly on a continuous news channel. On a major breaking story there's rarely time to Google the background. If it becomes obvious that you don't know anything about it, or that you should have been aware that something similar had happened before, you are sunk and your channel's credibility becomes a joke. A good general knowledge of twentieth century political and social events is essential, although too many among the younger generation in news regard the 1970s as ancient history.

Even with all the other attributes, there's one more that a presenter needs – sensitivity to the impact a news story may have. Varying the light, shade and pace of delivery shows that you are a sentient human being. Delivering a news story about a house fire in which children have died needs a different tone and approach to reading the football results, although a surprising number of younger presenters – across all channels – don't seem to be able to tell the difference. My feeling is that they are so distracted by all that's going on around them technically, that when it comes to reading the text they go into autopilot mode and take their eye off what the words actually mean.

Above all, a presenter must look comfortable on the studio set. 'Make friends with the stage' is an old theatrical maxim and it is just as important in live television. But it is here, in my view, that the BBC has made changes that could have been deliberately designed to make the job of its news presenters more difficult. Led by the obsession with 'branding' the BBC's entire TV news output, identical sets and desks are seen in BBC news studios up and down the land, and I found the design ghastly to work at. Sitting at that ubiquitous and soulless round plastic desk, it is impossible for the presenter to sit and work comfortably.

Ergonomically, with the desk curved away from you, the space for your scripts and notes is limited. If one falls to the floor, as often happens, it's invariably the one you need next and the most difficult to retrieve without disconnecting your earpiece and disappearing from sight. The computer screen, on which you depend, has been taken off the desk for purely aesthetic reasons and set inside the clear plastic tabletop, making it practically impossible to read because of the reflected glare of the studio lights. If you are over fifty years of age, and just beginning to find the *A to Z* difficult to read, text on the screen below your plastic desktop is even more difficult to decipher – another challenge for the BBC's older presenters.

If your eyesight is still perfect, it's just about possible to make the set work if you are speaking to a camera straight ahead of you. But a number of camera shots are taken from the side, so then only one arm can be kept on the desk, and no presenter seems to have settled on what to do with the other one. Not only is the presenter not sitting comfortably, he or she *looks* uncomfortable. Even shot from the front, some seem to find it impossible to sit upright – all because of the damn desk, on which someone has spent vast sums without first talking to the people who have to use it. The BBC News studio furniture is an expensive mess. The BBC 'presenters' slouch' has almost become their hallmark.

In contrast, when I launched *Channel Four News*, we went through all manner of desks, including having no desk at all. We settled eventually on a rectangular desk. It was simple and it worked, and essentially the same style of desk is still in use today. It makes the programme easier to direct and to present, in total contrast to the BBC's expensive Perspex creation behind which none of their presenters appears to be at home.

Incidentally, I received very little advice on news presenting when I was given the opportunity at ITN in the late 1960s, but what I was given I have never forgotten. For a few of my early on-screen appearances I too got into the habit of slouching to one side, leaning on one arm with the other outstretched – which is the default mode of many presenters today. My card was marked very quickly. I was told to sit up straight and keep my head and hands still while talking to the camera. In that way there is nothing going on to distract from what you are saying. But the fashion now, among some presenters, is to use their hands as much as their voice and facial expression. A finger held for a few seconds between pursed lips is a favourite gesture to indicate concern after certain news items.

Some newscasters are striking this pose three or four times a bulletin, varied by cradling their chin in a hand in sombre manner, as if we needed reminding when a story was a matter for extra concern. And if these pointless tics weren't enough, the needless waving of hands, for so long the prerogative of wandering reporters, has now also spread into the studio. I have lost count of the number of times people have come up to me and asked why reporters wave and walk so much. Without exception, viewers I speak to say they find it distracting. Some reporters, I am sure, wouldn't be able to speak if you tied their hands behind their backs. Out on the road, they are difficult to control, but there's no excuse for letting presenters in the studio get into bad habits. The sad reality is that in a modern TV news control gallery there's so much going on technically that no one seems to have the time or the will to give the presenters some helpful direction.

So much for the shortcomings of some presenters. But what about the defects of the medium itself? I have reluctantly come to the conclusion that the big flagship networked TV news programmes, of the kind which commanded such huge audiences in the 1960s and 1970s, are slowly dying on their feet. I would make an exception for *Channel Four*

News, which is still the one to beat. It has no more viewers now than it had twenty years ago, but it has done well to hold its audience despite the proliferation of other channels. Its news agenda is not a rehash of the morning newspapers, and the range and depth of its reporting, and the thoroughness of its interviewing set it apart. There is strong and imaginative editorial leadership and it shows on screen. I feel fortunate to have played a part in establishing it, and to have worked on it with two exceptional editors.

But there are danger signs even for *Channel Four News*. The bean counters are nibbling away, and it is beginning to affect morale. I believe also that it has to be careful editorially. Jon Snow, like his cousin Peter a journalist of phenomenal energy and enthusiasm, has strong views on many topics that are politically controversial. For the most part he maintains a high standard of impartiality, but there are lapses that let him and the programme down. I've heard Jon say that he believes that the viewers should know where he's coming from, but when someone accepts an invitation to appear on *Channel Four News* they may reasonably expect to be challenged on their political views, but not to have the presenter ranged against them politically as well. *Channel Four News* is keeping its head above water in the multi-channel age because of a credible and distinctive approach to reporting a complex world. A presenter parading his politics could make the programme vulnerable to political opponents who may be looking for an excuse to push it under or cut it down to size.

Channel Four News, of course, is made by ITN; and ITN also makes the *ITV News*, although you'd hardly know it from the subliminal glimpse viewers are allowed of the ITN logo. I, and many hundreds of former ITN employees, still have enormous loyalty to the *ITV News*, although none of us can understand why ITV thought it was a good idea to call it that when the ITN brand with its Big Ben bongs was so famous and evocative.

Fiddling around with the transmission time of 10 p.m., and surrendering the slot to the BBC, was also a massive own-goal – the biggest mistake ITV ever made, according to Michael Grade. I believe *ITV News* has also done itself no favours by wasting hundreds of thousands of pounds on studio presentation, starting with 'The Theatre of News' in 2006, and another facelift three years later – all a long way from the simplicity of Andrew and Reggie at a desk. Now the screen is cluttered with studio distraction, with the presenters sitting among it. But the ITN way of telling a story lives on, and, particularly on human interest stories, the reporters on *ITV News* regularly outscore their more ponderous counterparts at the BBC. With around a third of the BBC's news budget, ITN still punches above its weight.

All news programmes, however, have caught the entertainment disease. There has never been more airtime on news programmes devoted to celebrity, with no opportunity missed to cover stories that, in the heyday of TV news, would have been confined to the pages of magazines found in dentists' waiting rooms.

There was a time when both ITV and the BBC were fully signed up to the notion of a kind of airlock or 'Chinese wall' between the news programmes that informed their audiences, and the other programmes that entertained them. In the case of ITV, although the advertising revenue from these entertainment programmes paid for the news, the two sides never met. The ITV companies had directors on ITN's board, but they would have got short shrift – and fallen foul of the Independent Broadcasting Authority – if they'd pressured ITN editors to lard their news bulletins with show business.

Today, under commercial pressures, that airlock between news and entertainment at ITV has collapsed. But there's no reason why it shouldn't still exist at the BBC. The number of entertainment stories, and the rise of the entertainment correspondent, is of course justified by such stories being defined as entertainment *news*. But it is the thin end of the wedge and I believe such stories side by side with the big 'proper' stories of tragedy, politics, disaster, science and war, devalue all news in the public consciousness.

The conclusion is not new. The New York academic Neil Postman, in his acclaimed book *Amusing Ourselves to Death*, writes 'The problem is not that television presents us with entertaining subject matter, but that all subject matter is presented as entertaining, which is another issue altogether.' This, Postman argues, trivialises the once serious and coherent discussion of all public affairs.

Postman, writing in America twenty-five years ago, quotes Robert MacNeil, co-anchor of the *MacNeil/Lehrer NewsHour* (and also a former

BBC *Panorama* reporter) who described the assumptions controlling a news show as follows: 'that bite-sized is best, that complexity must be avoided, that nuances are dispensable, that qualifications impede the simple message, that visual stimulation is a substitute for thought, and that verbal precision is an anachronism'. That was an informed view of what was happening to TV news in America. Don't think it isn't happening here.

Even if it wasn't, even if the best editors and reporters that money could buy were put in a room and told to give us twenty-five minutes of television every evening on what they judge to be the day's most important stories, there are other big issues in play: the sheer complexity of the modern world, and the inadequacy of the medium in reflecting it. We live in the age of the computer and satellite, of the internet and the communications revolution it has spawned, of great medical advances, of genetic engineering, of controversial environmental concerns and new frontiers in the space age. Relations between nations are complicated by the new international terrorism, by unprecedented crises of global finance, by the shift in the balance of economic power, the collapse of communist ideology and the rise of militant Islam. That's in addition to all the old tensions, wars, hostilities and natural disasters that are always with us. Suddenly the twenty-five minute news bulletin seems hopelessly inadequate, and it is.

It is my view that none of these issues can be adequately reported by the stock-in-trade of TV news, the two or two-and-a-half minute 'reporter package', with its appetite for the visual, the violent and the sensational. TV news is still a powerful medium of communication, but it is increasingly an imperfect one. The BBC recognised this, and tried to do something about it. On some stories it puts a reporter in the studio to deliver a mini-lecture in front of a big screen, the words punctuated by a few sound-bites from interested parties. Some reporters make the best of it, others come across as didactic and patronising, jabbing a finger towards a word or number on the screen behind them like a teacher talking to a remedial class.

The other technique, in an attempt to make a complicated story more understandable, is to have the reporter sitting with the presenter in the studio, but preceded by the reporter's own recorded report – the 'package'. The presenter then asks the reporter a pre-arranged question, which enables the reporter to make one or two other points which didn't get into the package, usually because he or she ran out of pictures or of editing time. It may also be because of a new development that came too late to be included. This way of rounding off the reporting of a major story does, however, have one major fault. It has developed into a platform not for telling the viewers more facts, but for routinely presenting them with the reporters' opinions. If the words 'I think that' were banned from such staged conversations with the presenter, the viewer would be better served, and perhaps there would be fewer complaints of BBC bias.

Is the BBC biased? We have the word of the current Director General that it was thirty years ago, but it isn't quite so bad now. This is what he told the *New Statesman*, in an interview in 2010:

> In the BBC I joined thirty years ago, there was, in much of current affairs, in terms of people's personal politics, which were quite vocal, a massive bias to the left. The organisation did struggle then with impartiality.
> Now it is a completely different generation. There is much less overt tribalism among the young journalists who work for the BBC. It is like the *New Statesman*, which used to be various shades of soft and hard left and is now more technocratic. We're like that, too.

My experience of the BBC has led me to some conclusions about bias. Bias is too blunt a word to describe the subtleties of the culture at TV Centre. It's easy to take sides about bias – after all, one man's bias is another man's impartiality. The better word for what pervades the BBC is a mindset. This mindset occasionally breaks out into its programmes and viewers complain or congratulate – depending on where they themselves are coming from politically. But at the core of the BBC, in its very DNA, is a mindset, a way of thinking, and an approach to ordering journalistic priorities, that is firmly of the left but not defined in any conventional political way. By far the most popular and widely read newspapers at the BBC are *The Guardian* and *The Independent*, and the numbers of these newspapers bought by the BBC seems to outnumber all the other newspapers that it provides. Producers refer to them routinely for the line to take on running stories and for inspiration on which stories to cover. When I was presenting on the News Channel I lost count of the number of times I asked a producer for a brief on a story, only to be handed a copy of *The Guardian* and told 'it's all in there'.

What of the other newspapers? *The Times* is regarded as of limited use and is treated with caution, because it is owned by Rupert Murdoch. *The Telegraph* came in from the cold when it made the running on the MPs' expenses scandal, but BBC approval extended only to its news pages, not its opinions. The red tops are regarded as rags, but the *Daily Mirror* commands a soft spot for its unwavering opposition to the Conservatives. If you want to read one of the few copies of the *Daily Express* and the *Daily Mail* that find their way into the newsroom, they are difficult to track down and you would be advised not to make too much of a show of reading them. Wrap them in brown paper or a copy of *The Guardian* would be my advice.

I am in no doubt that the majority of BBC staff vote for political parties of the left. But it's impossible to do anything but guess at the numbers whose beliefs could be categorised as on the right, or even centre right.

This is because the one thing guaranteed to damage your career prospects at the BBC is letting it be known that you are at odds with the prevailing and deep rooted BBC attitude towards Life, the Universe, and Everything. And the BBC does have views on everything: anything the United Nations is associated with is good – it is heresy to question any of its activities. The EU is also a good thing, but not quite as good as the UN. Soaking the rich is a good thing, despite Arthur Laffer's demonstration that the more you tax, the less you get. Government spending is a good thing, although most BBC people prefer to call it investment, in line with New Labour's terminology. All Green and environmental groups are very good things, and have come to expect uncritical BBC coverage for any of their causes. Al Gore is a saint. George Bush was a bad thing and thick into the bargain. Obama was not just the Democratic Party's candidate for the White House, he was the BBC's. Blair *had been* good, Brown was bad, but the BBC has now lost interest in both. Trade unions are mostly good things, especially when they are fighting BBC managers. Quangos are also mostly good, and the reports they produce are usually handled uncritically. The royal family are a bore. Islam must not be offended at any price, although Christians are fair game because they do nothing about it if they are offended ... and so on.

I am sure my list is far from exhaustive, and it has elements of parody.

But inside today's BBC only those whose antennae are fully attuned to the corporation's cultural mindset, or if they are not, keep it quiet, are going to make progress. And making progress these days doesn't mean just achieving the influence and prestige of a senior job with the world's greatest broadcaster; if staffers do make that breakthrough into the senior ranks there's now big, big money and a gold-plated pension to be had.

Although there was plenty of grumbling on the shop floor about the way top pay escalated in recent years, it was muted. And it was muted because no one wants to wreck his or her chances of breaking through the cash and perks ceiling into the promised land on the floors above. The newsroom has many talented journalists of middle rank, who know what's wrong with the organisation but who don't rock the boat for fear of blowing their chances of advancement.

Even if they keep their noses clean there are two sets of obstacles: the annual appraisal and the promotions board. The annual appraisal is the less important: a face-to-face with your line manager once a year means you can establish your credentials as a reliable BBC person, while reminding your superiors of your ambitions, if you have any.

The really important milestones, however, are when staff are 'boarded' for a promotion. The key to understanding the system is that at the BBC, for every person who is promoted on talent, two are promoted because it solves a problem for management. Your talent isn't going to get you the promotion you seek if you don't fit the bill in other ways. That's why the representative from Human Resources is the most important person at most boards.

If Human Resources – or Personnel as it used to be known – advise that it's time a woman or someone from an ethnic minority (or a combination of the two) was appointed to the job for which you, a white male, have applied, then that's who gets appointed. But whatever your talent, sex or ethnicity, there's one sure-fire way at a BBC promotions board to ensure you *don't* get the job, indeed to bring your career to a grinding halt. And that's if, when you are asked 'which post-war politician do you most admire?' you reply 'Margaret Thatcher'.

One of the things that always puzzled me for much of my time at the BBC was the lack of inspirational leadership. Some of the people associated with recruiting me to the BBC had fine qualities. Perhaps my judgement was clouded because of the assiduous way they courted me. In any event they moved on and what contact I subsequently had with managers was with people who, with one or two exceptions, were not at all impressive. On paper they had status and rank; in reality they had little talent except the dark art of surviving at the BBC and alienating those who were answerable to them.

One of the reasons, I am sure, is that the BBC has become so big and complex that it is virtually unmanageable; managers, at the top of one of the world's greatest communications businesses, have no time, and accordingly have developed few skills, for communicating on a personal level with those who work for them. Many of them are former journalists, and were once convivial colleagues themselves, but strangely, few good journalists seem to make good managers. The dead hand of the BBC knocks the stuffing out of them, and the climate of fear – fear usually of making a decision – finishes them off.

I was fortunate in being able to spend a quarter of a century before I came to BBC news, in a totally different, albeit much smaller, organisation. The old ITN had an esprit de corps, and was led by editors whom you would follow over the top when they blew the whistle. For a trainee, as I was, there were valuable role models – and not just one or two. You were always aware that someone was in charge. When you looked to the boss for a lead, you'd always get it. If there was indecision there was always someone who would say the seven most important words in any newsroom: 'Here's what we are going to do.'

It wasn't always a bed of roses. I can remember fights and disagreements, strikes and setbacks. But I never felt the chronic lack of motivation that comes when you work for an organisation that is rudderless.

Perhaps it's unfair to make too many comparisons. ITN throughout the 1950s, 1960s and 1970s was to the BBC what a family dealership was to Fords of Dagenham. But although things have moved on, some things never change.

The BBC is one of our most important national institutions. It is revered around the world. Many of its products, in entertainment and drama, are unsurpassed. Its archive is prodigious, and goes on enriching our lives. But a core part of the BBC is News, and BBC News is an unhappy place, underperforming and directionless. Paradoxically, it's never had more people involved in journalist training and the laying down of editorial guidelines. But what it lacks is a leader whose lodestone isn't *The Guardian*; who will draw a line on political correctness; who will spend time in the newsroom leading by example; who's not afraid to hire some people who don't fit the BBC template; who will kick backsides when merited; promote solely on talent; who will remind all interest groups that they don't have an entitlement to BBC airtime; and who will do the job for the prestige and not the money. And pigs might fly...

Shortly before I left the BBC I spoke to some colleagues in the newsroom about the state of morale. It was around the time that the salaries, perks and pension pots of the BBC's top echelon were causing a high degree of adverse public comment. I suggested that the foot soldiers in the newsroom may have lost some respect for their leaders. I was told by a number of people, who felt they could confide in me, that it was not a matter of lack of respect. It was now a matter of total contempt. That feeling was widespread.

I was going to finish this book on that note, but I am going to try to cheer up the BBC's besieged managers and directors. The feeling towards them among those whom they command is nothing new. It is in the best traditions of the BBC. Indeed, they wouldn't be able to hold up their heads among the great BBC managers of the past if they weren't thoroughly disliked. They should not be downhearted – it goes with the job.

To find out what the BBC was like fifty years ago, I tracked down one of the BBC's most respected correspondents of those days. Reginald Turnill joined BBC News in 1956, and averaged 400 radio and TV appearances a year over the twenty years he spent there, mainly as aviation correspondent. I met Reg again recently, still extremely fit and sprightly, and spoke to him about his time in the BBC. After he'd retired, someone who still worked at the BBC had rung him up one day and said 'You wouldn't like it here nowadays, Reg; the BBC isn't what it was' – to which he heard himself reply; 'It never was what it was.'

Much of what Turnill told me chimed exactly with what people complain about at today's BBC. He found his bosses remote and uncommunicative – indeed he had no idea what some of them looked like. He and other staffers complained constantly about changes 'made by transient programme controllers, for no reason other than that they should be seen to be making changes'.

As for the great BBC tradition of The Morning Meeting, it was alive and well fifty years ago – with everyone afraid to venture a view on the previous night's output until they saw which way the wind was blowing. I asked him whether BBC managers all those years ago were held in contempt. 'No' he replied, 'they were just universally hated.'

But Reg Turnill also remarked on something I have mentioned in today's context, that through it all the BBC's international reputation for providing independent news survived relatively untarnished. And he put that down to 'the selection, persistence and integrity of the middle-ranking journalists doing the real work regardless of the struggles for power at higher levels'.

So, cheer up chaps. Nothing has changed. Except that the managerial defects of the BBC could be dismissed fifty years ago as idiosyncrasies. Perpetuated in the modern broadcasting world they are massive obstacles to the organisation unlocking its true potential, every scrap of which it will need to survive in the years ahead.

I'm glad I had the chance to be part of the story of broadcast news so far. I was given that chance by a loving mother who knew the value of education, some inspirational teachers and the example of some of the finest television journalists who ever lived. It would also have been impossible without the support of my wife and family during the many times when the going got tough. I never, ever, wanted to do more than not let any of them down. What's the most important thing I learned? That it's only a small step from a setback to an opportunity. When one door closes, it could be the best thing that's happened to you.

Index